Machinima

Machinima

The Art and Practice of Virtual Filmmaking

PHYLIS JOHNSON *and*
DONALD PETTIT

Foreword by PERSIA BRAVIN

McFarland & Company, Inc., Publishers
Jefferson, North Carolina, and London

Library of Congress Cataloguing-in-Publication Data

Johnson, Phylis.
   Machinima : the art and practice of virtual filmmaking /
Phylis Johnson and Donald Pettit ; foreword by Persia Bravin.
      p.   cm.
   Includes bibliographical references and index.

   ISBN 978-0-7864-6171-4
   softcover : acid free paper

   1. Machinima films.   2. Digital cinematography.   I. Pettit,
Donald.   II. Title.
   TR897.74.J85 2012
   777 — dc23   2012002929

British Library cataloguing data are available

Cover image © 2012 Shutterstock

Manufactured in the United States of America

*McFarland & Company, Inc., Publishers
   Box 611, Jefferson, North Carolina 28640
   www.mcfarlandpub.com*

Table of Contents

Acknowledgments

Phylis Johnson (known as Sonicity Fitzroy to the *Second Life* machinima community) and professional filmmaker Donald Pettit (more commonly known as Lowe Runo among his machinima peers and associates) have invested collectively more than a decade in virtual communities and media practices. Along the way, they have met many wonderfully talented and supportive people, who continue to push the boundaries of game and virtual film making.

The authors would like to first acknowledge the professional machinima community for contributing to this book, particularly those from *Second Life, The Sims,* and *World of Warcraft.* We dedicate this book to those who freely give of their time in the definition and evolution of machinima through their artistic pursuits and virtual filmmaking practices. Many names are mentioned throughout this book, several of whom are prominent and upcoming filmmakers, producers, talent, content creators, educators and advocates. The first two chapters offer beginning advice from some of them, and many more share their perspectives through essays and interviews. Special thanks to those who participated in the roundtable discussions that helped to inform the authors on the diversity of opinions with regard to machinima. Roundtable participants included Graceful Aeon, Juris Amat, Pooky Amsterdam, Larkworthy Antfarm, Asil Ares, Ataro Asbrink, Baird Barnard, Code-Warrior Carling, Penumbra Carter, Pamala Clift, Evie Fairchild, Clover Fenwitch, Moto Gamba, Kit Guardian, Chantal Harvey, Laurina Hawks, Brenda Jericho, LaPiscean Liberty, Alley McNally, Thinkerer Melville, Moo Money, Joel Savard, Almo Schumann, Kara Trapdoor, Cisko Vandeverre, ke Violet, Tikaf Viper, xox Voyager, Johnathan2007 Whitfield, Gene Williams, 1angelcares Writer, Gwenette Writer, and Suzy Yue, among others. Not all were cited but your views were significant toward formulating themes in this book. I would also like to acknowledge the talented producer Tony Dyson, who has contributed much filmmaking perspective to our thoughts on machinima in recent months

Hearty thanks to professional machinimist Ms. Sasha Rudie for her ideas, coordination of interviews, and her transcription skills that she offered to the authors.

∗∗∗

On a more personal note, the authors would like to dedicate this book to their respective families, who supported them during its research and writing. Phylis thanks her father, Dr. Philip T. West, for his timeless inspiration, and acknowledges the late Dr. Joan E. West for being a strong mentor and loving mother. She also acknowledges the support of her children, Nicholas (with his wife Jennifer), Jennifer Rosemary, and Julianna, for just being there and offering encouraging words. Special blessings to Alma and her daughter Rose for warm smiles along the way, and special thanks to Kim Pluskota, Kara Trapdoor, Jean Elder, and so many others. Phylis also thanks her co-author, Donald Pettit for his idea to write a book on this topic, and for introducing her to the world of machinima and involving her strategically in Lowe Runo Productions, LLC, and both the Machinima Artist Guild and Video Artist Guild in countless ways.

✳✳✳

Donald Pettit would like to acknowledge the many people that have become dear to him within the machinima community, from those who help to administer the Professional and *Second Life* Machinima Artist Guilds to the talented people he has worked with along the way. Among his machinima supporters has been Prism Haute Couture Fashion designer Cindy Landers (Journey McLaglen), who resides as a good friend in real and virtual life. He especially would like to acknowledge his family and friends who have supported him wholly through the making of this book and his machinima, and conference presentations, namely Keila, for her patience and encouragement, Ian and Lauren for their sense of creativity, Blanca and Barbara for their devoted care, and Sean and Brianna for their sense of wonder and love. He also thanks his old friend Jon who has shared countless adventures with him, and his new friend and collaborator Phylis Johnson for always keeping him on his toes. He thanks his sister Carol for letting him mess up her computer with all his virtual stuff and his brother Steve for setting an example of devotion to his family.

Finally, and most importantly, this book is dedicated to his late father and mother, Lowell Wayland Pettit and Vivian Jean Pettit. Both authors agree that it would be fitting to end the acknowledgments with recognition of lives lived well. Mr. Pettit was a generous and gregarious soul, a loving husband and father. Mrs. Pettit, who died January 25, 2011, brought humor to her family, along with simple and sage advice. No filmmaker would reject advice from parents who have seen many years of life and loved so much and inspired so many along the way. Their stories are told through those who knew and loved them, and such stories motivate us to pursue our dreams.

"When something unusual happens you will always remember it, but make happy memories if you can."—Vivian Jean Pettit (1928–2011)

Foreword

PERSIA BRAVIN

When I was first approached to write this foreword, my immediate reaction was to decline. Not for any negative reason, but purely because I was on a self-imposed break from both work and creative ventures; I was recuperating and allowing my muse to take a much needed mini-vacation. Only three days before, Pop Art Lab had wrapped production on a large machinima event within Second Life where a music video, filmed entirely in world, was chosen for the Danish electronica music band Giana Factory. This had been a groundbreaking machinima project on a fairly massive scale, involving months of hard work and creative collaboration with quite literally hundreds of people from across the globe, low budgets but high ideas and countless late nights spent forgoing sleep and any semblance of normality in exchange for sitting behind my PC and working, working, working.

But this is, in essence, what it's like to be involved in machinima, and I'm quite positive that the majority of people who have contributed to this book recognize the same symptoms that I have just described. Machinima makers are virtual pioneers, and along with that innovative spirit comes also the constant need to create, to once again forge something fresh and visually dynamic and to stretch your own personal artistic boundaries. For the uninitiated, or for those who are relatively new to machinima, it's probably best described as both an art form and a seriously addictive creative pursuit. Anyone with a modicum of inspiration and a reasonably powerful computer can become a machinima maker; this is filmmaking for the masses; it's democratic, requiring no extensive training or years spent at film school honing your craft. Machinima is classless, ageless and crosses the social divide more effectively and with greater power than any other current art form. Within a few hours, films can be made and uploaded for viewing by a worldwide audience, with many going viral, gaining huge numbers of followers in an exceedingly short time (a fact the large, corporately run media companies must anguish over.)

Savvy businesses, not-for-profits and educators now recognize the visual allure and value of machinima to attract key audiences and customers, and in these fiscally constrained times, machinima is becoming finally and deservedly

1

recognized for the beauty of its high-impact, low-cost production values. What originated only a mere decade ago as a by-product of early online gaming communities has now become a bona fide and respected genre of film production. Established movie directors, advertising executives and music companies are investing solidly in machinima as a worthwhile creative vehicle, and machinima makers are now being contacted directly in game by representatives of global corporations to produce videos, and incredibly we are even witnessing real-life news and politics presented via machinima programs. For getting the message across, for engaging with the online generation, machinima cannot be beaten.

These are exciting times to be directly involved in machinima, or to simply be an admirer of this powerful and very modern art form. Debate rages on its future and if the eventual and inevitable move from underground to mainstream will cause its decline or in some way weaken its credibility; I personally think not. Instead, we are witnessing an embryonic filmmaking revolution not seen since the early days of Hollywood, and to be part of it even in some small way is a privilege. This is the most definitive book yet produced on this gloriously vibrant and accessible art form, with contributions from people who are directing the very future of film production.

Persia Bravin of London is press manager for the international Pop Art Lab, a virtual journalist, television host, co-producer of Pop Vox *and CEO of Best of SL (BOSL) Radio.*

Introduction

Documenting Virtual Life in Machinima

PHYLIS JOHNSON

Just because [machinima's] so new or still working on its boundaries—what it is and what it isn't; it's not really in an early phase like Diary of a Camper anymore, but we still are trying to feel out what it is and how to do this and how do we turn this into something so awesome that everyone wants to be with it. So I think we're a bit on a pioneer edge here. Maybe we're the second phase of machinima and it's too early to answer this question"—Alley McNally [Roundtable Two, 2010].

How does one explain machinima to someone not familiar with the art and practice? Maybe we should begin with a description of the imagery of the amazing set of possibilities within virtual environments such as *Second Life*. It is a virtual world unlike *Blue Mars, The Sims* and *World of Warcraft* because *Second Life* allows the members to create their own landscapes and soundscapes from scratch, to create spaces to be inhabited by the Mad Hatter in a mock Wonderland to virtual playlands that encompass the ideas behind ILL Clan Animation Studios' *Tiny Nation.* The series *Tiny Nation* was set in an environment where Pixar-like bunnies, squirrels and other little creatures existed outside of the imagination in a fantasyland created for them—created for machinima, you might say. Once home of *Tiny Nation*, Locos Pocos Island became a well-visited tourist site in *Second Life.* The series and the island are gone now, but the machinima series remains a testament to the creativity possible through machinima. The authors and the contributors of this project have seen such virtual lands rich with inspiration for story settings.

Imagine walking into a storybook of a children's classic. But then again you can also experience with dark fascination an environment based on H.P. Lovecraft's novels—twisted trees, dilapidated buildings and homes, empty playgrounds—all waiting for one of his stories to come alive on the computer screen. Such dramatic settings are perfect for engaging students in the classroom, or anyone who enjoys seeing their favorite books pop off the pages. These environments, and many others, exist in *Second Life.* Some are created by machinima makers, while others are created for specific plots or purposes, maybe a music video. Imagine creating your own set for a video featuring an independent music artist at a fraction of the cost of Hollywood-style productions. With minor adjustments, you can achieve the feeling of romance through a water-colored skyline. Now add two people dancing on top of a skyscraper in New York City. Avatars are becoming extremely lifelike through improvements in virtual skin textures and advancements in sophisticated motion graphics and animations. Postproduction software can add a near-human appearance. All this can be done through machinima. This Introduction will look at what it is and where it is going.

Machinima as Cinematic Expression

At its root, machinima is a form of cinematic expression that documents life within virtual spaces, and draws connections between virtuality and reality. Machinima is virtual filmmaking, and the relevance of recent machinima to some is that it conveys underlying emotions and motivation for participants of virtual worlds like *Second Life* to express daily life, love, and art through the metaverse. Other machinima have originated from games and virtual worlds that are not designed to allow for content creation, and subsequently the producer is limited to whatever characters and sets exist within the 2-D or 3-D environment. Virtual filmmaking is minimally the process of capturing and constructing images within virtual environments to tell a story through iconic representation in various forms and genres. A good story line taps into the human soul, and machinima is not different in that respect.

Machinima is appearing on Vimeo, YouTube, and cable and television network shows, as standalone programs or segments. Even the established film festivals, like Sundance, are exhibiting machinima. Machinima does not necessarily fall into the film camp, nor should it be considered cartoon or amateurish in technique. It is closely aligned to the field of animation, but even then there have been some significant differences especially given the rise of machinima in massive multi-player online games that encourage the creation of custom avatars. *Second Life*, for example, allows residents of its virtual world to customize their avatars to accommodate the image they want to project to others. To machinima makers their avatars are actors, and some have several avatars that assume various roles. Others put out casting calls for avatars of a certain shape and type, and these become the actors of the machinima plot. There might be a separate casting call for voice talent. Other platforms like Moviestorm and iClone are popular among machinima makers, and are independent to virtual worlds or any game engine.

To date, machinima represents every genre, from drama, documentary, and romance to music video, news/sports, and the arts, as well as corporate productions. Its creators work individually or collectively as production teams, depending on the nature and size of the project. Some filmmakers, like Cisko Vandeverre and Donald Pettit (aka Lowe Runo of Lowe Runo Productions, LLC), have several avatars, with which they vary appearance as needed. Vandeverre worked in the field of computer animation for over 25 years in digital post-production. He discovered machinima in 2007 and "what I really like is the real-time capturing aspect — you grab it and you have it" (personal communication, 2010). He also makes use of the "computer generated content library in *Second Life*, more/less props for peanuts if you need it" (personal communication, 2010). Vandeverre is a moderator and event organizer for the *Second Life* Machinima Artist Guild.

Machinima makers are often their own actors, and some even voice all the parts. Machinima is not necessarily about competing with the major mainstream producers of Hollywood or the networks. It can be thought of as a form of expression that dates back to animation, cave and tomb sketches and flip cards — anything where people have assigned icons to human expression and emotion. Machinima, like other great productions of film and television, draws upon the innate desire to tell stories — and it is a form of digital expression that welcomes the amateur as well as the professional. Machinima also draws upon the art of capturing image through photography. Stills are sometimes incorporated into machinima, which can also be sequenced analogous to an animated film.

Understanding Machinima

In 2007, the first European machinima festival, Machinima Festival Europe (MFE), began to provide a hint toward the future of machinima. Based on award entries and nominations, two software engines rose to the top and consequently began to reformulate and redefine the state of machinima, especially as a vehicle toward storytelling. Moviestorm made a significant appearance, as well as several machinima that had been produced through the game engine of *Second Life*. The conference site defines *machinima* as filmmaking "within a real-time, 3-D virtual environment, often using 3-D video-game technologies…. Machinima uses video games and 3-D animation for making short films" (MFE, 2007). That definition can be traced to Paul Marino (2004), author of *3-D Game-Based Filmmaking: The Art of Machinima*. He was an experienced animator prior to his move toward machinima.

In 2002, Marino established the Academy of Machinima Arts and Sciences (AMAS), a non-profit organization, as well as co-founded the machinima production company ILL Clan. Part of his credits include director for the project *Hardly Workin'* that won a Best in SHO award in 2001 and in 2002 an award for best acting in AMAS's Machinima Film Festival. Among his credits, Marino created a machinima video for MTV2 on the action game *Half-Life 2*, and worked on a *Sims 2* machinima series. The premise of machinima, then, was described as derivative of "the player-producer culture, where the player uses his or her own story lines and humour to create new pieces, rather than professionally produce films. So cult has Machinima become, that it is now spawning a new era of computer games—and a new approach to computer gaming" (MFE, 2007).

Then as now, producers rely on characters and sets within a game, or totally start from scratch by creating their own actors and environments for the film. The end result is "a virtual film" (MFE, 2007). It is described as a "hybrid" (MFE, 2007) process that originated by capturing game play and evolved into a competitive means of producing sophisticated animated motion pictures. Machinima is no longer necessarily filmed within a game engine. A whole movie can be constructed within a virtual environment like Moviestorm, which is a stand-alone program designed for machinima and allows filmmakers to have control essentially over all their elements, as much as technically possible at this point in time.

Machinima is similar to animation, but scripting is defined by discrete events when capturing scenes. Animation producers generate continuity and motion by linking rendered images one by one. Each image is linked together to create a sequence of motion. Machinima, in contrast, is a faster process than traditional animation, and it can be recorded in real-time within a virtual environment, much like how filmmaking or video recording captures scenes. In essence, most machinima are created within 3-D environments, whether they are within a game engine or a computer program. The AMAS (2010) contends that machinima can be understood as the "real-time recording of human/scripted performance and events ... [that] eliminated the rendering process of animation." Like animation, however, it "allows total control over visual representation" of sets, characters and events (AMAS, 2010). It also provides a live or scripted setting for characters (or virtual-world actors or avatars) to interact with each other. Post-production further shapes the final look of the machinima, and the "hardware driven playback is resolution independent" (AMAS, 2010).

Saying that, over the past year, there has been a move to officially define or redefine *machinima*: what it is and what it is not. Some view anything filmed within virtual worlds as machinima, from game shows to newscasts to lessons prepared for education and training. In March 2010, the Virtual Worlds Best Practices in Education Conference brought thousands of educators together to explore new concepts and practices in learning, and how to extend those practices to real-life education. Several machinima discussions and demonstrations were facilitated through the conference. The type of machinima created among educators typically ranges from reconstruction of history and literary works to the filming of scientific techniques.

Problematic to its definition is the desire to label everything and anything recorded inside a virtual world as "machinima." A game show, for example, in the classic sense of a machinima definition, is not machinima. But a news report about a game show conducted inside *Second Life* would fulfill the "storytelling" component of machinima that many filmmakers hold dear to its definition. On the other hand, if we expand machinima to the chronicling of human drama inside virtual worlds, one might consider that same game show as an example of virtual life captured on film for archival purposes, similar to the role of a documentary and a slice of life as represented through avatars and controlled by their puppeteers.

Machinima Defined Philosophically

The authors begin by presenting the case of one of the leading machinima scholars, Michael Nitsche. He seems to be on a mission to not only track machinima from its origins, but to attempt to define it as a practice. Nitsche is the founder and director of Digital World and Image Group (DWIG) and associate director of the Experimental Game Lab at Georgia Tech University. More than once, he has wrestled with the definition of *machinima*, keeping in mind its historical evolution.

Machinima was birthed out of both the hacker culture of the 1980s, with some creating "signature" demos to announce their skills to the game world: "Notably, these sequences were not recorded like film but generated on the fly by algorithms. They very often used 3-D visualizations based on complex algorithms and thus gave birth to a form of grassroots 3-D computer animation" (Nitsche, 2005). Nitsche (2005) explains that machinima also originated, in part, from the real-time practice of cut scenes being embedded as elements into game plots or used to introduce a game. This practice among developers incorporated scenes into the game that somewhat propelled the story line without being a strategic part of it. To some, like Nitsche, these were the makings of machinima in its early crude form, and they were created in real time. The idea of capturing and archiving game action via machinima as virtual filmmaking would come later. The concept of storytelling through machinima would subsequently develop in years to come.

Nitsche (2009) has challenged the "utilitarian" definition offered by Marino, as well as Hancock and Ingram, a "technique of taking a viewpoint on a virtual world, and recording that, editing it, and showing it to other people as a film." He acknowledges the difficulty of defining *machinima* "based on a technique, which is one reason the term 'anymation' has been used as in parallel to machinima by artists such as [experimental machinist producer] Tom Jantol." He also points out, in his words, that "the connection to gaming is shrinking." He adds, "Tying it to a game in general has become equally problematic as special machinima creation packages like Moviestorm and iClone launched without any basis in gaming" (Nitsche, 2009). He perceives machinima as having a "much stronger focus on the cinematic presentation.... Where games play with the changes of the action, machinima plays with the changes in the cinematic narration" (Nitsche, 2009). In the end, Nitsche suggests that the definition process is just that, a process, an evolution.

Authors' Framework

To simply film random events in a virtual environment is not machinima; however, these events might be the ingredients to a story that could be constructed from those various filmed scenes. This book will concentrate on the storytelling power of machinima. It will not exclude television as a point of distribution, and it looks toward the rich history of storytelling through television comedy and drama on mainstream networks. Television is being redefined online through AviewTV, Blip TV, and similar services, and within *Second Life* on virtual television networks. Machinima can be viewed through home computers and home theater sets. Virtual film festivals simulate the cinematic feeling of real-life theaters, but, in reality, films are typically viewed by individuals on home computers as digital video. *Red vs. Blue* (*RvB*) has been distributed on DVD and online, and its story focuses on a parody of two opposing groups of soldiers in battle in a canyon. It premiered April 1, 2003, and its 100th episode, *Red vs. Blue: The Blood Gulch Chronicles*, concluded the series in 2007. The series relied on capturing motion within the original *Halo* and its sequels across various platforms, Microsoft Xbox, Xbox 360, and Microsoft PC. The series won four AMAS awards, and it became one of the first machinima series to be commercially successful.

The point is that the options for viewers have moved far beyond the standard mainstream fare provided by the motion picture and television industries. You might say machinima represents DIY (do-it-yourself) producers/viewers who want to make films based on interests within their communities of reference. Some producers might be inspired similar to those who make "fan" films of their favorite animated or television characters, sort of making tribute videos about them. Machinima has elaborated its form beyond paying homage to games to the development of original cinematic and television content.

For viewers, machinima is commonly and readily accessible for public viewing on YouTube and Vimeo. It is typically rendered and viewed as video, and the ability to deliver it in high definition (HD) has made it a competitive format in terms of production quality. The outlets for viewing continue to expand on and offline. The MaMachinima International Festival (MMIF) 2010 provided a mixed reality setting for attendees and filmmakers in Amsterdam, where a real-life audience immersed itself into a cinematic presentation of machinima. Simultaneously, a virtual audience gathered as avatars inside a *Second Life* auditorium and enjoyed the all-day viewing with multiple large screens set up across the theater complex.

Saying that, it is significant to mention that this is the first book-length exploration into the merits of modern machinima filmed in *Second Life* and other massive multiple-player role-playing games like *World of Warcraft* and *The Sims*, as well as other rival virtual worlds of the past and ones that are developing. It is not a matter of overlooking the historical and recent accomplishments by producers filming within action-based games, such as *Halo*, *Grand Theft Auto*, or *Call of Duty*. Notable machinima of every platform has paved the way for new forms, and not all machinima produced from action genres have shooter plots. Not all machinima produced from *Second Life*, for instance, refrains from blood and gore. Significant moments in machinima are discussed throughout the book, regardless of the platform on which they were created. The information presented is relevant to the extent that the art and practice of storytelling or creating art is central to the mission of machinima. The book seeks to share those machinima that move beyond the mere archiving of action footage.

The authors do admit bias toward virtual worlds where the producer has the freedom to create settings, characters, and animations for the sole purpose of creating machinima. There are role-playing and strategic action games embedded within *Second Life*, and those fairly recent additions offer the opportunity for capture of game play through machinima, similar to those game films presented on machinima.com. The advantage might be that the *Second Life* machinimatographer can more easily, within limitations, retain his or her movie rights provided the sim owner of the game allows him to do so. That becomes a matter of negotiation with an individual rather than a corporation. Yet, *Second Life*'s true advantage is its ability to provide a plethora of virtual filming locations or, at the other extreme, a blank canvas upon which one can build an environment quite inexpensively. Women machinimatographers, particularly, have gravitated toward *Second Life*, *The Sims*, and virtual environments where there is no game to win. Many *Second Life* machinimatographers interviewed for this book have argued that machinima has been traditionally defined by the capture of shooter game play. The authors move beyond that framework in this book.

Over the past 10 years, and particularly more recently, significant attempts have been made to establish professional societies among machinima communities like within *Second Life*. The Professional Machinima Artist Guild was formed in 2010 to establish guidelines and a society of membership that can advance the field. The work of the members can be viewed online at the organizational site. The *Second Life* Machinima Artist Guild, also based online, has focused primarily on the work of *SL* machinimists, whereas the guild seeks to showcase professional work from a variety of platforms. Weekly machinima screenings, such as those sponsored by MaMachinima's Chantal Harvey, are typically held within *Second Life*. Real-life international festivals are reaching out to all machinimatographers and inviting them to showcase their works.

Organization of the Book

In Chapter 1, "Machinima as Moviemaking," the authors take on the credibility issue of machinima, a form of cinematic expression that cannot be ignored, as major motion picture houses now employ machinima makers to create promotional trailers of blockbusters. This chapter provides an overview and brief history of machinima making through the 1980s and the early 1990s, focusing on how it was initially influenced by game play rather than moviemaking. Machinima began as a way for players to record their game performance and show it to their friends. It evolved into a means toward storytelling among players. At this point, as filmmakers began to explore the potential of filmmaking in a virtual environment, storytelling techniques employed in traditional cinematic production began to change the nature of machinima making. This chapter is essential to providing a historical framework to the field, which lends to an understanding of how machinima is advancing and challenging the movie industry. Many producers can attest to the cost savings afforded through using machinima. Chantal Harvey concludes the chapter with "Women Making Machinima," a look at women's accomplishments in a field where accessibility has translated to opportunity.

Chapter 2, "The Right Stuff: Geared Up to Make Machinima," provides an introduction into the vision, technology and process behind machinima creation, starting with the various game capture software and computer systems and then on to some thoughts regarding video editing programs. It also asks some professional machinimatographers how they became involved in the art and practice. Pooky Amsterdam discusses the potential of virtual filmmaking in "Machinima Unleashed."

Chapter 3, "Sounding Out the Story Line," contextualizes the art and practice of machinima sound as part of the rich history of Foley and audio design in filmmaking and points toward some exceptional award-winning motion pictures, traditional and animated. It also explores sound as a critical psychological component, assisting to create theater-of-the-mind moments in machinima. The chapter concludes with Phylis Johnson writing on "The Soundscape of the American Western," which looks historically at the use of sound in classic, contemporary and machinima Westerns.

Chapter 4, "Tell Me a Story," looks at the elements that help construct a good story. This chapter also reviews the various genres in machinima making. Machinimatographer Larkworthy Antfarm contributes "The Fine Art of Machinima," encouraging producers to stretch their vision beyond the Hollywood model of production, content and distribution.

Chapter 5, "Characters Come to Life," examines compelling ways to develop a story through strong characters. The idea is to make the avatar "act" as real as possible so that the viewer is engaged by the story line, not distracted by awkward movements. This chapter introduces techniques such as pose animations, lip-syncing, and some visual tricks to cheat the camera. It also introduces some film concepts that help to develop machinima characters. Actress 1angelcares Writer discusses the art of voice-over in "The Voices of Machinima."

Chapter 6, "Setting, Lighting and Composition," introduces readers to the principles of shot composition and spends much time on how to light and design sets and actors. This chapter explores the connections between photography and machinima, with a historical perspective on lighting presented to provide some context to the discussion. In "It's All About Pre-Production," machinima producer Toxic Menges shares her thoughts on lighting, set design and filming in a virtual environment. She is one of the few artists who intentionally work toward minimal post-production, relying heavily on pre-production to accomplish her machinima goals. She is often commended for creating cinematic settings within virtual environments, rich in atmosphere and emotion.

Chapter 7, "Post-Production: Bing Bang Boom," applies seasoned and cutting-edge filmmaking techniques to machinima, from editing to fixes to special effects. It covers some professional finishing touches to consider for any machinima project. It also revisits sound design. Sound engineer and educator Jonathan Pluskota, in "Aesthetics for Sound Design," discusses the science behind mastering the appropriately balanced sound mix at the post-production stage, so it greatly enhances the overall presence of a machinima.

Chapter 8, "Celebrating Machinima: It's Show Time!," examines exhibition of one's work and reviews the popular sites. It examines the leading machinima festivals across the globe and considers emerging opportunities. This chapter moreover discusses income possibilities for machinima makers, beginning with creating a demo reel. It also discusses the inclusion of machinima as part of installation spaces and art galleries in virtual worlds like *Second Life*, as well as the role of virtual living rooms with home theaters and virtual drive-ins as meeting places for audiences to enjoy watching machinima and for professionals to critique machinima. University of Western Australia's Jay Jay Jegathesan offers "Partnerships and Collaboration," to show how creative collaboration is elevating the art of machinima in virtual worlds.

The concluding chapters offer some best practice discussions. Chapter 9, "*The White Pigeon*: A Machinima Example," features a case study of a machinima production, from start to finish. In Chapter 10, "The Fine Print," copyright expert Todd Herreman sorts through the history and legalities of machinima creation and exhibition that arise around the use of digital assets and music in machinima. In Chapter 11, "Expression Through Machinima: The Virtual Classroom," Bryan Carter, an associate professor at the University of Central Missouri, shares his experiences with teaching machinima in his *Second Life* classroom. He geared his attention to college students who were fairly inexperienced on many levels with virtual media and especially with the concept of machinima as a creative and learning tool. He helped students internationally connect to each other, in the making of machinima, through university partnerships around the world.

In the conclusion, "There Is No Road," the authors offer words of encouragement for machinimatographers, no matter their level of expertise. Part One ends with "Curtain Call," with comments by renowned machinimatographer Phaylen Fairchild, who shares her perspective on machinima's potential as it bears on aesthetics and practices in the near future.

Part Two of the book features in-depth interviews with machinimatographers Al Peretz, Decorgal (aka Judy Lee), Iono Allen, Kate Fosk and Rysan Fall in addition to machinima reviewer Michael Gray and television network owner Wiz Nordberg. Following that are two Roundtable discussions with a number of experts, moderated by the authors.

An Inspiring Future for Machinima

Although the actual definition of machinima cannot be easily articulated by those working in the field, and those observing the format from the sidelines, it is clear that machinima is viewed as a means to create powerful stories for a fraction of the cost of major Hollywood productions—and it is a format that embraces new soft and hard technologies more readily than traditional processes. Virtual filmmaking is an art and practice that will continue to evolve and inspire others to participate in storytelling.

Harvey (personal communication, 2010) explains, "Inspiration is the stunning visuality of online worlds and games. How can one not film? Before *Second Life*, I could be thrilled by the little perfect images in daily life, like a rainy day — the drops making waves and colors in a puddle, or a child playing. I still am, of course, but virtual worlds are so inspiring; things people do there are amazing and never cease to inspire me. I see many people letting out the creativity that they have to withhold in daily life. Virtual platforms are a great opportunity for us all."

Hardy Capo would have us look toward how in a brief period "technology has moved on massively, and production values are increasing all the time. In the future I can see machinima providing the kinds of entertainment that TV can't. The guys at Pineapple Pictures started a websitezine called *Fallopian*. The first issue featured machinima makers who weren't just copying film narrative; they were trying to create something different. And this may be where we are heading — devising original, unconstrained drama that mainstream TV can't" (personal communication, 2010).

Draxtor Despres states, "I see machinima really as the tool for the young emerging filmmaker. The tools are now in your hands. There is no excuse to not get your feet wet and really hone your craft before you go to film school or before you knock on Hollywood's doors. We are talking about complete control over the environment. So that means an effect-type film or films with more elaborate visual effects can be done with compositing for instance for very little money. So it is just opening up this field for someone with imagination. This is just incredible, and again especially *Second Life* because it is focused on user-created content. You can create your scene, your set, anything to the smallest detail to your liking before you film it. That is just a complete revolution in filmmaking" (personal communication, 2010).

Yani Jowisz is optimistic about the future of machinima. "I see an especially bright future in hybrid machinima elements applied to other works for scene setting and special effects. I don't mean machinima as complete works but as small short segments to what would otherwise be created in other forms of animation. The key to this is not in the production of machinima itself but in the scripting and mocap animations and their sequencing" (personal communication, 2010).

Harvey states, "The future has already started; machinima is getting the recognition it should get. Sundance accepted its first machinima, Atopic Festival (France) has a machinima department now, Bitfilm does a great job. The World Expo in Shanghai has for the first time in history included virtual worlds and art; they have opened a platform for machinima in a way that was unthinkable in 2009" (personal communication, 2010).

Amsterdam, looking outward in the not-so-distant future, explains, "Greater use of motion capture will enable greater variety of movement, and hopefully facial expressions will be able to grow, as well as interoperability between platforms such as Moviestorm and *Second Life* for example" (personal communication, 2010). Amsterdam is a major proponent of machinima's use on various production fronts.

Despres, recalling what he said at one public event, states, "I see machinima in a similar way of when people laughed about digital animation as when it was so crude, and people said, 'no one will never watch that; it is just so choppy.' Look where we are now. The *Matrix* movies are all digital animation. I think machinima is going in that direction. We just need really good writing. We do not have that yet in *Second Life*. On the other hand in other games—*Smacky's Journal* for *World of Warcraft* is a comedy that is very, very well written, and that kind of quality of comedy is what I mean for example" (personal communication, 2010). "But where is it going," he adds, "it is going to the mainstream. Again my criticism would be that some of the writing is still too amateurish for prime time. I have seen some great stuff, but I am an editor. And if you want to do a machinima comedy for instance it needs to be as good as what is successful on TV right now, the flow of what the viewer is used to, the depth of characters; I am not suggesting to replicate this but successful shows like *30*

Rock on NBC should be the level of execution *Second Life* folks want to emulate! Machinima is not there yet, but it's going to the mainstream" (personal communication, 2010).

Harvey adds, "Research has shown that within the next three years, 80 percent of all kids will have an avatar. YouTube has the young people's attention, not cinema, not TV. Film festivals are welcoming machinima now, and festivals like the MMIF [MaMachinima International Festival] exist in mixed reality (*Second Life*, real-life Amsterdam and streamed on the Internet simultaneously) and will grow even more. Machinima is cost effective of course, and more important, the sky is the limit" (personal communication, 2010).

Despres states, "I think we will see in a few years a network machinima series" (personal communication, 2010).

CodeWarrior Carling sheds some light on the difficulty of positioning machinima among media forms in the future, saying, "As we all up our game and learn things, we start mixing it with other things. Real filmmakers aren't going to be limited into what techniques they can use, so machinimatographers are going say why can't I use real footage or full CGI or whatever tool I have available." In this way, machinima might have difficulty retaining its credibility as a distinct tool or filmmaking process as it enters the larger world of virtual filmmaking. On the other hand, it has a rich legacy that continues to withstand the test of time.

As We Begin Our Journey...

Some, like Amsterdam, would argue that machinima is nearly there, if not already, like Harvey states, and definitely one can witness its successful incorporation into television shows as segments or as a complete television episode, as demonstrated by the producers of *South Park*. As of 2010, machinima was finding its way into major international festivals. *Life 2.0*, the documentary, was screened at Sundance Film Festival. Some of the leading machinimatographers have had their work screened internationally at festivals and exhibitions across the world.

Machinima is both a tool and a medium of expression. Here the authors lean on the definition by machinima scholar Michael Nitsche (2009): "Machinima is digital performance that controls procedurally animated moving images in real time.... With that in mind, its differences to traditional CG animation becomes clear, as does its difference to games and classic film." What is more important to this discussion is what he says next: "The downside: this merely touches on the current practices ... the advantages of this kind of machinima can be exceptional. Machinima, here, is not described as a technique but as a media format" (Nitsche, 2009). The premise of this book is to demonstrate the practice and potential of machinima as a tool, an accessible and inexpensive means of storytelling, documentation, and artistic production, and a unique media format in and of itself. Add to that the ability of machinima to tell the story of virtual life from its filmmaking pioneers. The interplay between real and virtual worlds is one that shares the future with its viewers and producers— it is a world where all live increasingly, one in which we live in two worlds concurrently; a first and *Second Life* become one on the screen. So, one might say machinima need not find its identity in television or animation but has a unique place in the aesthetics and practice of motion pictures. It also has a unique place in understanding virtual life as expressed through film. With that encouraging note, the book begins.

References

Academy of Machinima Arts & Sciences (AMAS). Accessed March 19, 2010, from http://www.mach inima.org/

Fosk, Kate & Royce, Michael R. (2010). Pineapple Chunks. Blog. Accessed February 2, 2011, from http://pinechunks.blogspot.com/2010/04/moviestorm-or-second-life.html

Hancock, Hugh & Ingram, Johnnie Ingram. (2007). Machinima *for Dummies*. Hoboken, NJ: For Dummies.

MFE (2007). Machinima Festival Europe. This is Machinima? Accessed March 19, 2010, from http://www.dmu.ac.uk/machinima

Machinima Roundtable One. (2010). *Terminology, Technology, and Practice* (Sessions 1 & 2, June 25 & 30). Lowe Runo Productions, LLC, *Second Life*.

Machinima Roundtable Two. (2010). *Terminology, Technology, and Practice* (Sessions 3 & 4, July 15 & 16). Lowe Runo Productions, LLC, *Second Life*.

Machinima.com. Accessed March 19, 2010, from http://www.machinima.org/machinima-faq.html.

Marino, Paul. (2009). 3-D *Game-Based Filmmaking: The Art of Machinima*. Original edition 2004. Scottdale, AZ: Paragylph Press.

Nitsche, Michael. (2005). Film Live: An Excursion into Machinima. In Brunhild Bushoff (ed.), *Developing Interactive Narrative Content* (pp. 210–243). Munich, Germany: High Text. Accessed January 30, 2011, from http://www.lcc.gatech.edu/~nitsche/download/Nitsche_machinima_DRAFT 4.pdf

Nitsche, Michael. (2009). Machinima Definition. *Free Pixel*. Blog. Accessed January 30, 2011, from http://gtmachinimablog.lcc.gatech.edu/?p=291

Nitsche, Michael, & Thomas, Maureen. (2004). Play It Again Sam: Film Performance, Virtual Environments and Game engines. In Gavin Carver & Colin Beardon (eds.), *New Visions in Performance: The Impact of Digital Technologies* (pp. 121–139). Lisse, NL: Swets & Zeitlinger.

Tiny Nation. ILL Clan Production. Accessed March 22, 2009 from http://illclan.com/tiny-nation

1

Machinima as Moviemaking

*And if it is called video, film or machinima, I do not think it is impor-
tant for a filmmaker. He has to choose his platform or his tools. And if
the tool is called Second Life or it is called Virtual World or a video
engine game or whatever, then it's a tool to produce his story if it has
a story. So I don't want to be too strict on the meaning of machinima:
we have the machine, we have the animation, and we have the cinema.
These three combined represent the meaning of machinima for the
main public.*—Cisko Vandeverre [Roundtable One, 2010].

The credibility of machinima cannot be ignored as major motion picture
houses now employ machinima makers to create promotional trailers on blockbusters. This chapter provides an overview and brief history of machinima as
it has integrated with gaming and Hollywood. The growing awareness of
machinima's potential among game publishers and Hollywood producers indicates how much these industries and fields are interwoven:

> And while the genre has mainly attracted computer-savvy nerds, machinima is
> starting to pique the interest of mainstream, non-technical movie talent, who
> are attracted to the games-meet-Hollywood aesthetic exemplified by movies like
> *The Matrix* [Kahney, 2003].

This chapter focuses on providing a historical framework to the field, which
lends an understanding to how machinima is advancing and challenging, as
well as responding to, the movie industry. Strickland (2008) recalls the context
of early machinima; its fans were really other gamers, primarily because to
watch the machinima one had to own the game engine. *Dairy of a Camper* was
an early form of machinima, a two-minute fight capture, which made its debut
using the game engine *Quake*. The story line moved away eventually from shooting sprees to soap opera type plots with the introduction of machinima-making
tools built into *The Sims 2*: "Machinima began to explore psycho-drama,
infidelity and even porn. It also proved attractive to female storytellers, who
found the laser cannons of *Halo* a little too much like boys' toys" (Put Yourself,
2006).

Two of the most successful machinima, *Red vs. Blue* and *The Strangerhood*,
have been produced by the U.S. production company Rooster Teeth. They are

comprised of short-form series spoofing their respective games. For example, *The Strangerhood* plays off *The Sims* in a Big Brother house scenario. *Red vs. Blue*, which was based in *Halo*, is a series that made its debut in 2003. The game is situated on two military bases where players are positioned in opposition "at each end of a long, rocky canyon. Players have to attack and defend the bases ... and wrestle with pointless military bureaucracy" (Put Yourself, 2006). For *Red vs. Blue*, the production team used two Xbox consoles and editing software, and *Halo*'s popularity skyrocketed through the machinima. One hundred episodes were filmed over five seasons, setting a new standard for machinima makers and viewers across the Internet. The Lincoln Center in New York City premiered its second season.

Another interesting example of machinima was its use for a music video series on MTV2. The series was called *Video Mods*, debuting in 2003, and the mods were music videos made out of game engines: "In the Waiting Line," by the British band Zero 7, was "the very first machinima music video" to work its way into MTV's rotation (Marino, 2004, p. 14). Machinima from various platforms was used to feature songs from popular artists. For example, using footage from *Medal of Honor: European Assault*, a music video was created for Yellowcard's "Only One"; other videos were made using *SpongeBob SquarePants: Lights, Camera, Pants!* (Blink-182's "All the Small Things"); *Star Wars Episode III: Revenge of the Sith* (Franz Ferdinand's "Take Me Out"), *Fight Club* (Lil Jon and the East Side Boys' "Get Low"), *Half-Life 2* (Breaking Benjamin's "So Cold"), *The Sims 2* (Fountains of Wayne's "Stacy's Mom"), and *Star Wars: Battlefront II* (Foo Fighters' "DOA"), among others.

In October 2006, machinima was woven into the story plot of "Make Love, Not Warcraft," which was an episode of *South Park*. The connection between machinima and Hollywood (and other major studios) is an evolving relationship. Much of the machinima community, at large, is connected to the YouTube generation. Many producers post their works hoping to catch the viral waves of the Internet. It is difficult to navigate through this sea of videos about anything and everything. Other services such as AviewTV, Blip TV, and Daily Motion have attempted to organize machinima content, as well as other media, and serve to stream videos continuously on demand. These content providers inadvertently leave clues to the increasing popularity of machinima, and other indie film projects. Many producers can attest to the cost savings afforded through using machinima. The history of machinima, however, is an evolution and convergence of advances in filmmaking, computer technologies, and video games.

Brief History of Electronic Games

When one looks back, it becomes easier to see how machinima was a product of the visual effects of the early 20th century. Machinima would also be rooted in the computer gaming of the 1940s and 1950s, with the first notable interactive electronic game being the Cathode Ray Tube, a missile simulator conceptualized after World Word II radar.

Other games developed in the 1950s were computer chess, tic-tac-toe, and tennis. Three Massachusetts Institute of Technology students introduced a game called *Spacewar!* in 1961, and one of those students was Steve Russell, 50 years ago, who reflected on a time when "a cutting-edge computer-generated fantasy could be conceived, written, tested and packaged for distribution in a few months, just through the part-time efforts of a small group of friends" (Markoff, 2002). In 2002, Russell was interviewed by *New York Times* reporter John Markoff. Ironically, Markoff begins his article describing Russell sitting "in a darkened movie theater ... watching the army of credits roll by after a computer-animated Hollywood blockbuster" (Markoff, 2002).

Russell took a lead role in the development of what is likely the first shooter game and the world's first video game, although crude by modern standards. It did however motivate others to create their own versions. "Two tiny space-ships were locked in mortal combat as they swung around a simulated sun. The duel was called *Spacewar*.... It was an early hint that a powerful new entertainment medium was on the horizon, one that would ultimately bond Silicon Valley to Hollywood" (Markoff, 2002).

The game would also become a "driving force underlying progress in computing technology." Henry Lowood points out, *Spacewar!* "set off a chain of events that created companies and led to a whole idea of what Silicon Valley would be." Interestingly enough the game made its debut the same month of U.S. astronaut John Glenn's flight into space.

Springing off those early attempts, many advances went on during this era, particularly the early 1970s, among college students who had experimented using computer resources on campus. Some games that did surface beyond the dorm included a computer baseball game, a hide-and-go-seek adventure game, a flight simulator educational game and a fairly popular game series, *Star Trek*. By the late 1970s, Roy Trubshaw and Richard Bartle had created the first multi-user dungeon (MUD). These interactive predecessors would pave the way for truly immersive role-playing games like *World of Warcraft* and *Second Life*, for example. Meanwhile, Hollywood was integrating computers into movie production.

Pioneering Moments in Special Effects

The story goes back much further, before the rise of video games. King Kong in 1933 was recognized "as one of the pioneering films in the field of stop motion animation and animatronics" (*Brophblog*, 2007). With the 1968 release of Stanley Kubrick's *2001: A Space Odyssey*, Hollywood personified the computer

HAL. Computers would become integral to moviemaking in the decades ahead. In the 1970s, Hollywood embraced George Lucas' revolutionary experimentation in 3-D computer-generated interactive graphics (CGI) and animation, and the subsequent release of *Star Wars* in 1977. A few years earlier, Steven Spielberg's *Jaws* in 1975 was another landmark film notable for its special effects. Spielberg relied on an adapted version of the then-popular *Unreal* game engine to create animatics for his early films (*Brophblog*, 2007). He was able to edit and render in real time (Kahney, 2003), and did so using the painstaking CGI technologies of the day. One frame might take one whole day of production.

Industrial Light and Magic (ILM, 2010) is an Academy Award-winning motion picture visual effects company that has pioneered technologies and techniques since the early 1970s. The company was founded by George Lucas to create the special effects for *Star Wars*. Over the next decade, movies such as *Indiana Jones and the Raiders of the Lost Ark, E.T.: The Extra-Terrestrial, Poltergeist* and *Star Trek II: Wrath of Khan* astonished audiences on the big screen. Some of the notable advances included motion control photography for filming the air battles in the 1977 *Star Wars Episode IV: A New Hope*, which involved developing a camera system that could record and replicate camera movements repeatedly, and other camera features like pan, tilt and focus could be preprogrammed.

By 1985, the company had created the first completely computer-generated character in the motion picture *Young Sherlock Holmes*, and a few years later, the first morph on-screen was achieved for the film *Willow*:

> Utilizing puppets, live action footage of an actress, a tiger and other elements, the CG department created "Morf," a software program that ... allowed one image to progressively be altered to transform into another image. It would be almost two years before any ILM competitor could duplicate the technique [ILM, 2010].

Between the late eighties and early nineties, major advances in the development of computer-generated characters included the creation of a three-dimensional fluid-based character in *The Abyss* and the main character, T-1000, in *Terminator 2: Judgment Day*.

The company received its fifth Academy Technical Achievement Award for computer-generated human skin texture created for the movie *Death Becomes Her. Jurassic Park* became a landmark in computer graphics technology, and the movie earned recognition for its visual effects. Other movies that continued the evolution of CG excellence included *Jumanji, Casper,* and *Dragonheart*. Greater levels of realism advanced in subsequent years, evidenced by the pinpoint shadowing and directional lighting in the 2001 *Pearl Harbor*. Steven Spielberg used interactive virtual sets, primarily relying on the *Unreal* game engine, for his motion picture *A.I.: Artificial Intelligence*. In 2004, the digital baby Sunny became the first extreme close-up of a computer-generated character in *Lemony Snicket's A Series of Unfortunate Events*.

In 2006, ILM developed a new image-based performance capture system, Imocap, for the filming of *Pirates of the Caribbean: Dead Man's Chest*. Another recent advance included fluid simulation in the creation of a "virtual water tank" for the epic sea battle in the third *Pirates of the Caribbean* in 2007:

> The centerpiece of the sea battle is the half-mile wide CG Maelstrom that required the simulation of over 15.5-billion gallons of seawater and additional simulations to create subsurface bubbles, foam, spray, splashes and ship wakes [ILM, 2010].

This technology would be adapted for other movies such as *Perfect Storm, Terminator 3: Rise of the Machines*, and *Poseidon*:

> PhysBAM, the fluid dynamics engine ... was parallelized so it could be run across 40 processors and even so, it took quite some time to compute. The renders for these passes took anywhere from a couple of minutes to 20 hours per frame [ILM, 2010].

These advances are mentioned here to illustrate how Hollywood storytelling has relied quite successfully on the use of computer-generated technologies and techniques for decades. Computer-generated technologies have simulated human expressions and movements and have created new beings with realistic animations. The puppet has become real on-screen, and Hollywood has leaned on virtual technologies to simulate cinematic realism.

A Season for Machinima

Machinima has evolved from such advances, as has the larger cinematic world (*Brophblog*, 2007) become transformed by these new applications and programs. What we continue to see in the film and animation industry is a convergence of ideas and tools, and the purpose being varied depending on the goals of the producer. What machinima has done, similar to digital technologies in general, is open the playing field to the consumer and amateur professional, as well as the indie producer hoping to find an inexpensive and creative way to tell a story or communicate a message.

Machinima began as a way for players to record their game performance and show it to their friends. Paul Marino, in *3-D Game-Based Filmmaking: The Art of Machinima*, relays success stories on the early years of machinima from an insider perspective, being himself a major part of the early movement. At turn of the 21st century, the launch of the machinima.com site was revolutionary in that it provided the first collaborative forum for gamers interested in machinima and "served as a one stop location for anyone creating *Quake* movies and the like" under the direction of Hugh Hancock of Strange Company (Marino, 2004, p. 12). The name *machinima*, to which he credited Hancock and Anthony

Bailey, rose out of the need to "identify films that were created using the same production process regardless of the game engine technology used" (p. 12).

It would evolve into a means toward storytelling among players and began to garner the attention of the filmmaking community, even its critics. Marino points out that the initial evidence of a growing machinima popularity "came when renowned film critic Roger Ebert wrote an online machinima review on *Ghost in the Machinima* in June 2000 (Marino, 2004, p. 13). Ebert introduced machinima to the larger film community "as a new art form" (p. 13). As filmmakers began to explore the potential of filmmaking in a virtual environment, storytelling techniques employed in traditional cinematic production began to change the nature of machinima making. It would be soon afterward that machinima films would begin to compete and win awards in traditional and prestigious film festivals: "The ILL Clan claimed both Best Experimental and Best of SHO awards at the Showtime Network's Alternative Media Festival with its 'Hardly Workin' machinima film" (p. 14).

Marino pinpoints 2003 as a period of reawakening that would usher in a "machinima renaissance." Machinima articles began to appear in mainstream magazines like *Entertainment Weekly* as well as trade presses. *Second Life* made its debut in June 2003 during this renaissance. From fairly early on, this platform provided a means for filmmakers to use existing virtual cities or landscapes as interactive sets in the creation of machinima. As animations have become increasingly sophisticated in-world and could be supplemented via CG post-production techniques, the practice of machinima has become more concerned about how one can use such virtual platforms to tell stories in interactive environments.

The movie industry has not shied away from the inclusion of computer-generated technologies, and it would seem equally practical for its use in the evolution of machinima. Machinima can serve as a starting point for the launch of a major studio project idea, yet it might be considered both a tool and an art form. Computer-generated software and technologies merely expand the graphic opportunities for filmmakers and machinimatographers. This is all to say that, over the past decade, legendary filmmakers like Peter Jackson have considered machinima as a storytelling medium, as well as a path to experiment with story ideas in unique ways.

Pre-visualization in Filmmaking

The idea that 3-D movie set models, complete with settings, characters, textures and animations, can make filmmaking accessible, efficient, and afford-able to Lucas, Spielberg and the amateur is significant to the history of machinima (*Caligari Newsletter*, 2003). By 1994, Lucas employed visual effects artist David Dozoretz and a team that "used 3-D animation toolsets to create rough film shots, similar to animatics, that could be used both to guide the production teams on location and the post-production teams adding virtual creatures and scene elements" (Harz, 2006). The *Unreal* game engine, and then machinima, had opened up the possibilities for both planning big-budget movies and making low-budget films. Lucas' Industrial Light and Magic production company relied on *Unreal*'s 3-D engine as the platform of choice for pre-production. In fact, chief technology officer of Lucasfilm Cliff Plumer noted,

> It's almost like a game. The director can plan how to shoot a live-action or block a CG scene.... But, we can also record the camera moves, create basic animations and block in camera angles [Harz, 2006].

Plumer explains, the director can help the production crew pre-visualize the story concept of the director, and "instead of handing rendered animatics to the CG pipeline, we have actual files—camera files, scene layout files, actual assets that can feed into the pipeline" (Harz, 2006). In retrospect, *Unreal* was really the first engine that challenged the gaming world in its ability to offer modifiable scripting for a variety of games and purposes. Upon its debut in 1998, it did not allow for online play. By 1999, the game *Unreal Tournament* was developed to provide Internet interactivity among players:

> It was, at this time, when gaming as a whole began to make its shift from a mostly offline, single player experience to the online, multi-player experience that we have today [Brizz, 2010].

It was praised as a landmark game, and "the beginning of a series of communities, clans, ladders, and friends. The community has continued on, and so have the games" (Brizz, 2010). This communication among players would foreshadow the casting of unique avatars interacting among each other, uniquely, in a virtual environment.

As early as 2001, machinima began a way for Steven Spielberg to storyboard certain aspects of his film projects, leaning on the *Unreal* technology for the pre-production of his *A.I. Artificial Intelligence*. Marino noted that *Film and Video Magazine* "broke the story" that Spielberg used machinima "to pre-visualize camera paths for his special effects shot for his film *A.I.*" (p. 14). Other producers began to look toward machinima as a way to present rough cuts of major motion pictures. Harz (2006) called attention to the growing significance of machinima, stating that "the holy grail of previs [pre-visualization] lies in the use of videogame production technology, especially that of the game engine, the core of a game" (Harz, 2006). This core becomes the center of "all the movement and manipulation of modeled people and creatures within 3-D sets, together with lighting and camera moves—a process essentially the same as what pre-vis supervisors do before a major movie starts production" (Harz, 2006).

Hollywood typically sees game development based on forthcoming movies as a profitable venture, but much less time is provided for creation of the games and promotional machinima trailers. That being said, Lucas' *Star Wars* game series was ranked among the top 10 upon release. Moreover, he was aware that "ordinary storyboard techniques were insufficient to get his ideas across to his pre-production team — or to help keep the hundreds of creatures, characters and environments organized and moving down a timely pipeline" (Harz, 2006). For his first *Star Wars* film, he "cut together World War II footage of fighter planes dogfighting, as a moving storyboard for the attack on the Death Star. That approach evolved into using miniatures of the snow speeders, as well as hand-drawn animations, for *The Empire Strikes Back*" (Harz, 2006). For *Episode III: Revenge of the Sith*, Lucas would continually experiment with scenes, pre-shooting them repeatedly (Harz, 2006). More than 20 revisions to the first minute of *Episode III* were made, relying on "64-bit AMD Opteron-powered computers running Maya and Adobe After Effects to create an immersive environment" with a cost savings of $10 million (Harz, 2006).

Understanding Machinima as Virtual Filmmaking

The convergence of media is not unique to the film industry, for these trends have propelled the launch of thousands and thousands of indie record labels and musicians to break free from traditional corporate business models. In 2003, Paul Marino, co-founder of ILL Clan and executive director of the Academy of Machinima Arts and Sciences, noted, "This is machinima's moment." He was among the early machinima pioneers. Going back to those early days, according to Kahney (2003), "Gamers realized that instead of generating monsters to be blown away, game animation engines could be employed to conjure up imaginative sets, casts of thousands and spectacular special effects." Machinima would become the mini–Hollywood and an accessible alternative to major budget production animation movies like *Toy Story* and *Shrek*.

Hollywood contemporaries Peter Jackson and Michael Bay have discovered the utility of machinima, so much they are blurring the lines between film and machinima with both converging via computer-generated effects. For instance, the special effects for *The Lord of the Rings Trilogy* were created in such a way that the crowds were digitally comprised of unique characters. In Jackson's remake of *King Kong*, a flight simulator was employed as a capture tool in the scenes where the planes circle the Empire State Building. These digital inventions are changing the nature of filmmaking and the borders of reality.

Bay, producer and director of the films *Armageddon* and *Pearl Harbor*, has established his production house Digital Domain to keep one foot in the video game industry and the other in the motion picture industry. Part of the studio's mission is to develop game engines that will help to continue the evolution and creation of "low cost animation films using ... machinima" (Ransom-Wiley, 2007). Today, the CG world continues to move animated films and photography toward realism. The computer, as an interactive and immersive cinematic tool, connects the histories of film and machinima, as well as animatics and gaming more specifically. Machinimatographers wrestle with their goals and definitions for machinima; for the time being, it affords wonderful opportunities for both student and independent producers as well as for those directing and producing in Hollywood studios. Amazingly, machinima is propelling new opportunities and accessibility in India and Africa. A search of the Web will bring up Bollywood and Nollywood machinima projects, both independent and major studio productions. Christopher Harz (2006), new media consultant and video game filmmaker for blockbuster films like *The Fifth Element* and *Titanic*, espouses the practice as the marriage of machinima and cinema.

Its original intent was to create cinematic stories, yet somehow pre-visualization has become an offshoot of machinima; indeed, as Harz (2006) reminds us, "The process is basically the same—create sets and characters, move characters around in a certain way, try a different approach, repeat until satisfied." Elaborating, he adds, "The director of a machinima project can either use a game interface to move the characters around, or use the simple scripting of the game engine to plan character moves" (Harz, 2006). He acknowledged that machinima may not meet "Lucas' standards," yet one can find "a startling number of creative and even breath-taking short movies that are being shown in machinima festivals around the world" (Harz, 2006).

Marino looked ahead to an era "when people will only want to work on machinima for its own sake" (Put Yourself, 2006). That was five years ago, and machinima seems to be finding its own place in the art and practice of virtual filmmaking. Jackson, director of *The Lord of the Rings* and *King Kong*, stated publicly that he was "getting a little bored with films." His decision, by the way, "was influenced by a strange and growing trend in which film-school graduates, hardcore gamers and cutting-edge design studios are pulling apart the programming code of high-street video games to create a whole new style of moviemaking" (Put Yourself, 2006). Namely, machinima is what is changing the way filmmaking and television production is done in many aspects.

A Reference Point for Understanding Machinima

Leo Berkeley, in his article "Situating Machinima in the New Mediascape," clarifies the two distant views of filmmaking among those of machinima communities: "The first is its status as a new form resulting from a convergence of animation, filmmaking and 3-D computer games. The second is the opportunity it offers filmmakers with limited resources to enter the previously inaccessible, big budget world of 3-D computer animation" (2006, p. 67). Berkeley (2006), in his study of machinima, states, "The narrative possibilities of interactive, hypertextual and virtual environments are opening up but have only been tentatively explored" (p. 67). He goes on to explain that machinima typically is composed of linear narratives that do little in the way of experimentation or extending the craft: "It is a strangely hybrid form, looking both forwards and backwards, cutting edge and conservative at the same time" (p. 67).

Berkeley leans toward Bolter and Grusin (1999) in his critique of machinima, emphasizing that its state is neither progressive nor evolutionary, rather a "contested" arena with "newer and older forms" prevalent, borrowing from cinema and television styles of storytelling (p. 67). Berkeley exemplifies this, saying, "Machinima works certainly presented as highly remediated — the most popular series, such as Rooster Teeth's productions *Red vs. Blue* and *The Strangerhood*, are explicitly modeled on television sitcoms" (p. 67). Poster (1996), like Berkeley (2006), sees the influence of the Web as a social space on machinima, and any discussion on power shifts must be understood in these terms. Might machinima be viewed as a social narrative? It often becomes viral in its presentation. Machinima may be the work of one person or several in a crew. Whether its creation is the invention of one person, it is often at the point of its exhibition that it becomes linked to the machinima community — viewers and producers.

In the case of *Second Life*, understanding the difference in origination of a machinima, whether it emerges from the production of small indie film crews or those that require major production teams, contributes to its social evolution and distribution, be it grassroots or mainstream. Moreover, *Second Life* was built upon the ideas of many people, and their virtual landscapes become the settings for the machinimatographer, who is a member of the gaming community. That producer may or may not have created the virtual environment. As a player and/or virtual resident, the machinimatographer is invested uniquely into the world from which he or she produces (Berkeley, 2006).

Machinima can be conceptualized as a social discourse similar to Bourdieu's views of cultural production, as its producers struggle for independence and mainstream acceptance (Berkeley, 2006). Jonathan Sterne (2003) offers a conflicted view of the machinima community, seeing it on a continuum of rebellious independence and Hollywood idealism. "These contradictions reflect both an attempt to increase the symbolic capital of the movement ... but also reveal a disposition towards the large-scale production of the dominant Hollywood producers that is currently being denied them" (Sterne, in Berkeley, 2006, p. 68). Berkeley adds, "It is clear that machinima is an example of how digital technology has shifted power structures in the media towards the increased accessibility of production and distribution technology" (p. 68). The gaming industry has been particularly responsible for providing an interactive experience for its consumers. According to Mark Deuze (2005, p. 8), the computer game industry is embedded within "participatory media culture," apart from professional storytellers such as journalists and advertising creators, because it invites relationship building in media creation and usage.

Berkeley (2006), Deuze (2005), Leadbeater and Miller (2004) and Bruns (2005) point to the emergence of prosumers as producers in various media fields. Berkeley (2006) draws similarities in the rise of machinima and zines (Internet magazines). In both cases, the production process has provided accessibility to a fan culture. Machinima has "emerged as an essentially unplanned consequence of user interaction within the developing computer game industry" (p. 70). *The French Democracy* (Strickland, 2007), a 2005 machinima that centered on the French race riots, became a representative work of the open and accessible production process and subsequently its viral exhibitive nature.

Independent filmmakers have used machinima to express cultural and political perspectives, and this is reflective of the growing interest in the film genre in India and Africa. Nollywood and Bollywood have begun to see a strong emerging role of machinimatographers. Machinima is an accessible and economical medium that allows not only a competitive advantage to those without the resources of Hollywood producers, but levels the playing field for filmmakers across the world.

Moviemaking Exercises

Identify a machinima feature that is comparable to a Hollywood blockbuster or network television show.

1. What are some similarities and differences between the machinima you selected and a comparable-themed mainstream show or film?
2. How long does it take for the machinima to establish its main character? How long does it take for the character to be introduced in the motion picture/TV show?
3. Compare the pacing, characters, settings and special effects between the machinima and the selected movie/TV show.
4. Think of machinima that you would like to watch or produce, and has there been a comparable mainstream movie or TV show produced on that theme.
5. Identify a machinima producer that has a Hollywood/network style, and explain in what ways.

References

Atton, Chris. (2001). Approaching Alternative Media: Theory and methodology. Paper presented to the International Communication Association (preconference) at The American University, Washington, D.C. May 24, 2001.

Berkeley, Leo. (2006). Situating Machinima in the New Mediascape. *Australian Journal of Emerging Technologies and Society, 4*(2), 65–80.

Bolter, Jay David. & Grusin, Richard. (1999) *Remediation: Understanding New Media.* Cambridge MA: The MIT Press.

Brizz, Sir. (2005, May 31). History of *Unreal—* Part 1. Accessed August 8, 2010, from http://www.beyond *Unreal*.com/articles/history-of-*Unreal*-part-1/?page=2

Brophblog. (2007, November 28). Why Machinima is Good for Hollywood? Accessed July 27, 2010, from http://brophinator.wordpress.com/2007/11/28/why-machinima-is-good-for-hollywood/

Bruns, Axel. (2005). Some Exploratory Notes on Producers and Produsage: Snurblog. Accessed August 12, 20010, from http://snurb.info/index.php?q=node/329

Caligari Newsletter (2003, May). In The Waiting Line. Accessed August 10, 2010, from http://www.caligari.com/store/special/news_may03/waiting_line.html

Deuze, Mark. (2005). Towards Professional Participatory Storytelling in Journalism and Advertising. Paper presented at the *Media in Transition (MiT4) Conference,* Boston, MA. May 7, 2005.

Harz, Christopher. (2006, January). The Holy Grail of Previs: Gaming Technology. Accessed August 10, 2010, from http://www.awn.com/articles/machinima/holy-grail-pre-vis-gaming-technology

Leadbeater, Charles & Miller, Paul. (2004) *The Pro-Am Revolution.* London: Demos

Kahney, Leander. (2003, September). Games Invade Hollywood's Turf. *Wired.* Accessed August 10, 2010, from http://www.wired.com/print/science/discoveries/news/2003/07/59566

Marino, Paul. (2004). *3-D Game-Based Filmmaking: The Art of Machinima.* Scottsdale, AZ: Paraglyph Press.

Markoff, John. (2002, February 28). A Long Time Ago, In A Lab Far Away. *New York Times.* Accessed August 2, 1010, from http://www.nytimes.com/2002/02/28/technology/a-long-time-ago-in-a-lab-far-away.html?pagewanted=2

Poster, Mark. (1996) Cyberdemocracy: Internet and the Public Sphere. In Porter, D. (ed). *Internet Culture.* New York: Routledge.

Put Yourself in the Director's Chair. (2006, October 22). *Times* (Sunday edition). Accessed August 1, 2010, from http://entertainment.timesonline.co.uk/tol/arts_and_entertainment/article604292.ece

Ransom-Wiley, J. (2007, May 15). Michael Bay Eager to Put His "World Class" Images into Games. Accessed July 25, 2007, from http://www.joystiq.com/2007/05/15/michael-bay-eager-to-put-his-world-class-images-into-games/

Sterne, Jonathan. (2003) Bourdieu, Technique and Technology. *Cultural Studies, 17* (3/4), 367–389.

Strickland, Jonathan. (2008). How Machinima Works. Accessed August 10, 2010, from http://entertainment.howstuffworks.com/machinima3.htm

---

✦ COMMENTS BY CHANTAL HARVEY ✦

Women Making Machinima

I think the best way to talk about the evolution of women in machinima is to tell you a little bit about how I started myself, and about where I am today. Machinima is shooting film in a real-time 3-D virtual environment or game, using what I lovingly call PPP; pro-/pre- and post-production. Originally machinima started from game reporting; battles were recorded and then shared among the users of these games, without any editing at all. I believe the first machinima came from a game called *Doom*, and the first storytelling machinima was made in the demo function of *Quake*— but I am not a historian, far from that. I am a self-made machinimatographer. To this day, I have created close to 200 productions, in every possible genre.

I started machinima in 2007, in *Second Life*, the virtual 3-D world in which I create most of my work. *Second Life/SL*, like most online platforms, provides many things for many people. You can make it your own, and just like with any situation you encounter, you grab the opportunities that cross your path. Unlike video games, *SL* does not provide you with a purpose — just like life itself — and it is you that makes it work. My background lies in art school and television (I am a goldsmith, a painter, an editor, and a camerawoman). This has certainly provided the basics for what I do today. In the Netherlands we quote this famous national football legend (Johan Cruijff) who once said, "Ieder nadeel heb z'n voordeel," meaning any and all disadvantage has its own advantage. Not knowing the history and the rules of machinima production certainly did not hold me back. So, learning things the hard way, step by step, made me what I am today. And I had fun while I took these steps.

A visual production benefits from traditional rules for filming and editing. I will never forget the first sentence in film school; my teacher sat us down and after a profound silence announced: film is a close medium. *Machinima is a close medium.* Now, machinima is a new medium, and it needs a new language. Like Piet Mondriaan, who did traditional paintings before he developed his famous abstract style, I think it is important to master basics, while experimenting too. And when you are learning, you are trying new things too, and will develop your own style.

I have seen machinima develop in a major way, for it has grown from gaming reports to art and storytelling. What strikes me is the fun that machinimatographers have when creating their work, and the important role that women have taken. The fact that women directors are invisible in the film industry (oh, they are there, but not seen) is overcome in virtual reality. In virtual worlds, opportunities are truly equal — it does not matter where you come from, what color, gender, appearance, or age; we choose an avatar that represents us and thus overcome many prejudices. We are our mind, our actions, our art.

I have a strong hunch that this is why women do so well in machinima. Most of us focus on the emotion rather than on the car chases and gunfights. Also, the gaming world for a long time has been a boys' thing, even though girls are catching up fast. I find that my 14-year-old daughter will play *The Sims 3* and Mario games, as opposed to boys her age who play their favorite game: *Call of Duty.*

Machinima is a unique storytelling platform, and I certainly know some men that do very well — but among the true talents I find the larger part is female. Aesthetics, beauty, emotion (EQ — emotional quotient) — the urge to tell a personal story involving these characteristics is a traditional female thing. Of course, men can do this, and yes, women create exciting action machinima too. It is a dangerous path to take, dividing male and female as if they were categories. Are there dominant themes in female machinima? I see women taking a stand in digital media.

My opinion is based on what I see around me, not on science. I run several well-attended machinima groups. I founded and produce the MaMachinima International Festival and produce the 48 Hour Film Project for machinima. I teach workshops at high schools, and speak at congresses. I meet many people that are involved passionately in machinima. Among them include the following, and I present examples of their work here:

Phaylen Fairchild: *Harbinger*   This mixed-reality machinima has it all! Phaylen mixed not only reality, but found a perfect balance between storytelling and art, and deep personal emotions (fear) and fast action.

Rose Borchovski: *Lost in Counting, Susa Bubble*   A striking visual machinima, deeply sensitive and mysterious; it sets off your imagination in a way that most conventional films cannot. Rose writes art machinima.

Lainy Voom: *Push*   An experimental machinima, presenting how humans are tied to the mechanics of time. A moving, close to perfection, open for your imagination machinima.

Toxic Menges: *Little Red Riding Hood*   The not-so-classic retelling of a fairy tale. Funny and a perfect example of a woman's point of view. She deals with the wolf herself.... "Well done, Red, I knew you had it in ya."

Then there's what I consider to be my best machinima so far: *A Woman's Trial*, based on a short story by Louisa May Alcott, called *Happy Woman*, a story of a strong woman, caught in her own little world, walking the chosen path right until the end. Yet there are many, many more, to mention only a few is insane and not doing justice to the talented machinimatographers I have met. I am sure other parts of this book will take you on that journey. My own journey is one of passion and vision, and I made it my motto: I want to bring machinima to the world, show what it is and can do. Passion is the source of our finest moments. Without passion, all would be grim and gray. What women in machinima have in common is this passion; it is a fire that burns, and not one great machinima has been created without that passion. A film has never been great because of its technical aspects, but because of the way it has made you feel. I would like to finish with a quote by Laura Ziskin, a female producer whom I admire deeply. Laura Ziskin sees movies as the cornerstone to women as culture makers. She states, "Men have built the cities, made and defined the culture, interpreted the world. At no time in recorded history have women been culture-makers" (Gregory, 2002, p. 377). She adds,

> Movies are arguably the most influential, important medium in the world. Because women are now making movies, then women's ideas, philosophy, point of view will seep into that culture. And that's never happened in history. We can't even see the impact of that yet [p. 377].

With that I add, machinima is the medium of the future, and women are at the forefront.

References

Gregory, Mollie. *(2002). Women Who Run the Show: How a Brilliant and Creative New Generation of Women Stormed Hollywood, 1973–2000.* New York: St. Martin's Press.
Machinima Roundtable One. (2010). *Terminology, Technology, and Practice* (Sessions 1 & 2, June 25 & 30). Lowe Runo Productions, LLC, *Second Life.*

Recommended Machinima

A Womans Trial by Chantal Harvey, http://www.youtube.com/watch?v=V3l8eYPUZzo
Harbinger by Phaylen Fairchild, http://www.youtube.com/watch?v=6foiAz7iZFk
Little Red Riding Hood by Toxic Menges, http://www.youtube.com/watch?v=p5zZ6_RPYIg
Lost in counting, Susa Bubble by Rose Borchovski, http://www.youtube.com/watch?v=h1a3iIYrOE4
Push by Lainy Voom, http://www.youtube.com/watch?v=hLeK9Lanh94

2

The Right Stuff:
Geared Up to Make Machinima

Machinima is a craft and art form and has meaning. To make it relevant, it is important to study the work of people you admire and incorporate your own ideas into machinima. It is a passion as those of us who embrace film know — Pooky Amsterdam [personal communication, 2010].

Let's start by acknowledging some questions you probably have about producing machinima. Can you really do it? What gear is necessary to get started? What are some of the top game and computer engines for machinima makers? Those are some of the questions that the authors will take on in this chapter. Here we look at how these tools are creating a new group of filmmakers, comfortable with existing between animation and digital filmmaking, and real and virtual life. This chapter is divided into four sections. The first three sections— vision, technology and process— provide an overview of basic machinima production and some specifics on capture software and computer specifications, followed by tips on getting started from some machinima pros who share their thoughts. The chapter features Pooky Amsterdam's essay, "Machinima Unleashed."

Vision

In this book, themes discussed include relevant software and hardware to get started and to advance in the field, as well as timeless ways to conceptualize a story and to develop characters. Machinima artists are emerging as storytellers for the virtual generation. This book provides an overview of the prominent filmmakers, media mechanics and theory behind machinima making for beginning to intermediate producers, with some "secrets of the trade" passed along to the reader as well. It will provide examples from professional machinima makers. It is written by two media professionals who have nearly a decade of virtual-world experience (combined). It provides an in-depth look at machinima making in 3-D worlds, and has a particular bias toward *Second Life* (and similar new worlds on the horizon), as well as character and set designs that can be constructed within simulated virtual environments. This book offers a path around animation — or a way to redefine animation and filmmaking.

This book acknowledges the published works of legendary Paul Marino (2004), who authored *3-D Game-Based Filmmaking: The Art of Machinima.* Very few books exist regarding machinima, and most have become readily out of date. *Machinima for Dummies* (Hancock & Ingram, 2007) is a good reference book for beginning machinima makers. *Machinima: Making Animated Movies in 3-D Virtual Environments* (Morris, Kelland & Lloyd, 2005) acknowledges the need "for practical information on this fast-growing ... medium," and how Hollywood is looking toward machinima for promotion of movie blockbusters.

Our book attempts a fresh look at the evolution of machinima, from camera angles, acting, Foley, composing, lighting, and editing to advice from leading and on-the-rise machinima professionals we interviewed. It pays homage to film and animation by doing so, and solidifies the connections between them and machinima. But its purpose is to provide the reader with a conceptual understanding of storytelling through machinima. Our goal is to introduce and examine the techniques and thoughts of a new generation of virtual filmmakers immersing themselves as participants in virtual worlds and 3-D environments constructed to simulate human drama.

Technology

Game and computer engines rise and fall in popularity, as does post-production software and hardware, when technology advances. The authors address the technical components of machinima from an artistic and practical perspective, as one would anticipate in a book on the aesthetics and techniques of achieving professional filmmaking. Machinima is a format that exists somewhere between film and video and the industries of animation, film and television. Its uniqueness is established in its accessibility to novice and professional filmmakers and an industry overwrought with high production costs. Virtual filmmaking is an evolving process that is blurring the lines between formats and industries. It is digital media constructed in virtual environments that increasingly allow for individuals to interact with one another through role-play and simulation.

The process of casting actors as characters becomes a physical exercise in advanced graphic techniques, whereas the conduit to the avatar remains that supplied by human emotion and propelled through virtual reality. The credibility of machinima cannot be ignored as major motion picture houses now employ machinima makers to create promotional trailers on blockbusters. Machinima began as a way for players to record their game performance and show it to their friends. Eventually it evolved into a means toward storytelling among players. As producers began to explore the potential of filmmaking in a virtual environment, storytelling techniques employed in traditional cinematic production began to change the nature of machinima making. Significant technical considerations include sound design and music composition, setting and costume design, lighting, post-production, and legal considerations. These are discussed in the chapters ahead.

The Process

There are various components of a machinima production that will be discussed in the subsequent chapters. Our next chapter focuses on sound, the foundation of any good machinima project. Sound is a significant component in filmmaking, working hand in hand with image. We examine how sound is created and recorded in-world, as well as borrowed from the real world. Foley and music composition are important elements to machinima. Music machinima may very well be one of the best ways to engage newcomers in learning about the craft. Sound is often the last consideration, but in this book we consider it an essential element for machinima to have equally strong aural and visual storytelling components. So sound is at the top of our list as critical considerations in machinima production.

Machinima is a wonderful format for storytelling. Every good film — and machinima — needs a story line. Professional machinima makers can visualize the whole plot in their mind. For some, storyboarding can be a useful technique for laying out the plot. The bottom line, however, is that every machinima producer must carefully consider those components that make a good story — the plot, the characters, the props, the setting, the dialogue, etc. — all these elements must work together. Limitations in machinima compared to traditional filmmaking can be overcome when the story line is well developed and draws in the viewer. Regardless of the various genres—commercial, education, romance/drama, documentary, comedy, action — in machinima making, the end result should be meaningful to the audience. Even a machinima commercial has the potential to tell a story and trigger human emotion.

Let's not forget that behind every avatar is an actor! To make an avatar look, sound, and move realistically requires an understanding of various animation poses and scripts. The idea is to make the avatar "act" as real as possible so that the viewer is compelled by the story line. The machinima producer must do his or her homework and research and experiment with techniques such as pose animations, lip-syncing, and some basic scripting techniques. The brilliant machinimatographers are those that can express human emotion through avatars, and that requires knowledge and experience with sophisticated real-time animations in innovative ways.

Add to that, the setting is crucial to any project. Concurrently, lighting is a huge consideration that goes hand in hand with choosing the right location. With an understanding of some basic principles in shooting, framing and composition, the producer helps the story and characters come to life for the audience. Many photographers have transitioned into machinima, and that is most likely because there are similar guiding principles for capturing still and moving images. Once the footage is captured, then the producer edits the scenes to compile the story seamlessly, fixing and tweaking rough spots through creative post-production. New advances in software allow filmmakers and photographers to transform images of avatars to resemble humans to such uncanny degrees that one is not likely or easily able to tell the difference without considerable effort.

Getting Started

There are various programs that can capture game film, with some having advantages over others. Does your computer have the appropriate specifications for you to record and edit machinima like the professionals? Let's reconsider some of those questions introduced at the outset of this chapter. Can you really do it? Can anyone become a machinimatographer? What gear is necessary to get started? What are some of the top game and computer engines for machinima makers?

Not a day goes by that someone doesn't ask how they can get started producing machinima. The answer happily is that they may very well already have the tools on their home computer to begin making machinima in its most basic form. The formulas are simple enough, and not surprisingly many give it a try. You need some means to capture the moving animated frames shown on the computer screen and save it as data on a decent-sized hard drive, an editing program to cut and organize the captured footage into a logical presentation, and a means to render the finished work in a format that can be stored compactly and viewed on the computer's onboard media player or uploaded onto any of the numerous media sharing sites such as YouTube or Vimeo. As progress and experience increases, the user will probably invest more money in the software and hardware used depending on the quality of work produced.

Let's discuss these three basic steps further and the resources that exist to facilitate them. The first step, capture, is facilitated by special software that is available for Windows, Macintosh and Linux operating systems. At the time this book was written some examples of capture software for Windows include Xfire, WeGame, Fraps, Growler Guncam and Camtasia Studio. For the Macintosh there is ScreenFlow, Snapz Pro X, iShowU HD, JingPro, and also Camtasia. QuickTime X with Final Cut Pro is another option. Finally, Linux has record-MyDesktop.

All of these programs can effectively capture frame footage for editing; which one is chosen depends on the end user's needs. Some programs include basic film editors, and others even allow integration with presentation software such as Microsoft PowerPoint. The prices range from free to quite expensive; the authors recommend trying the lower-cost options while learning. Editing, which is the second step, may require separate software if an editor is not integrated in the capture program. Happily there often are some included with your operating system like Windows Movie Maker or iMovie for the Macintosh. These will suffice for basic editing, but be aware better editors can be purchased that can produce more polished machinima. These will be discussed shortly. Finally there is rendering software that compresses the finished product into a format that is usable with any number of media players or online services, and can even place a machinima on a DVD to be viewed on the family television. Some editing software includes basic rendering tools. The best ones offer high definition as an option since all of today's viewers use this improved format.

Considering the amount of gaming software available today, sources for capture are endless and are a veritable 3-D artist's palette for the machinima producer's imagination. *Second Life, Blue Mars* and *The Sims* are readily modifiable platforms, whereas using third-party software like *Garry's Mod* opens up the ability to manipulate other mainstream gaming platforms like *Black Ops, Counter-Strike* or *Half-Life 2*. Also there are sources that provide dedicated self-contained and fully controlled environments and integrated frame capture such as Moviestorm and iClone. As you select your favorite, bear in mind that there could be legal limitations concerning the use of content generated for machinima by the software platform maker. This ranges from simply mentioning the company in the credits to getting permission for use of captured footage. There also are issues of who has intellectual rights to the finished work. Always review the "TOS" or terms of service (the contractual fine print) of the platform you select. Often this information can be found online, but when in doubt contact the game platform maker.

Turning our attention to hardware and advanced software, it is recommended to use the best equipment and tools that are available. This is not to say that a great machinima cannot originate from a humble laptop and using the software included with the operating system, but shorter rendering times and fewer system errors are noted by using the fastest processors and the maximum system RAM on a dedicated graphic design computer. When looking for an "out of the box" solution, the "advanced gaming" models offered by mainstream computer companies are usually a good choice. The three things that will impact machinima production directly are using the latest CPU technologies at the fastest processing speeds, the maximum RAM installed that your operating system can utilize and finally the best graphics card you can afford. Improvement of any one of these three items will give you a noticeable boost of speed and efficiency.

Returning to the subject of software, a good high-quality editor will make life easier, once mastered, and gives productions polish and style. There are many to choose from with examples being, but not limited to, Adobe Premiere, Final Cut Pro and Sony Vegas. Most of these editors come in trial packages and the user can try them and judge them on their own merits. The more ambitious might browse the Web for other programs that continually surface as technology evolves.

The authors provide advice and other valuable information to help you stay abreast of the latest technologies, software, and legal considerations. Whereas the software and hardware vary depending on your finances and your skill level, this book focuses on the aesthetics and practice of creating machinima that goes beyond mere capture to that which captivates the viewer. If you are just beginning your journey, it might help to learn how some of the pros began and how far they have come, as they share with you their experiences in the next section.

How They Began

As this point, maybe you are looking for some inspiration from others who took the machinima challenge and have earned the utmost respect from their peers. Throughout this book, various machinima producers have been asked to share their thoughts on machinima practice and aesthetics. The authors thought it might be interesting to share how a few of them caught the machinima bug and have been producing ever since. Hardy Capo is a master at creating machinima as art and storytelling, although fairly new to its practice. His inspiration, he says, came "from outside the world of machinima.... I had no experience of machinima or animation. I have been a TV director in the UK so I know how to make shows and tell stories. He had been using machinima for a year when interviewed." He noted, "It was a while since I'd made a short film so I was looking to make one. But, in coming up with ideas, I realized I'd never get the locations I needed. At the same time I'd just discovered machinima when looking for a pre-vis tool for a corporate film I was making. So I shelved plans for the live-action short and decided to learn machinima properly." Capo uses Moviestorm "because it's very intuitive and mimics real-life filming very well. Anybody who has used time lines for video editing feels very at home with it." Hardy Capo's work *Sandstorm* and his series *Cafe Insomniac* were birthed through the platform Moviestorm. His works are amazingly seamless and his storytelling ability showcases the performative potential of machinima.

Then there is Chantal Harvey, founder of the MaMachinima International Festival, who recounts her introduction to machinima:

I was amazed by the virtual world of *Second Life* in 2007. I started pointing three RL [real-life] cameras at my computer screen (still have some hilarious pictures my husband took when I filmed the first gay parade in *SL* in 2007) and then found software to do that in-world. I use Fraps, and use my regular editing software that I worked with while doing RL television, Adobe Premiere. I treat machinima as I treat RL film work, using the advantages and working around the disadvantages [personal communication, 2010].

Aside from her formal training, she has specialized in "ENG, music clips, commercials, company films, documentaries, and live performances like ballet and concerts. I direct four camera shoots, still do, and love filming—but editing is probably my favorite occupation" (personal communication, 2010). She started machinima in 2007 and has "never stopped since. I have over 140 machinima online now. I never stick to one genre. I learn and work. I promote machinima when and where ever I can. I have been on TV in France and the Netherlands, and in newspapers and computer magazines" (personal communication, 2010). Harvey's notable *A Woman's Trial*, based on the short story *Happy Women* by Louisa May Alcott, and her first episode of a children's series, *The Joy of Music*, are featured in this book. Her production company is MaMachinima Europe. She mainly films within the virtual world of *Second Life*, but she has worked within the platform of *Twinity* and *Virtyou* (OpenSim), and has experimented with Moviestorm. She currently works with Tony Dyson, *Star Wars* R2-D2 creator and special effects legend, as a partner in Scissores, a film production company exclusively working in real time animation (machinima).

Pooky Amsterdam started machinima "doing Shakespeare productions originally in *Habbo Hotel*" (a social networking game aimed at teenagers that made its debut in 2001). "Someone came to me and asked to record it—we began to work together and I have on Blip TV those films. Here in *Second Life*, I started doing the science quiz show which is *The 1st Question*, and that is recorded and aired live too each week. I met a great film director in November of 2009 and we began working on films together—this led to more work and now PookyMedia is one of the top quality machinima production companies around; we are currently doing work for Linden Labs." Amsterdam states that her mission has been the same through the years: "to be a producer of great visual content—from early days of doing and writing plays and skits for friends to being a stand-up comedian and a regular at NYC's The Comic Strip" (personal communication, 2010).

She began making machinima in 2004, first through *Habbo Hotel*, moving onto *Second Life*, and now having also done voice work and character development for an iClone machinima. As founder and owner of PookyMedia, she works with many talented machinima filmmakers, and sees them as her mentors, with each having his or her area of expertise. Among those she has worked with is Russell Boyd (Rosco Teardrop); she states, he is "a great director and ... professional. I love his dynamic, depth of experience, his GREAT eye and his understanding of limitations of the platform" (personal communication, 2010). Others who have inspired her include machinima journalist Draxtor

Despres for his editing work, Jorge Campos for his storytelling, and Molotov Alva for his movie which really opened her eyes to many possibilities.

Amsterdam envisions machinima as an animation entry for an Oscar short. In the near future, she sees the legitimizing of other machinima categorizes beyond traditional cinematic definitions to include "web series, commercials, game shows, branded entertainment, training films, video e-mails, fashion shows, product development, book scenes in video form and more. I see machinima as a commercially viable art form" (personal communication, 2010). That is happening, as machinima is becoming an easy way to brand a host of video content relying on game and computer engines and other software and hardware typically thought exclusive to cinematic-oriented machinimatographers. Amsterdam acknowledges machinima is a powerful tool for storytellers: "I see it as an intimate recreation for short story exposition and deep storytelling" (personal communication, 2010).

Despres is well known as a machinima journalist in *Second Life*. He applies machinima to create news features and short-form documentaries. Admittedly, he is his own roving independent reporter within *Second Life*, and offers in-depth coverage of virtual issues only minimally covered by most reporters from mainstream news agencies that have little presence in-world. He has taken the concept of citizen journalism to a new level on the Internet, and his stories can be viewed online outside of *Second Life*. He is not only a virtual reporter, but also a longtime resident of *Second Life*. Some of his recent "news" stories have centered on education, the environment, and social good through machinima. He is an audio-video editor by trade. He composes music and creates sound design for corporate image films, big-budget and independent German movies, and writes jingles occasionally. As he entered *Second Life*, he noted that it was "completely amazing" and he said to himself, "How could I have missed this?" (personal communication, 2010). That was in 2007, and before then he had only made home videos:

> Obviously I became interested because I was working in film for the audio department. I didn't even know what machinima was. I just thought it would be cool to try to understand what was going on in this world, by way of doing these little video blogs and that's what I called them. So I got myself screen-capture software and I started interviewing people and putting my stories together in the format I was familiar with from my time at my NPR station [personal communication, 2010].

His video blogs "resonated with people because nobody was doing it at the time." Then in 2007, he began to write feature scripts for an in-world news magazine show, *Life 4 U*, founded by two real-life journalists from Berlin, Germany, that had a corporate sponsor. He explains his process of conceptualizing news and documentary segments using machinima, having started in 2007, after only being in *Second Life* for two months:

I did my first one in May 2007. I have a solid background in audio editing and writing for radio. I think that is the key because I approached these stories as if they were radio stories. That means for me they need to work in terms of flow as a radio story without any visuals. If that works from the quotes that I pull, the sound bites, the ambient sound, and the script, if it is compelling enough to work without pictures, then it is good enough for me to add the visuals. So that is how I approach it [personal communication, 2010].

Despres elaborates on his involvement in machinima, saying, "I didn't know that other people were doing this, beyond news features. Seriously, it was just this kind of ignorant cool sense I am the first one ever doing something like this. And then I realized, oh, there were people who have done this for a while and are extremely proficient" (personal communication, 2010). At one point, he was approached by Frank Dellario from ILL Clan. At the time, Dellario was involved with the 2007 launch of *I Am Legend: Survival,* a multi-player first-person-shooter role-play game. The game within a game was set on 60 acres of an eerie replica of New York City in *Second Life.* The movie was a promotional strategy for the launch of Will Smith's zombie thriller of the same title.

Despres explained,

I did a piece that explored why Warner Brothers would engage in *SL* and how game play is possible in a virtual world. Then after that came out, Frank called me and said, "You're pretty good. I am with the ILL Clan and we have been doing this since the mid late 1990s." I said, "What? That's awesome." I saw some of their stuff and I met them, the ILL Clan, also Kerria Seabrooke and Paul Jannicola and had gotten familiar with their work. Their sense of humor is really fantastic and I think their stuff could actually be put on network TV, but now they are doing a lot of promotional projects for the Linden Lab. I think they don't have time to continue with their *Tiny Nation* comedy concept in *SL.* There is a void there and it needs to be filled so definitely [personal communication, 2010].

On a side note, Dellario, writer of the award-winning machinima series *Tiny Nation,* has been instrumental to the development and professionalism of machinima. Beginning in 1997, he served as producer, director and cinematographer at ILL Clan. He had 20 years of film production experience prior to entering into machinima. His machinima clients included Paramount, Universal, CBS, Warner Brothers, Intel, Microsoft and MTV, and he has even won Best 30-Second Commercial at Machinima Asia. He is one of the founding members of the Academy of Machinima Arts and Sciences. Those who have worked with him at ILL Clan have equally impressive credentials.

Yani Jowisz, as he is known in *Second Life,* lives in a unique part of New Mexico, 22 miles southwest of Santa Fe in a village. The small artist community of Galisteo boasts some interesting attractions, many of which involve the art and movie industry: "I mention the village because these surroundings are very inspiring and foster creativity even for someone as technical as myself. I have no doubt that you have seen my little village Galisteo. It is primarily known for its sweeping vistas and has had a number of active movie/mini-series sets. Mostly Westerns are shot here but the occasional romantic comedy, drama and 48-hour film projects 'come to town.' Some examples are *Lonesome Dove*, *The Cowboys*, *Silverado*, *Into the West*, *3:10 to Yuma*, *Sin City*, the *Ted Binion Story*, and *Wild Wild West*" (personal communication, 2010).

Jowisz began his journey into machinima "helping a relative overcome some technical issues in her machinima. It revived a creative and inquisitive need along with a desire to recreate history and actions." He continued,

> I have had an interest in film that goes back to *Super 8* [film] days when I got a deal on a Beaulieu. At one time I actually spliced film! I have been making machinima for approximately two years. During this time there have been many obstacles to overcome in order to pay homage to the deity of machinima, frame rate. New Mexico is a beautiful place but is limited especially with ISP choices and bandwidth especially in areas like Galisteo where I live. Cell phones barely work, DSL is non-existent and cable will never come here [personal communication, 2010].

His computer platform of choice is currently Windows. "Not that I do not like Mac but I can get much more 'bang for the buck' with the Wintel platform than I can with a Mac. Besides in my professional life I am deeply involved with Windows especially on the server end. Currently, I use Fraps for captures, Camtasia Studio for initial renders and Pinnacle Studio for production" (personal communication, 2010).

When asked to name his machinima influences, he explained, "This is both easy and tough.... Robbie Dingo was probably my biggest inspiration as his video *Susan's Guitar* was the first machinima I ever knowingly saw." He adds, "That led me to his brilliant *Watch the Worlds* which in 2007 was way ahead of what anyone was doing." Additionally, Chantal Harvey, whom he refers to as "the master" had quite an effect on him with her piece *Orientation*. As far as machinima mentors are concerned, he says, he gleans "a lot from both Cisko Vandeverre and Lowe Runo. Cisko has a good eye and is willing to critique honestly, which is the best way to improve. Lowe just exudes machinima leadership and is always willing to share honestly in his machinima adventures" (personal communication, 2010).

Collaboration, Not Competition

A machinima, like a film, begins with a good story but must be crafted as visually and aurally stimulating to its viewers. More and more, machinima productions are competing with traditional film and animation features. Machinima festivals across the globe continue to thrive, and some features have been lauded in prestigious film competitions and exhibitions. Machinima producers increasingly collaborate on projects across the globe and virtual worlds, and the result is productions that bring together artists transnationally beyond physical restrictions.

Harvey (personal communication, 2010) offers some words of encouragement to beginners, saying, "I always advise people to start with a music clip. And be careful with copyrights! Study the machinima you like — on YouTube, and contact the creator for help and advice — most of us are friendly and sharing. In *Second Life*, join the Machinimatographers Group, MaMachinima, and Machinima Artist Guild — friendly and helpful people who are online most of the time. Why do I promote *Second Life* the way I do? It is simply because you can build your own sets there and work with real people instead of scripted avatars" (personal communication, 2010).

As we close out this chapter, special contributor Pooky Amsterdam reflects on her path toward machinima, having been a seasoned online explorer and contributor to socially mediated conversations and artifacts for a number of years. Her company is forward thinking toward the many uses of *Second Life*, from the corporate side to that of taking the platform to mainstream audiences. Some recommended machinima follows her essay, which is intended to help the reader toward understanding machinima as a meaningful form of expressing creativity, messages, and stories.

Throughout the course of this book, the reader will hear perspectives from various machinima producers, representing different game platforms as much as possible. Our journey resumes next chapter by examining the important role of sound in machinima production. Even silence is a choice.

Right Stuff Exercises

Browse through machinima on various online sites and identify producers that you would consider role models.

1. What is it that you like about their work?
2. What would you like to learn from them regarding machinima? Formulate five questions that you would ask them if you had an opportunity.
3. Identify, if possible, through their online sites, what types of software and hardware they use for machinima capture, editing, and post-production.
4. What types of genres do they produce?
5. Do they have a certain style or theme among their various machinima? Is it comparable to any mainstream television, film or animation that you have previously viewed.

References

Hancock, Hugh & Ingram, Johnnie Ingram. (2007). *Machinima for Dummies*. Hoboken, NJ: For Dummies.

I Am Legend. Video Game. Warner Brothers. Accessed March 22, 2010, from http://iamlegendsurvival. warnerbros.com/index.html

Marino, Paul. (2004). 3-D *Game-based Filmmaking: The Art of Machinima*. Original edition 2004. Scottdale, AZ: Paragylph Press.

Morris, Dave, Kelland, Matt, & Lloyd, Dave. (2005). *Machinima: Making Animated Movies in 3-D Virtual Environments*. Florence, KY: Course Technology PTR.

Tiny Nation. ILL Clan Production. Accessed March 22, 2009 from http://illclan.com/tiny-nation

Recommended Capture Software

Xfire, http://www.xfire.com
WeGame, http://www.wegame.com
Fraps, http//www.fraps.com
Growler Guncam, http://www.growlersoftware.com
Camtasia Studio, http://www.techsmith.com/camtasia.asp
snapz Pro X, http://www.ambrosiasw.com/utilities/snapzprox
iShowU HD, http://store.shinywhitebox.com/ishowuhd/main.html
Camtasia, http://www.techsmith.com/camtasia.asp
recordMyDesktop, http://recordmydesktop.sourceforge.net/about.php

✧ Comments by Pooky Amsterdam ✧

Machinima Unleashed

The mind boggles at infinity, a concept so great we can't comprehend it. It has been said that man did not create the universe so he cannot fully comprehend it. Virtual worlds and game engine platforms were created by people. We can and do understand of what and how they are comprised. By taking these powers of creation and crafting real-time experience, we make memories in film. This has the profound implication that what we do and create in these arenas is of our own doing. In this we are like the gods and can put our ideas and visions into pictorial form, moving among them and orchestrating what comes next into being.

It also means we have at our disposal anything we want, any way we want it. The filmmaker can also create the fantastic. It was Jean Cocteau in 1946 whose *Beauty and the Beast* had a surrealism that still inspires today. A filmmaker can envision creatures unseen to humankind; it used to be done with costume and makeup alone. Now they are created by computer graphics programs, with special effects that are expensive yet convincing.

What if you don't have a Hollywood budget, but you have the vision, drive and a sense of style? There is machinima, a genre of film and so also a craft. The materials may be less expensive, the equipment not as heavy, but the need is just as great. The fabric of the film must allow for limitations, and we need to plan around the inherent flaws in our engines of choice. We need a story, characters, plot devices, assets, animations, props, costumes, and soundtrack. Machinima is a beautiful medium; the question is how to create film that can stand up to the scrutiny of all audiences. Every element you work with on a film has to be analyzed before it can be considered. Machinima is never going to be CGI, but it has a fresh look and feel which is authentic. For audiences outside of a virtual-world or game-engine community to watch it, there has to be great thought and skill going into how the characters will look, relate and move. Limitations such as animations and movement have to be carefully thought out, and problems avoided. Do not accept less than you are capable of and do not make excuses to your audience. When you do that, you lessen the creation you are ultimately trying to render both literally and figuratively. The tools exist — the time to learn how to frame, edit and urge the character to deliver convincing dialogue has to be found. What machinima speaks to are the possibilities we all have inherent within us to envision or create a story, a memory or a classic tale.

Machinima has potential to transform your story, characters, plot device and dreams into a reality. The tools for creation are within your reach and your budget. What makes great film, though, will take a lot of work. It is more than merely turning on your program to record. Maybe it is, if all you want to do is capture that moment, the way anyone might wish to capture a moment in any reality, saving that memory for the day when you need pictorial recall. In other words your wedding is important to you; it might not be to everyone else or anyone else outside your family, but it has tremendous meaning to you. That legitimizes it for film; just remember it might not be for everyone. If it has meaning for you, it has meaning. If you wish to reach others with your story, view or opinion, it has to have resonance to a larger audience.

The potential for machinima on *Second Life* is endless, as any kind of asset or characters can be created for your films. What can be given a life, and more importantly an inner life, can also be made to connect with your audience. We have projected ourselves onto an "other" since the dawn of humankind. Thus is the nature of play, worship, love, and advertising as we can identify the doll, the idol, our romantic interest or a product with our aspirational selves. For filmmakers this other represents an opportunity, where use of avatars in a virtual-reality setting opens up the possibility of using real-time animation, which can be highly targeted, high concept and extremely cost effective.

The term *artificial reality*, coined by Myron Krueger, has been in use since the 1970s, but the origin of the term can be traced back to the French playwright, poet, actor and director Antonin Artaud. In his seminal book *The Theatre and Its Double* (1938), Artaud described theater as "la réalite virtuelle," a virtual reality "in which the characters, objects, images, and in a general way all that constitutes the virtual reality of the theater develops, and the purely fictitious and illusory world in which the symbols of alchemy are evolved" (p. 49). This dramatic interpretation clearly sets the stage for virtual entertainment. If we can give our avatars an internal life, and show them reacting in ways that mirror human drama and comedy, we have an acting force that is effective for story-telling.

Something which is important and among the best advice I ever got was from an aunt of mine — she said, "Why should I care about them?" in reference to some characters. This is the point — how do you make the audience you are trying to reach care about the characters and concepts you are putting forth? Will a close-up registering emotion do that? Will some humor contribute to this? How is the situation you are presenting ideally going to be remembered later on by those you wish to reach?

When I started entertainment on a virtual platform, it took the form of real-time avatar-based poetry readings, done weekly on *Habbo*; it is 2.5-D characters communicating only in text, and in turn. The excitement and meaning that this generated led me to try something else, something I now see as having been very ambitious but at the time seemed like the next logical step. I produced *Romeo and Juliet* in September of 2003 to much acclaim. In fact, it was so well received I went on to do Shakespeare festivals and an adaptation called *The Wizard of Habbo*. You haven't lived until you have performed a musical in text only. I also began the annual play that for the next five years would be called *The Chrimbo Carol*. Live entertainment that people could take part in became the hottest ticket on-site and led me to go on to other genres as well. I had a Friday-night comedy club, improv nights, a talk show, book clubs, a debate format and more. Having people from around the world that wanted to get together, in real time, acting and connecting from the tips of their fingers before an international audience amazed and inspired me. Jane Goodall, the famous anthropologist, said that we humans are meaning-seeking creatures. In text and each other, we find meaning, so it made perfect sense that this kind of viewer login entertainment would be important, and it is.

Today I am much enthused about this kind of play becoming one of the big stories for this decade. Viewer login entertainment is, I believe, a right of the populace. Today, for example, the power of the press is owned by those who hit submit; we are all bloggers, commentators and have opinions which we are not afraid to use. We have become an active and engaged population that is willing to share. What about being able to take part in entertainment which is live and tremendous fun? Sit back and relax has become lean forward and engage. We are not really suited anymore to passively watching and digesting a full five-course meal of "programmed by others" entertainment.

This is something that I have been pioneering for years, first on *Habbo* and now in *Second Life*. I ask, why watch TV when you can star in your own cartoon movie every night? A great question as the zeitgeist of today is turning toward the provision of entertainment in which the viewer takes an active role. Virtual worlds like *Second Life* provide a great platform for people to be able to log in and participate in real time. The shows I have originated and produce serve the audience because they are there in the Studiodome as the program is going on, such as *The 1st Question,* which is a 1950s quiz show but on an avatar-based platform and therefore in the future. During its filming, they can chat in text and react in real time to the things the panel is saying, providing feedback and indeed a lifeline at times for answers. People log in literally from all over the world and play right along. For the intelligent among us, this is where smart-ness is celebrated, and while not for everyone, I did originate this show because I was tired of being dumbed down by conventional media.

This avatar-based entertainment represents a lot of opportunity. I thought of how men and women must be able to tolerate each other's weaknesses as well as admire one another's strengths, and this had led me to create *The Dating Casino* (because love is a gamble!). The tools at my disposal for creating a matrix scoreboard and for creating game show kinds of furnishings are endless. That people log in to play right along, and the proceedings are also captured, means that we are creating high-concept video for a targeted audience.

Let's think about that for a moment-this means (and the growth of con-nected TV will bear me out) that people will be able to become part of their favorite shows, that people won't have to go to Universal City in Hollywood just to be in the audience, and that they can be in the audience from anywhere and play along live with other people. Just as we now have the citizen blogger, we will see the growth of the citizen entertainer. Not just in YouTube videos that capture a bitten finger or a cute kitten, but in shows online that people want to create and take part in.

The future, as I see it, has put the power to be a part of a bigger world at our virtual door. In the 1930s, D. H. Lawrence said in a great essay of his, "Why the Novel Matters," that our Rubicon is our fingertips—we end there. We no longer end at our fingertips, but use them to connect with countless others, making our self-expression able to reach further than it ever has before. Machin-ima and virtual entertainment means we are reaching out past all borders, where only lack of bandwidth will hold us back.

References

Artaud, Antonin. (1958). *The Theater and Its Double.* New York: Grove Press. Translated by Mary Caroline Richards. Reprint 1938.

Lawrence, D. H. (1977). Why the Novel Matters. In, David Lodge (ed.), *20th Century Literary Critics* (pp. 131–136). New York: Longman. Reprint 1936.

PookyMedia Films. (2011). Accessed January 31, 2011, from http://www.pookymedia.com/

Recommended Machinima

The 1st Question by PookyMedia, http://www.the1stquestion.com/
The Dating Casino by PookyMedia, http://www.thedatingcasino.com/
Time Travelers, Episode 1: The Time Machine by PookyMedia, http://www.youtube.com/watch?v=
 KCvktXDi6Z8
Time Travelers, Episode 2: The Future Will See You Now by PookyMedia, http://www.youtube.com/
 watch?v=6RR_xohMrvU
Troubleshooter, Episode 2 by PookyMedia,
http://www.pookymediafilms.com/2011/02/troubleshooter-episode-2.html

3

Sounding Out the Story Line

The sense of hearing cannot be closed off at will.... Our perception of sound is the last door to close and it is also the first to open when we awaken....The eye points outward; the ear draws inward. It soaks up information — R. Murray Schafer, 1994. p. 10.

Sound is one of those ingredients that helps to imprint a movie into our very being. No matter if the movie is an animated feature, mystery, or major motion picture production that suspends our disbelief for 100 minutes or so, every producer must contemplate his or her sound intentions. *The Lord of The Rings*, with its intriguing sound mixing, and *Finding Nemo*, with its well-executed sound editing, are two examples of extraordinary music achievement and sound design. For more than a decade, sound has surfaced as a key component of nearly every movie. There was a time when only a handful of movies took care to ensure that sound design was well crafted, but increasingly attention to sonic elements — music, dialogue and effects—can propel a movie toward recognition in the industry and among viewers. Moviemaking is part of the entertainment arts. That means there is an artistic component often embedded within entertainment media. This creativity, in part, can be fueled by our understanding of the sound culture in which we live our daily lives— but imagine it only magnified on-screen. Sound can make a movie seem larger than life and bring life to the visual elements. A great film soundtrack might be understood as comparable to the making of a soundscape.

Understanding the Soundscape

Sound artist R. Murray Schafer (1994), drawing from studies of media theorist Marshall McLuhan, espouses the often forgotten, yet cultural and ancient roots of sound. Why does a budding filmmaker need to explore the culture of sound? Films tap into our emotions, and our emotions are triggered by sound events in our life, past and present. Schafer (1994) reminds us that rural Africans dwell in "a world of sound — [a] world loaded with direct personal significance for the hearer" (p. 11). Soundscapes are defined uniquely by individuals within their respective personal, social and physical spheres: "Many of the most unique keynote sounds are produced by the materials available in different geographical locales: bamboo, stone, metal or wood, and sources of energy such as water and coal" (p. 59).

Microphones are designed based on how we hear sound. Hearing is omni-directional. Humans are immersed within sound at any one point in time or space, of course noting certain individual limitations. One can cue into a particular sound, and ignore others. But we can hear all around us. Hearing is comprised of sonic vibrations: the rumble of a truck passing by our house, for example, becomes part of one's listening space, even if that person is sitting behind a computer in the study room. One cannot escape sound as it emanates into our surroundings. We hear bass from a passing car as we walk through the neighborhood, dogs barking several blocks away during the late night, a train crossing our sonic terrain miles away on a foggy night, and so forth. Sounds creep into our listening space. As filmmakers, it is important to understand how sound invades our listening spaces, especially as we contemplate how to create credible sound environments in our productions.

Some lessons on sound are those learned along the way during the film-making process. "The cooling morning air was cold and still; a light fog lingered through the early afternoon," states Hollywood sound editor David Lewis Yew-dall (1999, p. 105). "I soon learned that such conditions are perfect for sound effect" (p. 105). This revelation came during the early shooting for the motion picture *Escape from New York*. Good sound designers are those who are very aware of their surroundings. They also know the difference between creating sound for reality versus entertainment films. By doing so, they acknowledge an appreciation for the human soundscape of daily life.

Sound Scenarios

Consider the following situational environments, such as soundscapes of a morning rush hour, a hotel lobby reception, and the checkout lane at a grocery store. How might we use sound to assist us in capturing the various scenes?

Morning rush hour: You walk out of your city apartment onto the sidewalk, turn left, and join the onslaught of walkers headed to the office. You stop at the intersection as you wait with 20 others for the signal to flash "Walk," and perhaps you hear five seconds of a chirp that beckons you to cross the street in step with the crowd. The early-morning construction has begun, yet you can distinguish words from one conversation to another. "Cubs lost again." "What's up with Brittany?" "Stocks up, Stocks down." Conversations fade in and out.

Meet and greet: The hotel lobby is filled with conference attendees, and as you step back from the activity, the many voices begin to separate from each other, allowing you to distinguish one from another. Sounds magnify and retreat, as your ears interpret the various noises across the room. Certain voices catch your attention, and you begin to focus on one conversation. You capture sonic snapshots within the room. Only moments earlier, it was a collage of indistinguishable sounds, a cloud of voices. You hear the voice of your best friend, your boss, and perhaps the sound of ice falling into a glass.

Checkout line: The grocery store is packed with after-work shoppers. You stand in line waiting for your turn with the cashier. The chatter blends the voices into one buzz. Then you hear a child's voice cry out, "Mommy," from across the store. Your ear cuts through the many voices and alerts and disturbs you, and all your senses focus on that one cry. It's not yours—so you fall back into the ambient noise.

Those situations represent daily life instances that many people can relate to in the developed world. Such "slice-of-life" scenes contribute to the notion of an omnipresent human soundscape. In actuality, we are immersed within a variety of concentric sound spheres, all competing for our listening. It is often our social and individual experiences that help us to seek out certain sounds. We interpret sounds within our experiences. Those days when the rain outside the window sounds like the sizzle of bacon in a frying pan, you begin to flash back to when your mother cooked breakfast on Saturday mornings. In a world of visual stimuli, hearing is sometimes considered a secondary sense: yet it is a sense that triggers touch and smell. Schafer (1992, 1994), internationally renowned sound composer and educator, states, one can touch sound:

> Touch is the most personal of the senses. Hearing and touch meet where the lower frequencies of audible sound pass over to tactile vibrations (at about 20 hertz). Hearing is a way of touching at a distance and the intimacy of the first sense is fused with sociability [Schafer, 1994, p. 11].

Theorist Keiko Torigoe (1994) speaks of a Japanese sound culture conceptualized through conscious sound making or listening as well as interpreted through perception of what cannot actually be heard: "Sounds of the past, sounds of the future, sounds in our memories and dreams" inform how we think we hear amidst our surroundings. Tadahiko Imada (1994) implicitly concurs with Torigoe, stating, "There is as many ways of listening as there are cultures and ears." He adds, the sound of the bloom of a lotus flower is below the frequency range of human hearing; however people still gather to listen to it in the early summer. They imagine they have heard it. Torigoe (1994) contends that, in this case, the unheard sound becomes part of "the total 'scenery.'"

Basic Questions: Planning the Sound

In a movie theater, one can feel reverberations from the motion picture's soundtrack. Hearing complements our sight, gives voice to our images, and gives depth to our experiences. Great sound editors and movie producers understand how sound triggers powerful emotional responses to how we experience a film. This chapter introduces the concept of listening as a pre-production technique: design of a sonic storyboard is one way to think about shaping the soundscape of a film. Each scene should be reviewed for sound opportunities. Of course, it might be more efficient to review each frame of a storyboard and consider how sound will be best employed.

Some basic questions might help to guide the producer through the process: How will sound be used to establish a scene? Is there a few seconds of lead-in music or sound effects that help the viewer to anticipate the scene? Does the sound intensify or diminish when the visuals in a scene are established? What sound elements are used to reinforce the story? Is there a consistent or recurring soundscape across scenes? How will sound be used as transitional devices? How might silence be used to draw attention to a scene? What is the mix ratio among the various sound elements—dialogue, music and effects? What scenes will be established without sound? What scenes require sound effects, and how will they be created to give an original but authentic feel to the film?

Your responses to these questions represent important decisions. The right answers are found through trial and error, along with observation and study of the classic movies and television programs. Within a film soundtrack, the producer considers the interplay between visuals and music, dialogue, effects, ambience and silence.

Crafting Sound from Memories

Kaja Silverman (1988) studies how women's voices and narratives interplay within a film to create a cultural soundtrack. We all bring listening and hearing perspectives into our viewing experiences and into the making of, let's say, machinima productions. Sounds trigger memories. Now let's pretend you once soaked in the acoustic vibes of a concert that you attended in your teen years. Do a simple test on your sonic memory. What do you remember from that concert? What do you remember about other events where sound helped to define the situation? When you think back, can you hear shouts of joy and murmurs of pain? These sounds provide context to our experiences—and in many instances, they define our experiences. In one of the author's sound surveys (adapted from Ferrington, 1995; Acoustic Ecology Institute, 2001), a student once reported that he remembered the sound of his mother's high heels walking across the floor when he was awakened in his bed by an argument between his parents one night. He never saw her again. The sound of those heels against the cool kitchen tiles became impressed upon his sonic memory. This event became part of his sound schemata, providing a building block within his personal sound history. It would serve as a cue for interpreting other walking sounds that would follow during his life. Walter Ong (1982) and Marshall McLuhan (1962) credit sound as the first sense, drawing us back to the communication of ancient civilizations. Still sound remains pivotal to our interpretation of events.

Sound as Composition: The Keynote

Schafer (1977, p. 9) refers to the keynote as the main reference point of any soundscape and defines it as "the key or tonality of a particular composition." Often, sound provides the emotional tone that drives the overall soundscape of a film. Imagine, for example, if you were to create a keynote for a Western film. Even without music, the sound editor might establish pacing and rhythm through various elements, like the hooves of horses pulling a stagecoach across the dusty road. Schafer introduces another term, *signals*, which should be thought of as foreground sounds that are heard and interpreted consciously (Schafer, 1977, p. 10). The whistle of a locomotive approaching a train station is one example. A town bell might indicate a community gathering. The low, powerful whistle of the North American train that crossed the Western frontier illustrates the principle of signal: "The train's whistle was the most important sound in the frontier town, the solo announcement of contact with the outside world. It was the stop clock of the elementary community, as predictable and reassuring as the church bell" (Schafer, 1977, p. 81). Trains were the clock keepers and the bells of society: "The church bell, as with the train, is an icon of civilization — although far more ancient" (Schafer, 1977, p. 54).

A sound mark, another iconic element, might be considered similar to a landmark, being that it is unique to a town or place. A foghorn calls out across land, expressing metaphorically the vastness of the sea. The soundscape helps at times to characterize space. A film, for example, sometimes allows us to rehear familiar sounds, although as somewhat exaggerated. It is the job of the producer to assure that a scene is experienced visually and aurally, even if the filmmaker wants us to believe we hear sounds that are not there. We fill in the blanks. Even a decision to use silence should be a contemplative choice.

We are surrounded by sound, and by what we perceive as silence. Silence is an illusion. John Cage (1961) discredited the notion of silence when he entered an anechoic chamber to seek absolute solitude. He could not escape the surface sounds of his body. Cage asked us to consider — what is sound? What is silence? What is music composition? Schafer (1994) notes that the very design of our bodies allows us to filter out deep body sounds (low frequencies) that would inhibit our ability to hear apart from ourselves. A soundscape is the environment which surrounds us that we hear, or we fail to hear for whatever reason.

That is why we are sometimes surprised, after we record the audio around us, about what we missed. Soundscapes can be recorded, amplified, composed or just enjoyed at the moment. For artists like Hildegard Westerkamp, the soundscape is a composition of the natural elements that she has recorded from various settings. She layers and organizes the sounds into musical performances, and the layered sounds bring expression to the natural. The layering and the construction of sounds become personal expressions and social artifacts.

At this point, it might be important to present some questions to use as a guide when considering how to create a soundscape for your production. What ways can you reinforce the setting of your filming environment? What elements are critical toward creating the feeling that the viewer is really there on location? Is there a certain species of bird there that has unique calls? Is the location urbanized or set in a remote region? How might outside sounds be heard within an indoor setting, and vice versa? What is the listening vantage point of the character? What is the overall keynote composition that represents the mood of the story? What are certain sonic signals and sound marks that should be considered as part of the larger soundscape of the film? Some of these questions might provide some hints toward how to design your sound.

Understanding the Basics

If a machinima maker wants to do only one positive exercise to improve his or her craft, it would be to seek counsel from experienced media professionals, perhaps on a regular basis. One way to accomplish this is to research professional motion picture or machinima web forums and establish a relationship with the local denizens. Newcomers are soon identified as novices but the community overall is accepting, and by respectful and consistent participation much knowledge can be gleaned from the pros. One such site is the Professional Machinima Artist Guild. Reading through the carefully scrutinized reviews, a consistent thread of truth rises to the surface, "Do not neglect sound!"

Sound is one of the main pillars of machinima production and one of the most useful tools for evoking emotions from a viewer. Machinima in its simplicity uses two categories: one is Foley or everyday noises embedded for effect, and the other is background music or musical scores that can stir emotion in the listener. It is fool hardy to suggest a repeatable formula for how Foley and the music score should be mixed relative with each other since the theme of the machinima will ultimately determine this ratio, but for new machinima makers a benchmark of 50/50 is a good start. This must be altered for effectiveness in certain situations.

A romantic piece will usually contain very little or diminished Foley and softer yet more pronounced music; in contrast scary features often have sudden loud effects with intermittent silence while sinister music plays in the background. Do not dismiss the power of short periods of silence; they speak volumes when timed correctly. It is perhaps the best exercise viewing then reviewing favorite and memorable films, listening to them with eyes closed to detect the sound director's mission, delivering a medley of tones that, combined, drive home the message of the scene.

Experimentation is recommended and encouraged. Never fear to ask someone with a trusted ear to review soundtracks of specific scenes. Thanks to the World Wide Web we have nearly unlimited sources of suitable-license free music and Foley effects. Another free resource is your own environment. Don't hesitate to grab an inexpensive digital sound recorder and hunt for hard-to-find sounds around the house. Recording with the integrated microphone, a steaming teapot sounds like a flying missile or a pair of hollow plastic coffee cups sounds like horse hooves when clapped hollowly against a hard surface. Again, let imagination be the key to creativity.

Just like editing captured animated frames, the recorded sounds and music must be synchronized and pieced together in harmony with the rendered scene. The best way to do this is with a multi-track sound editor. Prices vary from freeware to professional software. Many video editors offer an integrated basic sound editing system that works in conjunction with the film timeline. Often a combination of using a dedicated sound editor and then uploading finished edited effects and music to the integrated video editor gives the best results.

A Matter of Perspective

Microphone type and placement become critical for sound artists. They paint the canvas with their microphone. Among the experts who have written on motion picture sound is David Lewis Yewdall. In his book *Practical Art of Motion Picture Sound*, Yewdall (1999) shares advice from his experience working on more than 140 motion pictures. His sound credits include the movies *Chain Reaction, The Fifth Element, Starship Troopers, Escape from New York*, and John Carpenter's *The Thing* and *Christine*. His view on sound is very much like that of the authors of this book. He simply states, "Sound is sound," further explaining, "The recording of dialogue and sound effects, the style of editing, and the preparation of these sounds, as well as the philosophical talks and manner of mixing the sounds together are all virtually the same" (Yewdall, 1999, p. 1). Yewdall (1999) acknowledges that sound design is a process that begins with a gradual "hyper-awareness" of your "sensory perceptions" (p. 11).

That keen awareness takes the producer from just understanding technique to becoming a master storyteller, using sound to convey the appropriate mood of the characters and their environment. A point of view can be established through sound. What sounds work with what characters and what locations? To do this, one might consider a basic trick, creating sound profiles for the main character and those supporting him or her as needed. The larger issue is how the character fits within the plot and location of the story, and all the sound elements need to be integrated to achieve a sonic-visual continuity. Even the sounds of locations can be evaluated and profiled, for comparative purposes when deciding what works and what doesn't. It's a bit of research; that's all. No one said that this process would be easy, but eventually it becomes intuitive.

Sound educator Gary Ferrington (1995) stresses the importance of sound literacy. He begins by asking us to think back to the sounds surrounding certain defining moments during our childhood. It is equally important for producers and editors to become sound literate, and to learn how to listen to the world around them. Location is a critical element in sound design, not necessarily the filming location. It is far more important for the sound designer to think of how to sonically portray the story in a credible manner. The key is to know whose perspective it is we are listening to, whether it is an outside narrator or the main character, for example.

Consideration should be given to whose point of view needs to be represented in the movie. Knowledge of the types of microphones, along with an appropriate understanding of their characteristics, will help the sound person to portray a sonic landscape, rich in all its audio detail. Without even picking up a microphone, the professional sound designer should understand how various pickup patterns and microphone types help to shape sound. Many books and magazines offer such advice.

Microphone Considerations

The secret is to be able to stand in a certain location and understand what sounds need to be captured, and what is the best microphone for that purpose. Omnidirectional microphones help one to hear all around them, whereas a cardioid microphone rejects much sound from behind it. The difference in this instance can be heard as creating the feeling of being immersed in a jungle in contrast to a scenario where you only hear what is in front and on the side of your head. Other microphones, like shotguns, help the field sound person to narrowly hone in on a particular sound, like a bird in a tree. A shotgun microphone might be thought of as operating a sonic beam. These decisions need to be made by the sound person regardless of what the field recordings are intended for, be it a soundtrack for a motion picture or machinima production.

For recording voice and sounds, Shure Microphone's SM58 and SM57 are two of the most durable and affordable dynamic microphones on the market, with an XLR connection. The Shure Microphone 81 (SM81)condenser microphone offers a higher-frequency response and a warmer sound for voice and field recording. Other machinima producers may find a dynamic microphone with a USB connection as a good way to start, given that they might not have an interface unit for an XLR microphone. Condenser microphones are great for capturing sound in the field, but they require phantom power (electric or battery charge) and much care by the user. Single-point stereo condenser microphones run off external power, often a battery in its base. The microphone is more sensitive than the dynamic and should not be used for capture of loud sounds. The SM81 is a fairly inexpensive option for field recording. Do some research, and you will find numerous options; be sure to check the performance reviews to help you decide what microphones are best for your purpose.

In any case, a good sound producer will build his or her microphone kit to include a variety of dynamic and condenser microphones, keeping in mind the pickup patterns (shotgun, cardioid, unidirectional, omnidirectional, binaural and parabolic) that are available. At the minimum, an audio person should have at least two dynamic cardioid microphones (with a heart-shaped pickup pattern) and a condenser microphone for capturing subtle field sounds. Other considerations should lean toward microphones with omnidirectional pickups (all around sound), as well as microphones with narrowly focused patterns.

Experimentation with cheap to fairly inexpensive microphones can lead to some interesting sounds. Any machinima project requires some thought on the soundtrack. Let's say a production team was assigned with gathering audio for a machinima production of a science-fiction thriller, *The Attack of the Insects on Mellow Valley*. The sound of insects is a must for the film. In fact, the sound producer will need to record insects. Now, of course, they could search for prerecorded sources. A better route for those wanting professional sound recordings would be to build their own sound library. When time and resources are available, it is advisable to create the sounds. For inspiration, there is plenty of recording advice in books and on the Web. Take for example the work of naturalist recorders Lang Elliott and Wil Hershberger, authors of *Songs of Insects*; to produce their CD *Music of Nature*, they employed a variety of microphones to effectively record sounds from varied species of insects. In one instance, for the "quiet singers," the recording was done inside an anechoic chamber, described as a "carpeted walk-in closet." A short shotgun microphone was used for indoor recordings. Various outside microphones were used to capture the rich variety of insect sounds.

Binaural microphone techniques offer another means to capture sounds to simulate human hearing, allowing for realistic sounds with incredible depth. They are used especially with headphones, so that the sounds seem to pop out around you. You feel immersed within the sonic environment. Sound Artist Janet Cardiff (2004) is masterful at creating soundscapes through binaural recordings. Listeners feel they are in the midst of a location, but it is in actuality based solely on her capture, construction and placement of sounds in her installations and productions. She mixes dialogue and sounds, creatively arranging them in her productions. An inexpensive alternative would be to clip one or two lavalier microphones on a ball cap and tuck the wires inside. It is a simple way to capture sound without a lot of equipment or calling attention to the process of recording, especially when one is capturing ambience in a crowd. Another example of creative microphone technique can be accomplished by using cheap contact microphones and, for instance, setting them in the middle of a red ant hill. Of course you would need to be careful upon retrieving the microphone.

Tips on Recording Sound for Machinima

Here are some basic tips when recording sound in virtual spaces. Narration and dialogue should be recorded external to the game, whenever possible. Sound recorded in real locations should be isolated and mixed later whenever possible. Voice should be recorded on digital recording software, external to the game or virtual world. Recording voice through headsets into a game engine is one way to record voice. But when you want to craft the voices of your characters, it is always best to record them external to your game engine.

Captured voices within a game or virtual world should be isolated so that other sounds do not dilute the voice quality. Ambience of real and virtual locations should be recorded without voice and added later to the voice track. The sound of an object on location does not necessarily sound the same during playback. Sound producers often construct sounds through trial and error to create credible sonic representations. A good software program to get started, which is free and accessible online, is Audacity. Whereas machinima sounds can be captured internally, the best are typically imported into the mixing and editing software. These are field recordings recorded outside the game engine. The source is not as relevant as the ability to craft authentic soundscapes that lead to credible productions. "Story" machinima is dependent on sound effects and voice-overs. The voice-over is as critical in film as in radio.

Sound producers for machinima have more in common with radio producers than you might imagine. The BBC radio drama series *Hitchhiker's Guide to the Galaxy* is illustrative of well-produced voice-overs and a good sense of ambience. The sound allows the listener to "see" the story jump out of the radio. To further illustrate this point, Dick Orkin's Radio Ranch is a great place to start for ideas on how to create sound for short-form comedy. The Radio Ranch has a long history of professionally produced comedy commercials. The right voice-over helps to create a sense of personality. Sound should be an intimate experience for the listener. Some voice-over tips for machinima are provided on video by professional actor Ricky Grove (2011) on *CyberHermit*. That is one resource, drawing from Grove's long-standing reputation.

The Voice-Over

From a study conducted at the University of Copenhagen (*Scientists*, 2007), it was reported that sound, not electrical impulses, carries information through the nerves of our body. That finding suggests that what we hear, actively and inactively, is critical to our well-being. We inhale and then exhale. As we exhale, our diaphragm expands within our chest. When we lack confidence, our breathing becomes constricted, and our vocal cords become tense. The microphone, likewise, is designed to respond to the speaker. It responds to vibrations sent forth from us and around us. Sounds bounce off objects and walls of a space. Our voice is shaped by the space in which we record our vocals. The foliage in a dense jungle, the carpet of a living room, and aluminum lockers in a high school help to shape sound. You should anticipate a warmer vocal sound when recording in a room with wood paneled walls than in a space enclosed by glass.

When we speak with confidence, our voice emerges deep within us. When we are nervous, our vocals cords tighten and the pitch of our voice increases to a higher frequency, as vocal cords vibrate more quickly than at a relaxed state. So that is why professional announcers often have deep, resonant voices; their vocal cords are not strained and their breathing is relaxed. Knowing how to speak into a microphone is part of the process. Too much force on a microphone creates plosives, which can be especially heard on the consonants *p*, *b*, *d*, *g*, *k*, and *t* in the English language. A windscreen helps to prevent plosives, but often it takes the voice talent to learn how to properly breathe and pace himself or herself during a reading. Windscreens are effective as well for blocking out wind sounds in the outside environment. When we learn to listen to our own voice, we begin to understand the richness and layers of our personality.

Inside the studio, talent can experiment with his or her voice in comfort. By varying one's stance and positioning the microphone, the talent can shift the sound. There is a metaphorical dance that some voice professionals do with their microphones. With a microphone on a stand, as the optimal way to record, the talent leans into the microphone for emphasis but lowers the volume of his or her voice. When actors raise their voices, they move back from the microphone. This dance, or "give and take," with the microphone helps to avoid over modulation and provides richness in inflection variation. Some actors rely on headsets with microphones. The problem there is that most microphones work best when you directly speak into their diaphragm, and that might not be possible with some headset microphones. Some microphone headsets, however, are quite good and work fine. Just check them out beforehand, before there is any time crunch.

You might start with a small recording space with your microphone secured on a stand. Closets work best, or you might experiment with ways to isolate a makeshift sound booth. The idea is to eliminate those sounds that might bleed through your recording. That might not be entirely possible when recording on location. So dialogue would likely be recorded back in the studio. That is usually the case anyway. Prevention, not post-production, is the rule. It is difficult, if not impossible, to remove outside noises from your recordings.

In post-production, voices can be panned and doubled for certain effects.

Ways to "color" sound include playing with equalization and compression after the recording. However, sounds, including dialogue, are typically best when recorded dry, without any processing. All that can be added in post-production. There is sensuality about making good media, whether it is a romantic comedy or a thriller. A certain sense of timing is developed that comes with vocal experience and with understanding — to let go. Our voice is shaped by the ambience of varying environments; then when you add to that the different choices in microphones that come into play when you are recording in these different settings, you begin to realize the plethora of sound decisions that have to be made during the making of any production.

Casting and Coaching

The voices can make or break a piece. Casting just one wrong voice for an animated feature film or machinima can distract from your work. Moreover, it is not enough to cast the right voice for the appropriate character; ultimately it is a producer's responsibility to ensure that the voice talent is adequately coached and understands how the lines should be expressed. The voice actors should have some insight into the characters' motivations, and that can be shared with them through the director's conveying of the treatment, which should include a character summary of one sort or another of the producer's vision. The treatment will be discussed in the next chapter.

A good voice talent should not require much coaching, but he or she will need some understanding of the story line and interactions with other characters. Often dialogue is constructed in the post-production stage and some of the voice actors will never meet each other. They will record their lines often individually at their studios, especially given that many machinima companies work with an international base of talent. Some producers create a voice bank, and that helps them contact talent quickly and efficiently. Voice talent should be auditioned for each script and given some direction about the character and the story line; that will help to avoid any misunderstandings along the way. Voice actors should be accustomed to recording their own lines and delivering them as WAV files or a comparable format. The recording should be devoid of any room ambience. It should be a dry reading, with no compression or equalization. All sound coloring should be added in post-production by the sound editor. Voice talent should make sure that levels are not over-modulated or muddied, and that plosives are treated carefully so there is no popping of consonants in the reading.

Professional voice actors do not necessarily know how to use a microphone properly unless they have prior production experience in electronic media. So again, coaching by the director is always helpful. Voice talent should be amenable to advice, and if not, that is a reason not to hire them for the part.

Willingness to follow directions should be noted during the audition. Professional actors usually are skilled at knowing what sounds good and what does not, in terms of determining usable content to deliver to the director or producer. When you find good talent, make sure you keep them as part of your voice bank. Keep in contact with them between projects as well, and perhaps drop them a hello every now and then and say, "Hey, still thinking of the great job you did on my last project. Hope I get to do another machinima soon with you," or something along that line. Don't make promises, however, you cannot keep.

Many voice actors mark copy for appropriate points to breathe and underline key words that need inflection. There are various ways to do this, but the point is that marking the script will help you, as an announcer, to manage the copy in a way that is easy for the audience to understand what is going on, and what is important. Some directors provide voice talent with marked copy, particularly highlighting key words or concepts. A good voice-over should complement the visuals, not distract from the story. It is worth the time, in the long run, to carefully cast the appropriate voice talent and work with them along the way. Diversity of accents, gender, and personalities should be considered another way to make your characters interesting to the audience, whenever possible and fitting to the story.

Stuart W. Hyde (1995) offers some timeless tips for voice actors, which include reading copy aloud several times over for meaning, identifying the point of the reading concisely in a sentence, understanding the mood of the character's lines and noting shifts in emotion in the script, seeking punctuation as clues, playing with varying ways to inflect the copy, visualizing your potential audience, and asking about the director's vision for the character.

Creating a Sound Plan

Nevertheless, it is the role of the producer, director, or sound editor to execute a sound plan of action. Nearly a year before filming began, Yewdall was assigned by John Carpenter as the supervising sound editor on the movie *The Thing*. Production decisions were made even before any film was shot for the Antarctica scenes. Yewdall (1999, p. 18) explained, "He would tell me how he intended to cover the action and what kind of microphone he intended to use." The supervisors began to develop "the inventory of specialty sounds that were needed, months before sound teams were usually brought into a picture" (Yewdall, 1999, p. 18). He adds, "Oddly enough, the cold bone-chilling winds of *The Thing* actually were recorded in hot desert country just a few miles northwest of Palm Springs."

Sound effects and music should also be considered as contributing to the authenticity or the voice of a film. Beyond dialogue, according to Yewdall

(1999), sound effects help to define the "characters' physical being and action. Sound effects go right in at the audience.... They are proverbial — like music, they hit you right where you live" (p. 85). Both sound effects and music are "extremely powerful in the storytelling process. In the performance of a single note, music sets the tone for what you are about to see and probably how you are about to feel" (Yewdall, 1999, p. 85).

This chapter has elaborated on many of the qualities inherent in the big-studio concept of Hollywood sound. Along this line, Yewdall (2003) posits that sound in American motion pictures have often offered exemplary models of sound design to producers around the world: "When you ask a film enthusiast about sound design, the tendency is to recall legendary pictures with memorable sound, such as *Apocalypse Now* and the *Star Wars* series." Yewdall (2003, p. 203) cautions, "Let us remember that sound design did not begin in the 1970s," and offers examples of movies with extraordinary sound design, including *The Naked Jungle* and *The Day the Earth Stood Still*. He adds that the shrieks of the giant ants in *Them!* were made by "looping a squeaky, pickup truck fan belt" (Yewdall, 2003, p. 203).

Sound in the Virtual World

Machinima has been featured as part of Linden Lab's public-relations effort to exhibit the beauty, originality, and potential of the human imagination on the *Second Life* canvas. The *Second Life* home page entices web visitors to check out its many features, from dancing, socializing, shopping, role-playing and education. For residents of worlds like *Second Life*, sound triggers our emotions negatively and positively as we encounter the various acoustics employed in the construction of these environments. These virtual acoustics can be captured during recording, or sound can be later imported into a machinima from virtual environments or real world. There is a tendency at this point for producers to import real-world sounds into machinima, so as to create realistic human soundscapes. Needless to say, it is an important consideration depending on the purpose of the project. Each virtual world and engine has its unique sound qualities, and decisions must be made on whether the idea is to archive sounds or to tell a story. In the latter case, it stands to reason that recording sounds outside the platform is critical to creating credible sound, when storytelling is the goal.

Another world, *InWorldz*, is a spin-off of the OpenSimulator (OpenSim). It is comparable to early versions of *Second Life*, but it originated from OpenSim software. It continues to strive toward becoming an alternative to *Second Life*. At the time of this writing, it is reminiscent of the frontier days of *Second Life*. It offers opportunities, however, for development of virtual land and business, including virtual movie studios and environments. The authors came across a variety of regions under development ranging from medieval role-play to a frontier town in the spirit of the Old American West. The skins and clothing for avatars are not as sophisticated as what is offered by *Second Life* vendors. That will quickly evolve in this new world, as well as others on the horizon. The possibilities for filming and recording in acoustically interactive environments within virtual worlds likely will continue to expand, when these platforms build off the successes and failures of the previous ones.

One can expect the sound opportunities as well to prosper over the next few years, as sound artists paint acoustically across these 3-D landscapes. Such settings become the "natural" environment of virtual worlds. Consider the work of producers Doug Story and Desdemona Enfield. *Ripple* is the name of their late 2010 aural-visual interactive installation in *Second Life*. The visuals of the exhibit are stunningly engaging, moving with fluidity to an original sonic environment by March Debain. The work is responsive, as one touches the various settings, at its core. Its sound and visual design has been captured by machinimists, but as a sound work it also stands on its own. The sound waves in this installation piece, as visually and aurally represented, have special meaning, transformed and defined by the materials onto which they are emitted. In a virtual environment, one reconsiders the depth and breadth of sonic borders. *Ripple* was situated within *Second Life* at the New Media Consortium's Ars Simulacra. *Ripple* speaks to how science and art can be expressed collaboratively and creatively within virtual environments. Increasingly, we see artists and scientists come together for media projects, and sound seems to be at the center of this convergence. As sound design is perfected in platforms like *Second Life*, there might be more opportunities for screening machinima within interactive virtual environments. Look for the passion that arises from deep within and kicks in when you are totally engaged in what you are recording (or filming in the case of machinima). Cherish the idea that you are one with what you are doing—hearing and seeing and being all with all the production elements. Music can be that driving force, and its presence, if done well, can propel a film or machinima forward on-screen. A well-acknowledged scene in the 1979 motion picture *Apocalypse Now* opens "with the hypnotic beat of helicopter blades, the scene merges with Captain Willard's (Martin Sheen) view of a lazily spinning ceiling fan. In his Saigon hotel room Willard inhabits a private purgatory, unable to function at home in the States yet reluctant to return to the front line" (Cannon, 1997). It is the continuity of all the sound and visual elements that makes this scene work in this film.

Final Sound Thoughts

Sound foreshadows events to come in a motion picture. We hear the howl of the train before we see it. We also feel its vibrations on the track. The sound calls out to warn us—and to announce its arrival. In her book *The Acoustic Mirror: The Female Voice in Psychoanalysis and Cinema*, Kaja Silverman provokes us to listen to context. A few books should be considered must reads for those interested in sound as cultural studies, the art of deep listening, or the act of composing soundscapes as personal and social narratives. The first book is *Deep Listening: A Composer's Sound Practice* by Pauline Oliveros (2005). As a distinguished research professor of music, she has been hailed as a significant composer in the art of sound and music creation. Other books, surfacing only in recent years, attempt to reconstruct the soundscapes of the past centuries, including *Victorian Soundscapes* by John M. Picker (2003), *The Sounds of Slavery: Discovering African-American History through Songs, Sermons, and Speech* by Shane and Graham White (2006), and Emily Thompson's *Soundscape of Modernity* (*2002*).

Randy Thorn (2003), in "Designing a Movie For Sound," cautions us, "What passes for 'great sound' in films today is too often merely loud sound. High fidelity recordings of gunshots and explosions, and well fabricated alien creature vocalizations do not constitute great sound design." He adds that lots of dialogue, "well-orchestrated" music scores, and tons of loud sound effects should not be the goal. He asks, "Does every film want, or need, to be like *Star Wars* or *Apocalypse Now*? Absolutely not. But lots of films could benefit from those models."

Great sound is part of the film design; having sound for the sake of sound is not a good enough plan. In his discussion of pre-production, he states, "The degree to which sound is eventually able to participate in storytelling will be more determined by the use of time, space, and point of view in the story than by how often the script mentions actual sounds. Most of the great sound sequences are 'POV' sequences." Thorn is referring to the crafting of sound so the action within a scene represents the perspective of one or more of the characters in the story. For the sound crew, the location of the set has been selected, and most of the camera decisions have been made. A good sound person has to work within the boundaries already set by the producer.

We are defined by the sounds that surround us. In this sense, we are also sound makers. Michelle Comstock and Mary E. Hocks (2007), in *Voice in the Cultural Soundscape: Sonic Literacy in Composition Studies*, suggest that it is through listening that one begins to understand the role of voice in a soundscape. Soundscapes are cultural artifacts that represent the human past. It is through practice — listening and composition — that one begins to hear the soundtrack that accompanies daily spoken and written words. It is the participation in the hearing and making that invites the listener into the experience. Sound conveys meaning whether it emanates from a motion picture at the movie theater or the speakers of a computer featuring a machinima production on YouTube.

Sound Exercises

Critique the soundtrack of a movie, paying close attention to the dialogue, sound (natural and effects), and music. Consider the following questions:

1. What is the pacing of the dialogue and overall film?
2. What types of sounds (natural and effects) are used well in the film?
3. How does sound help to achieve the mood of the film?
4. How does sound serve as transitional cues entering or exiting a scene?
5. How is silence used? Or is it?
6. First watch a scene with no audio, and then listen back with the audio. How did the sound transform the viewing experience? Or did it?

Take a sound walk at various locations in your community, and note the differences in sounds. Sit down at one location to listen, or jot down the sounds you hear at various locations during different times of the day. Perhaps keep a diary of sounds for a month, noting how certain sounds trigger memories and moods. How might you use this listening experience in crafting your sound design for a machinima production? Consider how you might record these sounds using the appropriate microphones, given their various types, characteristics, and pickup patterns. You might also vary the sound walk exercise by taking some time to listen to sounds present within your virtual world or gaming platform.

References

Acoustic Ecology Institute. (2001). Simple Exercises in Acoustic Ecology. Accessed January 22, 2004, available at: http://www.acousticecology.org/edu/currintros.html

Beck, Henry. Cabot (2007, October 7). 3:10 to Yuma: On track. True West Magazine. Retrieved October 7, 2007, from http://truewestmagazine.com/archives/westerns/2007/western-310_yuma_10_07.htm

Cage, John (1961). Silence; Lectures and Writings. Middletown, CT: Wesleyan University Press.

Cannon, Damian. (1997) Apocalypse Now. Movie Reviews: UK. Accessed September 29, 2010, from http://www.film.u-net.com/Movies/Reviews/Apocalypse_Now.html

Cardiff, Janet. (2004). Her Long Black Hair: An Audio Walk in Central Park, June 17–September 13, 2004. Accessed March 22, 2007, available at: http://www.publicartfund.org/pafweb/projects/04/cardiff_J_04.html

Ferrington, Gary. (1995) Soundscape Experiences Questionnaire. Retrieved May 30, 2005, from http://www.acousticecology.org

Hyde, Stuart W. (1995). Television and Radio Announcing. Seventh Edition. Boston, MA: Houghton Mifflin.

Imada, Tadahiko (1994). The Japanese Sound Culture. The Soundscape Newsletter, No. 9, September. Eugene, Oregon: World Forum for Acoustic Ecology, University of Oregon.

Lang, Elliott, & Hershberger, Wil (2007). The Songs of Insects. New York: Houghton-Mifflin Company. Web site, accessed September 30, 2010, from http://www.musicofnature.com/songsofinsects/recording.html

McLuhan, Marshall (1962). The Gutenberg Galaxy. The Making of Typographic Man, New York: New American Library.

Oliveros, Pauline. (2005). Deep Listening: A Composer's Sound Practice. Lincoln, NE: iUniverse.

Ong, Walter J. (1982), Orality and Literacy: The Technologizing of the Word, New York: Methuen.

Picker, John M. (2003). Victorian Soundscapes. New York: Oxford University Press.

Schafer, R. Murray. (1992). Music, Non-music and the Soundscape. In John Paynter, Tim Howell, Peter Seymour, and Richard Orton (eds.) *Companion to Contemporary musical thought.* London: Routledge Press.

Schafer, R. Murray. (1994). *Our Sonic Environment and the Soundscape and the Tuning of the World.* Rochester, VT: Destiny Books. (New York: Alfred Knopf, 1977).

Schafer, R. Murray. (1977). *Tuning of the World.* New York: Knopf.

Scientists Say Nerves Use Sound, Not Electricity. CBC News: Technology & Science. Accessed March 23, 2007, available at: http://www.cbc.ca/technology/story/2007/03/09/science-nervessound-20070309.html

Silverman, Kaja. (1988) The *Acoustic Mirror: The Female Voice in Psychoanalysis and Cinema.* Bloomington, IN: Indiana University Press.

Torigoe, Keiko (1994). Nerima Silent Places. *The Soundscape Newsletter,* No. 9, September. Eugene, Oregon: World Forum for Acoustic Ecology, University of Oregon.

White, Shane & Graham White (2006). *The Sounds of Slavery: Discovering African-American History through Songs, Sermons, and Speech.* Boston, MA: Beacon Press,

COMMENTS BY PHYLIS JOHNSON

The Soundscape of the American Western

No matter the machinima genre, tradition and culture ultimately influence the design of the soundtrack. There are certain audience expectations for certain genres, and the interpretation of a genre is usually the job of the producer. One might look to the American Western film to understand how sound is contextualized within time and space. The soundscape is defined historically and culturally. The past is always present when you hear sound. The idea behind this discussion is first to look inward to the making of a Western machinima classic, only dating back to 2005. It was produced during the early years of virtual-world machinima. Sound in Western film has a rich history that machinimatographers would be wise to examine by watching and listening to the old movies. The sound basics can be discovered from those early films, and onward through the sonic evolution of the Western. It is within this context that our discussion will trace the sound decisions of those early days that set the stage for machinima.

The Machinima Western

Machinimatographer Eric Call, known inside *Second Life* as Eric Linden, was the senior artist for Linden Lab when he produced a Western machinima based on the poem *Silver Bells and Golden Spurs*, a parable about two gunslingers. The ring of the silver bells is a sonic theme that runs through the story. The machinima was titled the same as the poem, and its plot stayed true to the poem. The machinima was narrated and filmed completely in *Second Life* and made its debut in November 2005. The idea behind its production was "to use raw footage and let it stand on its own, using only simple dissolves and titles— which are common in most bundled software on off-the-shelf computer systems" (Linden, 2005). The point of the project was to encourage others that anyone could create "compelling stories and show interesting visuals if they approach their projects with creativity and thoughtfulness. That's really all *Bells and Spurs* is: a collection of sequential, cohesive images— put together in a thoughtful, creative and compelling way" (Linden, 2005). In fact, Linden (2005) defined *machinima* as the "art of making real movies in virtual worlds." The primary sound is the narration. Today, this piece would be easier to produce given the evolution of sound and animations in *Second Life*.

The story focuses on the gunslinger Dandy, known for a chain on his watch with a dozen silver bells hanging from it. Each bell represents someone who died from his bullet. The machinima is remarkably conceived and executed, given that it was made in 2005. At that time, custom avatars, costumes, and sets were constructed. The project involved directing a huge cast of avatar actors in the saloon. Animations had to be scripted or located that would allow the avatars to move realistically in the machinima. The machinima was screened at major film festivals in the United States and Europe.

The producer explained, at its showing, his search for the appropriate ingredients for the soundtrack: music, effects, and dialogue. Call (2006) emphasized that sound had a major role in his machinima:

> Sound is huge ... I wanted something cinematic, something rich — with a clear western theme. I searched extensively for just the right music, and after a month or so I stumbled on a piece on Dittybase.com called "Hang 'Em High."

Call needed some time to mull over his decision to be sure he had found the right music. He explains, "I loved it from my first listening, but wasn't sure if it was sinister enough for the emotion I wanted to elicit from the audience. I continued searching, but realized over time that this was, in fact, it" (Call, 2006). While doing so, he located sound effects and mood music to "round out the sound track." His next focus was "finding the right voice talent to read the roles of the Dandy, Stranger, and the Narrator. I found the perfect actor through an agency in Phoenix, set up a contract and e-mailed the dialogue. Bruce Miles' extensive range and experience were just what I needed" (Call, 2006).

"Recording the dialogue was a lot of fun," explains Call (2006). "Bruce did all of the recording in his home studio, and I directed him over the phone as he recorded it. He'd read a few lines, pause, and I'd direct him to slow down, speed up, change inflection, whatever I needed." The voice segments were e-mailed to him as MP3 files. Call (2006) noted that the recording was a "totally seamless, crystal clear voice-over that worked perfectly" to his editing timeline.

In the end, Call's work stood as an example of what could be done even in the early years of machinima production in *Second Life*. As in the early Westerns, Call created a soundscape that helped to shape his story. His work was among some of the early machinima produced in *Second Life*. He was also among some of the first to thoughtfully consider the sound design of his production. A strong narration and the right mix of sound required planning and much work to make it happen. The Western soundscape, or soundtrack, has a long history in motion picture production. Machinima producers may benefit from understanding the significance and tradition of the Western soundscape, particularly among its viewers.

In the Beginning

From its inception, the electronic media began to reinterpret the past through present technologies—film, radio, and television. *The Great American Train Robbery* made its debut at the turn of the 20th century, and other silent films soon followed. Grandiose frontier legends were being reconceptualized from literature and comic books to the big screen. Motion pictures, and soon radio and television, began to reinvent Western legends, scenery, and in some cases soundscapes. The free spirit of the horse and its rider encountered the heavy rhythmic sounds of the train and industrialization—a downbeat that offered entrance into mass culture. Industrialization, particularly 1890 to 1930, produced a new type of modern noise that challenged prior ways of interpreting life through one's sonic environment. The train, as an icon, became a sonic reference point on the plains and across urban regions, both east and west. This noise became assimilated into the soundscape of society (Attali, 1985; Keil & Feld, 1994; Thompson, 2002).

From the letters, journals, and notes of those traveling across the American frontier, it becomes evident the daily soundscape was one intermixed with wind, dust, and dirt. Clouds of wind and dust, particularly together, created a deafening pounding across the eardrums. The wagons pushed forward, with more than a dozen teams of horses leading the way. The constant pounding of hooves on dry ground created a sense of drone. It was impossible to see at times, and nearly impossible to hear — until the wagon train would settle down for the night. During winter months, snow brought a dangerous silence and solitude to the ground that warned of famine. In the spring, the whoosh of mud under wagon wheels was as much heard as felt and seen. As the travelers became settlers, the sounds began to change from the dusty trails toward town sounds. These were the Western sounds that would be reimagined on a big screen. By the turn of the 20th century, the Old West had become romanticized as a place of adventure, heroism, and individualism. The rise of the motion picture, radio and television industries would propel this myth. The dusty wind-torn frontier terrain, the steam from the locomotives, and the billowing and puffing smokestacks of the factories deafened listeners from noting the disappearing soundscapes of a wilder America. Emily Thompson (2002, pp. 1–2) demarcates this transitional era from the Old West to industrialization as pivotal to the making of the "soundscape of modernity."

In Old Arizona (1929), featuring Cisco Kid in a talkie, and Cimarron (1931), with its extraordinary land rush scene, have added to the sound annals of motion pictures. Sound recorded for Cimarron employed the RCA Photophone System which had become fairly perfected by then, compared to other systems of the 1920s: Lee DeForest's Phonofilm, Warner Brothers' Vitaphone, and Fox-Cades' Movietone. These two movies were very realistic in sound; hooves pounding on dirt roads and trails, rickety stagecoaches and wagon trains, and the constant popping of guns were recurring themes. In Old Arizona brings to mind sound theorist/composer R. Murray Schafer's discussion on the significance of bells and how they often serve as historical sound marks in communities.

The movie opens with mission bells, and then we hear the sounds of an incoming stagecoach, followed by street musicians. In the next scene, we hear the alternating "clucks" from the horse hooves of Cisco Kid and those of the coach horses. Interestingly enough, at the stagecoach station, we hear boisterous Americans whose voices grate against the soft environmental ambience of the dusty town. As the last tourist boards the stagecoach, we hear a loud bray from the donkey a few yards away. The timing might have been coincidental, but it definitely plays into the character of the American tourists. The Mexicans are characterized as quiet people rich with culture. Their soundscape is layered with violins, guitars and harmonica, and consequently we return to the sonic feel established by the ringing of the mission bells in the opening scene.

In the 1950s and 1960s, the acoustic feel of the motion pictures Shane and Magnificent Seven, and of course the masterful effects, music, and silence that would brand the spaghetti Western, served to heighten attention to Western soundscapes; whether these movies were nominated, won or did not win awards is not necessarily relevant (TV Westerns, 2007). They employed sound in creative ways. Through the 1960s, Westerns that won or were nominated in sound categories included How the West Was Won, Butch Cassidy and the Sundance Kid, The Wild Bunch, Magnificent Seven, and High Noon. Even the early 1930s' classics Stagecoach and Viva Villa were nominated for best sound. Given the limitations of technology, their sound design was quite amazing and competitive with today's best Westerns.

There is also a consistency in the themes present in Western movies that dates back to the earliest films. The sound of storms, stagecoaches, and saloons recur in early movies and those of later decades, and more recent movies do better to capture the hyperbole and legend of the Old West. For the most part, however, the first Westerns, like Cimarron, did well in recreating the drudgery of the 1800s and the expansiveness of the West.

Hearing John Wayne Movies

When we think of the Old West, we imagine glorious landscapes of majestic open plains and mountainous rocky terrain. We think of heroes and heroines who mapped the American West. John Wayne movies typically come to the forefront of popular Westerns. The characters have a song or two in their heart and exhibit the frontier spirit with true grit. In *Riders of Destiny* (1933), singing Sandy Saunders lip-syncs his way into our hearts. Many of his movies are classified under both genres "romance" and "Western." The first Wayne movie, *The Big Trail* (1930), provided a couple of catchy tunes—"Song of the Big Trail" and "When It's Harvest Time in Peaceful Valley." This film did little more than give Wayne an entrance into the sound era of the motion picture industry. It is considered by the Internet Movie Database (IMDb) as the first major release of a Western "sound" film.

Blue Steel (1934) filmed in Lone Pine, California, stirs up a bit of the classic weather that serves to signify the trials and tribulations of the human spirit — a storm within a storm — within the Western genre. John Wayne movies bring attention to the industrialization of America and its changing soundscape. Consider, for example, *The Hurricane Express* (1932) as a metaphor for this transition, which begins with sounds of technology as we see and hear wagon wheels evolve to trains, planes, and automobiles. The sounds segue into each other seamlessly over the opening credits. Wayne's movies contain classic sound marks, such as the rattling of the stagecoach and shuffling and pounding of horses' hooves against a dusty terrain, as heard, for instance, in *Winds of the Wasteland* (1936). Gun pops and horse trots create familiar rhythmic backdrops. The weighty combination of dust and wood often create a somber town ambience, somewhat like in the opening scene of *The Dawn Rider* (1935). In other scenes of Wayne's classics and other Westerns, we hear people walking across the wooden planks of the town walkways. We hear reverberations across the makeshift wood path. It served as an effect to spring the movie forward, and introduced a scene of good cheer or action. In both cases, the acoustics of the wood contributed to the unique sound of the Western, especially in movement and dialogue.

Stagecoach (1939) was a notable Western, in part through its cinematic beauty of Monument Valley. But it is impossible to ignore the powerful mix of dialogue, music and sound effects that recreated the glory and dangers of the frontier (although it would be difficult to converse in a moving stagecoach). A cinematic cattle drive gave rise to the Oscar nomination of the 1948 motion picture *Red River* for film editing (with filming on location in Elgin, Arizona). The sound of wheels, hooves, and guns in John Wayne movies adds muscle and forward motion to the films. Singing was used to slow down the movie pace, in counterpoise to the modern Western in which music and dialogue complement the visuals through a variety of techniques.

Sound in the Modern Western

In recent decades, a number of Westerns have won in the Academy Awards for their use of sound and music in motion pictures. In 1990, Kevin Costner won best original score and best sound for *Dancing with Wolves*, and Eastwood's *Unforgiven* in 1992 would be nominated for best sound. Technology had matured, as had the practice of moviemaking, particularly sound engineering. In *The Quick and The Dead* (1995), the audience hears all these elements and more of the West coming together to create a sonic text: the cocking of the pistols, the creaking of the saloon doors, the ticktock of the clock, bodies hitting the ground, the jangle of the boot spurs, the swirl of the wind preceding the Sharon Stone and Russell Crowe gunfight, and the storm at the cemetery. Stone received mixed reviews for her acting, but her character Ellen as a female outlaw brings a fresh spin to the male Western.

This is not a Doris Day portrayal of Calamity Jane. She is often quiet, and when she speaks, her voice is low and husky. Silence draws the viewer into the tension; the ticktock of the clock becomes the critical sound mark that leads into the gunfights. Listen closely and you will hear bell chimes mixed into the music score accompanying the ticktock. The chimes add credibility to the clock as a sound mark. The sound in the movie disturbs and excites us, reverberating as emotional triggers of those turbulent times. *Open Range* (2003) was nominated for best sound editing (for sound effects and Foley) by the Golden Reel Awards, with the prolonged gunfight as the keynote scene in the movie. Costner's climatic gunfight becomes a sound mark within the movie's soundscape.

The 1927 version of *3:10 to Yuma* received no notable mention for sound or cinematography. Its soundtrack and setting served to move the story line and dialogue forward with emotion and authenticity. The 1927 movie opens on the stagecoach robbery, and the sounds of cattle, gunshots, and horses work together to create the opening soundscape. Its tagline is worthy of note: "The Lonesome Whistle of a Train ... bringing the gallows closer to a desperado— the showdown nearer to his captor!" The train huffs and puffs its way across the screen; its bells and whistle are classic sound marks. The sound of the train seems to deserve a stronger presence given that the viewer has waited for this moment for nearly 80 minutes.

In the 2007 version of this movie, the second scene introduces the stagecoach and its robbers. Two soundscapes— birds and cicadas on the overlook and the jostling of the stagecoach — become evident. The lone gunshot echoes through the rocky terrain and foreshadows the meeting of Wade and the rancher. The modern *3:10* has acoustic depth and variety — long and deep gunshots, clangs of bullets hitting metal, thuds from bodies falling on dry ground, the rumble of the stagecoach, the give of wood as people walk and run across sidewalk planks, the slow spin of the wooden wagon wheel, the timing of whiskey being poured into shot glasses, and the scratching of an ink pen against notebook paper. The saloon is dark and quiet and provides respite from outside sounds. In the remake, the audience is haunted by Wade singing a gloomy ditty that puts a twist on the classic Western ballad. The movie comes to completion when the 3:10 arrives, albeit late. Its whistle becomes the keynote composition in the final soundscape. The whistle shrieks as it pulls into the station. It serves as a significant sound mark as well as part of the soundscape

Conclusion

To understand sound culturally and physically, a good reading of R. Murray Schafer's *Tuning of the World* (1977) would serve the producer well. It is a book that examines the role of sound in our lives, and its wisdom can be easily applied to understanding the dynamics behind crafting a soundtrack — one that taps into our sense of human drama. Machinimatographer Eric Call's work stands as an example of how sound is an extremely critical component of bringing a story and visuals to life. But producers should look toward the larger history of film and television and even radio Westerns to seize the emotional value that sound brings to a story line. Lessons learned in the early years continue to remain viable and valuable beyond the Western genre. Although the technologies have advanced, good sound principles are timeless.

References

Attali, Jacques (1985), *Noise: The Political Economy of Music*, Minneapolis, MN: University of Minnesota Press.

Call, Eric. (2006), Silver Bells and Golden Spurs Complete Making Of. Accessed September 29, 2010, from http://bellsandspurs.com/making.html

Comstock, Michelle, & Mary E. Hocks. (2007). Voice in the Cultural Soundscape: Sonic Literacy in Composition Studies. Accessed March 22, 2007, available at: http://www.bgsu.edu/cconline/comstock_hocks/

Grove, Ricky. (2011). Ricky Grove Voice Recording Tips Video. *CyberHermit*. Accessed January 7, 2011, from http://cyberhermit.com/?p=5505

Keil, Charles, & Feld, Steven. (1994). *Music Grooves: Essays and Dialogues*. Chicago: University of Chicago Press.

Linden, Eric. (2005, November) Silver Bell and Golden Spurs. Background and film. Accessed June 1, 2009, from http://www.secondlife.com/

Schafer, R. Murray. (1977). *Tuning of the World*. New York: Knopf.

Thompson, Emily (2002). *The Soundscape of Modernity: Architectural Acoustics and the Culture of Listening in America, 1900–1933*. Cambridge, MA: MIT Press.

TV Westerns. (2007). Retrieved October 7, 2007, from http://www.fiftiesweb.com/western.htm

4

Tell Me a Story

And that is really an amazing thing.... It's interesting that we control the content of what we do. We are not being told what to do by other people. And we're an amazingly creative group and that creativity spreads across every genre, every form of art. It is really something that we should all be proud of. And I think we're pioneers in what we're doing here"—Larkworthy Antfarm [Roundtable One, 2010].

Often vivid dreams occur and one awakens breathless, excited about the images and expressions that were released in the twilight of consciousness. What if at that moment, pen in hand, the story that was so moving was recorded before those intriguing flashes of the mind become nothing but lost possible realities or absurd abstractions, aberrations that soon vanish in the tide of daily life? What if that story were preserved to amaze and capture readers and viewers, and transport them to another world far more interesting than here and now? This is the challenge of the machinimatographer, to tell a story that captivates the imagination and gives respite from reality. Be warned, this vital part of the machinima-making process is fraught with pitfalls. Society has sadly become accustomed with overwhelming sensory overload from all sources of media. Minds are trained to be placed in trancelike emptiness awaiting input from advertisers, Hollywood excesses and media glut. We observe this in individuals who have lost their normal sense of wonder and imagination and must be spoon-fed every aspect of a story to be entertained.

Dealing with this becomes a study of modern-day media and society and making the best of what we observe. Let's say the average media-saturated audience loses interest in what they are viewing after one minute; we the storytellers must add a twist or turn within our story line every 40 seconds to retain their interest. Experience has taught that the ratio between viewer stimulation and loss of interest is even less generous. It is recommended that creators of machinima apply some form of visual or emotional stimulus to the viewer every 20 seconds. This is a challenge, but the best of the best know this fact and use it. Most machinima today is written to fill a 10-minute time slot or less. Longer features can be produced, but application of the 20-second principle becomes more challenging. For this reason many opt to break up long tales into a series of shorter story lines. Three 10-minute features to be viewed at the audience's convenience are more mentally palatable then one 30-minute mega-story.

Some creators are able to retain the full detail of their story in their minds, and this is fine when working alone. However if the project involves using different actors and voice-overs from all points of the globe, a script and perhaps even a basic storyboard will be needed to guide your cast and crew. Examples of scripts can be found on the Internet, and they may be produced with basic word-processing software. Storyboards can be handmade or very elaborate artwork. There is software that can be purchased to facilitate its creation as well. It should be noted that storyboards have the benefit of giving a potential client a way to see and approve of a project before the machinima-making process begins, saving time and wasted effort.

This chapter is designed to take you through understanding the process of planning a machinima project. The first step toward creating meaningful production is to know what it involves to take your idea and transform it into a blueprint for the final project. Consider the treatment, script and storyboard as that blueprint; it becomes at least a working plan that will evolve before and during filming, and even through the editing and post-production process. Part of the process also involves knowing where your story idea fits in a particular genre of storytelling (action, drama, comedy, romance, etc.). Nothing is more inspiring than watching some classics in your genre to learn from the best. For that reason, the chapter will conclude with a look at the role of machinima of various types and genres.

Meaningful Machinima

Many perspectives of what makes a good story exist, and the daunting task of sorting through them can overwhelm the producer. The difference between imagination and good storytelling is that the producer uses that creative spark to initiate the process. But machinimatographers must translate that spark and give it momentum, and that is done by an understanding of the craft as well as their own skill level. Some machinimatographers become so caught up in the tools that they forget about the central story to be told. So maybe the question is what makes a good storyteller, rather than what makes a great story. The best of storytellers can take any plot and give it that twist and turn to engage audiences.

You can find storytellers anywhere; even your grandfather probably has a tale to spin to the relatives over the holidays. Sometimes it helps to seek the support of groups like the National Storytelling Network (NSN). Its mantra is "connecting people to and through storytelling." The story, however, in our case must be translated to the screen. Knowing how to effectively use your medium is essential, but it starts with knowing the elements of a great story.

Let's not confuse our technology choices as a substitute for crafting relatable and authentic stories or messages. So whether you are making a film, TV program or machinima production, you have to contend with the fact that you have to create something worth the audience's time to watch. On the NSN website, it is said that storytelling is a language art that preceded modern technologies and an art form predating written history. Storytelling is not limited to a genre of film, TV or radio, nor by age or experience, for both professional and amateurs can "entertain audiences of all ages. Storytelling is a key tool in fields such as health and healing, business, law, education, religion, and environmental action" (NSN, 2010).

Storytelling carries that certain "power and intimacy of one-on-one conversation.... Storytelling, a life skill with enormous communicative powers, combines these qualities. Storytelling transforms lives" (NSN, 2010). The NSN mission has been to connect people across cultures and geographies through storytelling. It would seem that *Second Life*, and similar virtual worlds, with international collectives of residents and tourists, provides excellent potential in that regard. Machinima storytelling in virtual worlds facilitates people coming together across the world to collaborate on a project. Machinima can be used to tell a story, or perhaps to teach a cultural lesson. It can be used as a way to tell a company's story or to help its employees understand its mission through training.

Comparatively to other visual media, machinima is affordable and accessible. But like all visual media, the production must carry forth a message to engage its viewers. That begins with the development of the story through a treatment, the master plan for the script and project. Initial questions that producers must ask themselves include, What's the story idea?

Who cares? How will it be accomplished? Is it doable? The process begins by conducting some research on available resources for the project, as well as an honest assessment of who will actually care to view the production.

Who Cares? Your Audience Does!

Little Johnny stretches across the floor in his pajamas, tuned to every nuance in his grandmother's voice. A good storyteller knows his or her audience. On a basic level some stories are intended for people with inside meaning. They can respond to the story because they have "inside" information or connections to its meaning. These inside stories are built around a sense of community. The motivation of other storytellers is to reach beyond their immediate communities and make connections to the general public. For example, some of the action machinima plots in games like *Halo* or *World of Warcraft* are dependent on the viewer having a general understanding of the game. Early machinima productions typically gravitated toward a select community of game players familiar with the rules of engagement. Machinima films produced from residential types of role-playing games like *Second Life* and *The Sims* have been occasionally criticized for not relating to people outside of their membership. Producers should know what audience they intend to reach, asking themselves how they might achieve a story that moves beyond core users, particularly if they wish their plots to engage a general or mass audience. Machinima producers should seek common ground with their audiences and find ways to relate to these viewers. It might start with a good idea for a script, but it must also be conceptualized through the lens of the potential viewer. Your common bond with your audience might be driven by an awareness of the game, and your idea might totally relate to their interests.

But there are many considerations to ask yourself when beginning a new project. What types of character movements will drive the action of the game? Do animations exist that will create the continuity needed for characters to be viewed as credible and relatable on-screen? Is there an available set or location within the virtual world, or does the setting have to be constructed? What types of permissions must be acquired for use of in-game footage and virtual environments? Similarly, if the story is not original, what rights must be sought from authors on whose works your script is based? What about your source of music? Is it readily available, and what are the conditions of using it in your machinima? Is it possible to customize the appearance and gestures of your characters in the ways needed for the script? These are some of the questions that must be asked when deciding whether to take on a machinima project. It might be that the producer will need to revise the script, compromising on the original idea. The producer will have to determine at what point does compromise outweigh the original intention of the project.

People can sometimes suspend disbelief when they are privy to the game platform. That means maybe your viewer will accept the limitations of your machinima production. That too should to be weighed against the purpose of the project. Consider how sometimes one can enjoy the silliness of YouTube; some of the funniest videos can be amateurish. Sometimes we realize that the producer was having some fun with an issue, theme or song, and we accept that and go with the flow of that intention. It is the message we respond to in these cases, something relatable to our human experience. Also consider how well the *Scary Movie* (2000) spoof series has been received by audiences for more than a decade because there is a common understanding among viewers of the horror genre. In the gaming world, machinima producers occasionally make some leaps of faith, hoping that the viewer will connect to the story line, simply due to the fact that they are targeting first the game players and maybe other machinimatographers.

The challenge of good storytelling is best employed when one uses the craft of machinima in such a way that the story is timeless and crosses the boundary from *Second Life*, for example, to real life. When the story connects to an audience, it is because the plot touches upon a certain human cord in its audience. Sometimes a certain game platform might lack the expressive animations to make the plot credible to the viewer. The machinimatographer might see that as an opportunity to find work-arounds to help the audience visualize the story without such distractions. When a producer expects the audience to look past those awkward camera movements, for example, the burden is placed upon the viewers to remain engaged. Instead, the producer should look for creative ways to craft the machinima with the least distractive elements. It is not the machinima that needs to be noticed, rather the story that needs to rise above the means of production. Machinimatography is about the artistic use of a medium for storytelling, the essence of communicating a message or documentation of an event that is relatable to the viewer.

The Process

In his book *A Theory of Narrative*, Rich Altman (2008) points out, "Stories constitute the bulk of sacred texts, they are the major vehicle of personal memory" (p. 1). Yet, there is not one way to tell a story. He explains that the story or narrative "exists independently of the media," clearly illustrating that each medium facilitates a story in different ways:

> However different the media that serve as a given story's vehicles—however distinct the oral, written, illustrated, or film versions of a particular narrative—we readily recognize a story's ability to be translated into different forms and yet somehow remain the "same" story [p. 1].

Let's consider the pre-production process involved in the development of a story idea. This process involves expansion and refinement of the original concept, from initial research to script development and storyboarding to locating the settings and appropriate props and animations. An understanding of machinima genres (e.g., drama, comedy, news and documentary) and types of machinima productions (fiction, documentary, corporate, etc.) will help the producer frame his or her project. But first, the authors will introduce how to conceptualize a story during the pre-production stages, particularly focusing on the development of the treatment, script and storyboard.

Story Concepts

Media consultant Robert Hilliard (1997) is quick to point out, "The sources of the play—situation, theme, background and the character—are individually only germs of ideas. Explore, expand, and revise these elements to determine if they have any dramatic value" (p. 386). Hilliard reminds us that regardless of the means of distribution, big or small screen, the focus should be on the development of the story idea. The screenplay is the actualization of the story idea. Hilliard notes that script ideas can come from anywhere, and that for the television drama *Law & Order* "newspaper headlines for crimes and legal issues" (p. 386) were among the many sources from which plots were gleaned. A machinima story idea might originate from inside the game engine or external to it. Story ideas may come from personal experiences or from events and people that cross your life, virtual or real. Literature often inspires filmmakers, and machinima producers likewise draw from the classics on occasion. As a case in point, the authors call attention to producer Lainy Voom's *Dagon*, a well-received machinima based on H.P. Lovecraft's short story of the same title.

On the other hand, your machinima story idea might relate directly to action within the game. The purpose of most action games is to test your skill level as you maneuver through several levels to ultimately challenge some sort of entity, THE BEAST let's say. Each level is filled with challenges that might serve to provide story ideas for a machinimist. In multi-player role-playing games, players often choose their characters, and their characters are assigned to various opposing teams. The conflict between these teams, for instance, might provide fodder for story plots. In virtual worlds, like *Second Life*, there are also role-playing sims that attract large numbers of participants. From vampire and Gorean to fantasy and steam punk, a variety of role-playing-themed communities offer potential starting points for story ideas. *Second Life* and other emerging worlds are typically composed of communities of groups, such as fashionistas, artists and musicians, educators, and businesspeople. Other communities that arise are cultural or spiritual, with regions dedicated to sharing or showcasing customs of certain people and practices. Within these groups and across them, the rituals and practices of these communities lend themselves to story ideas—fiction and non-fiction. Remember that virtual worlds are comprised of international participants. Collaboration cuts across the grid for most activities, and cross-cultural machinima production teams and actors, as well as sponsorships, are becoming increasingly commonplace. That means the producers and their audiences should be considered part of an international media movement, breaking down barriers through machinima.

Research

In *World of Warcraft*, some of the best machinima producers are not necessarily those who are the regular players; however, they are familiar with the game structure and story line. They can maneuver around the game, being aware of the rules, practices, and the people. In this way, they can remain authentic to the game, if that is necessary. Others might make spoofs of the game, but again that requires familiarity with the game. *The Sims 3*, *Second Life*, *InWorldz* and others have vendors featuring clothing, vehicles, housing and furniture, and a variety of animations. Many of these items can serve as costumes and props for the machinima producer. The cost of these items should be taken into consideration during the pre-production stage. For example, what is the budget for the project and how much customization will be necessary to proceed with an idea. Cisko Vandeverre, a leading machinima producer, coined the phrase "penny for props." To him *Second Life* provides a vast playground of inexpensive props and resources that allow for professional productions, comparable to major studio productions filmed in real life. The limitations of *Second Life* and other worlds typically center on the quality of the animations. Pose animations, such as sitting and standing, have become sophisticated during the past several years. Likewise, motion animations, like running, dancing, fighting, lip-syncing, and others, have become more credible compared to only a few years ago. Yet they do not simulate every pose or motion of real-life beings. Animation scripts can be customized with some basic scripting knowledge, or a producer might pay for customization. Being familiar with the available scripts and animations is extremely important for a machinima filmmaker. A swaggering drunk animation can be repurposed to illustrate a pilot stumbling from a just-crashed plane, as demonstrated in the machinima *Le Village*. The more familiar you are with the existing animations, scripts, and props that are available, the more likely you will be able to produce credible machinima. When you can assess what you need to work around or have customized, you suddenly have a bigger view of the total project than otherwise before.

Research considerations also involve set design (do they exist or will they have to be built?), lighting needs (what is the mood of the overall story and the various scenes?), how many people are needed for this production and what are their roles? (e.g., the cast, the production crew, etc.), and many others as typically related to any type of filmmaking. These considerations should be included in the treatment. Any story line that involves myths, customs, historical periods, or scientific knowledge should be researched for accuracy, as one should attempt to do for any production. A credible project begins at the research stage.

Treatment

So you have thought through the story idea for its "doability." You made some initial assessments on what might be needed to accomplish the project. The treatment will help you organize your thoughts on paper. This master plan might be considered more or less a "working" contract with your production crew, the executive producer or the corporate sponsor of the project. A treatment is also used by a screenplay writer to sell an idea to a producer. Treatments vary in number of pages depending on the estimated length of the final production. The treatment summarizes the theme of the production. Is the story based on a historical event or is it a fantasy feature? Is the production a documentary or a music machinima? Consider the treatment as your pitch and your plan. It is the summary of your research as well as your project vision.

Your first two paragraphs should establish the goals of the project, including its genre, the basic plot and characters, and what makes this project significant to a particular audience demographic. After that, the set locations and the characters should be introduced. A separate section might be attached to the treatment that provides an in-depth character analysis of the cast. Major and minor characters should be mentioned, with more details given to the primary characters. The treatment can be very detailed to the point that each act is summarized, with set locations and character actions discussed. A basic guideline for any work, whether a short or long feature, is to think in three acts: the introduction (the establishment of the plot and the characters), the climax (the story leads to a major conflict, crisis or decision), and the resolution. Each of those acts can be summarized into a separate paragraph. You might elaborate here depending on the complexity of the story line. Finally, the treatment should discuss what resources are needed and outline the budget, giving consideration to payment of voice-over talent; the cost of clothing, props and animations; and any customization or technical considerations along the way. The treatment also helps the producer overcome limitations of the project. If a certain facial expression or body animation is not available, the producer can seek workaround or alternative solutions, such as shooting from a creative camera angle to compensate for the limitation. This technique is called "cheating the camera."

Overall, the treatment provides a detailed expression of the primary and secondary filming locations, and a profile of the major and minor characters (appearance, wardrobe, personality). The treatment is the foundation for establishing the what, when, where, how, and why in a film. The treatment is essentially a short story for the film, and it establishes the plot, setting, characters, and the scenes. It has a beginning, middle, and end. For short films of five to six minutes or less, it might range from one to three pages, depending on its level of specificity. Most machinima productions fall within this category. Feature-length scripts for movies are minimally several pages to around 12, especially for project pitches. Again, find out the needs of the executive producer or project manager, for they might want to be approached with a one-page pitch at first. This scenario is often the case when working through ideas with busy executives on corporate projects. Some elaborate treatments for a full-length film, documentary, or training video can average upward to 40 pages. That is rare. But there are times when directors want characters or a training process developed fully, and when the project is part of a series, there might be a call for a very detailed treatment. An average full-length script runs about 100 pages, approximately 100 minutes. A treatment for that script would likely average around 10 pages.

Script

The script can be written before the treatment or afterward. Often a producer receives a script and then writes a treatment for it. At other times, when a short story inspires the project, the producer might start with the treatment and then develop the script. In many cases, producers use the treatment as an outline to their script. For example, a detailed treatment helps the writer to understand the motivations of the characters. The treatment would likely need to be revised after the script is written to reflect any conceptual shifts. In either case, the script is a must for not only the producer but for those participating in the production, as crew or actors.

There are numerous types of script formats online and in professional books. The formats differ for commercials, documentaries, television productions and screenplays. When pitching a script, it is best to follow the appropriate format. Some scripts get rejected simply due to their lack of professional appearance. If your idea is good, then why not take the time to format your script properly, especially if it is not a project solely written, produced and starring you. A good script will provide not only the dialogue, but others should be able to visualize the script through the camera language (close-ups, long shots, medium shots, over-the-shoulder, crowd shots, panning to a side) to help the director translate the written words to screen.

Transitions from within the larger body of work and from scene to scene are established in the script as well. We see the introduction of characters, and their exit in scenes. The script tells us everything from location to the actions of the characters. A machinima might only have one location, as in a story that takes place in a café. This setting is identified as an interior location (INT). But once your characters venture outside of the building, the scene is marked as an outside or exterior location (EXT). Music and sound elements and lighting decisions are detailed so that we begin to feel the style of the director. Post-production elements are identified on the script, with visual and sound effects (such as explosions) and transitional scene techniques (dissolve, wipe, cut, fade, etc.) typically specified.

Storyboarding

Another part of pre-production is storyboarding the film, and again the level of this process varies in specificity. In John Hart's *Art of the Storyboard* (2007), he discusses the importance of the director's vision, and partly this involves an awareness of film techniques applied in classic films. Certain directors become known for their mastery of shot composition, lighting, editing, and special effects. An understanding of lighting and composition draws from the field of photography. In fact, several prominent machinima producers have had professional experience in photography. The treatment provides the rationale, but the storyboard outlines these decisions through illustration.

As a side note, Hart (2007, p. 1) states, "The film industry's current use of storyboards as a pre-production pre-visualization tool owes its humble beginnings to the original Sunday comics." Hart (2007, p. 1) elaborates on the origins of storyboarding in storytelling: "The concept of telling a story through a series of sequential drawings actually goes back to Egyptian hieroglyphics, even back to the cave men's drawings of stampeding cattle." Hart (2007, p. 2) states, "Artists who created those original Sunday funnies drew their cartoon in a logical narrative sequence; this, essentially, is still the task of the storyboard artist. The use of the storyboard is a premiere aid in planning a filmed, live action or animated feature."

According to Hart (2007, p. 2), storyboards are the hub of the film activity and "enable the entire production team to organize all the complicated action depicted in the script, whether being rendered for live action films, animation, or commercials. They will illustrate what action each lifted shot contains." And whether the action is rendered or sketched, storyboarding ultimately consists of "all the necessary action in each key sequence of shot" (Hart, 2007, p. 5). For example, in movies like *Pirates of the Caribbean* (2003), it was essential to describe the lead character and the settings in detail. A good reference to learn more about the history and development of storyboarding is Charles Soloman's *History of Animation, 1600s to 1990s*. Hart's book, nonetheless, also sets forth a well-construed road map toward developing effective storyboards.

The Pre–production of BloodSpell

Basically, the same pre-production rules apply for machinima as with television and filmmaking. For an excellent account of what is involved during the pre-production stages, we lean to Hugh Hancock's discussion on the making of his feature-length machinima *BloodSpell* (2006), which evolved into a three-year process from idea to execution. Hancock (n.d.) reflects back to the initial spark for the idea:

> Around about August 2003, a mad Frenchman named Francoise said that Strange Company needed to "get the punk back." The day after that the folder on my hard drive called "Gettin The Punk Back" (still the main hub of *BloodSpell* development) was created.

There was not a strong vision on how to proceed, other than that it would be a fantasy film and the team "wanted to use *Neverwinter Nights*. And that was about it." Hancock, as executive producer, and his team toyed with the game engine, and then sat down as a group to brainstorm the plot:

> Eventually, we narrowed our ideas down to a concrete story, which we then "broke" into acts (we were originally intending *BloodSpell* to be 6 acts of 5 minutes each), and then down to scenes within those acts [Hancock, n.d.].

They began to write up the story into a two-page treatment for what was originally intended to be a 10-minute film, but it had grown exponentially over the course of time. *BloodSpell* is the quest of a young monk, Jered, for his freedom. The treatment was very basic at its onset, with the plan to merely establish the story line:

> The prisoners are lined up in a row now, and two guards start to head toward the doors. Jered suddenly attacks the captain, knocking the fully-armored man to the ground, and starts up the steps, fighting through the guards. The older man stands up and orders for crossbows [Hancock, n.d.].

The treatment establishes the conflict, as it continues, "From the blood, an enormous monster, the size of the doors themselves, erupts, and the guards scatter, some trying to fight and being eaten, others running." Hancock recommends Robert McKee's *Story* (1997) as a good read for scriptwriters, and that book was influential in the crafting of *BloodSpell*. Hancock (n.d.) adds,

> For each scene, I first read my brief summary, in the treatment, then expanded that out to a sheet of story beats ... whether that's Jered running up on stage, the Captain ordering the crossbows to aim, Jered cutting his wrist, or much more subtle conversational stuff.

He would later rewrite each scene "as a short story first, with no dialogue but internal monologue from all the characters making it clear what they were thinking and feeling." Hancock (n.d.) explains, they "read badly as stand-alone stories, but they're invaluable for crafting a strong script, as they give you a strong handle on how your characters are thinking and feeling." The machinima, in its final form, was released in 2006 as a 90-minute machinima feature. It made its mark on machinima history, and much of the success should be attributed to their planning, scriptwriting, and rewriting. Hancock relied on feedback from his team throughout the process.

The Genres

Most of us can rattle off the names of movie titles if given a genre. Horror. Fantasy. Action. Drama. Romance. Comedy. Immediately titles, characters, scenes, and famous lines flash across our thoughts. Each genre has certain audience expectations. A comedy for example should be funny! An action movie better keep us on the edge of the seat. A romantic story should melt our hearts. A horror movie should scare us, by tapping into our hidden fears. And so forth, for different genres are associated with different audience expectations and reaction. Other than using machinima for raw game capture, the machinimatographer will find much in common with the television and film producer, with regard to the expectations of the various genres of storytelling

Machinimatographers increasingly take certain liberties in redefining their source of machinima content. They look typically at the game platform for their story ideas and even settings. A producer might capture footage from different action games and, for example, mix them into the plot of *Second Life*. Phaylen Fairchild produced a machinima series, *DiVAS*, that did just that, bringing her *Second Life* avatar into *World of Warcraft* to construct a multi-game machinima production. Machinimists can employ multiple platforms to create locations and characters for their broader story lines.

Machinima genres are endless, and really no different from categories offered in film, animation, and television. A fairly significant genre in machinima is abstract or experimental art. Such genres might feature interpretations of music, poetry, literature or a wide range of themes that tap into emotions. Given that machinima grew out of action video games, it is not surprising that action has remained a consistently popular genre. Comedy is another category that does well across all platforms, perhaps because it is easy to overlook imperfections in lip sync or other technological limitations when one is amused and ready to challenge reality through humor. Another popular machinima genre is music video. In *The Sims* and *Second Life*, for example, amateur and professional machinimists capture the mood of an audience by filming live performances and editing them into music videos, or they completely tell a story, playing off the mood or lyrics of the song using in-world footage. Some amazing music videos have emerged from *Second Life*, *The Sims*, and *World of Warcraft*, among others. Flimsey Freenote's work is one example of creative application of machinima to the music video concept. In one example, she filmed and edited Hazideon Zarco's original song *Lucky Stars*. Zarco constructed the set and avatars for the production. Such collaborations between machinimists and composers seem beneficial to all parties and are finding their way on the Web and making music news.

Many machinimists relying on advanced production techniques get lost in the technology, and forget that machinima offers communicative and cinematic expression. Cultural machinima can spring forth from tradition. In filming in-world ritual or cultural practices, the machinimist should seek those stories that define the people and their traditions, for example. In a diverse world like *Second Life*, there are specific challenges and opportunities for telling stories from varying perspectives, such as ones that elevate the voices of gender, race and ethnicity. Such machinima might be created for educational purposes and might help students engage in crafting machinima with unique cultural perspectives. Educational machinima can take the form of training films, or they might retell a classic short story or poem or reenact a historical piece. Documentary, as a machinima genre, can be educational, journalistic, or experimental. It can offer a slice of life of virtual worlds, for both those on the inside and outside. Political and cultural messages can be documented in ways that allow the producer to tackle an issue in a creative way and inexpensively. Commercial machinima can be used for training films or promoting products or services, from fashion to homes to real estate. Storytelling through machinima can be a powerful dramatic technique for nearly any genre. Dramatic series, from comedy to action, have become popular across many machinima platforms, and they serve as an effective means for building an audience base.

More specifically, machinima typically draws from action and fantasy plots that run parallel to the overriding theme of the game or virtual world. We will take a look at the popular fantasy element of machinima, followed by an examination of social and news machinima, types that are increasingly becoming relevant to residents of virtual worlds and multi-player role-playing games. We conclude the chapter with a discussion on dance machinima. It is a way for many people to begin to learn and understand machinima, and for some it is at the core of why they produce machinima.

Machinima of Legend, Literature, and Fantasy

An early machinima filmed on *Quake III* has become a cult classic for its sweeping imagery and color. In 2004, the film *Anna* was produced by director Katherine Anna Kang. Only four years prior, she had founded Fountainhead Entertainment. She was also the co-founder of the Academy of Machinima Arts and Sciences. The film tells the story of one flower's life. Kang had created this long-standing feature using an early version of *Quake*, and it has stood the test of time as an example of what you can do with machinima, even at its most basic level. Most would not believe that such an artistic machinima could possibly be birthed from an action game.

It is somewhat easier to be artistic within virtual environments, given the freedom afforded by *Second Life*, and many other virtual environments since then. Some environments/settings are created by machinima makers as part of their studio playground, while others are created for short-lived specific plots or purposes, like maybe to produce a music video. *Second Life* machinimatographers understand the value behind being able to use or create fantasy landscapes for movie sets. Celestial Elf's machinima based on the story *Jabberwocky* (2010) invites the viewer into a mythical space where the creatures roam and rule. The *Story of Susa Bubble* (2009), filmed and produced by Iono Allen, is a surreal journey into Rose Borchovski's amazing world — "the tale of Susa Bubble who went to bed single and woke up double."

Machinima can also become the celebration of one's culture that might be shared through music, language or story captured within *Second Life*. Attention to detail becomes highly significant toward achieving authenticity. Machinimist Larkworthy Antfarm shares a Japanese folklore in her piece *Urashima Taro* (2009), and *Club Noir* (2009) by Lowe Runo Productions, LLC, is a dramatic story with the narration in Spanish. Antfarm's film is drenched in color, and *Club Noir* was shot in black and white to capture a nostalgic feel. Both films are narrated by the filmmakers. The sets complete the vision of the machinimatographers, as spelled out in their story ideas, treatments and storyboards.

Settings will be discussed at length later on in this book; however filming location is an important aspect of the pre-production process.

Machinima for the Social Good

Machinima can tell a story that reveals a social condition to its audience. Take the next two examples. In the first example, Rysan Fall's *Across the Universe* (2010) is a machinima based on Craig Lyons' song of the same title. In *SL* machinima communities, some producers have sought out ways to communicate their social and political messages. Lyons collaborated with machinimatographer Fall to create a music video, *Across the Universe*, that made a plea to viewers for them to acknowledge their role in the devastation of the environment. Lyon's message underscores the consequence of humanity's irresponsibility in caring for the environment. Lyon's decision to use machinima as a medium was influenced by its low impact on environmental resources compared to the traditional filmmaking process. The idea is reminiscent of Sarah McLachlan's *World on Fire* (2004) music video, which criticized the excesses of Hollywood's film industry. Truly, machinima provides an interesting option for producers to consider environmental friendly productions.

Larkworthy Antfarm's *Spare Change* (2009) provides a glimpse of homelessness through the life of one woman living on the streets (in avatar form). In June 2009, Antfarm shared a similar message in *Blessed Are the Greedy*, a machinima that portrayed corporate greed against human needs. In these instances, social issues are framed as stories, and machinima is the medium through which they are told. Another machinimist, Gene Williams, drew upon the urban plight existing within New York City and portrayed the anguish of an African-American man through a music video filmed with machinima. The machinima production *Victim of Society* (2009) was set in Virtual Harlem in *Second Life*. Gene had composed the song years earlier, and later decided filming machinima in *Second Life* would prove the appropriate medium, being that it was an effective and inexpensive platform from which to communicate his message. *Second Life* provided him a means to tell his story in a creative and affordable setting. His professional animation training and education offered him insight into the cost and time benefits of producing his work in a virtual world.

Other machinimatographers have found this art form as a powerful and affordable strategy to communicate political messages through the Internet. Blogger Liz Solo (Lizsolo Mathilde) praised Ogogoro, a Nigerian producer, for his *In Pursuit of a Third Team*, a fictionalized plot that dealt with police corruption in his home country. The Moviestorm machinima can be viewed on the Nollywood Channel, and also was screened at the Second Annual MaMachinima Festival in February 2010. Machinima, like other forms of media, can be created for political and entertainment purposes. Solo noted that Moviestorm has been one of the tools increasingly used among machinima producers, but added, "These are not virtual real time spaces but machinima generators." She contends, these generators are not "as interesting to me as online spaces, because of the missing element of virtual embodiment — but the animations are quite seamless" (Solo, 2010). Solo observed that virtual storytellers are "exploring the classic 'fairy tale' through machinima, as well as examining the notion of idealized space and of reconciling our relationship to the natural world via the loving application of technology to nature (and vice versa)" (Solo, 2010).

News and Issue Machinima

The video *A Child's War* (2007) was created in *Second Life* by an organization known as Global Kids. It was the culmination of a yearlong non-profit project led by youth leaders in Queens, New York, based on research about the plight of child soldiers in Uganda. The youth examined, for instance, the circumstances surrounding charges made by the International Criminal Court related to the abuse. The project was sponsored by the MacArthur Foundation and was conducted in 2007. Former National Public Radio (NPR) producer Draxtor Despres, a virtual journalist, has been among the first to produce *Second Life* news machinima on a regular basis. He covers *Second Life* events and contextualizes them within real-world issues and situations.

In 2010, Despres created a machinima on how *Second Life* served as a social network for disabled veterans returning from war. The news machinima video *The Amputee Virtual Support System* (2010) investigated how *Second Life* helped soldiers handle isolation during long-term medical care. As a virtual journalist, Despres also reported on health and political issues and events in *Second Life* that are linked to real-world organizations and events. His real-world and virtual news actualities are seamlessly woven together into machinima reports, which can be found streamed online from web channels and sites, as well as watched on *SL* stations like Metaverse TV and Treet TV. News segments are crafted into short machinima features that can be viewed as an individual stand-alone piece, or as units within a larger virtual newscast.

Machinima Producer Rik Panganiban was among one of the leaders of the Global Kids project. On his blog, *The Click Heard Round the World*, he compiled a long list of social and political-themed machinima productions using various game engines as the filming platform. By far, it is not comprehensive but it does provide a starting point for understanding how machinima can engage communication on issues. One machinima of particular significance was produced by Josh Levy. Titled *A Better World in Second Life* (2007), it became the first documentary to truly focus on social and political uses of *Second Life*. It was produced as a five-part series on activist applications of virtual worlds.

Other machinima listed on Panganiban's blog include *Dead in Iraq* (2007), which was created using the online military recruiting game *America's Army* to create a protest piece against war. Machinima themes varied on the list from parody pieces (*Invisible Thread*, 2008) to commentaries on war (*An Unfair War*, 2006), environmental concerns (*The Greenest Console*, 2007), civil unrest (*The French Democracy*, 2005) and race and education (*Race to Equality*, 2008). *An Unfair War* (2006), using *The Sims 2*, was both criticized and applauded by viewers for its anti-war theme and its simple form. The story rests upon the experiences and views of one man, as he types on his keyboard throughout the piece. The words that he types are displayed across the screen, and they drive the cinematic story.

Getting in the Groove of Genre

One of the most criticized forms of machinima has been those based on capturing avatars in motion through dance animations. Dance machinima is considered, by some, one of the easiest forms of machinima, but that is not always necessarily so; many professional machinimists desire to challenge their skills beyond what they consider simplistic cinematic expression. Such machinima might involve filming a couple dancing or a woman or man dancing solo. Yet machinima centered on dance, when done well, has historical and cultural value. There is a rich history linking dance to cinema, worthy of note. Elizabeth Zimmer (2002, p. 1), in her book *Envisioning Dance on Film and Video*, states, "Early film pioneers were quick to realize that dance was an ideal subject for demonstrating the magic of their new invention.... In late Victorian times, film allowed audiences to witness dance at a socially safe distance, from the seat of a movie theater." Through film, Thomas Edison captured the "exotic" and "seductive ... vitality of 'dancing girls.'" (Zimmer, 2002, p. 1). One begins to see, through Zimmer's work (2002, p. 1), how "dance for the camera is a natural extension of the dance artist's skills— sensitivity to visual form, motion, space, time, and light, as well as a passion to communicate." Zimmer (2002) explains that the invention of film and video technology profoundly impacted the art of dance, namely its appreciation among viewers and its ability to cross cultural and geographical borders.

Dance indeed might be one of the most powerful forms of cinematic expression in a world like *Second Life*. Dance in a residential type of game platform, like *Second Life*, where socialization has a major role in the daily lives of members, offers a natural bond between the viewer and producer. Dance animations are created for solo performance in such virtual worlds, and are also continually improved upon to create a sensual and fantasy-like connection between couples. Machinima captures that connection, if it is well executed, allowing for the viewer to vicariously experience that moment in time, transcending the boundaries of technology. The viewers relate to the experience as they watch the performance and recall their own real and virtual encounters. It is a simple expression of the human bond. An effective machinima production is one that speaks to our humanity, or lack of it. The dance within the machinima, however, should be integral to the story or the message of the producer. The spirit of the dance (e.g., ballet, waltz, burlesque) captured in machinima might be considered a celebration of an emerging romantic partnership with new technology.

The Rise of the Independent Storytellers/Filmmakers

Chris Holmlund (2008), in his book *American Cinema of the 1990s*, starts with a screenshot of the late 1990s' low-budget film *The Blair Witch Project*, an independent project of student filmmaker Heather Donahue. Machinima producers would benefit from reviewing the work of those independent filmmakers who began to challenge mainstream movie practices in the 1990s. Some of these companies have roots going back to the late 1960s as "nontheatrical distributor[s] catering to [an] art and exploitation-oriented college audience" (Holmlund, 2008, p. 6). The motion picture company New Line "skillfully added sexploitation, gay films, rock documentaries, and 'midnight specials' to reach niche markets the majors ignored. In the 1990s, the company struck gold with the wildly successful *Ninja Turtles* series and franchise" (Holmlund, 2008, p. 6). Holmlund states, "Scores of big- and small-budget U.S. films testified to our fascination with, and fear of, these digital revolutions" (pp. 1–2).

Among the memorable movies of the 1990s were *Total Recall* (1990), *Terminator 2: Judgment Day* (1991), *You've Got Mail* (1998), and *Being John Malkovich* (1999) (Holmlund, 2008, p. 1–2). For the Hollywood majors, action was the defining theme of the decade, amidst a digital cinematic revolution. Holmlund (2008, p. 15) explains, "Action — broadly defined to include cop films, spy movies, certain epic science fiction films, gangster extravaganzas, martial arts movies, and more — was without question, the most popular 1990s genre." He adds, "Increasingly numbers of female viewers joined male viewers, delighting in the explosions, the special effects, the stunts, the buff male and female bodies" (p. 15). Meanwhile, there was a growth of independent productions and a rise of café screenings, and of course the digital revolution gave new life to old cinema. Holmlund asks us to consider the impact of the digital revolution, recalling George Lucas' astute observation that cinema is "dying," as he so "famously suggested in 1999 ... 'I love film, but it's a 19th century invention.'" One cannot ignore those cinematic influences upon the movement of machinima, still in its infancy:

As the 1990s ended, a marked digital divide partitioned the world into those without.... Previously unimaginable technological advances in connectivity were promised everywhere we turned [Romano, 1999, p. 37, cited in Holmlund, 2008, p. 1].

Jon Lewis and Eric Smoodin (2007), in *Looking Past the Screen*, present a series of case studies that ground early American cinema within culture. What emerges is a historical and social portrait of American culture, from the early days of cinema to the 1970s, using film (and its storytelling power) as a means to reexamine the past through multiple social lenses. The rise and growth of machinima might also be reexamined one day for its historical and cultural implications. It will likely help to shape and define the new cinema of virtual filmmaking across the world, from Hollywood to Bollywood to Nollywood. Filmmaking is about the transformation of stories into the language of visual and aural aesthetics, and such cinematic expression, at its best, can be shared among and across cultures to foster understanding and compassion. In the case of virtual worlds, machinima might truly offer an accessible means to share the stories of communities through news, information and entertainment that begins in-world but reaches toward the larger communities of viewers across the Web.

Conclusion

A powerful resource for helping filmmakers craft stories is Jennifer Van Sijll's (2005) book, *Cinematic Storytelling: The 100 Most Powerful Conventions Every Filmmaker Must Know.* Van Sijll establishes two fundamental requirements for achieving a superb script. First and foremost is having a "great story," but it is equally important to be able "to render the story cinematically" (Van Sijll, 2005, p. xi). She articulates the translation of the novel or short story into the film script, by clarifying that the distinction is based on the "technical elements that the screenwriter is expected to exploit" (p. xi). Van Sijll (2005) traces this practice in filmmaking to the mid–1920s, when screenwriters were asked to "master the technical aspects of film, such as editing, so that they could better create stories specifically for the screen" (p. xi). Moreover, she explains that it is not only important to know how to create a certain shot or scene, but one should know why it matters and what might be accomplished with such insight. The rationale behind making one technical choice over another must be clearly established by the director (2005). Technical decisions in machinima also involve an understanding of frame composition, lighting, and settings. Those decisions impact how a piece will be edited, from scene transitions to what sound effects and sound will be added. Other considerations up front include appropriate wardrobe and props and casting decisions. These elements should be considered in the machinima blueprint before capture even begins (perhaps except for some trial runs).

This chapter's goal was to elaborate on the pre-production process involved in the making of machinima, as in the making of a recipe to communicate a story to an audience. Regardless of the medium employed, the crafting of a good plot is essential. But that is only the beginning of the process, for the story must be translated to the medium of choice. Machinima producers can look toward the rich history of practice among filmmakers for inspiration. Yet there is a point of divergence, in which the machinimist must understand how traditional and virtual filmmaking might part ways.

Furthermore, the respective game engine helps to refine the process. A story crafted through *Second Life* offers unique challenges in preparation and production compared to perhaps another game like *The Sims 3*, *World of Warcraft* or *Halo*. The forthcoming chapters will present some of the technical and aesthetic considerations that must be accounted for before capture even begins, namely character development and lighting and set design. As noted already, the storyboard and treatment offer guideposts to the visual and aural translation of the written word to screen. The process itself becomes a wonderful transformation, from cocoon to butterfly, toward the emergence of a well-produced machinima, and those seeking to be inspired should look toward legendary producers of film, television, animation and machinima for inspiration and creative flight.

Story Exercises

Critique various machinima for effectiveness in story development, considering the following:

1. Identify the story plot in one sentence.
2. What is the genre of the machinima? Does it fulfill audience expectations of that genre as often portrayed in film, television and animation?
3. Create a rough storyboard and treatment for the machinima.
4. Explain why machinima was or was not an effective medium for the story.
5. Identify five machinima producers who convey a strong sense of storytelling in their work.

References

Allen, Iono. (2009). *The Story of Susa Bubble*. Accessed November 24, 2010, from http://www.youtube.com/user/Ionoallen#p/u/14/aJdVCqG3bZs

Altman, Rich. (2008). *A Theory of Narrative*. New York: Columbia University Press.

Antfarm, Larkworthy. (2010). *Spare Change*. Accessed November 29, 2010, from http://www.youtube.com/watch?v=dXJuzL8Dw6I

_____. (2009). *Blessed Are the Greedy*. Accessed November 29, 2010, from http://www.youtube.com/watch?v=2iIf4tzeVRM

_____. (2009). *Urashima Taro*. Accessed November 29, 2010, from http://www.youtube.com/watch?v=WhxelCORVcc

Despres, Draxtor. The Amputee Virtual System. Accessed November 20, 2010 from Http://www.you tube.com/watch?v=oUt2_C3SKIg

Elf, Celestial. (2010). *Jabberwocky*. Accessed December 1, 2010, from http://www.youtube.com/ watch?v=x1Wbcc0ntn4 http://www.youtube.com/user/CelestialElf—p/u/35/x1Wbcc0ntn4Fair child, Phaylen. *DiVAS*, Season 2 Episode 1— Phaylen Seeks a *World of Warcraft* Guild. Accessed November 12, 2010, from http://www.youtube.com/watch?v=zkZetBxaP2w

Fall, Rysan. (2010). *Across the Universe w/Craig Lyons*. Fall Films. Accessed November 21, 2010, from http://www.youtube.com/watch?v=MaRxjRlMTWg

Freenote, Flimsey. (2010). *Lucky Stars w/Hazideon Zarco*. Accessed December 11, 2010, from http:// www.youtube.com/watch?v=AgkPJfZA6Kc

Global Kids. (2007). *A Child's War*. Accessed December 4, 2010, from http://www.youtube.com/ watch?v=nK54WRu0jW4

Hart, John. (2007). *Art of the Storyboard*. New York: Focal Press.

Hancock, Hugh. (2006). BloodSpell: From Concept to Finished Scene Part 1. Accessed September 15, 2010, from *http://nwn.bioware.com/players/profile_bloodspell_anatomy.html?chl=en&*

Hilliard, L. Robert. (1997). *Writing for Television and Radio*. Belmont, CA: Wadworth Publishing.

Holmhund, Chris. (2008). *American Cinema of the 1990s*. New Brunswick, NJ: Rutgers University.

ILL Clan Machinima. (2008). *Tiny Nation*. Jannicola, Paul, Dellario, Frank & Fate, Damien (Executive Producers). Brooklyn, NY. Accessed December 11, http://www.youtube.com/watch?v=oQ6FqBD bgc4

Lewis, Jon, & Smoodin, Eric. (2007). *Looking Past the Screen: Case Studies in American Film History and Method*. Durham, NC: Duke University Press,

Lowe Runo Productions, LLC. (2009). *Club Noir*. Accessed December 1, 2010, from http://www.you tube.com/watch?v=C58AmU5zzD0

Lowe Runo Productions, LLC. (2008). *LeVillage*. Accessed December 11, 2010, from http://www.you tube.com/watch?v=SDt5L9iINsc

McKee, Robert. (1997). *Story*. New York: Harper Collins. National Storytelling Network (NSN). Accessed September 1, 2010, from http://www.storynet.org/

Ogogoro. (2010). In Pursuit of a Third Team. Accessed December 11, 2010, from http://www.nolly-wood.com/video/In_pursuit_of_a_third_term

Panganiban, Rik. (2008, October 23). Machinima that Matter: A list of machinima films with a Social / Political Message. The Click Heard Round the World. Accessed September 30, 2010, from http://www.rikomatic.com/blog/

Romano, S. (1999). DLP: A Report from the Trenches. *BoxOffice*, 138 (2) (February), pp. 36–37.

Machinima Roundtable One. (2010). *Terminology, Technology, and Practice* (Sessions 1 & 2, June 25 & 30). Lowe Runo Productions, LLC, *Second Life*.

Soloman, Charles. (1994). *Enchanted Drawings: History of Animation*. New York: Random House.

Solo, Liz. (2010, February 21). machine i am at MMIF. Accessed October 4, 2010, from http://machine-i-am.blogspot.com/

Van Sijll, Jennifer. (2005). *Cinematic Storytelling: The 100 Most Powerful Conventions Every Filmmaker Must Know*. Studio City, CA: Michael Wiese Productions.

Voom, Lainy. (2010). *Dagon*. Accessed November 1, 2010, from http://www.youtube.com/watch?v= CMOHpuxFbm0

Williams, Gene. (2009). *Victim of Society*. Accessed November 15, 2010, from http://www.youtube. com/watch?v=zizjpFNYZn0

Zimmer, Elizabeth (2002). *Envisioning Dance on Film and Video*. New York: Routledge.

✧ COMMENTS BY LARKWORTHY ANTFARM ✧

The Fine Art of Machinima

In a recent discussion of the future of machinima, film director Peter Greenaway declared cinema to be dead. He believes machinima, if it is to be a viable new art form, will need to "sever the umbilical cord" that ties it to the "Hollywood way of telling a story," which he calls "text based, not image based." He decries the stale and conventional direction cinema has taken, suggesting rather forcefully that machinima, its digital brainchild, represents a new and exciting "image"-based future.

Greenaway's comments resonate with those who have witnessed the development of digital kinetic art in *Second Life* where stunning visual imagery continues to astound with ever-changing new forms of expression. Its transitory nature, however, makes it next to impossible to recreate in real life or even to preserve for long in a virtual environment. Machinima directors have been quick to see unlimited possibilities for collaboration between artists, musicians and filmmakers in virtual worlds.

Artists have created rich and lavish environments in *Second Life*, many of which have been used quite effectively as sets in conventional storytelling; however, for every machinima director creating what Greenaway calls text-driven stories, there are others using the new media to experiment and push the boundaries of the art form with imaginative three-dimensional performance art that immerses the viewer in the sensory experience in a new way that goes light-years beyond what is even possible in real-life installation art. Yet even among some of the most talented avant-garde machinima directors, there is no agreement on a set of techniques or guiding principles for creating art machinima. If they do agree on anything, it is a passionate belief in the seriousness of their art.

Iono Allen — whose machinima *A Question of Honour* earned the rare accolade of being selected as one of 125 semi-finalists by the Guggenheim Museum of Modern Art in its 2010 collaboration with YouTube, "A Biennial of Creative Video"— knows more than most how seriously the art world has begun to take machinima. Allen's work is firmly "focused on the image" and reflects his own interest as a photographer in real life. He believes "machinima emphasizes the imagination: of the artist, who creates virtual artworks, but also of the machinima director who has a lot of freedom to film and compose with these artworks." His collaboration with some of *Second Life*'s most creative individuals has resulted in a number of award-winning machinima as well as praise for his vision.

His work with the installation art of Rose Borchovski in *The Story of Susa Bubble* and its sequel *Fears* are prime examples of the seamless mesh of art and machinima in *Second Life*. In her installations, Borchovski's character Susa Bubble is brought to life in a series of interactive vignettes both powerful and haunting. Allen brings the focused eye of his slow, deliberate camera work to Borchovski's ever-evolving story of Susa and allows Susa's consciousness to engulf the viewer in elaborate sensory imagery. The end result blends sight and sound in a way that evokes something akin to long lost memories which slowly rise to the surface as Susa struggles to break free of her own limitations in an amorphous virtual environment. A very unconventional way to tell a story emerges from the collaborative mashup of two fascinating artistic visions.

Perhaps more than most, Allen's camera work is reminiscent of early avant-garde cinematographers. One detects the influence of modernist art movements in his work as well. Nevertheless Allen does not look backward. He is enthusiastic about machinima's new possibilities:

> I am convinced that we are living in a more important age than people think: we are attending to the development of a medium which is, as its name indicates, a combination of many other media: animation, cinema, handmade animation, computer aided animation, video, etc.... Machinimas are a kind of morphing of all these media, made through modern editing tools. I would add that one of the characteristic of this medium is that it is improving quite quickly with technological developments (full HD, sharing platforms, editing tools, etc.). I think that this birth/development is now as important as cinema's birth.... I long to watch machinima which will stun me by melding all these approaches [Allen, personal communication].

If one seeks an artistic vision that has the power to "stun" the viewer as Allen puts it, one need search no further than the machinima of SaveMe Oh. In many ways, her work truly exemplifies avant-garde machinima's unconventional nature. "All my movies are in a way an extension of my performing and composing behavior; of the way my avatar has developed.... The only valuable art in *Second Life*," asserts Oh, "is performance art, and this is reflected in my movies." She describes *Second Life* as "the canvas" on which she creates. Her machinima "becomes the artwork."

Like her Dada and surrealist antecedents, Oh invites the viewer to become part of the composition, often forcing the audience to participate by reacting to her art installations which she captures as live theater in her machinima. Whether filming her audience chasing after flying dollars to remind them of the evils of consumerism, grinding them into hamburger to protest factory farming, or staging her own funerals in anticipation of rejection by critics of her work, Oh creates striking machinima that both challenges one's thinking and redefines the limits of the genre. Moreover, her art is rarely separate from her politics and provides thought-provoking underlying messages.

SaveMe Oh's persona, projected by her avatar, has become the vehicle for her art and provides continuity to her work. Among the most controversial of her works are those that explore hypocrisy and the traditional notion of sin and redemption. While machinima as a vehicle for social criticism is staunchly defended by some, others find the approach abrasive. SaveMe Oh's work elicits both responses in equal measure, reflecting her audience's reaction to her artistic vision.

One commonality of art machinima is that it typically represents a single director's orchestrated vision of his or someone else's art. The director most likely is solely involved in all aspects of production — script, acting, sets, lighting, camera work, and editing. The machinima becomes the art composed by the director, transformed into what Iono Allen defines as the creation of "a piece of a world in a time sequence and an ambience that builds upon existing pieces and worlds." Either alone or through active collaboration, directors seek to create art — not just film it as documentary. Whether focused on art installations or on performance art, the machinima is transformative, altering one form of expression to create another. Always, no two visions are alike.

Some machinima directors have used music as the focal point of art machinima. Collaborating with *Second Life* musicians, they have blended pop culture and art. One such artist is ColeMarie Soleil. Both director and musician, Soleil's experimentation with music, atmosphere, light and color palettes in *Second Life* combines the poetic and the painterly aspects of expressionism with haunting original musical compositions performed live in *Second Life*. Unlike other more conventional machinima directors, she distorts the reality of the virtual world she films in and creates an ambience that reflects her unique vision. The Machinima Artist Guild's 2009 award-winning *My Friends are Robots* and Soleil's entry at the Shanghai World's Fair machinima pavilion showcase her innovative style.

Distinctive stylistic differences continue to emerge, all strikingly innovative in their ability to explore space and time in unconventional ways; nevertheless there are those who create art in the more traditional cinematic style as well. And they are quick to defend its continued relevance as an art form. Machinima director Lainy Voom likens machinima to "the branches in a big tree with all the game engines and recording environments each doing its own thing, some being more conventional than others."

Says Voom, "Machinima has no rules, and for me that is important. I don't listen to anyone who tries to dictate what machinima should or should not be. I find that very arrogant. Being inspired by traditional media is fine by me, so is exploring other possibilities. I like to do both, and in that lies creative freedom." Voom's machinima *Push* is a fast-paced tour de force creation illustrating the unlimited imaginative possibilities in machinima. Computer-generated puppetry mimics animation in a fraction of the time. Machinima allows anyone with a computer, an imaginative vision and minimal technical ability to create art machinima. Voom shows what wonders can be accomplished by a machinima director on a tight budget ($50) using the vast array of tools available to her in a virtual world.

At the same time, Voom's use of traditional cinematic technique also shows her mastery of narrative form. Her innovative use of poetry in *The Stolen Child* by W.B. Yeats and her adaptation of an H. P. Lovecraft tale in *Dagon* serve as prime examples of the continued positive influence of conventional storytelling in art machinima, particularly stories mainstream cinema disregards as commercially viable. In a time when cinema has become excessively expensive to produce, those who finance the films are less inclined to let directors take many risks with their work. Cinema has grown stale, less innovative and more imitative as a result. Machinima, on the other hand, has flowered.

As virtual worlds continue to evolve, the genre of art machinima will undoubtedly change and grow more sophisticated. Advancing game technology will allow directors to develop innovative work more effectively with less cost. The art machinima will continue to gain respect and acceptance as one of the true modern multi-media art forms of the digital age. Accessible to a wide audience, fiercely independent, remarkably innovative and collaborative, machinima will transform the art of moviemaking.

Recommended Machinima

Allen, Iono. (2010). *A Question of Honour*. YouTube. Accessed November 25, 2010, from http://www.youtube.com/watch?v=YftouEm3CT4

Allen, Iono. (2010). *Fears*. YouTube. Accessed November 25, 2010, from http://www.youtube.com/watch?v=ByIIVpTvX38

Allen, Iono. (2009). the *Story of Susa Bubble — Rose Borchovski Artwork*. YouTube. Accessed November 25, 2001, from http://www.youtube.com/watch?v=aJdVCqG3

Oh, SaveMe. (2010). *Do It SaveMe Oh*. Vimeo. Accessed November 25, 2010, from http://www.vimeo.com/3300918

Oh, SaveMe. (2010). *Oh Lord*. Vimeo. Accessed November 25, 2010, from http://www.vimeo.com/6101317

Soleil, ColeMarie. (2009). *My Friends Are Robots*. YouTube. Accessed November 26, 2010, from http://www.youtube.com/watch?v=8h0sOIREUEo

Soleil, ColeMarie. (2010). *No Color*. YouTube. Accessed November 26, 2010, from. http://www.youtube.com/watch?v=L46IZKgI4mc

Voom, Lainy. (2010). *Dagon*. YouTube. Accessed November 26, 2010, from http://www.youtube.com/watch?v=CMOHpuxFbm0

Voom, Lainy. (2009). *Push*. YouTube. Accessed November 26, 2010, from http://www.youtube.com/watch?v=hLeK9Lanh94

Voom, Lainy. (2009). *The Stolen Child*. YouTube. Accessed November 26, 2010, from http://www.youtube.com/watch?v=g9hnUYV06t4

Personal communication with Iono Allen, SaveMe Oh, and Lainy Voom by the author of this essay.

5

Characters Come to Life

You are dealing with actors, you are dealing with other avatars who are your actors; they're your background actors; they're your principal actors. You direct them and that means you give them commands — go here, sit down, do this, do that, move your head while other people do other things in the background. That kind of real-time directing is so different from very solitary animation, frame by frame and painstakingly looking at incredible detail — Draxtor Despres [personal communication, 2010].

Roland Barthes opens his essay, titled "The Face of Garbo," with a striking description of the power of the human face on-screen. He states, "Garbo still belongs to that moment in cinema when capturing the human face still plunged audiences into the deepest ecstasy ... when the face represented a kind of absolute state of the flesh, which could be neither reached nor renounced" (p. 536). So what does that mean to filmmaking? Cinema makes heroes, creates moments, and captures the human spirit on camera. Your main character is the focus of your audience's attention. The face can become an invitation to viewers to get to know him or her during the span of the film, and beyond as they reflect on what they viewed.

In machinima, the face is a representation and construction. The human face is a metaphor of an idea or event, or both. Helen of Troy was said to have a face that launched a thousand ships. To sway an audience to an idea or event, one must provide a tour guide of some sort to entice them onward through the story. The character is the tour guide. Cinema, in many ways as with machinima, is about representation and metaphor. In a machinima, the avatar is an avatar until its character is defined. Its dialogue and action, as well as facial expressions, connect viewers watching. Audiences are interested in screen heroes, particularly those they can also identify with in some way. The hero is often larger than life in some aspects, but the best also endear us with their flaws.

Thomas Schatz, in his essay "From Hollywood Genres: Film Genre and the Genre Film," helps us understand how mainstream films serve as a "social" performance of American culture (p. 651). Hollywood propels the myth of the hero; whether the film is a "historical Western or a futuristic fantasy," the film becomes a cultural celebration on-screen (Schatz, p. 651). A machinimist should tap into those emotional (and cultural) connections between characters and audiences as they provide the common ground between them, even within the most idealized plots. There are some wonderful exceptions to the Hollywood approach. But in many cultures, nonetheless, audiences celebrate films that create screen heroes.

The main question to ask is, as a viewer, would I feel invested enough in this character to watch the whole film? As a producer, you must consider the audience's perspective. Other questions to consider: Is there something unique about this character that will draw audiences into the plot? What qualities does the character bring to the story that are relatable to audiences? When you look at the character, what do you like about him or her? What are those first and subsequent impressions? You get the idea.

This chapter discusses the concept of character, from the vantage point of the producer and the audience. Characters help the viewer to focus on significant plot points. Characters become memorable and provide reference to the viewer when comprehending and anticipating twists in the story. Inconsistencies and clues are derived from characters' actions. In a virtual world, finding animation scripts for appropriate expressions or actions is not as easy as it might seem. There are many generic animations. A producer must take extra effort to ensure that a machinima is expressed creatively and uniquely through appropriate animations, as well as situate believable characters within appropriate settings.

This chapter also considers the role of human perception and interpretation within the genre of art machinima, in which a story idea or an event is not necessarily expressed through the function of a character. For instance, one might consider the "character" of an art machinima to be that of the original creator of the work (painting, installation, or performance) — or the work itself — and perhaps the one who interprets the still work or installation into a film becomes integral to creating a sense of character, lending to the persona and having been invested now in the translation to screen. The creator and producer might be the same person. Yet, when they are not, the machinist moves beyond mere archivist to a translator or interpreter, a similar analogy being the novelist who entrusts her words to the screenplay writer. The story becomes interpreted through the machinimatographer's lens. There is no way to wholly avoid bringing in one's life experience into a film, as a producer or viewer. The producer, as an artist, seeks a way to connect emotionally to the viewer by calling attention to cinematic representations, be they ideas, beings, events or objects that have become elements of the machinima.

Hollywood-Type Machinima

Is it possible to develop machinima with the appeal of a Hollywood blockbuster? Machinima provides us with an affordable way to make great animated feature films. Beyond the limitations of machinima that grow less every day, and with the rise of external software that allows the producer to transform the ordinary into amazing avatars and settings, it always comes back to this question: what is it about the character that beckons us to watch a minute longer? That is the core to any good film. The action movie offers some advantages for machinimatographers, in that the intensity of the effects and rapid pacing of the genre carries the viewer forward to the ending. The action helps to suspend disbelief, with little time for the viewer to process the details. But to neglect the development of the character is a mistake. The audience wants a hero or heroine in these movies too, and that character must be credible throughout the film (although the concept of superheroes might be incredible to viewers).

Tom Bancroft (2006) challenges the producer when developing characters to consider their personality and role in the film, as well as certain aspects that define them through the plot. For example, is the character a hero or villain or perhaps a sidekick, and what parts of the story define his or her role? Bancroft (2006) suggests that Pinocchio's nose growing big when he lies is one example, and Shrek's ugliness offers another. He emphasizes the importance of staging the characters, for how you set up your characters at the onset of the story should prepare the viewer for what might happen along the way. The essence of a good film, according to David Bordwell (2006), is visual storytelling, and Hollywood still uses this formula for its blockbusters. Think *Jerry Maguire*, *American Graffiti*, and *The Lord of the Rings Trilogy*, and one begins to understand how plots are shaped through various characters' perspectives.

Bancroft (2006) states, "Seeing great films from the studio era can spur you to become a director; how many filmmakers were inspired by *King Kong* (1933) or *Citizen Kane* (1941)?" (p. 23). Lending some historical context, he shares, "Since the late 1910s, Hollywood cinema has constituted the world's primary tradition of visual storytelling, and ... this tradition has remained true to its fundamental premises" (p. 4). Kristin Thompson (1999) concurs that planned narrative structure, when done well, includes strong character development. She illustrates how films like *Hannah and Her Sisters*, *Tootsie*, *Alien*, *Amadeus* and *Desperately Seeking Susan* offer examples. Bordwell concludes, "The high concept movie, it's usually said, is one that can be encapsulated in a single sentence" (p. 6). Can you as a producer define your story in a sentence, and likewise can you describe your characters so succinctly that the audience could recognize them anywhere on-screen and offscreen? Machinima abides by these same rules of audience engagement, if connecting to the audience is key to your plan as a producer.

Identification through Character

What is it about the cinema that distinguishes it as a medium from literature and paintings? asks author Christian Metz (1999) to the filmmaker. While all forms may represent the imaginary, what other quality does cinema bring to the audience? There is a likely replication when cinema draws from a work of fiction. Through that interpretation there comes "a certain presence and a certain absence" (1999, p. 801). Given sensory information, the audience fills in the blanks with its own experience. Metz explains that cinema allows us to "see," "receive," and "release.... And I only need close my eyes to suppress it. Releasing it, I am the projector, receiving it, I am the screen ... I am the camera, which points and yet which records" (p. 805). It is the active sensory detail that releases our voyeuristic participation: "In order to understand the fiction film, I must both 'take myself' for the character ... and not take myself for him" (p. 807).

The viewer seeks to identify with the characters. Personification is one way this might happen in an animated feature, when characters are represented through animals or objects. In a general sense, characters, in all their forms, provide some predictability to a story that allows viewers to identify with them. Even the setting becomes important in developing strong plots. It is important often to situate the character. All these elements add to the "perceived detail," according to Metz: "The cinema involves us in the imaginary: it drums up all perception" (p. 802).

As active receivers, the audience continually processes and interprets new information. The producer should provide adequate information for the viewer to identify with the character. One way to do this is to build on the audience's existing cinematic experience when developing characters. Crafting archetypes, rather than stereotypes, allows viewers to relate to characters that remind them of people they have met in their life on or off the screen (Schmidt, 2007). For the most part, no one really likes to identify with a stereotypical image based on race, ethnicity, culture or physical image. Often many comedies lean on this approach, and some execute their story lines well; it is with great care that such decisions need to be made. Stereotypes often alienate your viewers, and most producers would like their work to appeal to as many people as possible. Archetypes can provide a framework.

In Phaylen Fairchild's series *DiVAS*, she plays a ditsy blonde "elf" — but more or less a human avatar that tries to gain admittance into a top *World of Warcraft* guild. In season 2, episode 1, Fairchild, quite fashionable in a majestic purple outfit, is interviewed by a beastly guild leader on her worthiness to be admitted into his group. Her character plays off the dumb blonde caricature, but the dialogue is brilliant. The conversation reveals two distinct personalities as she tries to understand his extreme dedication to the role-play. She begins by saying "Hi, hi," in a cutesy voice, admitting readily to not being familiar with the game customs and language, but still wanting to join his *WoW* guild. He responds, after a bit of reluctance, "OK, let's get this over with. I have a raid in 20 minutes." The characters drive the story. Her expressions are priceless, as are his responses. The animations are well chosen and executed. Her wit disarms the beast. That is the way an archetype can be employed to help situate the viewer into a context, with the scriptwriter or producer adding a twist or surprise to keep the viewer engaged and entertained. Linda Edelstein's *Writer's Guide to Character Traits* (2006) offers an interesting handbook for developing characters, by presenting profiles of human behavior and personality types. She includes appropriate body language, career traits, behavior disorders and other personality tendencies.

Orson Scott Card (1999) asks the producer to consider how and when characters arrive in a plot; is it serendipity? The point is your audience wants to see your characters as real people, to whatever extent that is necessary to the plot, and from there they can make assumptions about what will happen in the story. He offers the cinematic example of Indiana Jones in the opening of *Raiders of the Lost Ark*:

> Within ten minutes of the beginning of the movie, we knew that Indiana Jones was resourceful, greedy, clever, brave, intense; that he had a sense of humor and didn't take himself too seriously; that he was determined to survive against all odds. Nobody had to tell us [p. 5].

Card (1999) acknowledges that typecast roles are the ones that the audience feels most comfortable relating to during a film. But those are not always the most interesting; to know the rules is important, but sometimes it is important to violate a stereotypical/archetypical role to make that character more intriguing to viewers. The way to do that might involve playing with how the character responds to a range of emotions and situations that might intentionally contradict the archetype. At the extreme, it is a *Dr. Jekyll and Mr. Hyde* type of character; the viewer might be shown contradiction in subtle ways as well, as in being offered glimpses of the dark side of the character under stressful circumstances. Think of the portrayal of heroes in contemporary versions of the comic book character Batman, and the more recent movies *Iron Man* and *Watchmen*. Character is developed on-screen through a series of impressions, and some of the most important ones are at the very beginning of a film when the main characters are introduced. In a machinima, characters have to be developed in seconds rather than minutes, especially in short form. Archetypes, along with a twist or two of personality traits, help the machinima producer to speak volumes into their characters' personalities in seconds. Our initial impressions are formed immediately.

Achieving Character in the Character

It might be best to start with an exceptional example of how machinima can be developed from a work of non-fiction, bringing that story to screen. Consider the work of 19th-century transcendentalist author Louisa May Alcott.

Her writings and her life inspired producer Chantal Harvey, the founder of the MaMachinima International Festival, to produce a machinima. Alcott published a newspaper article in the *New Yorker Ledger* in 1869 that discussed the plight of single women. The machinima plot draws particularly from Alcott's short story *Happy Woman*. In her machinima, Harvey's main character has a customized face and appearance which reflects the age and wisdom of a woman from that time period. Harvey's machinima, *A Woman's Trial,* is a character piece that cinematically depicts what it meant to be an independent unmarried woman during that era. The character was the primary focus of the story. For the message to be received as credible, the appearance, voice, and setting had to be carefully conceived and executed. The nine-minute film follows the life of one woman's decision to choose career over marriage. That was the main message of Alcott's newspaper article. The strong narrative delivered by the main character is the voice of Harvey herself. The machinima opens with a close-up of a late-aged woman in a frumpy dress. The woman, Gwendolyn, explains that she was a rich man's daughter, "who was once pretty, accomplished, sensible and good." Continuing, she states, "I lived a fashionable life and found that it did not satisfy me." The machinima then transitions from color to black-and-white scenes from her younger days.

When the story returns to her present time, Gwendolyn is standing alone on the streets, against a backdrop of empty cafes in Paris, France. The narrator maintains her conviction and explains to the audience that Gwendolyn "never did find a suitable husband her father had hoped for." Her life was restless and ended tragically, with Gwendolyn eventually jumping off the ledge of the Eiffel Tower. The film continues to alternate between color and black-and-white images in its final scenes. As she falls from the tower, she is dancing with a man from her past (or a man that never was). The scenes—the dancing and the falling—overlap, until the past regains its color. The setting of the machinima was filmed in a simulated recreation of Paris circa 1900 within *Second Life*. As we see, the character is developed by not only the appearance of the avatar or puppet but through voice, setting, lighting, and animation, among other factors.

Character development presents special challenges to producers of films that feature strong women. Generally, and perhaps archetypically, the female, a social and physical icon, is represented sensationally across the screen. Linda Williams (1999), author of "Film Bodies: Gender, Genre, and Excess," adds that women's roles fulfill certain dualistic and conflicting social rituals, to which women viewers can relate when watching: "The woman viewer of a maternal melodrama such as *Terms of Endearment* or *Steel Magnolias* does not simply identify with the suffering and dying heroines of each." Williams continues, "She may equally identify with the powerful matriarchs, the surviving mothers who preside over the deaths of their daughters, experiencing the exhilaration and triumph of survival" (p. 709). Williams suggests that the point of identification among viewers is "neither fixed nor entirely passive" (p. 709). Harvey understood that developing character within machinima was challenging but ultimately rewarding, as she demonstrated the power of the form to create a relatable message. As one of the top women machinimatographers, she continues to forward the art and practice of machinima as a means for women to gain entrance into the world of film and storytelling.

Those Must-See Characters

Let's step back for a moment and consider this: what is it that draws an audience to the cinema? The story line might be intriguing, a must-see mystery. It might be a plot centering on a true story. Increasingly, documentaries have been included on the marque as box office draws. Then of course viewers might be in the mood for a hilarious comedy. Part of the success of the story rests on the actors, and the characters that they portray. The actors must offer a credible representation of the characters to engage the audience throughout the length of the movie. Comedies typically run about 90 minutes, whereas longer feature films can go beyond three hours. The characters, and the casting of them, determine the successful execution of the story line.

Think about your favorite characters in films and television shows. Who comes to mind? Many actors began their careers in Westerns. Clint Eastwood's first role was Rowdy Yates in the long-running series *Rawhide*. When that series ended, his next character, the *Man with No Name*, would propel his acting career. His lead role in Sergio Leone's spaghetti Western *A Fistful of Dollars* (1964), and the sequels that followed, made him an international icon. Throughout his career, he has starred in a variety of genres, beyond Westerns. For many actors, they find themselves typecast into particular characters and films. In the online magazine *Screen Junkies*, the editorial team featured *11 Great Terminally Typecast Actors*. On the list were Seth Rogen, Will Ferrell, Tom Cruise, Will Smith, Samuel L. Jackson, Morgan Freeman, Jim Carrey, Adam Sandler, Al Pacino, Robert De Niro and Jack Nicholson. Those actors tend to have similar or consistently predictable character traits across many of their films. The audience anticipates the character's actions in these cases, and it might draw some conclusions about the plot based on past screen performances. In other cases, the plot action drives the character, such as in novelist Ian Fleming's James Bond 007 series. Sean Connery, Roger Moore, Timothy Dalton and Pierce Brosnan were among the notables who played the British intelligence service agent. Each brought a slightly different interpretation to the role, but in a sense it was the Bond action that defined the movie.

One of perhaps the most well-known supporting actors is Jack Elan. He appeared in at least 200 Westerns, movies and TV shows. An eye injury as a child gave him a unique look that worked well for Westerns. Characters are typecast into certain roles; yet the audience finds comfort and familiarity with their presence. The more they are seen on-screen, the more we come to know them, or think we know them. *Gilligan's Island* introduced its weekly viewers to a cast of uniquely typecast characters that supported its well-written sitcom. In this series, the characters were fairly superficial, for the audience never really learned that much about their past. The sitcom centered on the mix of personality traits among the characters, and the weekly plot would offer a crisis that had to be resolved in less than 30 minutes. That was often difficult given the nature of certain characters, but in the end the cast worked together to solve the weekly problem. The show's entrance into millions of American homes regularly connected them to their audience. In *Gilligan's Island*, one begins to note each character as an archetype. Each character has a predictable role. The audience makes assumptions on the outcome of the weekly episode based on these roles. Without any one of the characters, the plot could not be fully implemented.

In the television dramatic series *Dr. Quinn Medicine Woman*, the main character is introduced as a strong-willed woman who leaves Boston in the 1870s to escape the prejudices of racism and gender inequality. She moves westward as a physician, and the weekly show revolves around the conflict she faces as a woman. The viewers anticipate how Michaela "Mike" Quinn, played by Jane Seymour, will resolve the crisis at hand. They come to understand the depth of her character and can then make assumptions on how she will solve the problem given her personality and her relocation to the harsh West. Similar challenges exist for machinima producers who want to develop characters that will draw audiences into the plot.

Challenges of Developing Machinima Characters

Barry Purves (2007) describes animators as possessing a "shared passion for a strange craft, and all the elements of design, storytelling, performance, movement and so on.... These elements often overlap with other arts and practitioners" (p. xvii). He asserts, through his professional observations, that it is somewhat "easy to say that all animators should be actors, but acting probably has certain connotations of the theatre and film, and is maybe too defined by scripts and human personae. These days I prefer to say all animators need to have the sensibilities of a performer" (p. xvii). The machinima producer will likely find that the best advice for character development falls between the crafting of film, television and animation. Kristin Thompson (2003) points out that much less is written on television storytelling than film, and the authors acknowledge that there is even less written about animation storytelling. Then, when it comes to books on machinima storytelling, producers will find little guidance along the way.

A few books provide an overview of the animation field, from story to pitch. All agree that character development is critical. Mike Wellins (2005), in *Storytelling through Animation*, encourages making emotional connections with the audience. Jean Wright (2005) states that it is all about brainstorming and creating memorable characters: "We can take our most childlike dreams or the wackiest worlds we can imagine and bring them to life. In animation, we completely restructure reality" (p. 1). Wright continues, "We take drawings, clay, puppets, or forms on a computer screen, and we make them seem so real that we want to believe they're alive" (p. 1). She suggests that animation is more visual than film, yet she advises, when planning and writing the script, "try to keep a movie running inside your head.... Keep those characters squashing and stretching, running in the air, morphing into monsters at the drop of an anvil" (Wright, 2005, p. 1). Wellins (2005) discusses particular concepts and techniques necessary for animation by sharing the theory behind the practice. He reminds us that motion in animation helps to define its characters and the plot. The importance of time and space becomes evident, for viewers process information on-screen rapidly in animation, in a matter of a few frames (Wright, 2005).

David B. Levy (2009), professional animator and author, states bluntly, "It's about character, stupid." He explains, "A quick survey of the top animated series cartoons since 1991 reveals that most have at least one aspect in common: a simple twist upon our expectations" (p. 6). He gives as examples characters such as Johnny Bravo, "a self-declared ladies' man that can't get a date," and Courage the Cowardly Dog, "a scaredy-cat who is forced time and time again into bravery against his own nature" (p. 6). This type of twist, according to Levy, is an appropriate beginning point for the development of a character, and this "leads to natural opportunities for conflict which, in turn, reveals character" (p. 6).

Machinima, similar to animated features, deals uniquely in time and space. The length of machinima varies considerably depending on the genre and goals. There is much debate and speculation regarding the appropriate length of a machinima based on various audience measurement tools, some of which are as simple as monitoring audience drop-off during viewings on YouTube. The filmmaker has a few seconds to catch the interest of the viewer and then about another half minute to keep that interest. Once you fully engage viewers, there are plenty of chances to lose them along the way. If the story is too predictable, then they might be off to other videos or ventures. What does your story offer viewers to maintain their interest? What signposts along the way keep them motivated to watch the whole piece? Signposts might be considered clues along the way that foreshadow a twist in the plot or the actions of a character. Organization is critical, even when the structure of the story might be unusual, such as in the style of the motion picture *Pulp Fiction*.

The depth of the character emanates from a well-conceived plot. However, it does take more than that to technically execute your story. It is interesting to note that Lainy Voom's recreation of H.P. Lovecraft's *Dagon* is an excellent example of how avatars can portray credible characters. Voom is a well-known woman machinimist, earning critical attention for her work as early as 2007 with the release of her production *A Tale from Midnight City*. Wagner James Au, in his daily blog *New World Notes*, praises her work:

> In every element — mood, photography, editing, storytelling, choice of shots, and more — it transcends *SL and* machinima as a medium. This is simply an excellent short film by an exceptional talent who just happened to choose those forms to tell her story.

The scene opens with a woman, the main character, in a darkly lit cafe. The audience hears into her mind, invited to listen to her conflicted thoughts. "I will never amount to anything," she thinks. A winged creature that we come to know as the soul catcher enters the room. The woman is expecting it. Near the end of the film, with a gun to her head, she shoots. A splatter on the floor below her is the last image the audience sees in the film as it ends. The complexity of the character is contextualized through the light, setting, animations, voice and the implicit and explicit relationship with the soul catcher.

Casting for voice talent is extremely important to the credibility of the character. It is good to have a pool of names associated with various types of voices, differing by accent, gender, attitude, and age. The right voice adds credibility to a character and might even help the viewer to overlook some minor flaws in the animations. Each character should have a defined role in the story. In an online virtual world, it is possible to collect an international pool of accents inexpensively. A voice bank, similar to a sound archive of effects and music, is a wise investment of one's time. Then in a moment, you know who to contact for the role. You have names and voice samples on file. On television and in motion pictures, certain actors become typecast to particular roles when they play that role well or long enough. That can be used to the advantage of the machinima producer too. In machinima, likewise, characters can be created to help the viewer anticipate their actions on-screen in seconds. Viewers like to feel that they can read into the plot, but only to a certain extent of course. No one likes to figure out the plot easily. When you reintroduce a popular character in a machinima series or genre, the audience immediately has a sense of expectation, which can be both good and not so good depending on how the story plays out on-screen.

However, characters can serve as tour guides in a sense, as if they are assisting the viewer through the story. Archetypical roles can be established in a story: the granny, the bratty sibling, the snob, the drifter, and so forth. These are starting points for the characters. Some writers provide a character analysis to help the producer cast for the appropriate voice or to customize an avatar to fit the plot. The more detail that is included in the analysis, the better defined the character will be to the viewer. That is not to say that the script will not change through the evolution of paper to screen, yet it gives the potential voice actors and the props crew some insight into what is needed to execute the story line by the most credible and efficient means. Whether one is working alone, or with a large crew, planning can save time and expenses along the way.

Realistic Animations and Scripting

Among the reasons people like to produce dance machinima is because scripts are continually updated and improved. In a social virtual world like *Second Life*, it is possible to achieve a sense of realism through dance. The avatars, particularly with animations organized in Huddles, perform before our eyes with fluidity and grace; it is as if they are romancing the screen. At the next moment, they can look like they are rocking out at a concert, bobbing their heads and tapping their toes. The best animations are those that replicate real life. When you cannot find the appropriate animation, it is best to rethink the scene than to use a poorly scripted animation.

A good animation is like a good virtual dance between characters—the audience needs to feel the action as they watch the avatars interact on-screen. Talking to individual producers will help a novice understand there is not one path to a good machinima. However, there is a need to carefully plan and execute the elements. Fast-action plots call for animations that take the viewer on a joyride with the character. The emphasis on dialogue might be less, although the producer must take care to establish a bond between the viewer and character through the establishment of some close-ups, mixed in with some medium and long camera shots. Facial expressions are critical on close-up shots.

Other producers of dialogue-driven machinima, such as sitcoms, might enhance the characters' personalities through a unique sound or music entrance segment. For instance, when the character enters the room, certain music might introduce her as she walks on the set. If the music starts a second earlier than the audience sees the character, there is an anticipation and expectation of her appearance. Another character may become distinguishable by the sound of his footsteps or the jingle of his keys in his pocket. Establishing characters through music and sound is one way to use repetition to involve the audience. The right props, clothing, and overall appearance of the avatar are all key considerations. How an avatar is animated to walk adds personality to the character. The customization of avatars is recommended, and much thought into what animations (e.g., action movements or lip-syncing) will enhance the credibility of a story is critical. Lip-syncing avatars can be challenging, but if the animation is used sparingly and skillfully, it can definitely add to the believability of the character. There is no reason to have a straight-on view of the avatar's face in every frame. Lip-syncing works well when the producer strategically considers the various ways to frame the shot and varies the camera angles and distance. A few well-thought-out close-ups of the lips moving to the dialogue might be all you need in a short machinima.

Best Practices in Virtual Character Development

In *Second Life*, the virtual world is designed to help in the customization of avatar actors. A variety of looks can be achieved through various hairs and skins, designer clothing, and period costumes, among the plethora of animations and sets available. It is a relatively inexpensive means of creating characters. The latest editions of *The Sims* offered some customization options as well. But in a world like *Second Life*, where content creation is at the center of the game, many machinima producers find options to allow them exceptional creativity in their films. The series *Tiny Nation* will be offered as an example of *Second Life* character customization at its best in a later section of this chapter. *A Woman's Tale* by producer Chantal Harvey has already been discussed in this chapter. Harvey's main character was carefully designed for the machinima. Aside from *Second Life*, Moviestorm provides a useful tool for developing some interesting characters, especially in association with other software like iClone.

Moviestorm has been a useful virtual tool in helping to construct movie sets and characters. Here are two machinima by the same producer that offer examples of strong character development and speak to a very planned narrative structure. The first is entitled *Cafe Insomniac: Episode #1*. One phrase, as coined by its creator Hardy Capo (2009), sums up the series: "*The Sopranos* meets *The Twilight Zone*." Capo produced the series using the virtual platform Moviestorm. It works as a stand-alone virtual environment and is not part of a virtual world like *Second Life*. The only community that exists is the one created by the producer. It can also be used in conjunction with other game engines to construct virtual films.

A machinima does not have to rely on the capture from any one platform or environment. Moviestorm, however, seems a popular alternative for some virtual filmmakers, and it has been accepted as a viable means for producing quality machinima. *Cafe Insomniac*'s script is well written, and the plot is character driven. The dim lights in a nighttime setting set the tone for the machinima. But it is the characters that intrigue and entangle the viewer into the plot. The main character's insomnia provides the perfect excuse for him to become owner of an all-night cafe that is open from 11 P.M. to 9 A.M. The cast of characters adds mystery to the story line.

Sandstorm is another machinima by Capo (2010). It centers on Private Harry Stone (voiced by Jorge Campos), who reflects on his final moments on earth. The film opens with a sandstorm clearing, and the viewer sees two chairs in the desert. The viewer travels through Stone's thoughts to the morning rush of a city, where people are busy dashing off to work. The machinima cuts back to his role in a military ambush. In his last moments, he envisions people on their daily commute, and he wonders what they will think about him dying in the ambush. Was his life and that of others like him wasted? The script is simple, spacious, and thought provoking, as Private Stone seizes his last minutes of life, waiting for someone or something (thus the second chair). The machinima closes with an angel arriving to greet Stone.

There are some striking scenes—the bustling street, the metro train, and the hospital, among others. Capo has a knack for transitioning between scenes. He is able to take the viewer anywhere, effortlessly—from the battlefield to a train ride to a captivating close-up as the viewer peers into the mind of the main character. The voice pacing, subtle gasping, emotional tone, and overall ambience in the desert work well to achieve the mood, along with the beige hues of the desert contrasted with the cityscape. Capo designed a machinima that would create the illusion of a soldier who was in purgatory and had not realized that he had died. Capo's scenes focus intentionally on the landscape, having made a production decision to refrain from too many close-ups of the soldier, as he has noted publicly on the Professional Machinima Artist Guild site. In both of his works, *Cafe Insomniac* and *Sandstorm*, there is pensive pacing that gives space to breathe, allowing the viewer to absorb the surroundings that define the characters.

Another Moviestorm film, *Death in Venice*, brings to screen an entangled relationship centering on the daughter of a brutally murdered mob boss, who seeks to avenge her father's death. The piece features many characters, and the work is driven strongly by dialogue. The directors Kate Lee and Sherwin Liu of Chat Noir Studio won several awards for this 20-minute machinima, including best mystery movie, best soundtrack and best long-form film at the 2010 Ollies; the film was also a finalist at the Shooot Fiesta Awards 2009 and nominated for the jury list of the Machinima Expo 2009. The directors took care to ensure that the avatars appeared unique, from wardrobe to accessories. The voices of the characters were obviously thoughtfully cast. In a story like this, the characters must be carefully developed to engage the viewer and to keep them attentive through the 20 minutes. Longer feature machinima runs the risk of losing an audience along the way unless the story line is tightly planned and executed.

Michael R. Joyce and Kate Fosk co-founded Pineapple Pictures in October 2007, a machinima/anymation movie company. Joyce's experience includes working in the Hollywood film industry for more than 20 years. As independent filmmakers, Fosk and Joyce continue to make strides in machinima production, relying on Moviestorm and iClone mainly. In fact, Fosk finds that iClone serves as a wonderful complement to Moviestorm for modifying avatar appearance, from body to clothing. One of the features by Pineapple Pictures is called *The Vampyre*, with sound design by renowned voice actor Ricky Grove. The machinima centers on the monologue of the main character. The duo experiments with new platforms and technology, but a large part of their professionalism is rooted in developing strong characters whether they are tomatoes, strawberries, guacamole or creatures of the night.

The Characters of Tiny Nation

Personification is when a non-human being or object is given human traits. It is through those human characteristics that the viewer can identify with a talking dog or rock, for example. A wonderful illustration of this technique can be viewed in the machinima series *Tiny Nation*. The season premiere launched what it described as the adventures of a band of cutesy, motley animals found in the average backyard. The series was an adult comedy, and a jury winner at Machinima Expo 2008. The first episode kicked off with the capture of a squirrel for a summer barbecue in a typical suburban neighborhood. The squirrel calls his furry buddies for a quick rescue. Captain Bob, the bunny, goes underground to bring together an animal army. The language is frank, and the producers play with gender roles and stereotypes, as well as toss in a few politically incorrect jokes. The series is geared to American audiences.

Numerous people were involved in the creation of the premiere. It was produced, directed and edited by Kerria Seabrooke. Executive producers were Paul Jannicola, Frank Dellario, and Damien Fate. It was written by Seabrooke and Jannicola (also the director of photography). Sets, props, animations and avatars were also the responsibility of Fate. Tom Donnelly handled the special effects and graphics. There was even a person assigned to facial animations: Sean Daniels. Fate worked on facial expressions and *Second Life* effects. The original music, score, Foley and sound engineering were also the responsibility of Jannicola. Custom scripting was done by Jason Crisman. Michael Johns created the custom skin. Jannicola and Seabrooke were the voices of the characters. The various puppeteers, those controlling the avatars, were Calamity Hathaway, Razzi Rockett, Stacie Ball, Damien Fate, and Michael Johns. The actual Tiny Avatars were supplied by Loco Pocos. As you can see, a look at the credits helps to reinforce all the important considerations that are involved in producing a machinima. Whether you produce it yourself or collaboratively, there is plenty to do to complete the production and to ensure the characters are not only crafted well but the surroundings in which they are filmed are worthy of the story line.

Character in Art Machinima

In other machinima, the focus may be a work of art. For example, machinimatographer Iono Allen has become well known for filming virtual installations in *Second Life* and then through machinima crafting his own interpretation from the artist's work. The originality that he brings to the work is his own response to it. He seeks the "character" of the piece (Allen, 2010). When he produced the Susa Bubble machinima series, his perspective emerged from the main character. He drew inspiration from the virtual installations, works of artist Rose Borchovski, but there is a point where he moves beyond her vision to translate and transform it into motion as machinima. He puts himself into the mindset of the little girl, and enters her imaginary world in order to take his audience along with him. When there is not a character, he invents one. As a producer of art machinima, he considers himself as both a storyteller and an artist. Identifying a point of focus in his work becomes central to his machinima (Allen, 2010).

His interest in machinima evolved from his love of real and virtual art. His passion for photography, and its transformation into art, gave him a unique perspective. A concept is illuminated in a frame through the right mix of light, color, and technique. As a virtual filmmaker, he searches for that connection to humanity, and that might be defined through an object or character. Art machinima has character, although not understood in the traditional sense of other machinima. But it must have a core that is reachable and taps into the experiences of an audience. Screenplays are often written from novels, and the two are never quite the same. In a similar way, Allen (2010) explains, "Well I think that firstly the exhibition has to 'talk to me.' I try to find a link for the whole machinima — a subject, something which is not obviously said in the exhibition, something personal but without betraying the artist."

In late 2010, Allen created a machinima based on the *Second Life* installation work of Betty Tureaud's *Nine Steps to Heaven*, a tribute to Stanley Kubrick's *2001: A Space Odyssey* (co-written by Kubrick and Arthur C. Clarke). "For Betty's install, it was a bit obvious," explains Allen (2010). "I wanted to have this old man, this astronaut as in the movie, who was not in the exhibition. It's a kind of personal interpretation, even if we both have been inspired by Clarke." In his YouTube description of the video, he continues, "I could not help but wear my space outfit and to dive in this Space Odyssey, like Dave Bowman did some time ago. Come with me?" Allen extends this personal invitation to his audience to enter his world and see what he sees through his lens. He challenges viewers to interpret art in their own forms. He claims art through his cinematic interpretation and takes what is often passive and gives it motion and life through machinima.

This is a skill that he has developed as he has progressed in his work. The difference is evident between his first machinima about Susa Bubble — *The Story of Susa Bubble* — and the second one, *Fears*. He invested more of himself into the sequel. It is not merely a matter of archiving an installation through machinima. Allen challenges other machinimatographers to reconstruct art through machinima. In essence, machinima is a different form of expression and unique in that it is accessible to the art machinimist. His builds upon the visions of others, such as the installation artist, while contributing his own ideas to it. In the book *Sound Unbound: Sampling Digital Music and Culture*, Paul Miller challenges his readers to understand all culture as sampled works; all work is built upon the former. Allen's work builds upon the former.

Film scholar David Bordwell (1999) tells us that the elements that shape art cinema, like other genres, are used to "advance the story" (p. 717). Montage editing, perspective lighting, camera distance, and narrative styles are some of the techniques that help to frame conceptual art films. Art cinema may vary in its level of abstractness and rely on the interaction between characters in a classical sense, but they lack "defined desires and goals.... Hence a certain drifting episodic quality to the art film's narrative" (p. 718). Bordwell (1999) elaborates, stating, "Characters may wander out and never reappear; events may lead to nothing. The Hollywood protagonist speeds directly toward the target; lacking a goal, the art-film character slides passively from one situation to another" (p. 718). Art machinima, like art cinema, employs the concept of character, but the core message is one to be defined by the producer and the audience. It is an open relationship.

Character in the Documentary

Life 2.0 producer Jason Spingarn-Koff, also director and editor, exemplifies a way that machinima can be expressed through the documentary genre. *Life 2.0* is his first documentary feature and it has been screened around the world, finding its way even to the Sundance Film Festival. The premise is based on his investigation, as an avatar, into the real and second lives of the people he interviewed. The goal was to produce a character-centered documentary that weaves reality and virtual-world footage to create a portrait of *Second Life* users. It takes an inside look at love and work in *Second Life*. The story centers on the lives of the people interviewed and profiled for this documentary.

Machinimatographer Draxtor Despres has created numerous documentary features in *Second Life*, mostly short news features under five minutes, using machinima as his storytelling tool. Many of his machinima productions are also styled as mixed-reality pieces, connecting RL and *SL* events. In his news feature, *The Kansas to Cairo Project Part #1*, Despres illustrated how more than 30 students experimented with urban design concepts in an expansive space situated between the Pyramids of Giza and the Grand Egyptian Museum in *Second Life*. The international collaboration happened all in the virtual realm. In one scene, the machinima portrays the organizational leaders of the project in the virtual world as they watch real-life news clips of U.S. president Barak Obama. The students are shown working together on design and implementation. Other features by Despres have investigated social, political and educational issues. He also produced a news piece on the European premiere of *Life*

2.0, which he noted was the first feature documentary that exclusively delved into life within the virtual world of *Second Life*. News machinima sometimes can be found in the form of newscasts, complete with avatar anchors who introduce event segments captured in the virtual world. The concept is basically the same as a real-world newscast. Some news organizations like Metaverse Television solicit *Second Life* opinions and perspectives from citizen avatars about real-world events, particularly regarding issues with global impact. The point here, however, is that real people are being interviewed in the form of avatars, and real people as avatars are delivering the news. *Second Life* news is about reporting on communities of people, no matter what form they take online. News and documentary machinima are based on the concept of storytelling, and stories need to relate to an audience. One way to do this is to understand how people relate to people. It begins with thinking of who, not just what, is significant to the story. Of course, there are similarities and differences between storytelling and portrayal of people through documentary and fiction.

Sheik Curren Bernard (2003), in his book *Documentary Storytelling for Video and Filmmakers*, points out the three act structure of documentary, as can be seen in the traditional film. The difference between documentary and other visual storytelling is "the conceptual process that begins at the moment an idea is raised and continues through production and post-production" (p. 5). Bernard (2003) continues, "Filmmakers routinely address story issues that are familiar to other types of authors, from playwrights to novelists. Who are your characters? What do they want? What are the stakes if they don't get it?" (p. 6). Filmmakers need to know up front what direction the story will progress, unlike the documentarian for which the script is the last element after gathering all the research. The characters reveal themselves through the investigation, and it might not be the ones that the documentarian actually planned on interviewing or focusing on at the start of the project. The story, according to Bernard, "begins as a hypothesis or a series of questions ... it has a compelling beginning, an unexpected middle, a satisfying end, and the kind of twists and turns that will get people talking" (p. 2). Bernard cautions that documentarians are "not free to invent plot points or character arcs and instead must find them in the raw material of real life" (p. 1). Elaborating on that, the authors suggest that rummaging the raw material of virtual life, and sometimes as it converges with real life, becomes the task of the documentarian machinimatographer. Virtual characters may or may not mirror reality, but they do offer unique story lines when based on authenticity that arises out of human connections, those behind the avatars.

Happy Endings

Tom Gunning starts off his essay "An Aesthetic of Astonishment" by calling attention to the audience of the early cinema: there was "the terrified reaction of spectators to *Lumiere's Arrival of a Train at the Station* ... [as] spectators reared back in their seats, or screamed, or got up and ran from the auditorium (or all three in succession)" (p. 818). He suggests that these accounts perhaps originate in myth, but they do underscore the viewer's lust for "thrills and spectacle, the particular form of curiositas that defines the aesthetic of attractions" (p. 831). The viewer agrees to participate in the film, by watching it. There are certain expectations that the viewer brings to the experience. They want some sort of resolution or reason for investing their time and emotions into the viewing. The protagonist should be transformed through the course of the story.

Victoria Schmidt (2007) advises writers to think carefully about the motivations assigned to their characters. In her book *45 Master Characters*, she notes that the character must be true to his or her nature, not because it is simply written into the plot. Schmidt (2007) proposes a series of guiding questions. Will the character run into a burning building? Will she rescue the cat from the tree? Will the teacher admonish the student? The answers to these questions should be rooted in the character's history and actions. A good character is memorable. Consider the likes of Dorothy, Xena, and Luke Skywalker, Schmidt (2007) adds, to understand the power of crafting strong characters. Schmidt (2007) explains that it is the characters, not only the stories, that become memorable to the viewer. The character depth of the protagonist is revealed to the audience as he or she is transformed by events along the way. It should be a learning process for the character.

All is well is not necessarily the appropriate outcome of every film, and audiences are not naive to expect such endings. But a good ending is one that gives a sense of resolution, or at the very least offers the audience some probable outcomes at the end based on the development of the characters and plot. There are some classic genre resolutions, as pointed out by film scholar Thomas Schatz (1999), as when "Cagney's heroic gangster would 'get his' or that Tracy and Hepburn would cease their delightful hostilities and embrace in time for the closing credits" (p. 650). Schatz (1999) explains, "the most significant feature of any generic narrative may be its resolution — that is, its efforts to solve, even if only temporarily, the conflicts that have disturbed the community welfare" (p. 650). An example might be illustrated through the Western genre: "Despite its historical and geographical distance from most viewers, [it] confronts real and immediate social conflicts: individual versus community, town versus wilderness, order versus anarchy, and so on ... seemingly timeless cultural oppositions [which] can be resolved favorably for the larger community" (Schatz, 1999, p. 650). In fact, Schatz (1999) acknowledges that setting and character drive Hollywood genre movies for the most part: "plot development is effectively displaced by setting and character" (p. 650). That means that our sense of acquaintance and a certain déjà vu feeling with that "familiar cultural arena and the players [ensure] we can be fairly certain how the game will be played and how it will end" (p. 650).

In contrast, he adds that in other types of films, what he calls the "non-generic," the characters and conflicts, and thus the endings, can be "unfamiliar and unpredictable, we negotiate them less by previous filmic experiences than by previous 'real-world' (personal and social) experiences" (p. 651). The machinimist negotiates between the traditional genre films and the non-generic. In one sense, virtual worlds can offer both a sense of familiarity and unfamiliarity, depending on the audience's experience with them and how the settings (and characters) are constructed. But the same general principles must be considered, because character, set, and plot development are critical elements of leading an audience toward an acceptable resolution or conclusion. Real-life and virtual-life experiences of the viewers will guide how they interpret the machinima. The more open a story line, the more the audience will fill in the blanks with their own experiences and speculations, and that might lead to a completely different interpretation than that of the producer, which might be good or bad depending on the original intent of the film project.

The machinima producer is a storyteller, not unlike those of other media forms. The difference is in the means of expression. Good producers learn from their predecessors, storytellers of various media, not only those of machinima. Yet machinima offers the unique advantage of inviting new forms of creativity and accessibility among those left behind by expensive gear and the Hollywood elite. Machinima lets the producer explore a new world of cinema on the horizon. It is a world of experimentation for character development and an opportunity for new producers to enter the storytelling arena.

Character Exercises

Critique various machinima for effectiveness of character development, considering the following questions:

1. Who is the protagonist (hero or heroine) of the story?
2. Who are the various characters of the machinima? What archetypes do they serve to bring to the plot? In other words, what are their unique contributions to the story line?
3. How do characters help to propel the plot?
4. How do the props and settings help to define the main character's role?
5. Watch an introductory scene and identify elements that help the viewer become acquainted with the main characters' motivations and actions.
6. What are some examples of art machinima that convey a sense of character, and how is the artistic vision expressed in relatable ways to tap into human emotion?
7. Critique the role of the interviewer and interviewee in a news/documentary machinima.

References

Alcott, Louise. (1868, April 11). Happy Women. *New York Ledger.*

Allen, Iono. (2010, October 3). Personal Communication.

Allen, Iono. (2009). The *Story of Susa Bubble.* Accessed November 24, 2010, from http://www.youtube.com/user/Ionoallen#p/u/14/aJdVCqG3bZs

Allen, Iono. (2010). *Fears— The Story of Susa Bubble.* Accessed November 24, 2010, from http://www.youtube.com/user/Ionoallen#p/u/l/ByIIVpTvX38

Allen, Iono. (2010). *Nine Steps to Heaven—* An Installation by Betty Tureaud. Accessed November 24, 2010, from http://www.youtube.com/user/Ionoallen#p/u/0/HJB4OYb_p58

Bancroft, Tom. (2006). *Creating Characters with Personality: For Film, TV, Animation, Video Game, and Graphic Novels.* New York: Watson-Guptill.

Barthes, Roland. (1999). The Face of Garbo. In Leo Braudy and Marshall Cohen (eds.), *Film Theory and Criticism* (pp. 536–538). New York: Oxford University Press.

Bernard, Sheik Curren. (2003). *Documentary Storytelling for Video and Filmmakers.* Boston, MA: Focal Press.

Bordwell, David. (1999). The Art Cinema as a Mode of Film Practice. In Leo Braudy and Marshall Cohen (eds.), *Film Theory and Criticism* (pp. 716–724). New York: Oxford University Press.

Bordwell, David. (2006). *The Way Hollywood Tells It: Story and Style in Modern Movies.* Berkeley, CA: University of California Press.

Capo, Hardy. (2009). *Cafe Insomniac—* ep. 1. Accessed November 27, 2010, from http://www.vimeo.com/4735924

Capo, Hardy. (2010). *Sandstorm.* Accessed November 27, 2010, from http://www.vimeo.com/10346196

Card, Orson Scott. (1999). *Elements of Fiction Writing: Characters and Viewpoints.* New York: Writers Digest Book.

Chat Noir Studios (2009). *Death in Venice.* Accessed November 27, 2010, from http://vimeo.com/6890750

Edelstein, Linda. (2006). *Writer's Guide to Character Traits.* New York: Writers Digest Book.

Eiselein, Gregory, & Phillips, Anne K. (eds.) (2001). Happy Women. *The Louisa May Alcott Encyclopedia* (p. 129). Westport, CT: Greenwood Press.

11 Great Terminally Typecast Actors. *Screen Junkies.* Accessed October 10, 2010, from http://www.screenjunkies.com/movies/movie-news/11-terminally-typecast-actors/

Fairchild, Phaylen. *DiVAS, Season 2 Episode 1— Phaylen Seeks a World of Warcraft* Guild. Accessed November 12, 2010, from http://www.youtube.com/watch?v=zkZetBxaP2w

Fosk, Kate, & Joyce Michael R. (2010). Machinima Frustrations: Moviestorm versus iClone. *Pineapple Chunks.* Blog. Accessed November 27, 2010, from http://pinechunks.blogspot.com/2008/02-/machinima-frustrations-moviestorm.html

Gunning, Tom. (1999). An Aesthetic of Astonishment: Early Film and the (IN) Credulous Spectator. In Leo Braudy and Marshall Cohen (eds.), *Film Theory and Criticism* (pp. 818–832). New York: Oxford University Press.

Harvey, Chantal. *A Woman's Trial.* Accessed November 1, 2010, from http://www.youtube.com/watch?v=V3l8eYPUZzo

Levy, David B. (2009). *Animation Development: From Pitch to Production.* New York: Allworth Press.

Jannicola, Paul, Dellario, Frank, & Fate, Damien. (2008). *Tiny Nation.* Premiere. Accessed October 1, 2010, from http://www.youtube.com/watch?v=oQ6FqBDbgc4

Metz, Christian. (1999). From the Imaginary Signifier: Identification, Mirror. In Leo Braudy and Marshall Cohen (eds.), *Film Theory and Criticism* (pp. 800–817). New York: Oxford University Press.

Miller, Paul. (2008). Sound *Unbound: Sampling Digital Music and Culture.* Cambridge, MA: MIT Press.

Pineapple Pictures. (2010). The *Vampyre.* Accessed November 27, 2010, from http://vimeo.com/9103336

Purves, Barry J. C. (2007). *Stop Motion: Passion, Process and Performance.* Boston, MA: Focal Press.

Reisen, Harriet. (2009). *Louisa May Alcott: The Woman Behind Little Women.* New York: Picado.

Schatz, Thomas. (1999). From Hollywood Genres: Film Genre and the Genre Film. In Leo Braudy and Marshall Cohen (eds.), *Film Theory and Criticism* (pp. 642–653). New York: Oxford University Press.

Schmidt, Victoria. (2007). *45 Master Characters.* New York: Writers Digest.

Thompson, Kristin. (2003). *Storytelling in Film and Television*. Boston, MA: Harvard University Press.

Thompson, Kristin. (1999). *Storytelling in the New Hollywood*. Boston, MA: Harvard University Press.

Voom, Lainy. *Dagon*. Accessed November 1, 2010, from http://www.youtube.com/watch?v=CMOH-puxFbm0.

Voom, Lainy. *A Tale from Midnight City*. Accessed November 1, 2010, from http://www.youtube.com/watch?v=PCSknY0Sa6I

Wagner, James Au. (2007, May 22). YouTube, Your obliteration: *Tale from Midnight City*. New World Notes. Accessed October 20, 2010, from http://nwn.blogs.com/nwn/2007/05/your_tube_your_.html.

Wellins, Mike. (2005). Storytelling through Animation. Boston, MA: Charles River Media.

Williams, Linda. (1999). Film Bodies: Gender, Genre, and Excess. In Leo Braudy & Marshall Cohen (eds.), *Film Theory and Criticism* (pp. 701–715). New York: Oxford University Press.

Wright, Jean. (2005). *Animation Writing and Development: From Script Development to Pitch*. Boston, MA: Focal Press.

✧ COMMENTS BY 1ANGELCARES WRITER ✧

The Voices of Machinima

Her stage name is 1angelcares Writer, and she usually goes by the name Angel. She keeps her real life private. In Second Life, *she is a well-respected actress and the former casting director for Suzy's Super Cast & Crew, a division of Running Lady Productions. She resigned from that position soon after the interview to pursue full-time voice-over work. The company assists filmmakers with actors and crew for their film and machinima projects, as well as works on its own productions. Angel was one of the primary go-to people in* Second Life *when it came to finding talent, or when people wanted to audition for machinima roles.*

In this segment she offers advice on everything performance-wise, from what is expected in an audition to the technology that she uses for recording her voice-overs. She also talks about how important it is for machinimators to build production crews and a reliable talent pool rather than trying to do everything as a solo venture, at least from her experience. Aside from her business relationship with Running Lady Productions CEO Suzy Yue, she has developed a rapport with some of the leading women of machinima, including Chantal Harvey, Evie Fairchild, Laurina Hawks and Toxic Menges, among others. Here are some of the lessons that Angel, as a machinima actress, has learned along the way during her travels through virtual worlds.

Lessons from Angel

Well, I consider myself much more of a talent scout than a casting director. Suzy slapped that title on me, but I've yet to cast anything. What I do is, well it depends on what she wants. Sometimes she just wants people. She wants me to just go and look up people's profiles to see if they have anything that says interest in acting, machinima, or anything like that. It's just kind of cold contact. But that was a couple years ago. Now she wants really more professional people who are actually actors. So we can afford to be a little pickier now that we have a good core group. We have a wonderful group of people already. So there's really not much need to continue to recruit, but due to the nature of *Second Life*, sometimes people leave. We want to make sure they are able to follow directions. So you need people who have a good head on their shoulders, who are not going to lose their cool, someone who's not going to become impatient. Basically, we look for somebody who's easy to work with, and available when you need somebody to be available.

The Audition Process

The way it works is Suzy meets a lot of people interested in acting and she'll send them to me. I'm her time-saver so she doesn't have to screen applicants all by herself. I interview them, sort of screen them. I see what they're about, and based on my recommendation, they go on to audition for us. It's very rare that I don't recommend somebody, but when I don't, Suzy listens to me. So I would say it's really about attitude. When I'm talking to a person, I'm interviewing them. Some really good advice that Suzy gave me a long time ago was that basically there are a lot of talented people out there, and what it often comes down to is not just the talent, because they're all talented. It's who do I think I could stand being around for this shoot. So I guess that advice is what I would give to other people. You want to go along to get along. You don't want to be the complainer. You don't want to be the person who's holding up the production. You want to just be very amenable to whatever the director tells you to do. Then you should be successful and be asked back a lot. As *Second Life* is skewed toward female users, it's no surprise that we would be skewed toward female voice-overs. We're always looking for male voice-over talent.

Building a Crew

Of course when you're the machinimatographer, and you're working with yourself, then you have full freedom to do exactly what you want, and take as much time as you want. I definitely see the advantage to that. But to me, when you're actually making a movie with a story line and many characters, it would really benefit you enormously to have people who know what they're doing and who have had experience in making movies. Everybody seems to want to round up their friends in a kind of Judy Garland, Mickey Rooney-style, "Hey, let's make a movie in the barn!" It's a lot of hard work, and a lot of movies don't get made because people don't realize just how much is involved. But we do. We're experienced people who have been in many productions, and so we know how long it takes. And we're willing to do that. We know what buttons to push, and where to move, and how to handle lag. To me, it's a great advantage for any director who really is truly serious about making a movie to just go ahead and bite the bullet. Hire the professional actors, and get the job done. Instead of it taking months, it can take days, and then you have a finished product that you're proud of.

With Suzy's Super Cast & Crew, we've done everything from work for very high-profile clients like IBM, doing a series for them — a promotional series for one of their products. Then other real-world universities wanted us to do promos too. Then we do comedies; we do fairly much whatever is asked of us. We have even done live performances that were taped. So we're very versatile in terms of what we can do, and have done. It's a new challenge for us when we get something we can really work on, and sink our teeth into. It's fun.

How It Started

It is a really good story of how I got interested in machinima in *Second Life*. Although I didn't start actually acting until 2008, on my first day in *SL* in 2007, on Orientation Island, I saw a machinima and said, "Wow! I would really love to do that!" I'd say within a month of me being in *SL*, I went to Susi Spicoli's sim. It's not there anymore, but she had little areas set up that were showing all different kinds of machinima movies from all different directors. I kind of lucked into Laurina Hawks' little area, which was showing a machinima with a woman walking in a cityscape. It turned out to be the *Matrix Offline: Wake Up*. At the end, it said, "Are you interested in acting in machinima? Contact Laurina Hawks." And so I did! I mean little newbish me, just all the moxy in the world, just like, "Yeah! I'm gonna contact this director! I would like to be in a machinima!" And she was so kind to me, and took me for a wild ride in her convertible. She told me about this incredible science fiction project that she wanted to do, but nothing ever happened. So I kind of thought, "Oh well. There goes that!" We still kept in touch occasionally, though. Then a year later, I was at a friend's, and the talent scout for Suzy's Super Cast & Crew saw that I had acting in machinima in the interests section of my avatar profile. He said, "Wow! Are you still interested in that?" "Yeah, I sure am." "Hey! Meet with Suzy." And the very next day, I was on the IBM shoot. That guy ended up stepping down as talent scout, and he recommended that I take his place. I guess he was impressed with my work ethic, and that's kind of how it happened that I became casting director for Suzy.

Another time, I was in a group called Brilliant Blondes, and a little blue notice came down on the corner of my screen that said, "Emergency! There's a director who desperately needs somebody who can read a poem in Spanish for their movie." I'm like, "Yo hablo espanol!" I contacted the director and she sent me the script. I didn't even know how to send an FTP file. She had to hook me up with her sound director. He got me all set, and I did the reading, and she liked it so much that she has cast me in nearly everything she's done since then. That was Chantal Harvey. So actually I got a lucky break and happened to be at the right place at the right time. If you don't do a good job, then obviously they're not going to call you back, so there must have been something that they liked.

On the other hand, I don't do any voice work in real life. I wouldn't consider myself a professional actress by any stretch of the imagination in real life. I come to the table with some experience. We'll just put it like that. But this was all new to me, for starting out and trying to figure out how do you act with an avatar. But the advice that I would give somebody who is interested in doing voice-overs— well, first of all, see me; I'll hire you for Suzy's Super Cast & Crew. But also build your contacts. Make it known that you're interested in doing voice-over work. I was very fortunate to get my voice-over break like you see on one of those Hollywood-type stories. Now I am Laurina Hawks' voice in that science-fiction series she's doing. As well as that, I was in the number-one award-winning University of Western Australia movie that we did, *No Tomb for the Arts*. She likes to use her avatar, but my voice.

All I can say, it sure beats watching TV. I was in a TV pilot. It didn't get sold, but that's amazing to me. It makes other things pale by comparison. It was called *St. Andrews*. Evie Fairchild was connected to it. That's how I ended up going to work for her as well. It was somebody's dream. He wrote it, directed it, cast it — everything. He asked Evie to come on board as an advisor and a builder, and scripter, and so forth. That's how I got to meet her. It was unfortunate that it didn't go anywhere because it would have been really cool. But my contact with Evie came out of that, and contacts are important in this business.

Achieving a Good Voice-Over

Since I've become this voice-over artist now, I've started really paying attention to voice-overs when I hear them in a movie, or a TV show, or what have you. I recently saw an animated move called *Tangled*. Wow! Mandy Moore did a fantastic job! I was really impressed. They all had really good voices. So I do pay attention. I want to get better at my craft, so I'm starting to really notice and invest more. As for audio software, I use Audacity. I'm using my cheapo microphone from Radio Shack right now, but I bought a couple of Sennheiser microphones. I moved over the summer, so my acoustics are completely off from what they were. Just "night and day" bad. So I'm trying to think, "Wow! How can I fix this so I can have the same awesome acoustic level that I had before?" So I'm going online and looking at sound muffling, baffles, and sound booths, all kinds of things. The more I have been getting into it, the more interested I am, and the more professional I want to be. So I could see possibly going to that arc of wanting to take it further than just *Second Life*, but for right now, that's where I am. For the most part, I'm doing my voice-overs without coaching. The director sends me the script and I make my best guess as to what he/she wants. For Laurina, in one movie, I think I was three different voices. One of them was a spaceshipboard computer, so I had fun working with the effects in Audacity trying to sound more like a machine. But mostly I leave it to the director or the sound engineer. Laurina writes her own music for her movies, so she's very into sound quality. It's almost better for me to send her the raw sound files and leave it to her to decide how she wants to tweak it. My involvement in these other areas might change in the future. We'll see.

The Community

Within *Second Life*, specifically, I consider us to be a creative community. I consider the directors that I'm working for to be friends. I'm not really sure if in the real-life acting world it works like that, but for me, if Chantal said, "Hey, Angel. I need you to do something or other," I'd drop whatever I was doing. Same thing with Laurina, and of course Suzy has been my mentor and my friend and has really changed my *Second Life*. Anything that she ever asks me to do, I would do it. I'm not really sure if that would equate in the real-life acting world, but certainly here in *Second Life*, we're all so close. That's how it is for me at least.

We cheer each other on. We share. We say, "Hey! Look what I did!" We encourage each other, and sometimes offer constructive criticism to each other. I think that contributes to making us more tight-knit. There's not a lot of money to be made here, at least not yet. So it is cooperative. That's something I really cherish. I hope that doesn't change. Based on the experience with IBM, that's where the money is, working for real-life clients. I got a kick out of saying, "Hey, in the IBM shoot, I played every single one of the heroes and I think three out of the four villains!" But that wasn't my voice, and that wasn't my avatar. It was me manning an avatar and being a puppeteer, and pushing buttons. So I got paid well, but it wasn't as satisfying as doing voice-over, even for free. So I guess, for me, I'll go on the record and say, "Although I enjoy getting money for my work, it's not about the money for me."

Thoughts about the Future

We are doing all these beautiful things, and I look forward to the rise of the female filmmaker really broadening what machinima means. Right now, if you say machinima to people, they instantly think of machinima.com. They instantly think about *Red vs. Blue Halo* stuff. And they're completely missing the absolutely gorgeous work that is being done in *Second Life* and elsewhere. They think that's what machinima is. And I'm like, "Are you kidding me?" You look at the beautiful cinematography that Toxic Menges has created through her work, for example, and then you compare it to the stuff that's on machinima.com. There's just no comparison. So people go away thinking that they know what machinima is because they've been to machinima.com. I say, "No. There's so much more to it than that."

I saw a really compelling machinima produced using *The Sims 2* or something like that for a 48 Hour Film machinima project. So they're definitely doing similar things using other platforms. In fact, I was an avid, addicted *The Sims* player. When I found out about *Second Life*, I kind of thought it was like a freeware *The Sims* Online. So I'm like, "Oh good, it's free." Then I found out, "Oh, no! This is not the same game! It's ten times better because now I get to (*be*) the 'Sim.'" I think in *Second Life* we have a lot more content, and a lot more freedom than do machinima makers in *The Sims*. There's something to be said for being able to be creative within such thin confines, but I would rather have the freedom. *InWorldz* is a newer open-source version of *Second Life*, still in its infancy. For example, *InWorldz* has no voice, so therefore we really cannot make the kinds of movies that we make in *Second Life*. Yet, as "not ready for prime time" as *InWorldz* is, it's so relaxing over there, and it has a pioneer spirit which has somewhat gone from *Second Life*. I have already helped Suzy to start bringing her studio to *InWorldz*. I'm not predicting the demise of *Second Life* anytime soon, but people are definitely looking at other places. There's OpenSim, and there was another one that I ventured to, just to register my name, but I hotfooted it out of there quickly. It was not really a good place. I don't know that I'd want to go on the record talking about it, but as a female over the age of 18, I was the opposite of their demographic. There's *Blue Mars*, also, but it has been too tightly controlled and too different from *Second Life* for me to really feel comfortable there. I love *SL*. I am a big *SL* fan.

Really, my main goal, always, is to get people to use my avatar along with my voice. It's a little frustrating to me at times that it's only my voice they want. It would be really nice to have both of them at the same time on the screen. It's the tickle that you get from seeing yourself up there. I get to hear myself, which is great, and I enjoy that, but for a next goal, I'd really like for people to want to cast me as me. We'll see. Then maybe, eventually, I'd love to see my name on a movie poster. Who knows! It's not about the money for me at all. It's the giddy feeling that you get. "Wow! That's really me up there!" I joke and I say, "I'm not an avatar in real life, but I play one on TV!"

Recommended Machinima

Cruise Control by RunningLady Productions, http://www.youtube.com/watch?v=Q5g-fyMjYWE
El Giafaron: An Incongruent Truth by Laurina Hawks, http://www.youtube.com/watch?v=LIAqFT3SK 4w
No Tomb for the Arts by Laurina Hawks, http://www.youtube.com/watch?v=QsrZgMA8SNI
Simulacron: Prologue by Laurina Hawks, http://www.youtube.com/watch?v=aM1UTigbj04

6

Setting, Lighting and Composition

Commercialization is what's putting it into the mainstream right now. In 2000, machinima.com was a small, niche group. Hugh Hancock was struggling with the server fees, sold it to Philip DeBevoise and the DeBevoise family — Aaron, Allen, Philip — worked and got funding — 4 million dollars of funding. I was part of their funding hires for a while. They strike deals with popular video games, first person shooters.... Hot Tub Time Machine has machinima. Lie to Me had an interesting segment where this guy had PTSD [post-traumatic stress disorder].... I'd say that's the kind of machinima. So you see this stuff on TV and you know it comes from a video game or an animation, or something like that, and you might be curious.... I'll bet that machinima was a very small part of that cost compared to hiring the greeters, hiring the builders, the sim costs, the development costs. I'll bet machinima was just a tiny chunk of that." — Moo Money [Roundtable Two, 2010].

In virtual worlds, the setting is crucial to the project — and those elements that bring the character to life within that environment. It is always more than capturing machinima footage to create a relatable, credible production that will engage an audience. Moreover, lighting is a huge consideration. This chapter introduces machinima makers to scene composition through lighting, and conveys some basics on choosing the appropriate virtual location or environment. It then offers some suggestions on how to create the right story mood, from lighting the characters to the props to the actual environment. This chapter explores the connections between photography and machinima, and how many photographers have transitioned into machinima. A historical perspective of the similarities between capturing still and moving images offers some conceptual ways of pre-visualizing your story lighting, and subsequently creating the ideal setting through lighting.

A Bit of History and Introduction to Lighting

In the late 1880s, filmmaking mostly happened outside. Funny today that in producing machinima, the creator's source of lighting in contrast draws from internal workings of the game engine and the producer's computer graphics and processing capabilities. The early studios relied on skylight, and "because these were silent films ... noise was not an issue" (Brown, 2007, p. 3). Author Blain Brown (2007) of *Motion Picture and Video* elaborates, "Some control was possible, with muslins stretched under the skylights to provide the diffusion of the light and control contrast" (p. 3). The "first artificial" light sources were used around 1905; they were mercury vapor tubes, and then "these were followed soon after by the introduction of arc lamps, which were adaptations of typical street lights of the time" (Brown, 2007, p. 3). So we see the producers were drawing from what was around them at the time, for their inspiration of lighting sources. Lighting has always been achieved best through improvisation, innovation and imagination.

Lighting sets the mood. It brings the emotional tone to a scene or film. The tone can range from black and white to a variety of hues. The concept of saturation is related and important to achieving a certain mood to the work. Most of the principles used in cinematic filmmaking are those related to photography, such as mood, tone, exposure, depth and dimension. The lighting artist knows how much and how little is essential to revealing the features of the character or the object. The shape, texture and fullness of a person or object comes to our attention from such efforts. Lighting can isolate a particular object in a frame as well as move it to the forefront, middle ground or background at any one point.

Kris Malkiewicz (1986) hosted a series of interviews with film lighting professionals working in Hollywood studio production in the eighties and arrived at some general conclusions. All in all, styles are influenced by personalities of cinematographers, as well as technology and film stocks. Malkiewicz (1986) recommends collaboration between the set designer and the cinematographer, at least as a start. A cinematographer, he notes, "must be as observant as the French impressionist painter Claude Monet, who painted the cathedral at Rouen from the same angle at various times of the day" (Malkiewicz, 1986, p. 1). A film, and its many scenes, should be conceptualized from any or all angles. He adds, "For a cinematographer, watching the light becomes second nature. Whether in a city hall, a restaurant, a nightclub, or in the woods, the cinematographer will file it away in his memory to be recalled when lighting a similar situation on a movie set" (p. 1). This knowledge and experience, reinforced by astute observation of art and practice, helps to delineate the "visual character" of a film. "The light is there to direct the viewer's attention, the darkness to stimulate his imagination" (pp. 1–2). The cinematographer works to light and darken the corners of our perception. Malkiewicz (1986) acknowledges that directors achieve lighting styles, and styles can be paralleled to technology and practice through modern cinematic history: "As in all arts there are styles in lighting that characterize certain periods or certain film studios. For example the glossy Hollywood pictures of the thirties were followed by the stylized low-key lighting of film noir in the forties," and so forth (pp. 2–3).

Painting with Light

So if you are wondering what lighting is all about, you might turn to John Alton's classic *Painting with Light*, one of the first books written on cinematography. Alton was a renowned cameraman who could tell a story through lighting. For many, lighting is merely a necessity, a way to see the characters, props and setting. But lighting can reveal hidden mysteries in a plot or illuminate a new relationship among friends in a romantic tale. The book *Painting with Light* was initially published in 1949. In 1995, it was reprinted with a special two-chapter introduction on Alton's professional life and lighting technique by Todd McCarthy. Alton is known for his film noir lighting in *American in Paris*, *T-Men*, and *The Big Combo*, to name only a few. In the 1940s and 1950s, he broke all the rules and challenged directors to look beyond available technologies and techniques to light the story by first visualizing it. His crafting of light into shadows, shades, and accents remains legendary as to what one can do by more or less thinking through a situation, then relying on available technologies. Alton painted first with his imagination, and then he sought ways to arrange the set and characters to tell the story. He challenged the conventions of other technical directors to the point that he angered some of them for his breaking of the industry practices.

Alton approached lighting as an artist, painting a scene through color, shadows, and innovation. He focused on what would best convey the purpose of the scene, rather than pre-conceived limitations of the technologies. In the middle 1950s when the noir era of film was coming to a close, one modest film of its time is still remembered to date for its exquisite lighting. That film was John H. Lewis' *The Big Combo* and it showcases Alton's lighting direction: "One last time, Alton pushed his impulse toward several black-and-white contrasts and silhouetting of characters to the limit," notes McCarthy (Alton, 1995, p. xxix). He explained, a considerable number of scenes "are clearly lit with only one source, and the final shot, with the figures of a man and woman outlined in a warehouse against a foggy nightscape and illuminated by a single beacon, makes one of the quintessentially anti-sentimental noir statements about the place of humanity in the existential void" (McCarthy, in Alton, 1995, xxix).

Alton's book is dated to the available technologies of his time yet still can be gleaned for some timeless advice to filmmakers. You begin to see how he sees, as he gives examples of various shots by providing the motivation for using them. Pictorial view shots are established to illustrate "the beauty of the countryside" (Alton, 1995, p. 120), for these wide shots set the mood for the story, sharing the larger setting with the viewer. Geographical long shots can be used to "orient the audience" (Alton, 1995, p. 120), and other long shots can be used best to display action, mystery, or a setting for romantic interlude.

Alton spent much time considering how to use the available light from outdoors, like most early filmmakers. But in machinima, the world is always internal in a sense. Lighting comes from within the context of a virtual set. The basic idea is the same, to use what is available, arranging the set, characters and camera angles to tell your story through lighting. In some virtual worlds, the producer might play with various camera angles and shadows. Regarding interior lighting sources, Alton once remarked, "We can use our imagination, we can style them" (p. 118). When conceptualizing a film, the story becomes played out through the various lighting of "sets, props and people" (Alton, 1995, p. 18). He explained, "Because the screen in the motion picture theatre is a one-dimensional flat surface, it is imperative that we photograph everything from an angle from which most surfaces of the subject are visible to the camera" (p. 30).

In virtual worlds like *Second Life*, machinimatographers have a range of environmental settings from which to choose. The advanced sky editor in *Second Life* allows a filmmaker to choose between various preset conditions, from blue midday, desert sunset, doomed spaceship, coastal afternoon, big fluffy clouds, ghost, and foggy, among others. These presets are also referred to as WindLight. The overall environmental settings allow the user to adjust for various times of the day: sunrise, midday, sunset, and midnight. The direction of the sun can be adjusted across a continuum from sunrise to sunset.

As part of the environmental settings, the atmosphere, lighting and clouds can be altered to varying degrees. *Second Life* offers many atmospheric moods through its environmental settings. If you want an overcast skyline, or an apocalyptic backdrop, you simply change your setting to create the appropriate lighting condition. That is the main way to light in *Second Life*, by relying on the game engine's source. Beyond that, the producer can use a photograph light, a scripted object with a light built into it, to augment the environmental lighting on ground level for close-up shots. These light sources are easy to create and script. For big scenes, it is always best to use the massive controls built into *Second Life*'s settings. Torley Linden offers tutorials on using WindLight and other *Second Life* tools that assist in crafting quality machinima and photography.

Location, Location, Location

Imagine sitting at the table with the Mad Hatter and his guests. Beyond the right costumes, the scene would not be so incredible if it were placed anywhere. It would call for an amazing setting to match the mood of the story. To be specific, there's the set and the setting. The set includes all those props that complement the environment, or the larger setting that creates the backdrop mood. The setting establishes location. As in a story, the plot must originate in a place, as it moves from the writer's mind to the written word. The producer translates the story onto the film. Settings can be expensive for real-life Hollywood productions, and even independent productions to an extent. Jeremy Hanke and Michele Yamazaki (2009), in *Greenscreen Made Easy: Keying and*

Compositing Techniques for Indie Filmmakers, acknowledge that the magic of Hollywood is increasingly at the convenience of filmmakers for a fraction of the cost. Sometimes producers rely too much on achieving the Hollywood effects without considering whether or not they are appropriate or necessary for the story to be told effectively and compassionately on-screen.

The cinematic tricks are at the fingertips of filmmakers more than ever before, especially when you consider what had to be done by the early producers, explains Hanke and Yamazaki (2009): "To be able to magically place your actors in steaming jungles, science fiction metropolises, or ultra-gritty city streets has been a pursuit of filmmakers since Florey and Vorkapich's *The Life and Death of 9413, a Hollywood Extra*, and Fritz Lang's *Metropolis* experimented with stationary mattes" (p. 1). They continue, "These early filmmakers used cut mattes to block a section of the exposure of the film negative and then used reversals of these mattes to expose only those sections to alternate scenes. Because these early effects combined portions of two scenes, they were the first composites." In later years, "motion mattes were utilized during the filming of movies like *Mary Poppins*, which allowed a background to be removed from behind a moving actor. These motion mattes were actually the first form of chromakeying" (Hanke & Yamazaki, 2009, p. 1).

In a virtual world, anything is possible, for it can be created in many role-playing worlds like *Second Life*. Fabulous settings exist in worlds like *Second Life, Blue Mars*, and increasingly new virtual worlds. Other games like *World of Warcraft* offer amazing fantasy environments for stories. Permission to film in these environments is specific to each world and game. But many machinimists make use of existing settings in virtual environments. For others, like Toxic Menges, they create filming environments on their virtual land. Her work in creating virtual environments will be featured directly after this chapter.

But what makes a good setting or environment? Some questions that one might ask include What permissions are necessary to use this space? Why waste your time building if or when some of the legal restrictions are too costly or burdensome? That is an individual decision based on your finances and goals for the project. Beyond that, does the setting complement the story? Is it the right fit for the characters and the story line? Can you create and modify objects in the environment? If you cannot, for example, place a prop in the setting, how will you work around it? Particularly how will you be able to light a set to your needs if you cannot bring in some of your lighting gear to the shooting location? A work-around might be to attach a portable light to the characters. In one instance, one of the authors asked an actress to wear a car on her avatar in order to get it into a virtual set that would not otherwise allow entry to objects. The woman, in avatar form, positioning herself lying flat on the ground, wore the automobile by attaching it to her back. She wore the prop as one would an item of clothing, and in the same way, an avatar can wear supplemental lighting. Of course, she was not being filmed as an actress at that point, but as a car with her body hidden from view. From face lights to fill lights, these considerations will impact how your setting will come across on film. Other considerations about deciding on a film location deal with the characters' ability to move freely within environments without obstacles. In *Second Life* and other virtual worlds, sometimes an environment that is graphically intensive is ridden with lag, a slowing down of the computer's processing capabilities. The result is a character that cannot move without noticeable resistance. Indeed, having more avatars sometimes translates into more lag. At this point, settings might need to be streamlined to only the bare essentials. The producer basically strips the environment of any non-essential scripts or particles that might slow down the processing power of the computer's rendering of on-screen images. Props and sets that adjust for this—for example, in *Second Life*—are those with minimal scripting. It is best to look for such props whenever possible.

The producer should ask, "Is the setting functional?" although it might look like the ideal locale. Of course, some settings are created through chroma keying, often referred to as green screening. The setting is constructed within a green box. The building and props are placed within the box; the whole set is enclosed with bright green walls or screens. The green surface allows software by any number of manufacturers to key out the green color and replace it with the background footage of one's choice. The footage can convey images and video that have been pre-shot internal or external to the game environment. Real footage of city traffic might provide the ideal backdrop for a scene in a virtual environment. It is the combination of real and machinima technology that sometimes creates an interesting work. The producer might have filmed a setting within a virtual environment that replaces the keyed out green surface with this footage. The keying software will replace the surface color with the new image, anywhere there is green. The virtual environment filmed for background, in fact, might have been imported from a different world or game.

Hanke and Yamazaki (2009) ask the producer, "Want to create a scene on a mountaintop but you're shooting in Indiana? No problem. How about a scene on Mars or aboard a UFO? Why not? You are no longer limited by your physical location" (p. 141). They describe the process of chroma keying "as simply removing any color that you designate and creating a matte in the shape of the removed color" (p. 2). The matte can serve as the replacement backdrop to any film, even a machinima. This might help the producer to create a sense of both virtual world and real life merging into one space, or perhaps a scene from another virtual world, as mentioned earlier, might be imported into the film. Any color can serve as the matte; for the motion picture *Mary Poppins*, yellow was used behind the characters. Florescent green and blue are the typical shades used for keying and replacing the scene with the desired footage, among most filmmakers and television news producers, respectively. "Green screening" is a phrase that refers to the concept of chroma keying typically in filmmaking.

Top: Illustration 6.1: The green screen. Notice that there is no background in the shot. Instead the actors are placed in a special green three-sided box to demonstrate how a filmmaker might create a background setting for a music video in post-production. *Bottom:* Illustration 6.2: Background replacement. Producer Donald Pettit replaces the green-screened box with a video scene in post-production.

Achieving Point of View, Framing and Composition

Blain Brown (2002), in *Cinematography: Theory and Practice*, states, "At the heart of it, filmmaking is shooting — but cinematography is more than the mere act of photography. It is the process of taking ideas, actions, emotional subtext, tone and other forms of non-verbal communication and *rendering them in visual terms*" (p. ix). Barry Braverman (2009), in his book *Video Shooter*, reminds us not to become too overly concerned with the latest technology or what format or medium we use; rather one should consider what is the best means to tell the story. The audience does not worry about all the technical stuff, but they do enjoy a professionally crafted film. So many choices, and yet the producer should not forget the rise of popularity of homemade videos that gain the attention of web audiences. The message is always central to the production, and the goal becomes how to bring that message to life on-screen. Brown (2002) explains, "Fairly early on, filmmakers began to realize that the flatness of the screen and its other limitations demanded more. Their first response was to break the action up into shots or sequences of shots: this is sometimes called separation ... shots are 'fragments of reality'" (p. 2). Brown continues, "It is the filmmaker who decides which fragments and in what order the audience will see the overall reality.... By choosing what pieces of this reality the audience sees and arranging them in a certain order, the filmmaker introduces a point of view" (p. 2).

"Point of view" is a term used loosely among producers. Of course, it is conveyed in a scene ultimately through the shot sequence and how the film is edited. But critical shot decisions by the director had to be made before that stage. Point of view is established when the camera identifies with the perspective of one or more of the characters in a particular shot, scene or series of scenes. Let's use the example of a spy thriller. A couple walking on the sidewalk below are being watched from a building rooftop across the street. The camera person might take the shot from a high ladder, with a camera attached to a jib. The point of view emanates from where the camera is located in a shot, or the series of shots within a scene. Maybe the story is about the reunion of a mother and young son. The camera might be situated at knee level to the child to achieve his perspective, as he sees his mother running toward him. The point of view can change through the movie, as in the instance of a car chase. We might have various camera perspectives, like an aerial view from a helicopter, a medium shot of the car, a close-up of the driver, and so forth.

Framing is a concept related to point of view that deals with the setup involved in introducing a scene. Perhaps a couple plans to meet in a café. One person is far across the street. The other is sitting at the table already. The person walking toward the café might be introduced in the setup shot of the scene. This shot is the point of entrance for the camera in the scene. In framing, you decide how much information is revealed to your audience, and this information can be expressed through long, medium, close and extreme close-up shots. Your framing provides important information you want to show your audience in a particular shot or scene. Long or medium shots often reveal time and place and introduce your viewers to where the characters are in the scene. In a close-up, the cameraperson is actually zooming in on the character and eliminating some of the information shown in the long or medium shots. The framing of the film involves two choices, according to Brown (2002): "picking a position from which to view the scene" and "isolating some part of it to look at" (p. 3).

He states, "We want to choose not just the angle from which the scene is viewed, but whether [the viewers] see all of it or just a part of it.... If the audience isn't always subconsciously asking the question, 'I wonder what will happen next?' well, you've lost them" (pp. 3–4).

Composition is what you do with the elements that you include within a scene, from people to objects to the overall backdrop of the scene. At its basic level, composition is where you place the characters. If you want to make sure that the moonlight is in a certain spot in relationship to the characters, those become elements of composition to consider when crafting a shot or a shot sequence. It is the practical aesthetics in making a shot functional and balanced to the viewer. Think about composition as furniture arrangement, plus the characters that will be using the furniture in that shot.

A classic rule of composition is the rule of thirds [illustration 6.3]. Conceptualize the shot by drawing a rectangle. Divide the rectangle vertically into three equal sections. Now divide that same rectangle horizontally in three equal sections. You should have drawn a rectangle with nine equal sections. The two horizontal lines are called horizon lines. Skylines and city streets, respectively, work best within the upper and lower tiers. Character placement is best somewhat off center in the middle horizontal region.

The two vertical lines of the rectangle serve as guideposts and represent the placement of the character in the shot. It is preferable, and more pleasing to the audience, when the character is placed off center, to the right or left of the center. The two vertical lines offer compositional guidelines for character placement. The idea is to imagine placing the character close to or on one of those lines. Another rule, the rule of empty space, is applicable to compositional

Illustration 6.3: The Rule of Thirds: Action Flick hero Vince Stryker is shown demonstrating the Rule of Thirds. He occupies the top third and left third of the frame.

placement. Draw another rectangle and then draw a character's profile in the center. The character's position should be adjusted somewhat by allowing for any empty space (more breathing room) around the front of the face.

Point of view, framing and composition all work together to execute a story that will draw in the viewer, as well as inform them. The director leads the audience throughout the film. A medium shot might establish a relationship between two people in a movie. A close-up of one of them might focus the story on the main character or redirect the action. The angle and distance of the camera in regard to the main character help define his or her placement in relation to other story elements and characters. The audience shares the camera perspective typically with the main character, and the producer can adjust that view accordingly, shifting or tweaking point of view, framing and compositional elements. One of the most critical elements in framing a story is its backdrop; it communicates essential information to the viewer. Braverman (2009, p. 21) states, "It may come as a revelation that backgrounds often communicate more than foregrounds or even the subject itself. This is because audiences by nature are suspicious, constantly scanning the edges of the frame for story cues." The audience seeks visual cues; "Is it supposed to laugh or cry? Feel sympathy or antipathy?" (p. 21). Viewers are always scanning for visuals to interpret to help them process the personalities of the characters, symbolic props in a scene, and any possible foreshadowing of adventures to come in the unfolding story.

Prioritizing Shooting and Lighting

On the matter of shot composition and sequence, Harry Box (2010), in his *Set Lighting Technician's Handbook*, brings the conversation back to the role of lighting, which can add emphasis or signify separation among on-scene elements. Lighting can call attention to characters and objects. Color, shading, outlining, depth and motion can direct the eye to a character in the forefront or in the background. Backlight is one way to create separation, but experimentation will produce the right impact depending on the goal. Box (2010) recommends this pre-filming sequence: block, light, rehearse, tweak, shoot. When blocking the scene, the actors or the objects are situated within the set. The lighting crew reviews strategies for achieving the desired impact. Then the scene is rehearsed with stand-ins and eventually actors. The process is tweaked and then the film is shot. As part of pre-production, the director must consider how lighting will play into the set location, and conduct some test runs if possible. The location will impact the lighting of the characters and props; in turn, the people and the objects will vary the location's look.

Box (2010) reviews some basics in establishing shooting sequence, acknowledging as a significant factor the length of time it takes when shooting for film compared to a television single-camera episode: "A feature film crew may shoot two or three pages of script a day. For a television single-camera show, the average is four to eight pages per day" (p. 12). Moreover, it is common practice to photograph the wide master shots to help determine the scene's lighting.

It is the close-up shots that will need adjustments. Box explains, "All the shots that look in one direction, requiring one lighting setup, can usually be shot before turning around. Once coverage from one direction is complete ... the camera is moved around to shoot the other way. The crew then relights for the new camera angle" (p. 12). Subsequently, the director blocks or sets up for the next scene. Of course there might be some exception to the shot order, depending on what action might be happening in the scene. For example, if a building has to be demolished on schedule, those shots might take priority, given that once destruction has taken place there will be no reshooting.

When thinking machinima, the producer must consider the unique variables involved in the setup of shots. How long will the producer have access to the virtual environment, and what are some of the lighting issues? What should be the sequence in shooting, given similarities or complexities in lighting and setup for characters, props or establishing mood in a scene or multiple scenes?

The mood of a story is a function of the shot sequence and scene setup and its interaction with the lighting so as to carry out the director's goals in creating a point of view for the audience, which uses that POV as a guide to interpret the action on-screen. Box (2010, p. 94) asks the producer to contemplate how light affects mood through a series of questions, such as "How is light treated by the character in the story? Would she invite sunlight to pour into the room like butterscotch or close it out, leaving us in a musty dark room, the sunlight seeping around the edges of thick curtains?" Then he asks, "Does the light connect the central character to his surroundings or does it isolate him? Is he surrounded by glowing human faces with whom he might interact, or anonymous figures who leave him alone and alienated?" (p. 94). Finally he challenges the producer to consider how lighting works itself toward the climax of the story, and throughout various parts of the film: "How does the space change in appearance and feel from one part of the film to the next? Is it a long day's journey into night, an emergence from darkness into light, or what? How will each scene in this progression be augmented?" (p. 94).

For Box (2010), classic lighting decisions should involve two other elements, aside from composition and mood: visibility and naturalism. These two elements help the director to craft the way the character or critical objects in a scene are revealed to the audience. Visibility involves the degree and direction of lighting and contrast: "Much of the artistry of cinematography is ... selectively exposing objects and characters to appear bright and glowing, slightly shaded, darkly shaded, barely visible, or completely lost in darkness, as desired" (Box, 2010, p. 91). Naturalism, on the other hand, helps the viewer to locate the scene "in time and place" (Box, 2010, p. 92). He continues, "Often unconsciously, we recognize lighting that portrays time, season, place, and weather conditions. The lighting is evocative of the way the air feels and smells, whether it is dusty or clean, foggy or clear, cool or hot, humid or dry" (Box, 2010, p. 92). There are reasons to have unnatural lighting, such as when a director wants to call attention to a strange phenomenon. When these principles are applied to machinima, one can begin to explore the possibilities of creative lighting in virtual spaces.

Specific Lighting Techniques

As in real life, creativity is a must when attempting to light under difficult conditions. In a *Second Life* photo shoot on Tempura Island, for example, one of the authors found there was no way to supplement the virtual lighting. The model, however, required additional lighting to soften her face and body and the area around her. Without any means to import fill light into the region, the producer was left with only one option. Inspired at that moment, he attached an additional face light to his avatar, and the light from it softened the harsh shadows around the model. Lighting is something that must be positioned appropriately when filming; it is nearly impossible to fix badly lit characters and scenes during post-production. This section will review some fundamental sources of lights: key light, side light, fill light and backlight.

Key light is the main light on a scene. It establishes the primary mood of the shot or scene. Whatever is central to the shot must be revealed through lighting. In *Second Life*, producers mainly deal with key light, and its source is from the game engine. To achieve dramatic lighting, a side source positioned at an oblique angle to the subject might be the solution. For example, if one wanted to create a harsh look on a villainous character, the director might adjust the side light to achieve that effect. That effect tends to work better on men's facial features than those of women. Dramatic side lighting on women often takes considerable experimentation in order to achieve a proper balance. A fill light might be a side light, or a reflector or even a reflective surface, and it is typically placed opposite of the main light to help fill in shadows. Weaker, less powerful lights might be considered fill lights that help to eliminate or lessen harsh shadows.

Rembrandt lighting typically refers to the frontal key light that illuminates the character's face: "The shape of a face is revealed to the eye by the way the light falls on the curves and planes of features. Tonal variations—the shading and shadows—tell our brains the shape of an object" (Box, 2010, pp. 96–97). When the character's face needs some lighting to adjust for shadows and harsh angles, secondary lighting usually is considered. A face is mainly lit by a frontal key light, and fill lighting is typically necessary. Some features might be hidden or look less than flattering without a fill light. A key light when placed on the opposite direction than the actor is facing seems to do the trick. Common practice is to use a "far-side key light" as an addition to the frontal lighting (Box, 2010, p. 97).

When a filmmaker or a photographer lights for a fashion shoot, a supplemental source often comes from a light box placed over the camera person's head. The beautiful model is set against a bright postery background, and in this instance you can bet a soft light was added above the camera lens to create this warm effect. Generally light in *Second Life* is soft on its own, and the light comes from directly over the camera angle, from where the camera person is shooting. Additional soft lighting can enhance the shot. Perhaps a soft light box can be placed nearby the object or character being filmed.

Varying the camera angle changes the mood of the character. When the camera is placed above eye level of the character (e.g., the hairline), the person looks more contrite or humble. A camera shooting below eye level (e.g., chin or neck) creates the illusion that the character is powerful or strong. The camera angle and the lighting help to craft the personality of the character and the mood of the scene. Photographers refer to the combination of key (frontal), fill/side and back light as part of the lighting triangle in a shot or scene. Box (2010) explains that side and back lights separate characters from the backdrop and help to bring facial features and props to the foreground. Ambience is the finishing touch to a shot or scene, and it provides a "general fill throughout the set" (Box, 2010, p. 107).

Filming the Virtual Environment

Ready-made sets and lighting are convenient options for machinima makers. *Second Life*, *The Sims*, and *Blue Mars* are filled with a variety of potential filming locations. Elaborate sets can be purchased as well for minimum cost in *Second Life*, a world where online content creation is at the heart of the virtual experience. In *The Sims* series, there have been a number of downloadables, including a camera, to help with everything from character and set creation to lighting. But the basic lighting and camera native to the game in the recent updates are more than sufficient for *The Sims* machinima maker. *The Sims 3* revolutionized its lighting, allowing the user to adjust for environmental settings. Interior lighting can be adjusted for color and brightness, and shadowing looks more natural as do the avatars (*Sims 3*, 2009). In *Second Life* and other virtual worlds, your best source of light is usually from the platform's engine.

Massive multi-player role-playing games, like *World of Warcraft* and other action games, typically provide adequate key lighting or work-arounds that help to accommodate lighting needs. *Second Life*'s WindLight settings, as mentioned earlier, offer a plethora of preset sky conditions. Moviestorm works a bit differently than *Second Life*. As a 3-D environment, it has much more in common with software programs like 3ds Max than virtual worlds like *Second Life*. Such programs offer 3-D modeling, animation, rendering and compositing, and the lighting can be specifically tailored to a shot or scene.

In Moviestorm, virtual lights can be programmed to act and react as real lights similar to those on real-life movie sets, and that offers some real advantages to classically trained filmmakers who are comfortable with having more control over their sets and lighting. On the downside, Moviestorm offers less spontaneity than *Second Life* in terms of setting up a scene. What might take an hour in *Second Life* could take hours or days in constructing a virtual environment in a program like Moviestorm. However, that is not to say one way is better than another; each platform must be evaluated based on the goals of the machinimatographer in achieving a story that effectively captures the audience's attention.

This chapter is followed by a machinima spotlight by Toxic Menges, a talented machinimatographer with an eye for dressing a virtual environment.

Setting, Lighting and Composition Exercises

Identify a machinima that has strong set design, along with good use of lighting and composition.

1. Describe the settings of the machinima. Is there a main setting, and what are the functions of the other virtual environments?
2. Critique the use of lighting in one or two scenes.
3. Identify ways in which the producer achieves composition, in relation to the placement of characters and objects in a scene.
4. How does the producer use various shots, from close-ups to medium and long shots?
5. What are some other aesthetics employed in this machinima that help engage the viewer? How do these aesthetics help to support the main character(s)?

References

Alton, John. (1995). *Painting with Light.* 4th edition. Los Angeles: The University of California.

Box, Harry. (2010). *Set Lighting Technician's Handbook: Film Lighting Equipment, Practice, and Electrical Distribution.* 4th Edition. Boston, MA: Focus Press.

Braverman, Barry. (2009). *Video Shooter: Storytelling with HD Cameras.*Boston, MA: Focal Press.

Brown, Blain. (2002). *Cinematography: Theory and Practice: Image Making for Cinematographers, Directors, and Videographers.* Boston, MA: Focus Press.

Brown, Blain. (2007). *Motion Picture and Video Lighting,* 2nd Edition. Boston, MA: Focus Press.

Hanke, Jeremy, & Yamazaki, Michele (2009). *Greenscreen Made Easy: Keying and Compositing Techniques for Indie Filmmakers.* 2nd Edition. Burbank, CA: Michael Wiese Productions.

Machinima Roundtable Two. (2010). *Terminology, Technology, and Practice* (Sessions 3 & 4, July 15 & 16). Lowe Runo Productions, LLC, *Second Life*.

Malkiewicz, Kris. (1986). *Film Lighting: Talks with Hollywood's Cinematographers and Gaffers*. Whitby, ON: Fireside Publishing House.

McCarthy, Todd. (1995). The Life and Films of John Alton. In (John Alton, ed.) *Painting with Light*, p. ix–xxxiv. 4th edition. Los Angeles: The University of California.

Sims 3 and Machinima. (2009, January 21). Decorgal's Blog. Accessed December 12, 2010, from http://decorgal.com/blog/?p=349

✧ COMMENTS BY TOXIC MENGES ✧

It's All About Pre-Production

Toxic Menges is very comfortable online and in virtual environments. She is a machinimatographer, and really it all began with her real-life work as a manager of online communities. Menges has been online for nearly two decades. She has been very involved in community development in Second Life, with her focus these days on virtual filmmaking. From her sim in Second Life, she experiments with natural effects and techniques to achieve quality machinima with minimal post-production, during a time when many machinimists are turning to external programs to complement or supplement the capabilities of the game engine or platform. She is an advocate for understanding the potential of virtual worlds like Second Life, and pushing past what some see as perceived limits of machinima. This conversation focuses on her work in Second Life, as a visionary of machinima in its true form. With a powerful new computer in her machinima arsenal, she has discovered the richness of Second Life as an interactive medium.

Exploring Boundaries

Having a powerful computer really opened up a completely new world for me. It is designed particularly for machinima, and was fairly much top of the line because I wanted to keep abreast of what was going on, and what I could do to make sure that I could stay current and that really opened up a new world of using shadows and creating textures. I really have enjoyed pushing the boundaries of what we can do in here. Saying that, I am really trying to think out of the box, like when I did *Little Red Riding Hood*. I used textures rezzed in-world that were basically 3-D objects, breaking the fourth wall to an extent I suppose. In this way, the characters of my machinima interacted with the walls, walking through them. Even the titles were done in a very different way. So what I am doing is integrating things that would not be possible in real life and making use of the unique space within *Second Life*, allowing me to push the boundaries.

I love that we can do that. I love that I can rez letters to make a title and my titles are done completely in-world. I don't use the post-processing effects to create them. Aside from that, anything I do is completely done in-world, and that is completely unique in the sense that I am moving away from the post-production practice of many machinimatographers. I think there's a trend for them to go, "Oh, I can use after effects for what I make." What I think is so beautiful is the raw footage that we can get from this engine. And *Little Red Riding Hood* is absolutely gorgeous to look at. There are only two pieces of post-processing used in it. One is a transition. The other one was a bit of green screen that I had to use. One of my avatars was two characters, so I had to green screen in the end titles.

Because we are in such a malleable world, we can change everything — we can change the sky, the direction of the sun, we can remove the water, we can add the water, we can do anything. We should be making the most of that. Someone called me a bit of a purist, and that is quite interesting because I really don't do any post-processing at all. What you see is what you get. I'm fortunate to have a machine that allows me to show exactly how beautiful *Second Life* can be. I actually enjoy the challenge of just using *Second Life*.

My post-production is basically editing and transitions, if there are any transitions in my work. I use them as needed, but I have moved away from a lot of them mainly because I prefer to avoid them, simply that. I think *Little Red Riding Hood* has one transition — a dissolve — in four minutes. I suppose that makes me ultra-minimalist.

I am not really a builder per se in *Second Life*. I make pretty pictures and that is about it. If anything I love pre-production in which I enjoy dressing a set. I do build, but I am lucky enough to have lots of friends that are very good at building, and I can describe what I need from them. For example, I have a sim for my machinima. I rent a portion out, but the residents there are very encouraging if I need to change the land and dress it for a machinima.

The Rotating Ball

I really enjoy that aspect of pushing boundaries as in *Little Red Riding Hood*. The chase scene was almost happening like the Keystone Kops because, basically, I had this big ball that rotates at various angles; the avatars — the girl and wolf — don't move but the ball gives the illusion of running. The little girl appears to be moving, when it is actually everything around her that is rotating through the use of the ball animation. To an extent, I am using some sort of trickery, but it is all done in-world. You can do that, and that is what makes *Second Life* so amazing. Indeed, pre-production for me is sitting down and figuring out what I need, and being able to explain it to someone else, so they will realize why I wanted it. The person who was building that rotating ball was certainly incredulous until the creator saw it working. Though I probably have lots and lots of crazy ideas for similar items in my head, and it is not until they come to fruition that people realize why I wanted them. I can also see to a certain extent what the limitations are here.

In one particular project, I completely changed the texture of the sea to match the land to give this certain effect. We should be doing more of that, pushing the boundaries. Projected texture is a new feature, which will completely change our machinima. It's so otherworldly and yet we don't completely understand properly how to use it at the moment. In another way, it is the same with lighting in general. The rules of lighting in real life really do stand up in *Second Life*. I use WindLight primarily, but you can attach lights to prims in various ways. You can use backlight for effect for instance, and how we have shadows now we can use that as well.

You can evoke so many moods in *Second Life* fairly naturally, virtually. That's one of the things over which we have much more control and a lot more power as compared to real life, as when backlighting someone to achieve a certain emotion or by side lighting them for things like that. But those real-life tenets of lighting still stand. To a certain extent, we do rewrite the rules here. It's the same as if you have two avatars looking the same direction; you can evoke emotion with lighting. That's because as people we are programmed to feel like that because we have seen TV and films throughout our life. That's what we see; we've seen that, and we respond in those ways to the lighting. So perhaps to an extent it is time to rewrite some of those things. We have so much control over our virtual environment. It's a matter of thinking outside our comfort level.

Virtually Elsewhere

As for other engines, in terms of OpenSim obviously that is going to work, but the producer does not have the breadth of versatility. It is not as friendly or controllable as *Second Life*, and plus you cannot use the space navigator. It is kind of ridiculous really because you have this huge vista and the UI simply isn't there to take snapshots and things. And of course, people are doing some amazing things like on Moviestorm and iClone. But those do not have the collaborative feel. I could be sitting in my basement if I had one, working with iClone and not talk to anyone for six months while I create something. And it's not real time.

We are in a unique position in *Second Life* where everything we film is real time. And iClone I think does not have that — the immediacy and control level I like. *Blue Mars* isn't there quite yet. If they came and talked to me I could give them a big list of what I wanted them to do. I admit it's pretty.

Setup

People storyboard a lot. I tend to keep it all in my head as a vague idea. Although let me say in *Little Red Riding Hood*, I generally tested every single shot until I did it. If you set up each scene in your head, set your WindLight, and you save everything to a folder for each scene, then you know exactly where you are. To me the most fun is the pre-production anyway, and I sort of revel in that. I will do a set list of people and tell them when I need them at such and such time and tell them what we are going to do. I will use a share camera HUD and show them rather than just explain to them. So basically what they do is they share my camera. I show them where I want them to walk and where to stop. And I am always explicit about the time and place. The groundwork you do is important.

I take a long time over the look and feel of things. I do lots of tests so I don't have any surprises about what I actually ended up filming and the quality that I have gotten. That's going to save you a lot of heartache, if you filmed your movie and realize that you have the wrong resolution or something like that. Or you can't get the frame rate, and you end up trying to get the frame rate. I think that is really important, and I think it is also important that you know how to encode and get to the point where you want to get. If you say you want to do a 720 HD video, and it comes to encoding what you have done and you don't know how to do that, you have all this footage and all this time you spent, and you may waste it if you cannot get the resolution you want. If you haven't covered every single eventuality and in the middle of the scene you just have to stop everything for six hours and have to film again — you have wasted your time.

Final thoughts

All in all, in terms of me with regard to no post processing, my machinima *A Petrovsky Flux* has only minimal transitions and titles. That particular video will allow you to understand my minimalistic approach to machinima post-production, and my desire to capture the beauty and potential of *Second Life*. There is a definite trend lately to have huge amounts of post-processing. I prefer to explore the capabilities of *Second Life* and virtual environments in their raw forms in real time.

Recommended Machinima

A Petrovsky Flux by Toxic Menges, http://www.youtube.com/watch?v=lM4CAOyse_g
Decay by Toxic Menges, http://www.youtube.com/watch?v=j_ndjsqu5FI
I Surrender by Toxic Menges, http://www.youtube.com/watch?v=Q-PIh3AWvn0

Little Red Riding Hood by Toxic Menges, http://www.youtube.com/watch?v=p5zZ6_RPYIg
Morning Sail by Toxic Menges, http://www.youtube.com/watch?v=doEg_4Cdhkc
The Water Horse by Toxic Menges, http://www.youtube.com/watch?v=2GjXyDcD3G8
Toxic Menges is an award-winning machinima producer, and her work had been screened at World
   Expo 2010 Shanghai around the time of her interview.

7

Post-Production:
Bing Bang Boom

"Bling has no worldly or any business in Second Life and definitely not in machinima. There's nothing more terrible or distracting. That's just part of my learning curve back from my old days. And now I have a list, and believe me, all of my actresses or actors get their bling off before we start shooting because they all look like airliners coming in for a landing with that stuff on. Where I am now with post-production, I could remove it, but why have to bother with it in the first place.— Donald Pettit, CEO of Lowe Runo Productions, LLC.

All the chapters have led to this point — editing, organization, adding those effects and making those corrections and adjustments that were perhaps not possible in the course of shooting the project. It is here, during post-production, that the producer has a second chance at enhancing the character, action and effects, crafting the story through editing and organizing elements, correcting for color balance, and ultimately mastering the machinima so it is ready for an audience to view. The process of mastering ensures continuity in the machinima, visually and aurally. To some extent, some of these topics have been touched upon, including the concept of lip-syncing — where lips of the characters move according to dialogue or monologue.

Disclaimer Before We Start

Some purists in machinima do not like to use too much post or use no post at all. One of which is machinimatographer Toxic Menges, who provided an alternate view to heavy-handed post-production in the spotlight of last chapter. And of course that's fine. Machinimists like Menges try to use as much of the scripting within the game, relying on scripted effects, and keeping things as they are. It's kind of a challenge for them. Nothing is wrong with that. It depends on what you like to do and what kinds of machinima you are attempting to create in this way. For others there is a definite appreciation beyond the game itself to what computers can add to the project. For those who use post-production in real-life video and film, it seems quite a regular practice, with no pause or compulsion against using it for machinima, as long as it reinforces the story. It always comes back to the story. The producer might feel a need for something to be added to the story to complete it, a special effect inserted, like an explosion or sound effect, or a combination thereof, flashing and all that, and some particles effects. If that drives home, even more effectively, the story that you're trying to bring in, and adds a little drama, it improves viewability and quality, and the viewers' experience. If it fulfills all of those things, most would see no problem with it.

"I love those movies where they have a lot of action like Jon Woo movies. I'm a typical guy. I like to sit and watch the guy movies with the fighting, the Kung Foo, and all that," notes machinimatographer Donald Pettit. "I can't really name a favorite machinimator, and I won't, because I'm friends with so many. They all have influenced me one way or another. And I don't want everybody to just think I'm all into that one genre. I like some of the romantic stuff out there, some of the artistic stuff, where they use colors and stuff. I just love that. My interest goes all over the place, but I love the post-production that goes into my action machinima," he continues. Many machinimatographers open their arms and embrace post-production, adding effects into their movies. That's the general position.

At other times, a machinimatographer might refrain from post-production techniques, as when producing romantic music-type videos, or music videos per se. That genre might call for very little post because there might be someone that is singing a cover of a favorite song, or they have their own song they have written, and that is part of the story that is being conveyed in that machinima. In that instance, the audience should hear the tenderness or the emotion that is inherent in that song. The producer likely does not want to cover it with a lot of effects or things like that. One might put a moon in the skyline of the set. Make a nice little fractal moon and throw it up in the air behind the singer somewhere. There is no need for a whole lot of post with that scenario. In that case, the story one is bringing home is the song itself.

Now if one is producing an adventure-type thing, doing comedy, or anything, the producer may want to have a pie fly in and hit someone in the face. The director might want that character to fall off of a cliff, and that can be done by using a green screen behind the avatar (such as illustrated last chapter). Post-production might also be useful when the producer wants to add a realistic explosion or gunshot (illustration 7.1). Or in that situation, the producer might want to show the blood associated with the gunshot, depending on how graphic one wants to be. If it brings home the story, again, it always comes back to the story, and that's when post-production techniques are best applied. It should not be used for the sake of using it; this additional process often slows down the project workflow, making the turnaround time significantly longer. Obviously, the producer does not want to waste time. If it enhances, then the guideline is go for it.

Illustration 7.1: Post-Production Effect: This scene from *Action Flick* shows an effect that has been added through post-production, giving the illusion of gunfire from the sniper's rifle.

Filling the Animation Gap

Let's follow up on the idea of one avatar throwing a pie in the face of another. As in the case of many game platforms, there are limitations to what animations can accomplish, without having them customized for a special project. There will be movements or expressions, for example, in the game or virtual world that are not possible to do internally during the filming or readily in that environment. In those instances, some of those movements would be created in post-production. But the question becomes, how much post-production is necessary? Should the producer rewrite the story?

In the best-case scenarios, the producer will already have forethought. It would be wise for machinimatographers to have planned for the particular sequence of the story, so they would have already anticipated making the enhancement through post, and then tack it into the movie. That might also be discovered during storyboarding. Producers should not conceptualize post-production as always fixer-upper, but really they need to spend more time on pre-production. It would be remiss to not say that post kind of wiggles into pre and during production too. If one really, really wants to create a pull-out-all-stops machinima and have everything in it that one would want, it typically means that the producer should plan on post-production.

Like the authors have discussed throughout the book, or through the narratives of the machinima community, this medium is fast, it's cheap, but it also has its limitations. The producer often must work with the animations that are available, such as with vehicles and scripting that are on hand or commercially available. When those fall short, the producer is likely going to create through post-production, adding visual effects, sound effects, and other things like particle effects. If one wants to blow a vehicle off the road and have it spin through the air, the machinimatographer is going to have to spin that vehicle in probably After Effects, or using a program called Combustion, to get it to twist through the air and make that tire fly off, for instance. In actuality, the producer is not going to get that effect otherwise, although one might be able to get someone to script it in *Second Life*. Yet that will likely add to the cost of the project and will not look as professional as when created through a post-production software environment.

Keeping the Character in Mind

Post-production allows for the mastering of the project. It helps to provide continuity in the story line, and it can help keep characters consistent in appearance, such as making sure color stays true throughout the whole piece. The good thing about shooting machinima and being in the virtual world, the producer can dial in the environmentals, particularly through *Second Life*. Sometimes environmentals will go haywire, and the shading and the colors become a bit off because of whatever. Maybe the sunlight setting moved out of place while the filmmaker was shooting the machinima and the producer did not pay attention. So it becomes wonderful to be able to go into post and make sure from frame to frame that all the colors blend in and at the appropriate times.

As for the character, especially close-ups and all, the producer needs to have certain continuity in the feeling conveyed — for example, through the use of colors and other elements enhancing what the character is doing. If the character needs to be shown crying, one might be able to work around using post-effects, and do that instead in-world. Some good tear scripts in *Second Life* are available, and that is a good touch. However, a good example of when to use post might be a portrayal of an evil character. In post, the producer might add electricity coming out of his or her hair or hands, or a certain black or blue glow around the creature might add awe and credibility. That could be done in post-production, and for the action genre, the main character looks through binoculars, for example, then shoots, bullets are shown coming out of a rifle, ricocheting all around the walls, and subsequent blood spatter follows. These are all done in post and are added to enhance the movie. Such additions really make the scene realistic and fuller than otherwise possible. That was the case of *Action Flick*, a machinima by Lowe Runo Productions, LLC, previously mentioned. When the producer has good post with good editing, bing bang boom, the machinima is strengthened through a really powerful action sequence.

Pettit explains, referring to *Action Flick*, "I guess the best compliment I ever had was I shot an eight-minute machinima — which to me is a long one —

and I've had people say they were able to finish it out because they couldn't quit watching it. It kept them occupied, and it kept their attention throughout the whole eight minutes. They said even the titles were entertaining, so see? That's what you want to go for. Credits and titles that are even entertaining, along with all the elements. Then you know you've done a really good job of it."

It's the Details!

The number-one reason post-production is important is fixing stuff. Sounds simple, but it goes deeper than that conceptually. The two reasons for post-production are fixing those elements or scenes that look terrible and adding to things that are not otherwise available in the filming environment. At that point, one is not fixing. It becomes a matter of substituting, or adding to make enhancements. Whatever platform the machinimatographer is using, there comes a need to enhance that which is not otherwise available. Often those elements can be done through post-production equipment and software.

And then, through post, super enhancement takes the machinima to a new level, like making vehicles spin, or even a hand grenade spin and fall. They are not easy to do and require painstaking effort and time, especially the first time one attempts this well-crafted magic. For instance, first the producer has to find a way to take the hand grenade and make it go 3-D. Make it rotate. And of course it cannot tumble perfectly or predictably. It should hobble. It should wobble. The producer has to add a wobble expression on the hand grenade while it is spinning so that it wobbles randomly — and one has to consider the camera angle in which it is shown.

So these are all things that have to be considered and carefully executed. It becomes a very complicated process. Speaking from experience, Pettit adds, "You think that it's going to be an easy thing. 'Oh, I'm gonna have my guy toss a hand grenade down on these other two guys.' No. You must make it wobble. You've gotta make it wobble randomly. And then there's the need to change the scale of the grenade as it nears the camera." It is all the elements in a proper sequence which must be done that makes this process very challenging. People do not realize what goes into this type of work, and that is a little part of a movie like that.

The Romantic Machinima

One thing that has become clear through the authors' process of inter-viewing machinimatographers is that increasingly many of the producers and crew members are women. Even in *World of Warcraft*, many machinima makers are women, and most prefer to produce less action-oriented stories than their male counterparts, as stereotypical as that sounds. In such instances, some of the post-production techniques that become useful besides fixing things might be in the way of swirly lights or props. One could have a magical romantic story and use post to improve the backgrounds, such as adding fractal-type effects to give the illusion of a heavenly or an out-worldly atmosphere behind a couple. One can always make a beautiful moon. If the character is on another planet, if it is a *WoW*-type platform, it might be three moons. Those are niceties that add to the environment. This type of effect is commonly found in After Effects—Adobe—and it is called Fractal Noise. It is basically thrown on a solid surface and then one can also make a sphere with it. Add a sphere effect, and that will make it appear like a moon or a world. It is a very handy enhancement. By changing the settings, one can do very interesting backgrounds with it, so it is just one of the effects or add-ons among the many available in After Effects.

At the time of this writing, the two leaders of post-production software are After Effects and Combustion, the latter of which is made by the same company that does 3ds Max and Maya. Autodesk Combustion is as powerful as After Effects, and with particle generation, it is actually more powerful in many aspects. To some, it has better tools that are handy to the producer. Probably a lot of what one sees on television today is done either in After Effects or Combustion. Other programs are available, but those are tools that are commonly accessible to machinimatographers, although they are reasonably expensive. The cost is actually a limitation for many machinimatographers, and there are additional programs that can actually work inside of After Effects. Yet After Effects is a stable program with market longevity, and its potential seems limitless for what it can add to a film. Interestingly, it is common for producers to utilize only 20 percent of the program. It also becomes a matter of having enough memory to handle its potential, and with that requirement met the producer can make anything—romantic, action-wise, or whatever he or she dreams of for a machinima. If one has an older computer, it might be a good idea to use some older generations of the program, and they seem to still work fairly well.

Her Lips Are Moving...

Lip sync is perhaps one of the most challenging aspects of machinima. The concept is that the characters' lips are moving appropriately to their lines in the film. For some, it becomes a matter of some trickery, sleight of hand, as when you include some distance shots. The rule of thumb is that if the characters are distant and at least full frame, where the viewer can see them full frame, the machinimatographer can probably use the existing platform's lip sync that is built into the game engine. But as the camera gets closer to the character, from that point on, there must be enough distance that the average viewer will forgive the filmmaker if the machinima is little bit out of sync here and there. A rule of thumb is that from waist up to the head of the avatar, or character, monster, or whatever it is, viewers will no longer forgive the producer if off timing becomes noticeable. One of the big complaints about *Second Life*'s beta lip sync was its inability to sync appropriately, particularly when the slightest pickup noise from a microphone made the lips move, and that does not translate to a good visual.

For a music video for example, the producer might feed the song in-world, and the character would subsequently move her lips to the song, if all other noises have been isolated and the proper function has been chosen. Or the person behind the character might read/sing his or her lines in-world on voice, with no intention from the machinimatographer of using that audio track for the production. It only exists as a way for the character to simulate lip movement in a realistic manner. Another trick that might provide a better solution without having to involve an audio track or to actually read lines is this: if one can be really quiet while the avatar is on the set doing the scene, instead of talking, kind of think the dialogue, and tap your microphone. Tap. Tap. Tap as you think the dialogue. And that makes the lips move with the tap. And if all is quiet on the set except for the tap, then that actually achieves a bit better sync than otherwise. And one is not even talking, simply tapping in rhythm to what is being read mentally from a piece of paper. It is kind of silly, but you know what? It works. And if it works, then hey, you're there.

A program that is popular is CrazyTalk. It has its limitations. But that works for close-ups. If performed very long, viewers do not enjoy it because the head seems almost frozen when characters are engaged in the program, but it does make lips run perfectly. The producer can actually add eyes blinking and some facial gestures, and these enhancements distract a bit from some of the limitations. But it looks fake when used for very long, so the best advice is to use CrazyTalk for some very quick responses or phrases, like "yes," "no," "sure," "right away," and so forth. Now if one is capturing face to face, like in dialogue or in the instance of an interview, such as going back and forth from the face of each character, then it would not be too distracting for the viewer. But again, new and old-timers appreciate that lip-syncing is very difficult to accomplish in machinima at this time, and at least in the virtual world of *Second Life* it takes a lot of effort, thought and work-arounds.

Trial and Error Through Rendering

Nonetheless, post-production is more than simply fun and fantastic effects, for it establishes the core of the machinima — it is a process that helps the filmmaker arrange and organize the various production elements. In fact, a producer should never consider a piece to be complete, even when it is rendered.

Rendering can also be conceptualized as a preparatory stage for the producer to determine how the audience might view the work. In many instances the machinimist will create a rough cut of the editing and render it to the desktop for personal viewing, to help in the visualization toward achieving a complete piece. Renders can be uploaded to others privately on various video services to allow for feedback from others. When the work is in its various rough stages, this practice might be thought of as pre-rendering. It is often necessary for the producer to pre-render the production and examine it with a critical eye. If it does not look convincing to the producer, why would he or she put the work out there for an audience to view.

So if it is not convincing, then the producer needs to go back into the machinima, and perhaps that becomes where one can use some other enhancements and things that can help improve the work. It is a simple philosophy. You want the machinima to look good. You don't want it to look bad. It depends on how picky the person is that is editing—and in this case, the authors will assume the producer is not the editor. The producer should require the editor to be very attentive, and really picky about this final stage of the process. Much work has been invested into the project thus far; why compromise at this point in the production? Some viewers will forgive certain things, but they will not forgive bad audio. They will not forgive bad video. The machinima has to have strong visual impact, and the audio has to be good. Then after that, viewers will not forgive the producer for very long for poor lip-syncing or bad timing on certain things. So it becomes very important for the editor to produce a rough cut, or a rough rendering, and look at it. Really show it to some people that do not mind telling the truth. Those people might include family, and Pettit adds, "People in my family look at it, and they don't have any problem hurting my feelings. They go, 'Oh, that looks terrible.'" So it is a place to start for feedback. Ask for opinions from professionals as well as average viewers. When someone says, "I'd click away; I wouldn't even look at that," that tells the machinimatographer right there, "Ut oh, That's not going to work." Then it must be redone, for what is the point of moving on with a piece that no one will appreciate on-screen? Or maybe there is need for the machinimatographer to enhance it somehow, as long as it is not a matter of solely adding effects and junk with no real plan on how to improve the piece.

Imagine as the producer you have all your scenes ready for editing. Of course, it is necessary to have chosen an editing program already, as discussed earlier in the book. As an editor, one has choices between cutaways, hard edits and dissolves, and all these transitional devices. It can become confusing to the novice. The bottom line is to understand the pacing of the story, and consider that as a means to determine whether a fast cut or a slow dissolve might work best between scenes. The romantic ones, like music videos, might call for fades and dissolves, more or less than hard edits. If it is an action-based machinima, those transitions might be distracting. For that genre, the machinima must jump right into the next scene, and the scenes should flow together, often rapidly within an action sequence.

If the evil queen is talking to the hero, the machinimist has a behind-the-shoulder shot of her. When she is done talking, it should be over the hero's shoulder looking at the queen now. It should be this sort of interaction going on during the editing process. If that isn't there on-screen, action viewers might not be as receptive to seeing a fade or a dissolve. They will want to see boom, boom, boom, boom, going back and forth because the dialogue is central in that scenario for propelling the action. That is an extremely important principle. A dissolve involves some kind of transition in time or space, and the pacing between scenes subsequently slows down. The straight edits, hard edits as they are called, must be bam, bam, bam, bam! It is a matter of pacing to generate the mood. In an action genre, one should not plan on too much dissolving unless it involves a flashback such as when a character remembers a dramatic incident that happened during childhood. For example, consider how a flashback becomes a critical moment in the movie *Braveheart*, where the producer takes the viewer back in time to experience events pivotal to the story's plot and motivations of the main character. Those moments are often treated as distinct segments, more or less presented as dream states, while most of the other scenes will transition quickly — bing, bang, boom! That is essential — remember the bing, bang, Boom!

Sound in the Machinima Mix

The mix of all the sound elements comes together in the editing stage. The thing about formulas for sound mix, there is usually a recommended voice-to-music ratio, and many suggest a 50/50 balance. Often the producer will tweak that formula based on the genre and story line. When audio is available as discrete tracks, as in a multi-track sound editing program, it becomes easier to listen to it in multiple ways. With a few guidelines, and if one has the sound elements at the right levels, along with any kind of decent editor, it is easy to edit using the timeline. Nowadays, the editor can scroll back and forth on a scrub tool. The editor simply scrubs back and forth, and watches and listens to ensure proper placement of the sound. But it is more than editing; it is how all these elements come together with each other and how they help to establish and define the visuals.

During the making of this book, the authors came across a machinima that sounded like the announcer was speaking through a barrel. This person had a great machinima, as far as the visual components and it was very interesting, but the way that the sound was originally recorded, edited and mixed totally ruined it. So that took away from the machinima; remember that 50/50 rule from the very beginning of the production. No one will watch bad visuals or listen to bad audio. Audio is typically the weakest area of most machinimatographers, from getting the most out of one's voice actors and helping them to convey emotion through the microphone, to the application of Foley, music and sound effects. Post-production is an extremely critical stage for the audio of the machinima. In most cases, audio is recorded external to the machinima filming.

To avoid bad audio, as in the instance mentioned above, there are different strategies that the producer might do, as discussed in the sound chapter. One is to pay attention to the acoustics of the actual room in which the voice talent is recorded. And another, among others, is to record audio without any sort of processing. Audio with no sweetening, such as compression or equalization, is called dry sound. Processed audio is considered wet sound. The sound enhancements come during the final stages of the mix. A voice-over that has been sweetened during the recording runs the risk of being overly processed when the producer wants to enhance equally the whole mix in the mastering stages of the production. The voice-over should remain raw until decisions are made on the overall feel of the sound during the mix. Those who process their sound as they record it, with any kind of processing such as adding reverb or echo, should be advised to wait until they hear a rough mix and hear all the audio as one.

Even when making Foley, it is best to wait before enhancing those created elements. Those tweaks can be made later with a number of plug-ins. Additive processing impacts the quality and perception of audio levels, with sometimes that cool compression or reverb actually reducing the highs and lows of a voice, sound or effect. Those pleasant nuances become major obstacles to overcome when bringing all the sound elements together in a mix. It might make the voice-over talent happy, when listening back to his or her audio track at that moment. But keep in mind it is the mix that matters. Once the sound is wet, it is difficult, if not impossible, to subtract those effects in a vocal track. It is always easier to add processing than to remove. There must be continuity within a scene and through the entire audio mix. Try to accomplish a pure recording, good levels and clean sound. Then play later. That however goes back to understanding some basics of sound recording. Pettit explains,

> And something I'm learning, and if you're like me, and you live in a square, little box, where you do a lot of your office work, and you're editing, if that also is your sound room, we all know that the worst place that you can be is a square, plain-walled room when you're doing sound. Something that you can do is if you have any of these blankets, I call them Christmas blankets, because here in Florida, we only bring them out at Christmastime, you can use them to sound-proof for recording and listening back. Those little blankets can be easily purchased locally. And this is something that we can throw in as a tip. You tape those up on your walls; they're real lightweight, like a little throw blanket that you put on your couch, or whatever. That's what they're for. But they're so small and lightweight, you could tape them or hang them on your drapes, in your

office or in your room on the bare walls. That takes away a lot of the echo that's in your room while you're recording. So you can have kind of a makeshift recording studio. You'll get fair quality if you do that. So that's a good hint.

Consider also hanging those blankets across wall corners to reshape the acoustics of a square room. In this way, it changes the dimensions of the room, as well as different types of materials help in shaping the acoustics of a room. A wood-paneled room has completely different acoustics from a room with more reflective surfaces such as glass. By understanding how acoustics are impacted by different materials, one can consider where to record and even craft a room by adding various panels, glass or wood. Experimentation is the rule. Such strategies might alleviate the need for post-production in some instances, especially when the producer does not have sufficient plug-ins to achieve the audio effect desired for a scene. Regardless, it is still best to record and listen back in a dead room. That is not to say that one should not listen back to their audio mix in a variety of locations. It might be a good idea to listen back on the speakers of desktop computers in addition to studio speakers. A car stereo sometimes offers a good reference point for detecting if the audio mix is balanced.

Many ask, what is the music-to-voice ratio in a balanced mix? A formula of 50/50 music to voice was provided by the authors as a starting reference point. In reality, that balance is often determined by experience, and it is frequently something that professionals can do by ear. Sometimes it is matter of listening to a mix over and over again. It is sometimes a guessing game. It can be a gut feeling or instinct; like in a romantic scene, one would probably want to emphasize music over effects, so the Foley might be quieter than the music — crickets lightly chirping in the background while the music is heard in the foreground. Then again, if the machinima plot involved a war theme, a particular scene might include explosions with people yelling and screaming, "*Ahhhh!*" The crowd sound, layered over the effects, creates what is called "walla" or "walla walla" among media professionals.

Background noises, in this case, might be stronger than normal, with music a bit more diminished or exacerbated depending upon what emotion will help to thrust forth the mood of the scene. Foley has its own special considerations, particularly its placement in a film. One of the rules often employed in Hollywood cinema is that a particular sound might signal a visual event is about to occur. Think about that squeaking fence in the wind. Similar to the way that music might introduce a scene a second or two prior to the introduction of a visual, Foley can be used to foreshadow what is to occur at the end of a scene. One might start the sound a bit before the producer actually switches to that scene with a squeaky fence. In the same way, there might be a lead-in to an explosion although such effects are fairly much instantaneous. It would be a very, very small factor on an explosion. But in many instances, there should be a little bit of lead-in to the scene through the sound elements.

To be able to accomplish a good mix, the editor needs to isolate the voice track(s) from the music so that individual sound tracks—voice, music and effects—can be manipulated until the final mix is achieved. Because once the elements are mixed down, the producer cannot change their balance. Once it's in there, one cannot extract the voice or effects. For that reason, a multi-track editing unit is definitely needed for a machinima. There are two ways of conceptualizing such a system. The sound and video editing systems can be separate from one another. The producer works on the audio and visual elements separately, bringing the sound into the finished product. Some professional video systems allow importing of different tracks of sound, and then the producer can record and mix within them. Some producers incorporate two methods, importing the sound into the movie, and then adding extra sound effects in the video editor when necessary and finally making some last minute touches within the video editor as well. That is possible when the video system has a multi-track sound editor in it. One can create a complex bed of sound on the bigger projects, and then bring that sound into the video editor by sequence or scene. The producer might work on a scene on a multi-track sound editor, import the sound bed into the video editor (with its own multi-track sound capabilities), and then make the transitions—music or sound—between scenes. In this way, the producer still has the original tracks of the mix in the sound editor and they can be reedited or remixed when needed.

One might configure a transition from fast-paced action to slower scenes by way of calm music or sound that seems to drift between scenes, as a means to establish a new mood. The producer might maintain continuity by using the same music that was employed in the prior scene, but on a slower tempo, or one with a calming effect. The sound beds are connected to the scenes in this way, and likewise connected to each other. Often, new producers do not understand why it is essential to avoid positioning sound tracks to compete, such as when a strong voice-over is layered on top of song vocals. It becomes confusing for the viewer/listener to comprehend perceptually, as to what is the important element—the song or the narration. In most cases, people would tune out the narration and listen to the song.

Consistency in Sound Quality

Before rendering, instead of looking at the visuals, producers should get into the habit of listening intently to the sound, closing their eyes and tuning in the aural elements. That's very important. Just run the sound track through with eyes closed and listen to how it flows. As a matter of fact, it might be best to shut the video portion off, and that is possible on editing systems. As you listen to the sound, there should be a nice flow. It is through this process that the producer will likely hear if something is out of place, needs a little doctoring or pitch shift, or anything like that. That's when the producer is going to hear it. For the most part, if the producer has been organized, he or she will not likely have to change too much. Usually, at that point, it becomes a matter of adjusting the volume down, or up, a few decibels, to mix well. The sound mix should be at least CD quality at a 44 kHz (kilohertz) sampling rate — that is more than double the maximum frequency level of human hearing (20 Hz to 20 kHz). Except for specific circumstances, rarely will the producer need sampling rates beyond 48 kHz. Sampling rates help to achieve a natural contiguous sound; an analogy might assist here. Each sample of sound might be conceptualized as a frame in a film chain. A greater number of frames per second achieves higher production quality. But there is a limit to how well the viewer can hear and see some of the miniscule differences, so when the producer goes beyond a given sampling or frame rate, there are no real benefits to the overall quality of the work — and in fact such adjustments simply require additional storage space and slow down the computer.

To achieve and maintain good-quality sound, the producer should also avoid using MP3 files when recording or importing sound elements. Such files are highly compressed and they lose their distinct highs and lows. A better option might be to work with WAV files when importing and exporting elements to sound and/or video editing systems. A number of online sound sources provide options between MP3 or WAV files; choose the latter for better quality. In this way, the sound elements will likely maintain a higher level of quality and stay within what some refer to as the sweet spot. It takes experience determining the appropriate audio levels at various stages of achieving a good sound, and even more talent to be able to craft a pleasing final mix for the rendering. On the other hand, notes Pettit,

> Sometimes if you discover someone that has a really good, rich voice, and you need that voice characterization, you'll do anything to get it, they'll even sound okay on MP3. I'll take it. My editor will take anything. I would rather have it as uncompressed as possible. I think WAV is better, but again, sometimes you have a limitation with where your stuff is coming from. If my voice person is over in Europe somewhere and her equipment is basic, I might have to take the MP3 and make do with it.

Some systems help with improving audio quality, allowing all the various elements to play well together in the sound program. Some people might struggle with level differences. As long as it sounds good in the end, when you do the closed-eyes test, that is what counts.

Most machinima are screened within an online environment, and differences in quality often become noticeable when works are exhibited in high-fidelity spaces, and that is becoming a serious quality consideration among professional machinimatographers seeking new venues. Perhaps this will be an issue of greater concern for producers in general in the near future.

Beginnings and Endings

Titles are an important part of one's machinima, and it allows for creative opportunity to catch the attention of the audience. It is a place where one also can be creative. A good beginning can definitely introduce a mood. Some of the greatest movies have plain black-and-white titling. It is not an absolute need to have effects scroll out — as if the words are revealed through an unfolding scroll — or to have titles in Sanskrit, or raining down on-screen. The effect might add a nice touch. When the machinimatographer only has a few minutes to tell the story, the title can be designed to lead into it. When titling is done artistically in that way, well, the producer is ahead of the game. Sometimes it is one of the things that can really save a machinima, or at least help it, when the titling falls right into place with the story that is about to be told. So let's just say as a rule, if one wants to make rules, titling plain is as good as titling fancy, or with effects. It works well when it blends into the story. Otherwise, don't go crazy. Don't worry about it.

And endings have some specific considerations, especially for commercial work. Often sponsors want to see their logos, and some of them actually provide the producer with the artwork. They want their logos to be included in the credits. Also, anything one can do to make the end credits more entertaining is always value added. Who likes to hang around for end credits? Nobody, but throw in some bloopers or make up some bloopers, and the ending might keep the viewer watching through the closing credits. That is of course if that is necessary, or one can make the ending blend in with the movie. Some machinima include colors and beautiful things, anything that keeps people watching it. The producer owes that to the people who helped in the making and financing of his or her machinima. By making the credits interesting, the producer encourages the viewer to hang out and look at those credits— the sponsors, actors and actresses, and others who helped by providing set locations or design elements. Someone who is clicking on it on YouTube might not otherwise view the credits, so the producer should consider making the ending credits viewable.

Less Is More

Post-production — less or more. It really depends on what the producer wants in the machinima. Always look at the story — that has to be the main driving force of this chapter. There is no need to add anything more or excessive if it does not support the story; in fact to do so ruins the machinima or takes away from it. If one is excessive on anything, or heavy-handed, it distracts from the story. Consider how a good artist might have some bright colors, but she knows how to subtract or not use them until it is the appropriate time. That is basically how one should think about post-production. Try not to be heavy-handed with it. Know that the audience wants to believe in the machinima. They will engage with their mind's eye. They want to watch the story. So they're going to forgive some bad lip sync here and there. They going to forgive a little bit of a bad explosion where they might see a little falloff or something, but if the effects are excessive, they will not forgive that overindulgence that pulls them away from the story. So always try not to do anything excessively out of character of the story line.

It takes time to develop good filmmaking skills, particularly at the level of high-end post-production, so do not become frustrated for any lack of experience. Continue to develop skills and acquire tools, while watching some good machinima and taking notes on various producers' approaches and techniques. Beginning machinimatographers should concentrate on developing their stories and building their skills. Many people continue to produce machinima with Windows Movie Maker or the built-in video editor of their operating system — and they do quite well for their needs. There is much free stuff available, and it simply takes some time to figure all that out. When someone is on a limited budget and starting out, it makes sense to use some of the freebie software. There is nothing wrong with that. The authors, in addition to sophisticated audio programs, use Audacity, occasionally for various reasons; for one, it is a simple and accessible program. It is a reliable program and has some good features as well. That's a freebie. Similarly, other public programs should not be discouraged from being part of a machinimatographer's tool set.

But at some point in one's evolution as a machinima-type producer, it will be necessary to enhance the repertoire of tools. There is intermediate software, like Pinnacle Pro-HD, that is reasonably priced, yet offers some effects and a little bit more tools than available in the typical out-of-the-box computer. Later on down the road, when a machinimatographer considers taking on clients for hire, that might be the time to upgrade to a higher-end editor or equipment, such as Adobe Suite, Final Cut, AVID, Sony Vegas and those kind of editors. That increases the costs substantially for the machinimatographer, but the features are geared for professional needs. Some discounts exist for top line programs, and many are offered at educational discounts. It is not necessarily the case that a producer has to pay premium price to acquire really good licensed software.

And to begin the voyage in virtual filmmaking, simply start someplace, with something, with a vision to create — and the rest will come. Pettit concludes,

If you're really doing a big piece, or a big project, it's gonna kick your butt. You will likely spend long hours, not sleep a lot, and you will have to do things over, but I want to encourage everybody to hang in there. It really is worth it once you get it done, and to get that little extra edge of perfection through post, it will reap benefits later. I want to encourage people, when they think that they're really going nuts with something, just keep on going nuts. You will get to the end. So persevere. It's worth it.

Double-Check Before Posting— Did You Ask for Permission?

The authors felt compelled to close this section of the book with some serious considerations on the legal aspects of producing and posting machinima. We discussed the importance of giving credit, when credit is due to the sponsors, animation scripters, virtual landowners that generously allow filmmaking, the various actors and voice talent, and all those people who assisted in some way toward the production of the machinima. Next chapter will deal with where machinima is viewed and exhibited, and the subsequent chapter will introduce and hopefully untangle, as much as possible, some legal aspects through a lengthy invited discussion by a copyright expert.

Fair use is a significant legal concept that machinimatographers should definitely know about. Machinimatographers, as a rule of thumb, doing anything for pay, especially for another company, are either better off making their own tracks, buying sound or music tracks, or making sure they are working with a reputable company that can give them rights to a track. Better yet, if a producer has friends that are musicians, make a deal. Pay them. Saying that, however, producers must make sure they have the rights to use the music on the machinima. Newbies tend to get away with using music sometimes, only because their work might not be viewed by many people. It is not shared, for example, to the degree that other videos might be viewed on public sites. They could get in trouble, and when they typically don't, they mistakenly assume that the risk is not there.

When making anything that will likely be seen on public sites, it is necessary to take precaution. Aside from acquiring music rights, permissions/releases should be obtained from the actors, all the people in the machinima. The rule of thumb for photojournalists and videotographers, for example, is they can generally take a photo or video without consequence (within limitations) when they are basically in an environment where people cannot expect privacy. In that respect, the machinimatographer might not worry about obtaining signed permits from all 50 people who showed up at an event when it is unquestionably a public gathering in a public area. Other conditions might apply of course, and the authors strongly advise machinimatographers to seek legal counsel when in question and depending on the unique circumstances of their project to be produced and viewed. On the other hand, when the machinimatographer is filming in a room with some kind of acting going on, or some kind of interview taking place for a documentary or something of that nature, there must be consent, written or recorded. And if the machinimatographer needs release statements from avatars, it becomes trickier, and it might be the case that special arrangements need to be made to secure permission.

Many machinimatographers have relied on using their own avatars and alternate avatars—creating a cast of characters that requires no releases because the producer owns all the avatar actors that will be used in the project. It often becomes so difficult to acquire permits and permissions that it is easier to create one's own actor avatars. The producer can bring in different people for the voice-over, with their consent recorded on the audio track: "Yes, I give so-and-so permission to use this voice-over for the financial consideration provided to me." At that point, the clip or voice-over belongs to the producer. The recording can be played back in court if ever needed.

At the other end of the spectrum, as Pettit explains,

I've actually had people that have given me their schematics and I've reproduced their avatar in a movie, because they're not available. They're so busy. And I don't want to disrupt their schedule, but I want them in the movie. So I've actually reproduced their avatar. That's kind of the cool thing about an avatar. They are reproducible if you have the shape dimensions and the skin — and all the other parts. Of course, you're never going to have their personality per se, but for a movie, you do that through the voice.

Reference

Lowe Runo Productions, LLC. (2010). *Action Flick Part One, Rescue and Perdition*. Accessed December 11, 2010, from http://www.youtube.com/watch?v=g9OI5E2A00o

Post-Production Exercises

Browse online for some machinima that interests you, and consider the following questions.

1. How much did the producers rely on special effects and were these accomplished through post-production?
2. How might some machinima have been improved with specific post-production techniques, and in what ways?
3. Might certain machinima have been improved by removing some post-production elements?
4. Identify a machinima that has the proper balance to accomplish the story's overall message.

✧ Comments by Jonathan Pluskota ✧

Aesthetics for Sound Design

Sound engineer and assistant professor Jon Pluskota relates the science behind mastering the appropriately balanced sound mix in the post-production stage so it greatly enhances the overall presence of a machinima.

As technological processes, storage, and delivery methods continue to improve, the potential for virtual and interactive computer-based environments seems limitless. Interest in virtual environments has grown over the past twelve years (Bainbridge, 2010). Those who experience these environments have been empowered through recent technological advances and software innovations to not only capture their experiences, but to create stories in the form of a low-cost alternative to full-production animation known as machinima (Elson & Riedl, 2007).

The creation of machinima by a machinimist involves two distinct parts: the visual component and the aural component. The purpose of this section is to concentrate on the latter from both a technical and a creative facet. To understand the necessities required for an effective transmission of story line via aural design aspects, it is necessary to understand the basics of auditory perception as it relates to visual cues.

The Technical and Perceptual Considerations

Both visual and auditory cues are initially routed through the same part of the brain, the thalamus, but end up in distinct processing centers, the auditory cortices and the visual cortex respectively (Waxman, 2009). The auditory nerve is ultimately responsible for carrying the signal in the brain, but the perceptual value of the sound is processed throughout many parts of the brain en route to the cortices. The values perceived by the brain include pitch, tone, loudness, localization, time elements, and more (Brynie, 2009). The different areas of the brain responsible for processing, in this case, auditory and visual cues are distinct but related. Scientists are quick to point out that while the actual path sound may take in the brain is unknown, there are definite links between the auditory and visual functions of the brain (Brynie, 2009).

Beyond the cognitive aspects of sound, there are technical differences to consider. Sound itself is analog because it is created by the disturbance of air molecules. This disturbance of air molecules is known as acoustic energy. When sound needs to be amplified, recorded, edited, or played back (to name a few), it must transform itself from acoustic energy into electrical energy. It is at this point that sound becomes audio. Audio is the electrical energy equivalent of sound's acoustic properties (Connelly, 2005).

Because sound is processed by everyone's own brain, several of its characteristics including loudness, tone, perspective, and localization can vary from individual to individual. With slight exception, the electrical characteristics of audio do not vary. Therefore, sound is considered to be more subjective than audio, since it relies on individual perception and interpretation as opposed to technical guidelines (as in the case of audio). As will be discussed later, there are methods one could use to minimize the subjectivity of their sound design.

The preceding discussion is of significance to anyone interested in creating effective machinima. While the visual component contributes greatly to the story, the importance of creating effective sound design from a cognitive, perceptual, and technical view cannot be ignored. Good sound design will not only enhance, but aid in the communication of the story line.

Telepresence

While science has not been able to clearly define the relationship between visual and auditory processes from a neurological perspective, other research indicates a positive relationship between visual and auditory cues. To understand the relationship as applied to machinima, it is imperative to draw a parallel between machinima and other moving-picture media, such as cinema or television. Perhaps one of the most important theories of moving-picture media is the concept of telepresence, or in some cases, presence.

The difference between telepresence and presence is a semantic one. For the purpose of this section, presence will be used. The most comprehensive definition of presence was constructed by Lombard and Ditton (1997), who defined presence as "the perceptual illusion of nonmediation" ("Presence Explicated" section, par. 1). Simplified, presence is the perception of realism of the content (measured through physiological means), delivered by a medium, that the subject may otherwise fail to perceive or acknowledge. Achieving a high level of presence has the potential to create a realistic experience with little or no distraction from the medium itself.

The significance of presence to machinimists is twofold. First, the screen size and technology of the medium has been determined in past studies to be positively correlated with the level of perceived presence by the viewers (Lombard, Ditton, Grabe, & Reich, 1997; Lombard, Reich, Grabe, Bracken, & Ditton, 2000; Ijsselsteijn, de Ridder, Freeman, Avons, & Bouwhuis, 2001; Bracken, Pettey, Guha, & Rubenking, 2010). As screen size increases, so does the viewer's perception of "realism" of the work. Interestingly, some delivery methods used in machinima utilize smaller screens, such as computer monitors, or even smart phones. The fact that the machinimist will not know the size of the medium on which his or her work is being viewed leads to the second point: the importance of sound cues.

The value of sound cues to visual information must not be underestimated. Studies have found greater salience of visual events (Noesselt, Bergmann, Hake, & Hans-Jochen, 2008) or increased presence (Larsson, Vastfjall, & Kleiner, 2002; Sanders & Scorgie, 2002; Riecke, Schulte-Pelkum, Caniard, & Bulthoff, 2005) when sound accompanies visual content. Other studies have explored other related auditory attributes and found that (1) enhanced multi-channel sound systems increase spatial attributes of the viewers (Hamasaki, Nishiguchi, Okumura, Nakayama, & Ando, 2006; Zhou, Cheok, Qui, & Yang, 2007); (2) quality of audio content enhances the sense of immersion into the environment (Bonneel, Suied, Viaud-Delmos, & Drettakis, 2010); and (3) identification of visual stimuli is quicker when accompanied by a perceptually consistent auditory cue (Doyle & Snowden, 2001). Ultimately, the quality of the sound can affect viewers' attention to the visual work. This includes recording quality, mixing quality, and overall technical quality of the work.

The Mix Basics for Sound Design

With the significance of audio's role in enhancing visual stimuli established, some basic audio principles should be considered by the machinimist. In doing so, it is necessary to point out that there are three major components to cinematic (or, in this case, machinimatic) audio: voice, music, and sound effects. Regardless of the amount of each, the following considerations apply universally.

First and foremost, it is essential to reinforce the concept that auditory processing is individualistic, and hence, subjective. Previously, it was mentioned that the technical aspect of audio varies only slightly and therefore is not as subjective as the perceptive aspect. The slight variation that does occur, and theoretically could be controlled for, is coloration due to manufacturer-specific nuances. While machinimists may not have control over the audio reproduction method or system (method as either via headphones or speakers), they do have control over the recorded or sourced material. When machinimists record their own sounds, it should be completed using professional-quality microphones and recording equipment. Likewise, if the content is sourced, it is worth purchasing high-quality sound effects from a sound effect library. The less coloration by means of the equipment or source, the more objective the audio will be from the start.

Second, music selection can have an immense impact on the machinima. Specific attributes of music, such as pitch and spatial sequence, are detectable by all humans, though at different accuracy levels (Warren & Griffiths, 2003). Similarly, the efficiency of music processing can be increased and sped up when music attributes match neural templates, in essence the musical/listening preferences or culture of the audience members (the intended viewers) (Tervaniemi

& Brattico, 2004). Summarily, the music must be used in an effective manner at appropriate times, and within cultural parameters to contribute positively to the visual content. Music that violates such principles runs the risk of distracting the viewer to the point that interest is lost.

Lastly, variation on the reproduction end of machinima, whether through speakers or headphones, cannot be controlled. But by applying certain sound principles, even the novice machinimist can overcome some of the output variability issues. One of the most basic audio principles to employ is the principle of equal loudness. Under this principle, the perception of frequencies depends on how loudly the sounds are played (Rumsey & McCormick, 2009). For example, bass frequencies at low levels tend to be unnoticeable, whereas mid-high frequencies, such as some vocal characteristics, appear to be louder. The easiest way to compensate for the equal-loudness principle is by making sure that the mixing level (the audio level when listening as the voice, music and sound effects are mixed) is at a somewhat normal level, also known as a reference level. While some professional recording environments are balanced using 85 decibels as the reference level, Huber and Runstein (2010) suggest a moderate mix level between 75 and 90 decibels, depending on the individual's preference. As a reference point, normal conversation occurs at around 60 decibels (Connelly, 2005). Huber and Runstein (2010) put the concept of mixing level into perspective by suggesting that "if you have to shout to communicate in a room, you're probably monitoring too loud" (p. 531).

Related to the equal-loudness principle, yet different, is consideration of reproduction techniques and simple acoustic principles. Unless absolutely necessary, avoid mixing in headphones due to *Unreal*istic reproduction when played back through speakers. When mixing and listening through speakers in a room, characteristics specific to the room will introduce artifacts that, while not necessarily the same as what the listener will experience, are more representative of a typical listening environment. These characteristics include early reflections and reverberation of the sound (Howard & Angus, 2006). A room should not be too live (i.e., like a church) or too dead (i.e., like a small closet full of clothes). Rather, a medium-sized room with average reflective properties is ideal. Furthermore, when using loudspeakers, mixing should be done using speakers that are equidistant apart, with the machinimist positioned directly in the center. This ensures an accurate representation of the stereo field, which will be similarly replicated by headphones should the audience choose to listen back in such a manner.

Finally, as previously discussed, the use of auditory cues has been shown to enhance the recognition of visual stimuli, and therefore accurate placement of the sound effects (and dialogue) is necessary. Most dialogue should remain in the center of the stereo field (pan set to 0), unless the dialogue takes place offscreen. In such a case, the dialogue should be panned according to the side from which the actor will enter the screen. If the actor will not enter the screen during the scene, the placement becomes purely based on preference. Regarding sound effects, they must be positioned within the stereo image relative to their position on the screen. For example, if a gun is fired on the middle-left of the screen, the sound effect should be panned aesthetically to the middle-left of the stereo field.

The Cinematic Value of Audio

Machinima provides a unique opportunity for those who are interested in animation to tell their story without major investment in technology. Oftentimes, audio is left as a last-second consideration in numerous visual productions. While research indicates that screen size has an effect on presence, advances in technology have made screen sizes smaller on devices that are capable of handling cinematic (or machinimatic) releases. If machinimists cannot count on the size of the screen on which a viewer will watch their works, the importance of audio becomes even greater as a method to increase audience presence. By carefully considering the technical and aesthetic principles of sound and audio, a machinimist will most certainly improve the value of his or her production.

References

Bainbridge, W. S. (2010). Introduction. In W. S. Bainbridge, & W. S. Bainbridge (Ed.), *Online worlds: Convergence of the real and the virtual.* (pp. 1–6). New York, NY: Springer-Verlag London Limited.

Bonneel, N., Suied, C., Viaud-Delmos, I., & Drettakis, G. (2010). Bimodal perception of audio-visual material properties for virtual environments. *ACM Transactions of Applied Perception , 7* (1), 1–16. doi: 10.1145/1658349.1658350.

Bracken, C. C., Pettey, G., Guha, T., & Rubenking, B. E. (2010). Sounding out small screens and telepresence. *Journal of Media Psychology , 22* (3), 125–137. doi:10.1027/1864–1105/a000017.

Brynie, F. H. (2009). *Brain sense: The science of the senses and how we process the world around us.* New York, NY: AMACOM Books.

Connelly, D. (2005). *Digital radio production.* Long Grove, IL: Waveland Press, Inc.

Doyle, M. C., & Snowden, R. J. (2001). Identification of visual stimuli is improved by accompanying auditory stimuli: The role of eye movements and sound location. *Perception, 30,* 795–810. doi: 10.1068/p3126.

Elson, D. K., & Riedl, M. O. (2007). A lightweight intelligent virtual cinematography system for machinima production. *Proceedings of the 3rd Conference on Artifical Intelligence for Interactive Digital Entertainment.* Association for the Advancement of Artificial Intelligence.

Hamasaki, K., Nishiguchi, T., Okumura, R., Nakayama, Y., & Ando, A. (2006). Influence of picture on impression of three-dimensional multichannel sound. *28th International Conference: The Future of Audio Technology — Surround and Beyond.* New York: AES.

Howard, D., & Angus, J. (2006). *Acoustics and psychoacoustics (2nd Edition).* Boston, MA: Elsevier: Focal Press.

Huber, D. M., & Runstein, R. E. (2010). *Modern recording techniques (7th Edition).* Boston, MA: Elsevier: Focal Press.

Ijsselsteijn, W., de Ridder, H., Freeman, J., Avons, S., & Bouwhuis, D. (2001). Effects of stereoscopic presentation, image motion, and screen size on subjective and objective corroborative measures of presence. *Presence , 10* (3), 298–311.

Larsson, P., Vastfjall, D., & Kleiner, M. (2002). Better presece and performance in virtual environments by improved binaural sound rendering. *22nd International Conference: Virtual, Synthetic, and Entertainment Audio* (pp. 31-38). New York: Audio Engineering Society.

Lombard, M., & Ditton, T. (1997). At the heart of it all: The concept of presence. *Journal of Compuer-Mediated Communication*, 3 (2), doi: 10.1111/j.1083-6101.1997.tb00072.x.

Lombard, M., Ditton, T. B., Grabe, M. E., & Reich, R. D. (1997). The role of screen size in viewer responses to television fare. *Communication Reports*, 10 (1), 95-106.

Lombard, M., Reich, R. D., Grabe, M. E., Bracken, C. C., & Ditton, T. B. (2000). Presence and television: The role of screen size. *Human Communication Research*, 26 (1), 75–98.

Noesselt, T., Bergmann, D., Hake, M., & Hans-Jochen, H. F. (2008). Sound increases the saliency of visual elements. *Brain Research*, 1220, 157–163.

Riecke, B. E., Schulte-Pelkum, J., Caniard, F., & Bulthoff, H. H. (2005). Influence of auditory cues on the visually-induced self-motion illusion (circular vection) in virtual reality. *Proceedings of 8th international workshop on Presence 2005* (pp. 49–57). International Society for Presence Research.

Rumsey, F., & McCormick, T. (2009). *Sound and recording (6th Edition)*. Boston, MA: Elsevier: Focal Press.

Sanders Jr., R. D., & Scorgie, M. A. (2002, March). *The effect of sound delivery methods on a user's sense of presence in a virtual environment*. Retrieved February 13, 2011, from Naval Postgraduate School: http://edocs.nps.edu/npspubs/scholarly/theses/2002/Mar/02Mar_Sanders.pdf

Tervaniemi, M., & Brattico, E. (2004). From sounds to music towards understanding the neurocognition of musical sound perception. *Journal of Consciousness Studies*, 11 (3–4), 9–27.

Warren, J., & Griffiths, T. (2003). Distinct mechanisms for processing spatial sequences and pitch sequences in the human auditory brain. *The Journal of Neuroscience*, 23 (13), 5799–5804.

Waxman, S. (2009). *Clinical Neuroanatomy*. New York, NY: McGraw-Hill Professional Publishing.

Zhou, Z., Cheok, A. D., Qui, Y., & Yang, X. (2007). The role of 3-D sound in human reaction and performance in augmented reality environments. *Systems, Man and Cybernetics, Part A: IEEE Transactions on Systems and Humans*, 37 (2), 262–272. doi: 10.1109/TSMCA.2006.886376.

8

Celebrating Machinima: It's Show Time!

Some want to make money. Some want to make a combination of art and money. Some want to just reach people and teach lessons. So I think that even though it's not that new, it is new in terms of being part of an art form or a new way of making films — it is still, I think, an individual choice as to where we want to go with it and what we want to do with it like any other filmmaker — Suzy Yue [Roundtable Two, 2010].

In this chapter, the authors look at the payoff for producing machinima. It can be personally rewarding as well as profitable. Some income possibilities for machinima are introduced. The leading machinima festivals across the globe are examined, as well as machinima acceptance into established film festivals. Machinima is increasingly featured in art galleries in virtual worlds like *Second Life* and across the world in prestigious museums and galleries in major cities. Pop Art Lab within *Second Life* links the real and virtual world together to showcase machinima and has established partnerships with universities, museums and international artists. On an informal level, virtual living rooms with home theaters and virtual drive-ins have become viewing spaces for audiences to enjoy watching machinima. The chapter concludes with a feature segment from University of Western Australia's Jay Jay Jegathesan, who discusses his experiences in building partnerships and collaborations in *Second Life* and how machinima has helped to solidify his goals. He speaks from the vantage point of working within an educational institution that has built a strong virtual presence within *Second Life*, and has developed international relationships with universities, artists, and a variety of other entities extending across and beyond the Internet.

The Personal Payoff

The payoff for making a machinima might be personal satisfaction, the accolades of peers or some extra income. For many beginning machinima producers, simply putting a song or story to film and showing it to friends might be a rewarding, personal accomplishment to be appreciated by others. There is absolutely nothing wrong with machinima as a hobby. Many professional filmmakers began their careers by merely playing around and having fun. It can be an inexpensive hobby for many, who refrain initially from the advanced production techniques discussed in some of the chapters. YouTube and Vimeo might be ideal places to upload your machinima as video in standard or high-definition formats, provided you pay attention to the appropriate copyright regulations. Your hobby might turn into a way to make extra money, as your friends begin to ask you to film their virtual weddings, songs, or special occasions. Word of mouth might get you a few more side jobs, and before you know it you are earning a few more dollars here and there in a gaming environment. If you are new to the gaming and virtual worlds, you would be amazed at the number of virtual activities, including weddings, that are filmed.

Other filmmakers come into *Second Life*, for example, with the intent of using the platform to start a business that requires low overhead compared to real-life filmmaking. A number of businesses seriously consider machinima as an effective way to showcase their company image or create training videos in a creative and affordable means. Machinima might be thought of as quick, affordable animation. An experienced machinimist knows how to create professional productions using *Second Life* and post-production software. The results from virtual filmmaking, particularly within platforms like *Second Life*, can be comparable to traditional animation, which takes much more time and money to create.

In the corporate world, time is money, and the turnaround for machinima commercial or corporate video is relatively fast compared to traditional means. Virtual sets can be constructed and characters can be crafted in much less time than needed for an animated film. Whereas a short promotional video might cost 5,000 to 10,000 US dollars to make in real life, a machinima might be produced at a fraction of the cost. Machinima commercials have the look and feel of traditional animation, with a little tweaking here and there. As already documented in this book, a good producer knows how to compensate for the shortcomings of machinima, such as limitations in animation scripting. A combination of creative shot angles and other work-arounds, plus some post-production skills, provides enough tricks to make the corporate machinima producer or storyteller competitive in the marketplace.

For-profit machinima spans quite a few genres, from professional music videos, to training videos, to commercials. The first move from personal to corporate machinima production might begin by producing a demo reel, a sample of work demonstrating one's skills. Voice talent should also consider creating an audio demo representing his or her various accents, characterizations, and moods through a sampling of work, from commercial to dramatic performances. Moments in virtual life are created and/or captured through machinima, and the right voice-over is essential to convey the appropriate mood of the piece.

The Virtual Community

Probably one of the most powerful and collaborative aspects of *Second Life* is the development of a machinima community within its virtual platform. There are a number of organizations that host screening events and lecture series on machinima. MaMachinima founder Chantal Harvey has sponsored numerous such events, from Machinima Mondays to the 25 Days of Machinima, to a series of impromptu machinima events. The Machinima Artist Guild has also sponsored similar events in the past. Machinimators are also considered visual artists within *Second Life*, and machinima exhibitions are increasingly being hosted by virtual art galleries and museums. Audiences in their avatar representations participate in such events, through critique sessions or simply enjoying the work shown on huge virtual screens. The person behind the avatar can zoom in on the virtual screen and watch the machinima in high definition with no noticeable sacrifice to the quality of the film. The machinima fills the computer screen, and at that point the virtual screen showing the film is no different than watching a film on any other personal viewing monitor. In fact, through the lens of his or her avatar, the viewer often reports feeling immersed into the virtual environment, with a sense of being there in the audience watching the film live in the auditorium. The discussion after viewing a machinima film segment brings the audience together virtually in real time. In this way, viewers can watch the machinima from the comfort of their homes while participating within the interactive discussion taking place around the screening. The machinima audience is typically a global one, bringing producers and fans into one virtual space from across the world. That Parisian producer can view the work of a Canadian or Brazilian machinimist without leaving home, office, or studio.

The 2010 MaMachinima International Festival is one example of a large-scale event that attracted viewers from around the world to a screening of machinima that represented work from *Second Life*, Moviestorm, and other platforms. This festival had a physical real-world screening in Amsterdam, while much of the world's machinimists attended the event from home viewing it from *Second Life*. Their avatars sat in red plush theater seats within a massive machinima auditorium in *Second Life*. The auditorium might be described as a huge theater-in-the-round, with large screens positioned strategically for all to see the works conveniently from any seating angle. As each work was screened, individual producers took to the stage in their respective avatar form. It was quite an impressive event, with many avatars decked out in the high fashion of *Second Life*, and similarly a real-world audience watched from theater seats in Amsterdam.

Machinima might also be viewed on virtual televisions within virtual homes. TV networks like Treet TV and Metaverse Television fill the virtual airwaves with machinima programming, including serious discussions, live events, game and comedy shows, news events, documentaries, and other forms of creative production. Treet TV CEO Wiz Nordberg shares the story behind the birth of his television network in the interview section of this book. Machinima viewers have more options than ever before to watch content within *Second Life* or across several online services and networks. One of the top online networks, AviewTV, is owned by LaPiscean Liberty and features machinima on demand, including dramas, comedies, recorded live concerts, music videos and about everything that one would anticipate seeing via a cable or satellite programmer — but only in the form of machinima.

Some viewers watch blockbuster movies on their *SL* viewers or at in-world drive-ins. Machinima screenings might take place at a drive-in, a virtual residence, or a huge performance arena. The point is that machinima is being viewed within *Second Life*, beyond YouTube, for example. Some machinima has found itself on real-world television, particularly as segments worked into plots of popular series. The classic example of machinima on network TV is the *South Park* episode "Make Love, Not Warcraft," airing in October 2006.

The most well-known content website, machinima.com, had maintained a comprehensive archive representing a variety of games and platforms including *Second Life*, *The Sims*, *World of Warcraft* and many shooter games. In late 2010, the company decided to focus primarily on machinima constructed from action-based games, featuring speed runs, in-game sessions, game trailers, favorite plays or best kills ("frag" videos), and content along this line. A source of rich machinima content is the Machinima Artist Guild — the professional site and regular site. The content of the *Second Life* Machinima Artist Guild is dedicated to machinima made using primarily *Second Life*. The Professional Machinima Artist Guild features *Second Life*'s advanced machinima and welcomes top machinima from other platforms. The Pro-MAG continues to expand in that direction, filling the gap left behind by machinima.com. These sites are mentioned again simply to reinforce the importance of exhibiting work and allowing for critique and collaboration.

A number of university-sponsored machinima events exist in both virtual and real-world spaces, and one of the first and most dedicated of education institutions to the art of machinima is the University of Western Australia, which has set up a virtual campus in *Second Life*. Under the leadership of Jay Jay Jegathesan, the founder of *SL*'s UWA presence, this university has sponsored regular design and machinima challenges within *Second Life* for hefty contest prize monies and recognition. It has created a strong community of artists, designers, and filmmakers who come together and often collaborate on entries for these competitions. At the end of this chapter, Jegathesan discusses the birth and evolution of his university's sponsorship of these challenges and the larger significance of these cultural activities.

Real-World Machinima Exhibitions

The showing of the *Second Life* documentary *Life 2.0* in the Sundance Film Festival is one example of the increased acceptance of machinima as a legitimate form among its film counterparts. A number of other festivals have embraced machinima as a genre of animation. In *Second Life*, machinima producers are familiar with the aforementioned MaMachinima International Festival and its real-world impact on propelling machinima to the public eye as a significant storytelling medium. In late November 2010, professional and amateur machinimatographers met in-world to view screenings and learn from top producers and vendors at Machinima Expo. The platforms featured at the expo go beyond *Second Life*, and the exposition is conducive to learning various tools and environments. Machinima Expo features a variety of works at its annual event and on its online portal, including a Latin/Spanish reel as an outreach to cultural diversity. The executive committee for 2010 was comprised of award-winning machinima producers Kate Fosk (of Pineapple Pictures) and Phil Rice, and award-winning actor and sound designer Ricky Grove. Rice and Grove manage machiniplex.net, which is host to both the best of contemporary and classic machinima. Another venue worthy of attention is the Laval Virtual International Conference and Exhibition held in France annually; it offers a forum for works and research in virtual reality and converging technologies. The International SIGGRAPH conference has increasingly exhibited machinima works.

The FMX is the long-standing Conference on Animation, Effects, Games and Interactive Media, and in 2011, its 16th year was held in Stuttgart, Germany. Other machinima competitions/screenings include the Shooot Fiesta in Singapore (in conjunction with Asia SIGGRAPH) and Atopic Festival Prix Machinima in Paris. In 2010, machinima was featured in the World Expo in Shanghai, China, and that drew a lot of media attention to the virtual world of *Second Life*, where some of the top art and story machinima have been created in recent years. Real and virtual exhibitions were set up for screenings and related events.

Machinima can be seen as feature segments on mainstream and virtual television, as well as at real-world and virtual festivals, such as in the World Expo. The boundaries are disappearing between film, television and machinima. No matter how and where machinima is viewed, it is watched by a growing audience becoming familiar with alternative forms of storytelling, where they have the opportunity to archive their virtual memories and to craft their own stories on a relatively inexpensive and accessible medium.

Show-Time Exercises

Consider what are the top sources for exhibiting your future works as you review the following:

1. Identify various online services that exhibit machinima and compare their advantages and disadvantages, including technical specifications and rules associated with uploads.
2. Identify three festivals or exhibitions at which you would like to showcase your machinima. Review the top-placed machinima at a festival that interests you. What are some elements that you liked about the winning machinima?
3. Identify organizations you might join that would help you network with other machinimatographers. Explain why you picked these groups.

✦ Comments by Jay Jay Jegathesan ✦

Partnerships and Collaboration

Now the heading for this may be "Partnerships and Collaboration," however my story on this is a weave starting with 3-D art and how that has led to collaboration for machinima, not only between machinimatographers, actors and their fans, but also between the "universes" of *Second Life* artists and machinimatographers. Well actually it goes beyond that. It starts with 3-D virtual worlds, and this is my story.

I am the manager of the School of Physics at the University of Western Australia. In the 1990s, I graduated from UWA with a bachelor of commerce degree and set out working in Malaysia, Japan, Singapore, etc. However, UWA, with her enchanting grounds and architecture reeled me back, and in 2004, my alma mater turned into my employer. By 2006, I was struck by the idea of the UWA campus grounds in 3-D up somewhere on the Internet in all her glory, the architecture, the grounds, the trees, the peacocks, the ducks and everything that makes this campus one of the finest on earth.

Of course I had no technical skills whatsoever to do it, just the grand plan, and failing to raise the $180,000 I thought I needed to get it done; it sat in the back of my mind, until Dr. Chris Thorne (then Mr. Chris Thorne, mature-age Ph.D. candidate with the School of Computer Science and Software Engineering) sent me the following e-mail at 3 P.M. on the 15th of May 2007:

Hi Jay Jay, I am running an online event on the show floor at the SIGGRAPH conference in August. It will be an online public participatory event where people can login, choose an avatar and join others in a virtual world. Do you think that you could sponsor me a little by providing server resources—I will be using a number of servers across the world. We have some servers from a Finland sponsor available already.

And with that I knew I had found the man to help me achieve what I wanted. The response from me 30 minutes later is what led to the five sims that UWA are operating now in *Second Life*, the Linden Prize nomination 2010, the UWA 3-D Art and Design Challenges, and the UWA Machinima Challenges. I simply said, "Chris, how can I call you, need a quick discussion on this."

This led to a $1,000 National Science Week grant which was put toward building what we called the UWA Virtual Universe, which was a 3-D world featuring only UWA sitting on a single server. With this, while there was amazing collaboration in getting it set up with undergrads, post-grads, academic staff, technical staff, admin staff, retirees, and even acquaintances from Thailand, the United Stated and the UK who inspired us; the collaborative capabilities via the system itself were impossible as one could only see one's own avatar when logged in.

This dynamic team then went on to win the Google Earth Build Your Campus in 3-D competition in 2008, gaining coverage in the national press, among others, and recognization within the university as a team capable of delivering on what were once seen as lofty promises. This led to the funds being secured by May 2009 to create a UWA presence in *Second Life*, which we were convinced had the necessary elements to implement the full vision for the university's 3-D presence first dreamed of in 2006.

The initial idea for the campus was to just have a replication of as much of the campus as possible, including the creation in *Second Life* of UWA's magnificent Moreton Bay Fig, sunken gardens and reflecting pond. It was meant to be a place where prospective students, staff and alumni could visit and enjoy in three-dimensional space. I did not have any immediate plans to have research, arts or teaching or machinima for that matter factor into the presence. In fact at the time of creation, I had not even heard the word *machinima*.

By the time of the full campus launch, however, on the 2nd of October 2009, serendipity had stepped in, and we had visualization research in full swing through collaboration with Paul Bourke, director of UWA's West Australian Supercomputer Programme; we had actual university degree teaching utilizing *Second Life* via collaboration with Professor Wade Halvorson of the School of Business; and critically for the development of machinima collaboration downstream, we had launched the biggest 3-D art and architecture challenge in all of *Second Life* via collaboration with Professor Ted Snell, director of UWA's cultural precinct and Quadra Pop Lane, a UWA arts alumni.

Starting with a modest 27 entries in the month of September 2009, by the end of it all in August 2010, the UWA 3-D Art and Design Challenge had attracted 841 entries from around the world, bringing together artists and architects from Venezuela, Belgium, Mexico, Wales, Canada, the USA, the UK, Uruguay, Scotland, England, Spain, Switzerland, Italy, France, Brazil, Argentina, Chile, Denmark, Holland, Ireland, Portugal, Austria, Cuba, Serbia, Tunisia, Germany, Japan, New Zealand and Australia. My monthly offer of a huge reward for someone bringing to us an artist from Antarctica (the only unrepresented continent) had come to be anticipated by those taking part.

UWA's machinima journey began quietly on the 20th of October 2009, when UWA 2nd second-year business student Matt Jilley thought out of the box in submitting a class project and created a machinima of the UWA presence. I was enchanted as I had never seen a machinima before. However things did not crystallize until the 8th of December 2009, when French machinimatographer Iono Allen, with encouragement from *Second Life* 3-D arts promoter, White Lebed, created an amazing machinima of the artwork sent in for the November round of the UWA 3-D Art and Design Challenge. The 3-D Art Challenge had already brought much collaboration. Apart from the global interest and flavor that developed, partnerships were formed with the University of Texas at San Antonio and even a Peruvian university as to matters relating to art and beyond. Machinima was to take all of this to the next step.

Moving at more than triple the speed at which things happen in real life, the support of White Lebed and the Machinima Artist Guild had by the 18th of December 2009 driven me into launching "MachinimUWA: The UWA Machinima Challenge." The goal of this challenge was to create a machinima that captures the four main elements that make up the heart of the University of Western Australia in *Second Life*, these elements being architecture, teaching, research and arts. The goal here was to use machinima as a battering ram to break down the barriers between *Second Life* and real life, within the upper echelons of the university in particular, and to provide a tool through which greater collaboration and partnerships could be fostered. It had crystallized very quickly in my mind that this was the perfect vehicle to introduce the uninitiated to 3-D virtual worlds and their potential.

It was rough going getting machinimatographers interested in this challenge, as we started off with only a $20,000 Linden [*SL* currency] prize pool, and the theme was particularly restrictive, with a number of individuas telling me that the theme made it more an advertisement which they were not interested in. I spent at least three to four hours with each machinimatographer explaining the motivations behind this challenge including my feelings that this was necessary to break the dam wall and allow for proper funding for 3-D art and for machinima to be secured. By the closing date, 13 entries had come in, by machinimatographers hailing from Texas, Massachusetts, New York, Florida, Barcelona, San Sebastian, Paris, Maastricht, Berlin, Toronto and Perth.

One of the biggest reasons the machinimatographers agreed to create the machinima for this challenge was the presence of the 3-D art platform carrying the wonderful art creations submitted to the UWA 3-D Art Challenge. These works featured prominently in all the machinima.

A judging panel was assembled made up of people who I thought would be able to influence decisions as to the next stage, to be able to provide the necessary funding for art and machinima and to provide resources for partnership and collaboration: an impressive lineup, led by Professor Alan Robson, vice chancellor of the University of Western Australia; Kelly Smith, director of the International Centre; and Jon Stubbs, director of Student Services, none of whom had more than a fleeting exposure to *Second Life.*

The plan succeeded beyond imagination. So taken were the panel with the quality and elegance of the machinima that the prize pool had increased to L$250,000 by the time the last reel ticked over. Berliner Cisko Vandeverre took top prize over Bradley Dorchester and ColeMarie Soleil. These machinima have since then been used numerous times in building collaboration with groups intending to start having presences in virtual worlds being played at national and international education conferences, among others.

This had further positive consequences. The success of the machinima led directly to funding increases that has seen the UWA sims funded for the next three years, with L$1,000,000 being available in each of these three years for arts and machinima prizes. With at least four sims being available, a 200-seat amphitheater was built (a UWA and *Best of SL Magazine* collaboration) with many machinima events being run at this location under the tutelage of initially Taralyn Gravois and now Chantal Harvey. The availability of the theatre to machinima events led to collaboration between UWA and the Library and Archive at NASA for their National Space Society Machinima Showcase.

Iono Allen had been appointed as the "official machinimatographer" for UWA, and he produced a monthly machinima bringing together all the winning artworks for each month, masterfully weaving together unrelated art pieces submitted by artists of various influences into a dynamic whole. Seeing their works so wonderfully captured as machinima was something of great value and inspiration to the 3-D artist community.

As the grand finale of the UWA 3-D Art and Design Challenge approached, the magic that the monthly machinima had weaved through the artworks kept urging me to do something more, and out of the blue, MachinimUWA II: Art of the Artists was launched, with the theme "Create something that will take our breath away!" the challenge being *to create* a machinima featuring some of the winning artworks from the UWA 3-D Art and Design Challenge.

Thus it was that the world of the machinimatographer, and the world of the 3-D artist, hitherto already aligned (due to the need for set design, prop creation, etc.), was brought into the one sphere, leading to an amazing 45 machinima being made featuring the 35 artworks that had made it to the grand finale round. Machinima gives immortality to the transience of the 3-D art creations, and as such is amazingly powerful.

Once again, Germany and Australia took the top prizes, with joint winners Laurina Hawks and Bradley Dorchester being declared. Interestingly, these two creations are polar opposites of each other both by theme and even length, the former being the longest and the latter being the shortest submission. Pondicherry (India) based Frenchman, Tutsy Navarathna, took third prize with a surreal interpretation.

I now cannot imagine having art events without a machinima component connected in some way. The UWA Art Challenges have kicked off their second year, and an early announcement was made as well, that a second Art of the Artists will run concurrently, with all entries across the year being eligible for filming.

How do I construct a conclusion to this little story on my journey through the virtual world riding on the back of machinima? For a university presence in *Second Life*, the creation of local and international partnerships and collaboration would be one of the key components of what we would consider a successful venture. To this end, machinima has proven to be the ultimate arrow in my quiver.

References

Allen, Iono. (2009). A Selection of Artworks Presented in UWA in November 2009 UWA Presence. YouTube. Accessed January 27, 2011, from http://www.youtube.com/watch?v=Dame2q6mcPg

Jilley, Matt. (2009). UWA in *Second Life*. YouTube. Accessed January 27, 2011, from http://www.youtube.com/watch?v=AyQ8hMOocbE

Machinima Roundtable Two. (2010). *Terminology, Technology, and Practice* (Sessions 3 & 4, July 15 & 16). Lowe Runo Productions, LLC, *Second Life*.

MachinimUWA: The UWA Machinima Challenge. (2009, December 18). Blog. The University of Western Australia. Accessed January 27, 2011, from http://uwainsl.blogspot.com/2009/12-/machiniuwa-uwa-machinima-challenge.html

Recommended Machinima

An Art Form is Born by Tutsy Navarathna, http://www.youtube.com/watch?v=xr1JGXuXs_U&feature=player_embedded

Art of the Artists by Bradley Dorchester, http://www.youtube.com/watch?v=q3HzHUNREno&feature=player_embedded

MachinimUWA : Art, Architecture, Research, Teaching by Bradley Dorchester (Perth), http://www.youtube.com/watch?v=YN1k80dA3I8&feature=player_embedded

No Tomb for the Art by Laurina Hawks, http://www.youtube.com/watch?v=QsrZgMA8SNI&feature=player_embedded

SEEK by Cisko Vandeverre (Berlin), http://www.youtube.com/watch?v=H6zbFx3-Dxws&feature=player_embedded

UWA Machinima by Colemarie Soleil (Florida), http://www.youtube.com/watch?v=KdIQP-YrYLw&feature=player_embedded

9
The White Pigeon:
A Machinima Example

Her heart broke into a million pieces and she cooed softly to him from behind the glass. He would not lift his head. She hid her tears and cooed yet more determined for the sound of her voice to penetrate the darkness and find him, wherever he had gone — Skylar Smythe [2010], author of *The White Pigeon.*

The producers were contacted by the Aview TV founder LaPiscean Liberty about the possibility of crafting an emotional tale, *The White Pigeon* by Skylar Smythe, from story to machinima. The story was far more complex than its first read, and the producers decided to take the challenge, namely to be able to communicate the passion behind the story using machinima and the *Second Life* platform. Aview TV is a leading network for machinima distribution and forum. *The White Pigeon*, in its original literary form, made its debut in October 2010 having been posted on Smythe's blog. It has been well received by online readers. This chapter demonstrates the transformation of the story to machinima.

The Original Story:
The White Pigeon *by Skylar Smythe*

The mornings were dark and cold flying past the downtown buildings full of strangers who never said hello and never cared whether you lived or died so long as you did not interrupt their day. The white pigeon flew slowly watching the magical twinkles of a million lights being turned on as people with different lives than her own rolled over for their morning kiss.

Sometimes she would find herself staring up at the window and wondering what that felt like. To belong to someone.

"I do that too" said a man and startled her briefly.

"Do what?" she responded carefully backing up from the strange man lest he should strike out at her the way that most did.

"Watch them. Envy them."

"It is nice to have someone" she replied wistfully.

"Yes. It really is." He said.

He invited her to his home and she was fearful to enter. It was a beautiful home full of beautiful things and she felt unworthy and frightened. She was after all only a pigeon and although she was a brilliant bright white with soft feathers she was not a dove. She was just a pigeon who liked to watch from street level as the world passed her by.

He began to leave seeds outside his window in the hope that she would grow to trust him. Slowly she began to visit his balcony more and more and partake of his generosity and kindness. In a city full of alley cats that would just as soon make a meal of a pigeon with a broken wing, she began to see something tender and protective in the man. And when she sat upon his window sill she could feel the warmth of his heart through the glass wall and distance between them. And she began to sing a low gentle coo that traveled straight to his ear even when he rested far from her touch.

And so the friendship grew between them. Sometimes when she visited and alighted upon his window sill she would find him angry. Throwing fits of rage about the unfairness of life and complications not of his doing. About change and being forced to change. He was a man who did not like surprises and yet it seemed his life relentlessly threw elements requiring mass adaptation. Sometimes he would be drunk and only then would she truly grow to know the depth of his sorrow. At four or five in the morning when all the fight had left his body and all that was left was a poet's bleeding heart.

She sang to him from behind the glass to draw out the venom. Her breath dispelled the cloud impeding the brilliance of the full moon.

In his moments of triumph he would excitedly share his vision and goals realized and she stood tall on the perch of his window sill smiling. Staring quietly from gentle eyes that shared in his victories as she shared in his sorrow. As she shared in all things with him every day.

Soon he began to build a cage for her. A lavish beautiful home on the other side of the glass full of comforts and promises that he would never harm her. That he would always keep her safe. She was not a songbird or a regal peacock but her coo had become the thing that soothed his angry heart. It became the thing that stopped bad thoughts and brought peace and poetry and every romanticism he thought was dead in him returned. Now that he had found her how could he not have her in his life when she made such beautiful music that fed his very soul?

And he painted her a dove in his heart.

He never did finish building the cage for her. One day she flew to his window and noted that the entire room had gone black. A fire had ravaged the sanctuary and left him sitting alone in a corner with his head buried in his hands. He wept. Her heart broke into a million pieces and she cooed softly to him from behind the glass. He would not lift his head. She hid her tears and cooed yet more determined for the sound of her voice to penetrate the darkness and find him, wherever he had gone. She knew she could bring him back if only he would open his ear to her.

He would not.

Over the months she continued to fly to the window. Sometimes she would see him staring out at her and he would leave it slightly open so that he could hear her moving about her business, his ears straining to hear her soft cooing as she went about so as not to disturb his thoughts. But there was no more bird seed placed lovingly outside to sustain her and yet she returned convinced she could hear his voice calling to her in the darkest hours of the night. Dreaming of her perhaps and when she sensed him calling in her head ... wherever she was at the moment she cooed her broken hearted retort.

One day she flew by and cast a woeful look upon his window. It had been months since she had stood on the sill and thrust out her downy warm chest to sing her love to him and chase the darkness from his eyes. The window was barred and shuttered closed. There was no light inside. Her heavy heart vowed to never return.

To this day if you ask him he will discount her worth. She was nothing of impact or comfort or consequence. Of loyalty of faithfulness and patient forgiveness. But if you ask her she will tell you stories of a beautiful man that sustained her once. And a friendship she thought should span a lifetime until he broke her wing and dained her to fly through revisionistic history which repainted a guardian as a villain. A dove as just a pigeon.

She understands why this is easier now that the alchemic melody is lost; she weeps each misspent note in retrospect.

The Treatment

The producers reviewed the story for main points, deciding what was critical to the plot, in an effort to remain true to the author's original intent. They would need to ensure the story was told in a credible manner that would be possible through machinima. Initial scouting for animations, sets, clothing, skin and hair helped the producers determine what was available within *Second Life*. Other considerations were how to portray this story within a reasonable length for machinima, most likely three to five minutes. The team attempted to summarize the story, by retelling its gist back to one another concisely. With a one-page treatment, summarizing the key points, a draft script was created and then revised until the script was finalized pending approval by the original storyteller. Further revisions refined the script. The authors focused on the flow of dialogue initially and how to convey the metaphor of the pigeon's transformation to woman/dove within the story. It was a process of give and take between the scriptwriter and the producer as well as the author. A storyboard was developed to help visualize the scenes and conceptualize how the dialogue and narration would be executed within those scenes.

The Script

*ACT I: *The Introduction**
FADE IN:
EXT. CITY APARTMENT BUILDING—DAY
Dawn is approaching. Sky is gray and wintery. PIGEON flies across the sky, past downtown buildings. People are walking solitary in the city on sidewalks, city streets.
INT. APARTMENT WINDOW
MAN looks out window. There is a small balcony for potted plants and such.
EXT. PIGEON
PIGEON flies slowly. Stars begin to fade against a backdrop of a million lights being turned on in the city.
INT. BEDROOM
MAN looks out window toward neighboring apartment.
EXT. PIGEON
PIGEON has landed on the balcony ledge of the MAN's apartment.
EXT. NEIGHBORS' APARTMENT
MAN looks out window, seeing COUPLE rolling over for morning kiss. PIGEON faces NEIGHBORS' apartment. Both catch a glimpse of the COUPLE.
EXT. BALCONY
From the PIGEON's perspective, she sees the MAN as a dark shadow standing near his apartment window.

MAN
I do that, too.
PIGEON
(STARTLED) Do what?

Camera has moved closer to reveal MAN's face to PIGEON.

MAN
Watch them. Envy Them.
PIGEON
It is nice to have someone.

PIGEON replies wistfully, but more confidently. PIGEON is now a dove-like woman, but only revealed from her back.
MAN
Yes, it really is.
INT. HOUSE
The MAN motions for the PIGEON to enter his house through the window.

The house is quaint, but well furnished. The shadow is now on the PIGEON (still not revealing her face), as she humbly takes a step back from the window ledge in awe and fear. Camera focuses on her brilliant bright white body with soft feathers. As the act closes, PIGEON looks at the window, as if thinking about flying away. She does not enter his house.

*ACT II: *The Friendship**
EXT. WINDOW LEDGE — NEXT DAY [AND OVER TIME...]
MAN leaves seed on window ledge. Camera focuses on PIGEON on ledge, and MAN watching from INSIDE the apartment. *Pigeon's low gentle coo is heard.*
EXT. APARTMENT — DAY
MAN paces inside apartment. PIGEON looks on from ledge.

NARRATOR (PIGEON)

And so the friendship grew between us. Sometimes when I visited and landed upon his window sill I would find him angry, throwing fits of rage about the unfairness of life and complications not of his doing. About change and being forced to change.

INT. APARTMENT — NIGHT(S)
MAN on sofa/kitchen chair/floor, in exhaustion and despair.

NARRATOR (PIGEON)

Sometimes he would be drunk and only then would I truly grow to know the depth of his sorrow. At four or five in the morning when all the fight had left his body, all that was left was a poet's bleeding heart.

EXT. WINDOW LEDGE — FULL MOON
PIGEON (in non-human form) watches from ledge. The PIGEON *sings* to him from behind MAN's apartment window. PIGEON's face/body is revealed as beautiful woman in the window's reflection. MAN builds cage. PIGEON watches on.
INT. MAN'S APARTMENT
Man contently looks toward the window. PIGEON's face is now revealed to him, and she appears as a beautiful woman (as dove-like). The glass remains between them. Zoom in on a framed art work, with the words, "And he painted a dove in his heart." Transitions into next scene.
EXT. BALCONY
A dove flies off the balcony through the sky.

*ACT III: *The Fire**
EXT. WINDOW LEDGE — DUSK
View into MAN'S APARTMENT from BALCONY.
INT. MAN'S APARTMENT
Room black with fire. MAN sits in corner of room. Head in hands, MAN *weeps.*
EXT. BALCONY
Transition from weeping to gentle coos, as camera looks through the window

at MAN, with his head hung low in despair. PIGEON (as woman) hides her tears. The *coos become louder, and trail off under NARRATOR.*

NARRATOR (PIGEON)

I felt that no matter what I did, I had lost him to his darkness. I continued to sing.

INT. MAN'S APARTMENT

MAN straining to hear her *soft cooing.*

NARRATOR (PIGEON)

He strained to hear me. I would call out to him, but my voice grew distant.

EXT. BALCONY — DAWN

Birdseed is gone. PIGEON (as woman) stands outside window. MAN staring out at her.

EXT. BALCONY — DAY TO NIGHT SEQUENCE

(Returning to the opening scene of Act I). Dawn is approaching. Sky is gray and wintery. PIGEON flies across the sky, past downtown buildings. People are walking solitary in the city on sidewalks, city streets.

The window is barred and shuttered closed. The PIGEON (as woman) is shown from the back, facing the window.

NARRATOR (PIGEON)

To this day, he dares not look back, and may not even realize the beauty of what he had — a special friendship that might have spanned a lifetime. It was lost in the darkness. I have no regret except the gifts of warmth I gave him, freely, but it was my strength that he used to get through his night. My wings are tired but still in flight. I will not return, but I will not forget either.

FADE OUT

The Setting

After some scouting, a building was located that would be fitting for an apartment, complete with city fire escapes to provide a sense of reality — and a landing for the pigeon. The building was placed on a platform in the sky of *Second Life* to minimize lag from the producers' company site below.

Two rooms were decorated in the building. One of those would be central to the relationship between the two main characters — the pigeon and the man. The other room was related to a brief scene of a couple in a neighboring apartment. The man and the pigeon would look out from the balcony into that apartment. Actually, the producer would shoot within a room of the same building providing the illusion that the apartment was across from them. The rooms were furnished as needed, simply but effectively to achieve enough realism and minimal clutter. The building was situated within a three-sided green screen box. The producers had decided upon a "city view" video that would replace the green chroma key.

Characters

The man was cast in his 40s, with a seasoned appearance. The viewer would see the transformative metaphor behind the pigeon — a young, caring and vibrant woman, a dove in disguise. To make the conversation credible to the viewer, it was necessary to show the pigeon as a woman. The woman was dressed in white, with matching hair, to assist in her characterization as a bird-like being. She would be very much human in her overall representation to the man and the viewers, with occasional shots that would reestablish her in her non-human form. The only other characters, a loving couple, appeared early on during a bedroom scene in a nearby apartment, when the man and pigeon looked across their balcony. The script relied mainly on narration by a female voice, with only several lines of dialogue from the main characters. The visuals would be critical to the execution of the story. The voice was recorded external to *Second Life*, being added during the editing process.

The Storyboard

The storyboard provided a rough example to the producers on how they might conceptualize the story as a machinima. For space reasons, this book illustrates only a sampling from the final storyboard for *The White Pigeon*, highlighting an opening shot sequence [illustrations 9.1–9.4]. The process of storyboarding can be as minimal or as detailed as the producer needs it to be. In this case the producers were also the actors, and both shared the vision on how the story would unfold. Storyboards for other projects might be more elaborate to help a larger crew to visualize the intent of the producer. In that case, many more frames might be illustrated within a storyboard than otherwise.

Filming in Second Life

Lighting was factored into the set design. The producers conducted some film tests, checking on what angles would work best under what lighting conditions. At one point in the filming, the script called for a burned-out room, after a fire. Lighting would help to convey that image. A variety of close-up, medium and long shots were used, with close-ups establishing a bond between the audience and the characters, as well as the emotives of the characters. Medium shots of the man and the woman (the pigeon) helped to convey their relationship. Long shots were used to establish setting and to show distance when needed.

Top: Illustration 9.1: Opening Shot of Building: The frame is representative of the opening shot of the building. It establishes the setting for the story. *Bottom:* Illustration 9.2: Balcony Meeting: Here the main character talks to the pigeon on the fire escape balcony.

Top: Illustration 9.3: Couple Embracing: The main character and the pigeon happen to notice a couple cuddling in a nearby apartment, setting in motion a conversation about how nice it would be to have someone special in their life. *Bottom:* Illustration 9.4: Pigeon Woman: The pigeon in her transformative state is shown in this frame.

Post-production and Final Thoughts

The "city" video would replace the green screen and establish the setting for the apartment building. That was part of the post-production process. The pigeon-woman transformation was created through the magic of After Effects Adobe software. The editing process other than those elements followed regular video practice, with pacing established through transitions. Music was added in post, along with dialogue and narration. Titles and credits finalized the piece, giving acknowledgments where due.

Remember that there are many ways to conceptualize a story visually, and the authors simply present one way as a case in point.

Reference

Smythe, Skylar. (2010, October 22). *The White Pigeon.* My Imaginary Brief. Accessed February 15, 2011, from http://microfictionbyskylarsmythe.blogspot.com/2010/10/white-pigeon.html

The White Pigeon Exercises

Consider other ways that the story might have been told through machinima.

1. In what other ways might the characters have been portrayed?
2. What are some possible ways to convey emotion through machinima, giving consideration to this story?
3. Identify the key elements of the story that are visually critical to establishing the relationship between the main characters, as well as the pigeon's transformation.
4. How might this story be produced without use of chroma key or special effects specific to post-production?

10

The Fine Print

TODD HERREMAN

You know, I was thinking about when SL was brand new. The people that were here all went out of their way to help each other to learn the tools and were incredibly generous. Everybody would help EVERY-BODY.... We're still in the learning stages and we'll develop the content and the tools and the thoughts about it and then other people will come in and try to make the money off of it, and in a way, ruin it for all of us. Or make it different. Maybe I should say it that way. Make it a dif-ferent atmosphere—Evie Fairchild [Roundtable Two, 2010].

The authors asked Todd Herreman, a copyright expert, to weave through the machinima fine print and provide some interpretation and guidelines for machin-ima producers. He also offers them advice for the blind spots on their journey. In his essay, he reviews various policies of popular game platforms, and contextualizes those polices within court decisions. Herreman, a 20-year Los Angeles-based music industry veteran as producer, songwriter, composer, engineer and session musician, with a client list including Prince, Michael Jackson, Brian Wilson, Jeff Beck, Jodie Watley and Adam Ant, in 2004 turned his attention to teaching audio engineering, producing and music business at Southern Illinois University. He holds a degree in music and philosophy from Indiana University and a master of legal studies from SIU School of Law, with a concentration in intellectual property. Industry affiliations include the Recording Academy (NARAS), voting member; ASCAP, writer and publisher; Audio Engineering Society (AES), professional member; and member of Music and Entertainment Industry Educators Association (MEIEA).

Introduction

The creation of machinima potentially puts the artist in the undesirable position of being liable for copyright infringement. Such a threat can result in costly litigation or cause the artist to not create for fear of being sued. While no litigation has yet resulted from the creation of machinima (at the time of this writing), as the art form receives more widespread attention, gains accept-ance and becomes more commercialized, the possibility of the rights holders (read: game developers) demanding control of their property may increase. This section will explore the legal implications of using copyrighted works in the creation of machinima, how some manufacturers have responded to such use, and whether fair use is a viable defense for the machinima artist. (Note: this inquiry is in the context of U.S. copyright law.)

Copyright, Licenses and Derivative Works

Video games are software. Software is subject to copyright protection (Merges, Menell, & Lemley, 2006, p. 970) as are music, sound recordings, literature, movies, photography, painting, sculpture, architectural works and choreography (U.S. Code 17, 1976).[1] This means that the rights holder (the game developer) has exclusive rights (with some exceptions, such as fair use), which include the right to copy, the right to create derivative works, the right to distribute the work, and the right to publicly perform the work (U.S. Code 17, 1976).[2] By capturing screen play to create machinima, the artist has implicated the first two exclusive rights: copying and creating a derivative work. The definition of a derivative work is "a work based upon one or more preexisting works, such as a translation, musical arrangement, dramatization, fictionalization, motion picture version, sound recording, art reproduction, abridgment, condensation, or any other form in which a work may be recast, transformed, or adapted" (U.S. Code 17, 1976).[3] The issue regarding the distribution right and performance right depends on what the artist does with the machinima. For example, posting the movie to YouTube or even to one's own site would be considered distribution to the public, and implicates the third exclusive right. (Note that it does not have to be a "commercial use" to implicate the aforementioned rights.) When the work is then viewed on that site, the playback of the work constitutes a performance of the work. Hence, the machinima artist, if using software without the express permission of the rights holder, may be liable for infringing the game maker's copyright. However, the rights holder can grant licenses (exclusive or non-exclusive) to others; that is, a rights holder can give permission to copy, to make derivative works, to distribute the work , and to publicly perform the work (certain conditions apply, of course).

Red vs. Blue: *Not Black and White*

Not so long ago, in our very own universe, a seemingly strange and unlikely event occurred: Microsoft not only didn't seem to mind when the guys at Rooster Teeth used content from *Halo* (developed by Bungie, owned by Microsoft) to create the wildly successful machinima *Red vs. Blue*, they let them continue to produce content using *Halo* and did not demand a license fee. On top of that, Microsoft even hired the production team to create *Red vs. Blue* videos to be used as advertisements (Thompson, 2005). In August 2007, Microsoft codified its machinima policy in its "Game Content Usage Rules" (Phan, 2007). Blizzard Entertainment (developer of *World of Warcraft*) followed suit within weeks by publishing its own guidelines for machinima (Phan, 2007). While some of the language differed, and other companies did not openly address machinima use, machinima creators were no longer operating completely in the dark (more like twilight).

The "End User License Agreement"

Generally, when you pay for software (including video games), you don't actually own it. Rather, you are granted a license to use it. The license is "permission" to use the copyrighted work, and such "permission" will come with restrictions on what you can (and can't) do with it. Such a license includes language that determines the scope of the license (i.e., the rights granted along with restrictions) and goes by the name "End User License Agreement," hereinafter referred to as "EULA." (Not only does it sound cooler, it does save a bit of typing.) Whether you are creating machinima or simply playing the game, as a "user" you are subject to the terms of the EULA.

One of the challenges a machinima artist is faced with is that there is not a standard industry practice regarding EULAs. The scope of the grant of rights can vary widely from one developer to another. For example, the Microsoft Game Content Usage Rules directly address machinima creation, which state, "Microsoft grants you a personal, non-exclusive, non-transferable license to use and display Game Content and to create derivative works based upon Game Content, strictly for noncommercial and personal use" (Xbox, 2010). However, the same agreement does not allow one to "create pornographic or obscene Items, or anything that contains vulgar, racist, hateful, or otherwise objectionable content," or to "sell or otherwise earn anything from your Items," which includes posting it "on a site that requires subscription or other fees" (Xbox, 2010). Similarly, Blizzard openly addressed machinima creation by allowing non-commercial use (Letter, 2010). Like Microsoft, the use cannot be sold and cannot be posted to a site that *requires* a fee to view content. However, Blizzard explicitly does not object to the posting to a site that accepts fees as long as the site provides a "'free' method to see their machinima content" (Letter, 2010). Blizzard also has a decency requirement, but utilizes the Entertainment Software Rating Board (ESRB) standard "T" rating (Letter, 2010), whereas Microsoft does not expressly rely on the ESRB standard.

Contrast Microsoft and Blizzard EULAs and acknowledgment of machinima to Turbine, Inc.'s, *Lord of the Rings Online* (lotro) EULA, which strictly prohibits any modification of or creation of derivative works "based on the

Game Client or any portion thereof" (*The Lord*, 2010). Even Electronic Arts (EA) does not address machinima, per se, in its EULA; it simply says the licensee "may not otherwise copy, display, distribute, perform, publish, modify, create works from, or use the Software or any component of it" (Electronic, n.d.).[4] However, it goes on to claim, "In exchange for use of the Software, and to the extent that your contributions through use of the Software give rise to any copyright interest, you hereby grant EA an exclusive, perpetual, irrevocable, fully transferable and sub-licensable worldwide right and license to use your contributions in any way and for any purpose in connection with the Software and related goods and services including the rights to reproduce, copy, adapt, modify, perform, display, publish, broadcast, transmit, or otherwise communicate to the public by any means whether now known or unknown and distribute your contributions without any further notice or compensation to you of any kind for the whole duration of protection granted to intellectual property rights by applicable laws and international conventions" (Electronic, n.d.).[5] Does this imply that machinima creation would be permitted as long as these latter conditions are met? Further examples suggest that EA does not vigorously enforce the former restrictions when viewed in the context of machinima creation for certain uses. For example, in 2004, EA encouraged fans to post their own *The Sims 2* movies by creating a website to display their work (Thompson, 2005, p. 5). In September 2010, USC's Interactive Media Division announced a student machinima contest sponsored by EA, using "Game Assets" from *The Sims 3* (Brinson, 2010). The contest rules give students narrow rights to use *Sims 3* content: "By providing any Contest Assets for entrant's use Sponsor is granting entrants a limited, non-exclusive, non-commercial license to use the Contest Assets solely in connection with, and as a part of, the Contest" (Brinson, 2010).

To further blur the lines for creators, Linden Lab's (creator of *Second Life* or "*SL*") machinima policy is more complex, in that actual ownership of content (and, therefore, permission to use) is not always exclusive to Linden Lab. For example, Linden Lab allows use of snapshots and captured machinima "that is displayed in-world" (i.e., in *SL*) (*Second Life*, 2010). Such content can be used "within or outside of *Second Life* in any current or future media." The policy further clarifies "Use" to mean "use, reproduce, distribute, modify, prepare derivative works of, display, and perform" (*Second Life*, 2010). While this is extremely broad, it does not include use of content "on another Resident's land," certain use of avatar's names or likenesses, music performed "in-world," or video content that originated outside of *SL*. All such uses require consent (*Second Life*, 2010).

Additional restrictions that the machinima creator must consider, which the EULA may or may not address, include use of music from the original game, and products featured in the game that are trademarked. Music for games is often not owned by the developer but licensed from a third party. Such a license agreement may prohibit the licensee (the game developer) from allowing any use of the music outside of the intended use during game play. Similarly, in games that incorporate trademarked products, the game developer would have a license agreement with the owner of the trademark to use that mark in the game, but may not allow the game developer to transfer that license to allow the machinima artist to use the mark. Microsoft directly addresses these issues in its Game Content Usage Rules with the following language:

• You can't necessarily use the soundtracks or audio effects from the original game. We often license those from third parties and don't have the rights to pass them on to you. We might mention on the community website for a particular game whether you have these rights, so you'd do well to check. And you might need permission from a third party, especially for games with licensed music. But we'll confirm right here that the music from *Halo 3* is available for your use in non-profit ventures thanks to an arrangement with O'Donnell/Salvatori, Inc., composers of this iconic theme.
• You can't infringe anyone's IP rights in your Item, even if the IP rights being infringed don't belong to Microsoft. Among other things that means you can't use any of Microsoft's trademarked logos or names except in the ways described in the pages linked from www.microsoft.com/trademarks [Xbox, 2010, p. 8].

Microsoft also points out that in games like *Flight Simulator* and *Forza Motorsport*, "Use of individual vehicles may require permission from their manufacturer" (Xbox, 2010, p. 8). For example, use of a Ford Mustang in a game would require a license from Ford to the game developer to use the trademark. That license would probably not include the game developer's right to allow other uses of that mark by a third party. You need to get your own license.

In Blizzard's "Letter to the Machinimators of the World," content they will allow to be used in machinima (subject to the aforementioned conditions) includes, "video images, footage, music, sounds, speech, or other assets from its copyrighted products, including '*World of Warcraft*'" (Letter, 2010, p. 10).

The Use of Outside Materials: Music

If the machinima creator adds outside music (i.e., music not from the original game, but from an existing outside source), permission is required from the rights holders. This includes non-commercial use. Yes, really. Just because the use may be non-commercial, you still need permission, as the exclusive rights mentioned above make no distinction between commercial and non-commercial use. And, for use of music in machinima, it requires two separate permissions: use of the underlying work (the "song"), and use of the sound recording of the song (the "master"), as they are two distinct copyrights. The first license is called a "synchronization license" (or "synch license," for short), because the use of the song will be synchronized to a moving image. The rights holder(s) for the underlying work is the music publisher. It must also be noted that some songs have multiple publishers, and permission is required from all of them. The second license is called the "master use license" and must be sought from whoever controls the master recording, typically a record label. There are no set fees for these licenses; they must be negotiated on an individual basis. Issues that are considered in determining a price for the license include how the song will be used (is it featured or background? is it a major studio feature film or a small independent production company with limited distribution?), how much of the song is used, which part of the song is used, and the current value of the song (a current hit by a major artist will cost a lot more than a relatively unknown work that hasn't seen any licensing action for a while). And there is no compulsory license for these uses, so the rights holder(s) can say no.

What About "Fair Use"?

Some uses of copyrighted materials without permission may be excused. The fair use doctrine allows for exceptions to the exclusive rights granted to the rights holder(s) (for our purposes, the right to duplicate, create derivative works, distribute and perform). But what conditions qualify for such an exception? The challenge for the machinima artist (or anyone relying on a fair use defense, for that matter) is that there are no clear-cut rules. The U.S. Supreme Court ruled that fair use "requires a case-by-case analysis rather than bright-line rules" (*Campbell*, 1994). Therefore, sometimes there is little certainty that a particular use would exempt the user from requiring permission. Furthermore, even if the user ultimately prevails with a fair use defense, the cost and time of a legal battle is beyond the means of most artists.

Awareness of the factors involved in determining fair use, along with a brief analysis in the context of machinima creation, may prove illustrative. Section 107 of the Copyright Act outlines the "Limitations on Exclusive Rights: Fair Use":

> Notwithstanding the provisions of sections 106 and 106A, the fair use of a copyrighted work, including such use by reproduction in copies or phonorecords or by any other means specified by that section, for purposes such as criticism, comment, news reporting, teaching (including multiple copies for classroom use), scholarship, or research, is not an infringement of copyright. In determining whether the use made of a work in any particular case is a fair use the factors to be considered shall include —
> (1) the purpose and character of the use, including whether such use is of a commercial nature or is for nonprofit educational purposes;

(2) the nature of the copyrighted work;

(3) the amount and substantiality of the portion used in relation to the copyrighted work as a whole; and

(4) the effect of the use upon the potential market for or value of the copyrighted work. The fact that a work is unpublished shall not itself bar a finding of fair use if such finding is made upon consideration of all the above factors [U.S. Code 17, 1976].[6]

These are called the "four fair use factors." One factor does not necessarily carry more weight than another. Rather, all four must be considered together, not in "isolation" (*Campbell*, 1994, p, 579). In applying the first factor to machinima, "the purpose and character of the use" (i.e., how the copyrighted material is used), if the use is non-commercial, there would be a greater likelihood of a finding of fair use. However, a commercial use does not necessarily bar a fair use defense, depending on the outcome of the analysis of the other three factors (*Campbell*, 1994, p, 579). If the use is sufficiently transformative, such use would support a finding of fair use. Transformative use can be defined as adding "something new, with a further purpose or different character, altering the first with new expression, meaning or message" (*Campbell*, 1994, p, 579). Similarly, if the use is a form of commentary, including parody, the greater the likelihood that the use would be considered "fair." These principles balance the conflict between the limited monopoly afforded to the rights holder on the one side, and the purpose of copyright protection (to benefit society by promoting the "Progress of Science and useful Arts"[7]) and free speech, on the other. Given the fact that the content in machinima comes directly from the original, protected game software, the look and feel of the resulting video would probably not rise to the level of transformation necessary to claim that the use is "sufficiently transformative." However, some machinima creators could claim that their work is a parody of the original. Could *Red vs. Blue* be considered "commentary" on the banal life of the characters and situations facing them in *Halo*?

The second factor considers the degree of protection afforded to the original work. Not all works are treated equally, as a higher degree of originality deserves greater protection. For example, facts are not protected (as they are not original), so a biography (which is based on facts) deserves less protection than a work of fiction. Game software is highly original and therefore qualifies for a high degree of protection, which will work against the machinima creator in establishing a fair use defense, unless the other factors lean in his or her favor.

The third factor is a quantitative and qualitative inquiry: how much material from the original is used, and how important is that material? If, for instance, only one character is used, but that character is the most important element in the game, it goes to the "heart" of the original work and would weigh against a fair use claim (*Harper*, 1985).[8] Regarding the quantitative inquiry, the more elements used from the original game (including characters, images, sounds, speech, story lines, etc.), the less one could rely on a fair use defense. Using *Red vs. Blue* as an example, it is clear that not only are the characters instrumental components of the original, almost everything else comes right out of the original work. Factor three would work against the creative guys at Rooster Teeth, if they had to rely on a fair use defense (fortunately, they did not have to).

The fourth factor considers the economic impact of the use to the rights holder and on the value of the original work. Has the owner lost sales because of the unauthorized use of their work? Is the use a "substitute" for the original? Has the value of the original been diminished by this use? If the answer is no, the fourth factor weighs in favor of the machinima artist. Clearly, the creation of machinima is not a substitute for the game itself. And, in the case of a viral success, the game developer reaps the benefit of exposure to a wider audience. "There are people out there who would never have heard about *Halo* without 'Red vs. Blue.' It's getting an audience outside the hardcore gaming crowd" (Thompson, 2005, p. 5). This would support the machinima artist's claim that the rights holder has not been economically harmed.

However, licensing income, particularly for commercial uses, could be a significant income stream for the rights holder. Here, the game developer has to make a choice between the possible income loss versus the free advertising, exposure to a wider audience, and the perceived gesture of good will toward artists and fans. Does this exposé crystallize whether machinima would qualify for fair use? Absolutely not. Most current uses could go either way, without a definitive answer as to what would qualify for fair use and what would be considered infringing. As mentioned in the early stage of this fair use discussion, there are no bright-line rules. (Thanks a lot for clearing that up...)

So, Now What?

With such uncertainty, the best thing the artist can do is some homework and due diligence. Completely read the EULA for the game from which the content will be used, and if applicable, the community website for the particular game (as Microsoft suggests). A few phone calls and/or e-mails to the licensing department of the rights holder may quickly clarify the answers, and grant permission for your intended use (or not). It is certainly a lot cheaper (and faster) than defending a lawsuit. Remember, even if you prevail in a lawsuit, you might not recover your legal fees and court costs (it is up to the court) (U.S. Code 17, 1976).[9]

Looking Forward: Establishing Best Practices for Machinima

Machinimators of the world, unite! One approach to help clarify machinima artists' ability to use copyrighted works for certain uses would be to establish "best practice" guidelines for the genre. While it is not simply their choice to determine what is fair use (that is left for the courts), it would serve as a valuable educational tool, as well as a statement from the community as to what they consider "reasonable" while they pursue their art. It could also help unify the industry in its support of the genre.

As a parallel example, in 2005, a group of documentary filmmakers established guidelines for practitioners of the genre by publishing "Documentary Filmmakers' Statement of Best Practices in Fair Use" (Documentary, 2011). The statement serves to educate filmmakers as well as content rights holders why certain uses should be permitted under the law. Documentary film may deserve a broader application of fair use than some other forms of media (such as machinima) because of the inherent nature of the genre being "commentary" (similar to "critics who work in print media and by news broadcasters," as the statement suggests) (Documentary, 2005). However, using this example as a model may serve the machinima community and game developers and bring them to the table to generate a creative environment that benefits everyone, from artists to game developers and consumers.

Some best practices examples within the machinima community have already emerged. Shannon Bohle (n.d.), an educator, archivist and MLIS librarian (specializing in science), uses *SL* to create machinima for educational purposes, such as online tutorials. She has compiled "Machinima Best Practices" guidelines "for the creation, distribution, and long term storage of machinima video" (Bohle, n.d.). In addition to the *SL* terms of service, when using existing elements in *SL*, Bohle (2010) recommends that the machinima creator:

1. Always request permission of a sim owner before filming in their sim;
2. Always respect copyright by using material that are either in the public domain, fall under a Creative Commons license, are materials you create yourself, or that you have written permission to use;
3. Always credit people who:
   • Own the sim
   • Create content appearing in the video
   • Appear in the video as avatars
4. Play music or created audio heard in the video.

As a further example of the community educating the community, a *Second Life* Bar Association (*SLBA*) has been formed that guides *SL* members through the *SL* "legal landscape" (About, n.d.). The legal issues that arise in a virtual community pose some challenging questions that may have no real-world legal precedent. How do you enforce a contract in a virtual world? What about jurisdiction? Is virtual property treated like real property? The *SLBA* states:

1. to educate the public and profession concerning legal issues arising from the *Second Life* virtual world;

2. to study the legal, business, and technical implications of the 3-D Internet, including virtual worlds, and the *Second Life* virtual world in particular;
3. to offer our members opportunities to meet and discuss the association's interests with professionals from around the world; and
4. to promote justice, professional excellence, and the rule of law in *Second Life* [*SL* Bar Association, 2011].

While some of these examples are exclusive to certain communities or genres, they do demonstrate that an organized forum for dedicated users can develop and promote practices that advance the art form and the artist's freedom, while respecting the rights of the original copyright holder(s). Perhaps more contests, festivals and conferences will expand to incorporate panels, discussions, demonstrations and seminars on these topics to promote machinima and support education of the medium, which would link artists globally and encourage them to communicate, collaborate and share their work. One such effort is MMIF (MaMachinima International Festival), which "is an event for the celebration, promotion and education of machinima arts creation" and aims to "create a community of machinimatographers around the world" (MaMachinima, n.d.).

Consortiums could be formed that offer a bridge between machinima artists and game developers. This potentially creates a synergistic/collaborative relationship whereby artists and developers help each other. The result is mutually beneficial, whereby more creativity is supported, the artist does not have to be as concerned with intellectual property issues (some would most likely still exist), and greater awareness and exposure is generated for both the games and the machinima works.

Ultimately, the goal is to have broad and clear guidelines for the creation of machinima that are supported by the industry and artists alike. Whether this is achieved through a unified licensing scheme adopted by the industry (which, as already shown, may be difficult to achieve), a strong unified voice representing the global community of machinima artists, or a combination of these approaches, the world of machinima would be positively served if the artist(s) were allowed to more freely create, without the underlying fear of infringing.

Notes

1. U.S. Code 17 (1976), § 102(a). Subject matter of copyright.
2. U.S. Code 17 (1976), § 106(1), (2), (3), (4). Exclusive rights in copyrighted works: to reproduce the copyrighted work in copies or phonorecords; to prepare derivative works based on the copyrighted work, to distribute copies or phonorecords of the copyrighted work to the public by sale or other transfer of ownership, or by rental, lease, or lending, and in the case of literary, musical, dramatic, and choreographic works, pantomimes, and motion pictures and other audiovisual works, to perform the copyrighted work publicly.
3. U.S. Code 17 (1976), § 101. Definitions.

4. Electronic Arts Software End User License Agreement, Section 1, subsection C. (n.d.).
5. Section 1, subsection E.
6. U.S. Code 17 (1976), § 107. Limitations on exclusive rights: Fair use.
7. U.S. Constitution, art. 1, sec. 8, cl. 8.
8. Harper & Row, Publishers, Inc. v. Nation Enterprises, 471 U.S. 539, 564-565 (1985). The Nation published parts of Gerald Ford's memoir without permission (and before it was published), and was sued by Harper & Row, the publisher. The defense argued that the amount used was insignificant in relation to the work as a whole, but the publisher argued that the portion used went to the "heart" of the work (i.e., why Ford pardoned Richard Nixon). Harper & Row prevailed.
9. U.S. Code 17 (1976), § 505. Remedies for infringement: Costs and attorney's fees.

References

About the *SL* Bar Association/*SL* Bar Association. (n.d.). Accessed February 10, 2011, from http://www.slba.info/about.html?current=two

Bohle, Shannon. (n.d.). *Machinima Best Practices: Preserving Virtual Worlds through Video Documentation.* Accessed February 10, 2011, from http://www.learningtimes.net/innovation/bohle

Bohle, Shannon. (2010). *Machinima/Archivopedia.com.* Accessed February 10, 2011, from http://archivopedia.com/wiki/index.php?title=Machinima — machinima_best_practices:_preserving_virtual_worlds_through_video

Brinson, Peter. (September 17, 2010). *The Sims 3 Toyota Prius Machinima Contest by Electronic Arts.* Accessed February 10, 2011 from http://interactive.usc.edu/blog/?p=6000 (also see link to *Sims 3 Machinima Contest Rules,* Electronic Arts, Inc.

Campbell v. Acuff-Rose Music, Inc., 510 U.S. 569, 590 (1994).

Documentary Filmmakers' Statement of Best Practices in Fair Use. (November 18, 2005). Center for Social Media. Accessed February 10, 2011, from http://www.centerforsocialmedia.org/sites/default/files/fair_use_final.pdf

Documentary Filmmakers' Statement of Best Practices in Fair Use. (2011). American University Center for Social Media. Accessed February 10, 2011, from http://www.centerforsocialmedia.org/fair-use/best-practices/documentary/documentary-filmmakers-statement-best-practices-fair-use

Electronic Arts Software End User License Agreement, Section 1, subsection C, E (n.d.). Accessed February 10, 2010, from http://tos.ea.com/legalapp/eula/US/en/PC/

Harper & Row, Publishers, Inc. v. Nation Enterprises, 471 U.S. 539, 564–565 (1985).

Letter to the Machinimators of the world. (2010). Accessed November 7, 2010, from http://www.worldofwarcraft.com/community/machinima/letter.html

MaMachinima International Festival/MMIF.org. (n.d.). Accessed February 10, 2011, from http://about.mmif.org/

Merges, Robert P., Peter S. Menell & Mark A. Lemley. (2006). *Intellectual Property in the New Technological Age.* New York: Aspen Publishers.

Phan, Monty. (August 28, 2007). Machinima Licenses Spell Out New Rules For Creators. *Wired.* Accessed February 10, 2011, from http://www.wired.com/culture/art/news/2007/09/machinimalicenses

SL Bar Association. (2011). Accessed February 10, 2011, from http://slbarassn.ning.com/

Second Life "Terms Of Service," Section 7.7. (October 6, 2010). Accessed February 10, 2010, from http://secondlife.com/corporate/tos.php), which links to Linden Lab Official Snapshot and Machinima Policy.

The Lord of the Rings Online(tm) End User License Agreement. (2010, June 28). Section 1, subsection c and d. Accessed February 10, 2010, from http://www.lotro.com/support/policies/218-eula

Thompson, Clive. (2005, August 7). The Xbox Auteurs. *N. Y. Times Magazine.* Accessed February 10, 2011, from http://www.nytimes.com/2005/08/07/magazine/07MACHINI.html?_r=1

U.S. Code 17 (1976), § 101; 102(a); 106(1), (2), (3), (4); 107; 505.

xbox Game Content Usage Rules. (2010). Accessed February 10, 2011, from http://www.xbox.com/en-us/community/developer/rules

(Authors Johnson and Pettit: One might say, loosely, that machinima is an art that began by a group of computer hackers, who capitalized on their skills to tap into game engines to create films on game play. That is a rough interpretation, but it drives home the point that it is becoming more difficult than previously was the case to protect content in such a fluid environment. What is possible is not always legal. The irony of the situation is that machinima often relies on in-game content for its creation. That too is changing through programs like Moviestorm. Machinima makers collaborate on projects within *Second Life* and at times other virtual worlds, and the result is productions that bring together artists transnationally beyond physical restrictions. The legal restrictions at times, however, become contentious, and must be attended to by the machinimatographer.)

11

Expression Through Machinima: The Virtual Classroom

BRYAN CARTER

The authors asked Dr. Bryan Carter to share his experience with teaching machinima in the classroom within Second Life. He geared his attention to college students who were fairly inexperienced on many levels with virtual media, and especially with the concept of machinima as a creative and learning tool. Although this essay is directed at educators, there are some valuable lessons for all beginning to learn machinima, or those seeking ways to train newcomers to virtual worlds and virtual filmmaking. Dr. Carter is an associate professor of literature in the Department of English and Philosophy at the University of Central Missouri, Warrensburg. He is particularly well known in Second Life for his creation of Virtual Harlem, which replicates the cultural experiences in art, music and literature during the Harlem Renaissance era. It is the hope of the authors that this essay inspires machinimatographers to mentor up-and-coming filmmakers on the creativity afforded through virtual worlds.

Introduction

Machinima is not an entirely new form of artistic expression. Introduced in the early 1980s through a variety of video games, multimedia creators used this form as a cost-cutting alternative to high-cost 3-D rendering platforms. There is no doubt, with the graphic evolution of video game engines and online virtual worlds that machinima has solidified itself as an expressive way to explore filmmaking within virtual environments.

One area where machinima is just beginning to make inroads is in education. Academics have explored performance studies in a variety of disciplines since the early 1970s. Although hotly debated as an actual "field," the idea of "performativity" as explored by Judith Butler suggests that "the reiterative power of discourse to produce the phenomena that it regulates and constrains" allows "actors" to understand the text as reality, performing it countless times

197

through their actions, thus increasing understanding of the text through their performance (Butler quoted in *Identity: A reader,* 2000). Machinima helps address some of the criticisms in Butler's concept of performativity in that the space where the machinima is filmed adds to the overall understanding of the piece, along with how other actors are involved in the overall shot. Furthermore, the interpretation of those viewing the machinima, whether live or recorded, is in part dictated by their overall experience, where hardware, networking and user experience all come into play as integral parts of understanding the text/machinima itself.

This essay adds to the growing body of knowledge of how machinima is being used in the humanities. When incorporated properly in a Digital Culture course, machinima has the potential to not only change the way students understand a text through performance but it also helps to create memorable experiences in a class, thus increasing retention. The concepts in our text include topics such as safety, privacy and identity, and it is through machinima that students are offered a creative outlet to express their understanding of these ideas. What are good examples of how machinima can be used in a Digital Culture course being taught in *Second Life*? In what ways does a period-based project like Virtual Harlem, or any themed sim, enhance the "performativity" of a text? Finally, what is the typical workflow of students participating in a course designed to be taught in *Second Life* that focuses on Digital Culture and meaningfully relevant concepts?

Course Design and Objectives

Those who know of machinima often consider it a niche genre, relegated to shorts found on YouTube that focus on satirical subject matter, some training or even music videos. Exploring how machinima can help students demonstrate their understanding of a text or concept is a rather recent use of the technology. In Fall 2010, I designed and taught a course on Digital Culture where the primary medium of communication and expression was *Second Life*. The objectives of the course were described as follows:

> During this term, we will learn, study and use a tool that has changed the landscape of communication, collaboration, journalism and social networking. We will also put to use our newfound skills, reaching out to students in Sweden, France and universities in the US, to discuss "modalities of identity and presence" along with other topics identified by popular and mediated culture. Through the Machinima you create you will exemplify your understanding of complex ideas, and express them in the most creative way possible using this medium.

This rather broad set of objectives was intentional so that students would be encouraged to explore the limits of their learning and use of machinima while focusing that creativity to express concepts found and discussed in our textbook *Born Digital: Understanding the First Generation of Digital Natives*, by John Palfrey and Urs Gasser (2008).

There were 25 students enrolled in the course, and a majority of them only had a basic understanding of virtual worlds, a handful considered themselves "gamers" and some had very little computing experience beyond basic web surfing, watching YouTube videos and checking e-mail. I saw the diversity of this audience as a plus, however, because the varying skill sets of the students encouraged them to assist one another, as small groups consisted mostly of students with a variety of skills. Out of the 25 students in class, only three had heard of *Second Life*, and only one of them had an account (she was a student previously enrolled in a composition class that I taught in *Second Life* the previous semester). The course met one day a week, and because of the way our fall semester began, I did not see them until the second week of classes. They were, however, e-mailed instructions on how to create a personal blog using Blogger, how to create their *Second Life* account and download the client to their personal computers to test and ensure it worked on their machine (those without personal computers were able to use those in a lab/classroom reserved for the semester where *Second Life* is installed and maintained). They were also instructed to place their real name and avatar name on a Google document to which they all were given access and editing privileges. These step-by-step instructions were provided both via e-mail and in the course syllabus and in the welcome e-mail sent to the students. Finally, the students were asked to respond to a VoiceThread with their thoughts on initial reactions to the course based on the syllabus, *Second Life*, blog creation and the use of machinima and voicethreads. (VoiceThread is an audio/video discussion board application where students can respond to prompts made by the instructor using their voices or video.)

The first official class meeting was chalked with excitement, anticipation and in some cases a bit of skepticism. This was all expected. Course objectives were explained, and after some questions on grading and other assignments, we all logged into *Second Life*. Of course, the organized chaos centered around avatar modification, basic navigation, communication, landmarking, friending, and teleporting. When all of the students were finally in our virtual classroom on Virtual Harlem (one of the two islands I own in *Second Life*), we were able to ensure everyone exchanged friendship, landmarked the location (the Dark Tower), and knew the basics of communicating using text (both public and private IM) and voice. Students were told that if they planned to use *Second Life* at home for our class, they must have voice communication capability beyond a built-in microphone on a laptop computer; otherwise, they must either purchase an external mic or come to the library for class. This choice of "physicality" for class seemed to intrigue some members of the class.

The class meetings last an hour and 50 minutes, and after the first initial exposure/orientation to *Second Life*, we jumped directly into our course content and activities. Readings were assigned from our text, and the flow of class included discussing the readings, exploring locations in *Second Life* related to those readings, and encouraging students to consider how the readings could be expressed through short machinima created in *Second Life*. These mini-brainstorming sessions were crucial because they helped move students toward a common mode of thought regarding both machinima and *Second Life*. Instead of *Second Life* being seen as a "game" or 3-D social network, students began to consider its usefulness as a creative mode of expression where their understanding of the text could be realized.

Mechanics of Machinima Creation

Because of cost, a desire to maintain an initial level of consistency, and ease of use, a standard set of tools was introduced to students in order to create their group machinima. Those who were a bit more advanced or who were familiar and comfortable using more advanced tools were encouraged to do so and to show their group members how to use them. However, because some of those tools come at some expense, only free or basic versions of all software used this term were installed on the lab computers and their use taught in class. Machinima involves screen capture, individual and system audio recording and video editing the screen and audio recordings. For screen capture, we used Fraps (which limits captures to four minutes for the free version) and Screenr (with a five-minute limit). The basic difference between the two is that Fraps is a stand-alone application and only runs on Windows-based machines. Screenr is a web-based application that is cross-platform (a Twitter account is necessary in order to export screen captures to other formats). Students were given other options to use such as Jing, Screenflow, iShowU, and Quicktime X, but again, for the sake of consistency, we focused on Fraps and Screenr.

Clean audio is an important part of good machinima, and students were required to use external microphones in class and as they recorded their group machinima projects. This, however, proved to be more of a challenge than initially expected. Those who purchased their own mics bought microphones or headsets of varying quality, and as a result, machinima audio was of the same varying quality. Some was very rich and full sounding, while others were very thin and metallic, like talking in a cave or tunnel. One other unexpected issue with audio was a consistent capture of system audio. This is a crucial part of machinima if "live" audio is to be used as part of the screen capture. System audio allows one to record others who are speaking in the same area, ambient sounds and system music. Students who ran into this difficulty, either in Fraps or Screenr, worked around the problem by capturing avatar movements and then later recording and adding their audio track during the video editing process. In some cases, this was a much better solution as it brought back more consistent audio quality to the final output.

After initial screen captures were complete and audio was recorded, students were introduced to an online non-linear video editing program called JayCut. This Web-based non-linear video editing program offered the most useful, elegant cross-platform solution for students to learn. It is also free, which was a plus. After students captured their video, which contained good audio, or they recorded their audio, they then were shown how to import their content into JayCut. This program allows for one video track and up to four additional audio tracks. According to the JayCut site, the advantages of using an online video editor include the following:

• No need for downloads or installs
• Instant access via any web browser
• No specific hardware requirements
• Access uploaded content anywhere, anytime
• Works on all computers and browsers
• Use content on the web in movies, e.g., YouTube videos
• Collaborative editing, work together with other users from around the world.

Given these tools, students were now ready to begin their group machinima projects. They were required to create at least one individual practice machinima to acclimate themselves to the screen capture, audio recording and video editing process, and one group machinima practice. We "peer critiqued" these projects in *Second Life* using HTML on a prim after these videos were uploaded to YouTube, offering suggestions for improved audio and video as well as camera movements.

Group Machinima Projects

The group machinima projects were a central part of the course requirements in the class. Students signed up for a collaborative group on Google Docs. Each group consisted of three to four members of the class. Requirements for this assignments were as follows:

This project requires that you work with a small group of your classmates (of your choosing) that consists of at least two other members of our class. (If you work with students from one of our partner institutions you will earn extra credit. This includes students from France, Sweden, or a university in the States). Your project must focus on a topic/theme of your group's choosing yet found in our course textbook. Suggested topics include but are not limited to:

Identity within a virtual environment; Extending your presence; Acceptance as it relates to your digital identity; Material culture as it relates to your digital identity; Defining friendship in a virtual environment; Safety, virtual and real life.

Once recorded and edited, this assignment should be posted on a video sharing site like YouTube, Blip TV or Google Video (there are several available from which you can choose), and it should be at least 3–5 minutes long. It should include meaningful dialogue with your group members or at least meaningful participation by all members. Your topic should be posted on your personal blogs, and your script should be posted on Google Docs, accessible by your group members and me (I will show you how to do this if you are not familiar with Google Docs). The link to your small group project should be posted on our small group sign-up Google document in the appropriate area and embedded on your personal blog.

These were quite hefty requirements for students just learning *Second Life*, some with little or no experience with machinima, video editing or advanced computing. In order to make efficient use of our time in class as well as to provide ample time in class to film, edit and receive instruction and feedback from me on the use of these tools, our class incorporated a rather unique workflow throughout the semester.

Our class made rather extensive use of the course textbook. Weekly readings were assigned and students were required to post VoiceThread responses to prompts that I gave them. Their responses had to be either audio or video so that students could become more comfortable using their voices to express their ideas related to digital culture with support from the text. All of our class sessions after the second week of school were held in *Second Life*. By this time, students were minimally comfortable with voice communication in *Second Life* and we experienced very little if any audio issues throughout the term.

During our class sessions, we initially met on Virtual Harlem, one of the islands I own in *Second Life*. Our classroom there is rather traditional with two rows of seats, two screens at the front of the room capable of presenting images (slideshow presentations), and web pages (for rich web media on a prim). At the beginning of class, I gave announcements and answered any questions that students asked about the reading, some technical aspect of one of the tools we used, or some experience they had in *Second Life*. I always encouraged a light and conversational atmosphere in class so that students would liken their *Second Life* experience with that which goes on in a more traditional classroom, *on steroids*. The enhanced aspect of *Second Life* allowed very unique experiences in just the first part of our class, even before we worked on machinima projects. Several times, when students shared some interesting place they visited in *Second Life*, I asked them to share the landmark in a teleporter I had set up in the classroom, and we all simply went there, with the student serving as a field trip leader so to speak. These impromptu excursions served to not only broaden the students' view of *Second Life* but also encouraged students to be one of those leading the trip for the next class.

The next part of class was spent briefly discussing the reading assignment. We began listening to one or more VoiceThreads and commenting on the ideas that the student(s) expressed and how that related to the reading. Students offered feedback and ideas of their own based on what they saw or heard from the VoiceThreads played in class. These were all played on the screen in our classroom in *Second Life*. This part of class was also used to bring in guest speakers who were experts in machinima and who answered student questions while showing examples of their work.

The lion's share of class was spent with student groups working on their machinima projects. Students dispersed to the various locations in *Second Life* where their video shots were taking place for that class period. (I say that period because their videos were shot over a period of several class periods at a variety of locations.) As students were shooting, planning video shots or practicing their machinima, I traveled to each group location and observed, answered questions, and/or offered suggestions. Usually, groups had at least an hour or more during each class to shoot their video footage. Students were instructed to shoot several shots/angles of the same dialogue or scene so that they could then mix/edit that raw footage into their final video. This process continued for the next eight class periods (approximately two months). Students were also encouraged to meet outside of class in *Second Life* to work on their projects, shooting video, practicing dialogue, scouting video shots or filming technique and camera movements.

After video footage was captured and audio was recorded, students were taught how to use the online video editing program JayCut. This program is great because students can log on at the same time and chat while editing their video. Some used Skype to communicate instead, and others used traditional instant messaging. One group chose to meet in a small media preview room in the library to edit their video as a group, face to face. After meeting initially in *Second Life*, students would then move to JayCut to edit their video footage. During these meetings/editing sessions held during class, again, I would drop in and offer suggestions, comment, and answer questions using whatever communication method the group was using. This schedule was maintained for four class periods, using a majority of the class for this editing process. The peer teaching and learning that took place during these sessions was phenomenal. At the end of the term, students expressed an overall increase in their technical skills as well as an acquisition of skills that they felt they would use outside our class as they moved into their careers.

Further Discussion and Conclusion

I must say that, overall, the machinima projects in this class were a success. Not only did students demonstrate creative ways to express their understanding of concepts found in the reading assignments and discussions related to digital culture, but they also learned new skills. However, the semester was not without some problems. The most significant problems occurred when there were issues with *Second Life*. Unexpected updates, voice communication issues or lag related mostly to bandwidth at our university or with a group member's Internet service provider were sometimes a challenge. Bandwidth also proved to be a problem at times when students were editing their videos on JayCut. One student would make a change but it would not appear for a few moments, causing another student to make a different change, and when the original change appeared, it caused some confusion. Audio consistency was also a challenge. Students with inferior mics or headsets were not able to clean their audio well enough to match that of those with better audio input devices. The difference was quite evident in some cases. Finally, and most surprising to me, some students had a difficult time being creative in their machinima projects. Initially, there were a few groups that designed "presentation-like" machinima, those where students were basically standing in a park or other location taking turn reading dialogue. It took several class periods, countless examples and quite a bit of prodding to encourage more natural dialogue, creative camera shots, scene changes and overall creativity before students understood what I was looking for. As much as we would like to believe that students of this generation exude creativity and are technologically adept, I found this to not always be the case in this class with this group of students.

Machinima is one of the most creative ways in which students can express their understanding of complex ideas while learning new skills, all within an environment that encourages interactivity and engagement. The activities, requirements, organization and flow of our Digital Culture course is only one example of how Machinima can be effectively used in a course like this. Success hinges on not only good organization but also consistent technology and equipment. Most importantly, faculty teaching a class like this must be comfortable and familiar with all aspects of the programs being used. Any hesitancy or confusion on the part of the instructor will transfer to the students, which, in my opinion, will create a tense learning environment. If, however, the faculty member is knowledgeable in not only the tools but teaching pedagogy and methodology in a virtual environment, the environment in the class will be lively, communicative and interactive.

(Authors Johnson and Pettit: Truly machinima has assumed an important presence in society when it finds itself within the educational sector and becomes a means of expression of what students have learned about themselves as well as those before them. Machinima appears to be an accessible tool and creative force of articulation for those in humanities, those who would not otherwise have had an opportunity to connect moving images to the great ideas and concepts of the past and the hopes of the future. Machinima is a medium that helps to engage a new generation of learners, no matter their age; for it is the willingness to learn, reflect, and experiment that propels virtual filmmaking. Machinima is an active process, evolving, and involving those who care to partake in its reflection of virtual life, the extension of what is and what will be. Machinima is not the only way, but it is becoming a credible source of entertainment, learning, journalistic reports and documentary, life experiences, and so forth. And it is lots of fun for students, instructors, and the professional machinimatographers who share their time and talent in the classrooms with the intent of forwarding its art and practice.)

Reference

Machinima Roundtable Two. (2010). *Terminology, Technology, and Practice* (Sessions 3 & 4, July 15 & 16). Lowe Runo Productions, LLC, *Second Life.*

Conclusion to Part One:
There Is No Road

We need the writing, and the story, and we need to get it out there, just sort of have the faith that it'll attract an audience. It doesn't always happen. Go look at Broadway, or movies, or whatever, there's a lot of failures of good things. Even if it's good, and it's consistent, you put it out there for a long time, it's still a roll of the dice — CodeWarrior Carling [Roundtable Two, 2010].

It might seem cliché, but everyone does have a story to tell. Saying that, however, machinima will challenge the budding media makers, depending on how complex the story. At some point, if they stick with it, they will be able to tell their story through machinima. And yes, there'll be an audience there to see it. That's even more important. They'll leave a little bit of a legacy behind. Machinima is far from a static medium, and its producers will be faced with ongoing challenges as technology advances. The future of machinima is summed up in *Back to the Future*. Near the end, Dr. Emmett Brown said, "Where we're going, we don't need roads." The same thing here. The sky's the limit.

One should anticipate even more realistic avatars — both animal and mineral, and female and male, and so forth — than the present technology allows. The cityscapes and landscapes will likewise increase in authenticity. The authors hope that the creators of these virtual people and places will lean toward machinimators as the archivists and that they take advantage of such skills. Of all these wonderful changes that are coming up, it will show how far machinima has evolved and help its viewers and makers appreciate its historical value (while we also laugh at a lot of the old machinima). There may be remakes, which would be funny, of classic machinima. Machinima is part of the larger move toward virtual filmmaking. Whether it finds itself one day absorbed into mainstream television or film production, machinima is a cost-efficient means to creating programming. It is not dependent on any particular virtual world or platform; those environments that allow for flexibility in set design and creativity will be those that attract serious machinimatographers and virtual filmmakers. Archiving game play and virtual experiences are relevant uses of machinima. But it offers much more for the digital and virtual storyteller and artist.

The Heart and Humor
of Machinima Storytelling

The authors asked machinimatographers and those interested to gather for a final screening of favorite and meaningful productions in *Second Life*. The nominated machinima are not necessarily the best in technical achievement, but they illustrate the power of communicating through machinima — the essentiality of great storytelling. Of course, those selected represent only a handful of the machinima available today, and some of these examples date back several years and represent platforms in and outside of *Second Life*. The screening sessions were conducted Thursday and Friday, July 22–23, 2010, within *Second Life* at the offices of Lowe Runo Productions, LLC. The moderators, Phylis Johnson and Donald Pettit, facilitated the screening and discussion. Attendees included Asil Ares, Dimitrio Lewis, Knowclue Kidd, Mellisano Brandi, MinDBlinD Setsuko, Pamala Clift, Pooky Amsterdam, Rhiannon Chatnoir, Rosalynn Weatherwax, and Rosco Teardrop.

It was an opportunity for the machinima community to discuss their favorite machinima, particularly those that trigger an emotional response — whether happy, funny, sad, or angry, but those that evoke strong emotions within them.

Nominated Machinima

A Woman's Trial by Chantal Harvey
http://www.youtube.com/watch?v=V3l8eYPUZzo
Faith, Hope and Charity by Wingmen Productions
http://www.flightsimmachinima.com/faith-hope-and-charity-by-wingmen-productions
Fall by Lainy Voom,
http://www.youtube.com/user/firstAMF2009#p/search/4/BUCSQs9hIHc
Life on Life by The Life Factory
http://www.blip.tv/file/1047096/
mAdvertising, A take on Mad Men by PookyMedia,
http://www.youtube.com/watch?v=KPzIIpizTXo
Moonlit Senata by Dimitrio Lewis
http://www.youtube.com/watch?v=vAuSAzXMDpM
My Spirit's Only Home, by Anna Pera,
http://www.youtube.com/watch?v=nIiqywDaJmk
Naumakia by Ars Navalis,
http://www.youtube.com/watch?v=ocYbrD181e4
Out in the Cold, by Legs Machinima,
http://www.youtube.com/watch?v=qIDBe2UyHS0

Requiem by Serpentblade and XPC — *2002*,
http://www.youtube.com/watch?v=YWULYfP3sVc
The Kiss by Tikaf Viper
http://slmachinimaarts.ning.com/video/the-kiss
The Snow Witch (*The Sims 2*) by britannicadreams
http://www.youtube.com/watch?v=uX5C2MrpBbo

A Call to Women Machinimatographers

My Spirit's Only Home by Anna Pera served as a moving piece for all who attended, although several years old. It won second place in the 2009 Machinima Artist Guild Awards. It stimulated a discussion on the significant role of women in machinima. Donald Pettit explained,

> This is the first machinima to make me cry. I have other ones I like, but this is the first one that got me. It was a very good job. This is an oldie by today's standards. What makes that an all-time favorite, at least for me? What would you think makes that special? Why does that make me cry, because I don't cry very much. I guess the common thread on all of the machinima that we've watched is the story. That was an old machinima and it's kind of basic. So they had to rely mostly on camera angles and editing. But still, in me, when I first saw it, it evoked an emotion. We still always come back to the story. That's what gets the emotions going, and how we portray that story, and the lengths we take to get it to work. Well, I'll tell you, it's definitely the hardest to — whether you're trying to come up with something romantic, or action or whatever, coming up with a good story that people will buy into by watching it and getting emotionally involved, that is a tremendous thing that we can do. I think that the people here that I'm talking to today — a lot of you have accomplished that in your machinima. I think I'm very proud to be associated with you. I think that's what sets you apart. You're starting to scrape on the pro level when you're getting at someone's heartstrings.

Rosco Teardrop noted the number of women involved in *Second Life* machinima, with Moo Money adding, "In *Second Life*, there are a lot of female machinimators — outside of *Second Life*, it's mostly men. The machinima.com crowd is like 13-year-old *Halo* first-person shooter kiddies. The *World of Warcraft* community is mostly men. There are very few women outside of *Second Life*, with exceptions like Legs, Demachic and Selserene, that make machinima. Most of the games that they make machinima with are catered to men."

Rosco Teardrop concluded, saying, "There are a few famous names of women who make machinima. So there seems to be a place for them in machinima, but I say bring on more into making films in machinima as well as in the real business of making films."

The very fact that many women have become machinimatographers makes machinima an interesting medium to watch. Machinima has become part of the online and virtual life of many artists and storytellers and has opened up the world of filmmaking to people with absolutely no prior media experiences as well as provided the means for professional filmmakers to afford experimenting within their craft. Virtual filmmaking can be a way to create features and programs at a fraction of the cost of the traditional process.

Uncharted Virtual Future

More than that, machinima, at its best, is an expression of a growing virtual culture of prosumers who understand media as central to their life. Machinima prosumers are consumers/viewers of visual artifacts and choose to participate in content creation as well. There is a parallel universe to contend with today; it is the virtual life where educators, artists, journalists, storytellers and businesspeople come together to experience interactivity, internationally. It is an uncharted world that documents virtual environments simply through machinima, and machinima shares in the larger media convergence that brings artists, storytellers and content creators together into the same forum.

Machinima requires the same basic skills to create any visual media work — beginning with vision and writing and shaped through design considerations (setting, lighting and audio) and arrangement and editing of elements. But without an audience with which to connect, the machinima lacks its ability to evolve to the next level. Machinima is a medium, and as such, it is intended to create a bridge that draws the producer and viewer together to explore a concept, idea or story. As a community, machinimatographers are increasingly sharing ideas on how to ensure the acceptance and professionalism of machinima. But there is nothing wrong with merely producing virtual film for the fun of it. So go play! On behalf of the authors, Pettit offers these final words of encouragement to beginning machinimatographers:

> I got into machinima at the very beginning as a lark. I saw a Torley Linden tutorial on machinima, and I thought "that's cool." All my life I had the desire. I started out with still photography. That's my background, and I did that for many years enough to be considered a professional. I taught photography throughout the state of Florida as the chief instructor in it. But I always wanted to get into motion photography. But such is life, because we have our 8–5 workdays, and families, and all that, one doesn't really get to do often what you'd like to try to do. Machinima offered me a way to get into that and try it out without taking too much of my personal time. That being said, now it has taken a lot more of my time. So I would encourage people — in the beginning — to give machinima a try, just to see if that's something that they like to do. And it brings the skills of video editing and audio editing, and all these other things into play.

They can learn these valuable skills that they can take into real life someday, if they so desire. So it actually has value. See if it intrigues them. And they may find that they have something that's a creative outlet in their life. You don't ever want to do any of this stuff for money. You do it for your personal enjoyment, and your personal fulfillment. If they really find that — having gone through this book — machinima is a way to find personal fulfillment in doing something that they love, well then we've accomplished our goal.

Reference

Machinima Roundtable Two. (2010). *Terminology, Technology, and Practice* (Sessions 3 & 4, July 15 & 16). Lowe Runo Productions, LLC, *Second Life.*

Curtain Call

Phaylen Fairchild

The Soul of Technology Is Human Expression

This is the story about a girl, Phaylen Fairchild, who grew up to be an avatar, and lived happily ever after. She never lost her sense of adventure and wonder, and came to enjoy living life in the real and virtual, until she thought one day, I can bring these worlds together. That remains her vision, and she continues to project her imagination onto others who also seek new paths toward telling stories. She arrived for her interview with a beautifully fresh princess face, sparkles lighting up her emerald eyes, and her body shapely in the form of a teapot. Her beautiful blonde hair adorned with an intriguingly cute teapot top, which was curious no doubt to the occasional onlooker who half anticipated a gentle to rowdy whistle to escape from her head at any moment, being that her personality was truly animated and full of life and energy, even for an avatar.

When one sees Phaylen Fairchild on-screen or has a moment to chat with the up-and-coming filmmaker of virtual worlds in the here, now and soon to be, they are charmed by her personality and natural comedic sense of timing. She is a down-to-earth storyteller with a knack for developing strong characters, and some of her work has already been discussed in this book. Filmmaking has always been a way of life for Phaylen Fairchild; only now she creates in the virtual aspect of it. She wrote her first novel at 16, her first screenplay at 18, and by 19 she had an agent. By 20, she won her first award. Being around movie directors is not new to her; what is unique is that she is the movie director— and producer, talent, sound person, and of course writer, as well as whatever else it takes to make her virtual movie or feature.

The authors began this journey with seasoned filmmaker Chantal Harvey and conclude the main thrust of this book with a woman dressed as a beautiful teapot with lovely human appendages. This relatively young woman has helped to launch what one might consider the new Hollywood of virtual worlds. And what might one call this new twist in the art and practice of machinima bringing together women online to produce filmmaking into an inspiring virtual community (with and without its tie to the once foundational

211

gaming community)? Perhaps Mollywood. That is in jest, a quick descriptor, not of Fairchild's words, but the term does speak to the 21st-century evolution of machinima to virtual worlds, and to the emergence of strong women film-makers who use machinima as their means to advance the larger practice of virtual filmmaking.

Fairchild is mentor to many women who consider entrance into filmmak-ing, and somehow the accessibility of online makes it possible for many of them to learn and to eventually participate. She speaks to the necessity of community building, but the truth is that it is difficult to maintain such efforts when the machinimist is often the producer, editor and talent — and in the case of Fairchild also the writer. But she and other women machinists have made great inroads to building a strong machinima infrastructure. For the newcomers, it is initially a place to play and experiment, and then they may begin to see what stories from their experiences will emerge to attract a larger machinima com-munity and virtual-world audiences more generally.

A long-time gamer herself of strategic role-playing, she realized the impor-tance of making connections between the various machinima communities and the respective audiences of the games connected to those communities. Within that frame of reference, the authors turned over the microphone to Phaylen Fairchild, machinimist extraordinaire, peacemaker to the worlds of *Second Life* and *World of Warcraft*. Her machinima, *Phaylen Seeks a World of Warcraft Guild*, launched a series that intersected both multi-player platforms. To Fairchild, it is all about machinima — and *virtual filmmaking* is perhaps a more relevant and useful term these days.

Beyond Hollywood: The Insatiable Desire for Creativity

I have always had this visually, intensely creative desire, a little more than being satisfied beyond how some people are quite content working in regular jobs. I was eccentric and flamboyant, loud and obnoxious, and intrinsically creative, and that took me to Hollywood. Imagine this: at one point I was in Hollywood being chased by a producer in a towel — the stereotypical story, right? I went home and said, "I am not ready for this." So I thought I would spend some time honing my craft.

I went into *Second Life* when I was 23. It wasn't until I was 25 that I acci-dentally did my first machinima. I say that because I didn't intend to do it. On behalf of Linden Lab, I was putting together a meta-verse awards show that honored top content creators on the grid through a voting process. I noticed that there was a way to capture video, and that led me to produce a video, using some of my real chops in a virtual environment. Let me clarify that; in real life I was more known as a writer, not as a filmmaker. I had been on film sets; I just never had been a director. I ended up making a short film. And it was called *Welcome to Your Second life*, an introductory celebratory virtual-world video.

I uploaded it on YouTube and from that moment on when I saw the potential in this environment to create coherent, cohesive stories that have a function, beginning and an end, with a potential audience, that's when I was sold on machinima. I started making films immediately and learning first Windows Movie Maker, and subsequently Sony Vegas and then After Effects, and tripping through light fantastic over these wonderful tools.

The vast majority of my adult life has been spent in *Second Life*; I have been here for nine years. *Second Life* was an education for me, the ability to step into a world in which I did possess control and some anonymity to experiment in the regard that I could be unafraid. I didn't have to abide by the Hollywood standard. It became this grand experiment really in storytelling in an entirely new medium. If you said the word *machinima* back then, not too many people knew what we were talking about. It is like the kids of today, who have no clue about the term *record player* and no concept of "Can I borrow your Walkman?"

Machinima, however, gave me this outlet that I really needed at the time. After my Hollywood experience, *Second Life* was there — this beautiful lovely enthusiastic utopia of infinite promise of creative potential, and for someone like me that was the best thing I could have asked or hoped for really. It made me better at what I did in real life. It made me a better writer in the area of imagination, and it helped me develop better characters. Originally when I began my series, it was an exercise in short-form storytelling without words because we didn't have voice at that time in *Second Life*. I began to realize that machinima in a virtual environment would start very much the same way as silent film did in the early 1900s. There was no vocal track, yet people were doing great comedic stunts to make an audience laugh. It was about reaction and entertaining more than storytelling at first. Then when it did tell a story, these word panels would move it forward and evoke an emotion, and there were those classic expressions on the characters' faces that told the rest of the story. When the talk film arrived, one could make punchy one-liners and provoke people to roll in the aisles or weep in their seats.

We have evolved in the same way that silent film did; there is no question in my mind. *Second Life* and virtual platforms like *Second Life* are an expedited industry, exponentially moving at the speed of light. It took us a century to advance from silent pictures to *Avatar*. In *Second Life*, it has taken us eight years to get from "Oh look, I have a little image capture thing here on my screen" to creating an entire series that is transcending virtual worlds with a character that one can virtually feel, touch, and that resonates with audiences around the globe. We have already seen major Hollywood types reach into *Second Life*. We have seen them reach into its toolbox; we have seen it in films and more recently on television with an episode of *CSI*; we have seen it run the gamut from little snippets to larger documentaries. I think it is not going to be long before the larger industry realizes the potential.

I really have a different approach to this because a lot of people say everyone is going to run to *Second Life* because you can create "very cheaply." Whereas you spend 100 million dollars on a Hollywood budget, in *Second Life* you can do the same thing for 10,000 dollars. I don't think that is going to happen, but I do think what will happen is that Hollywood will largely be seduced by this alien planet that is mostly untapped. They will come here to see what we have done and what we can do with the tool sets that we have here, and determine what we can produce and what we can achieve. And the same way that *The Guild*, a web-based series, was crafted, I think it will not be too long before we see a *Second Life* series or comedy that transcends its platform boundary, and that may be when Hollywood would truly take notice. Hollywood will not come to exploit *Second Life*, rather to celebrate and endorse the platform as a viable tool for valuable media production.

Maybe in the future, the far future, it will not be entirely impossible for someone to come into *Second Life* to produce a full movie. For now, we have an enormous technical hurdle to jump over, and Hollywood just can't come here and say I am going to make it happen. There is a learning curve for filmmakers, for one, who come into virtual platforms, as they become familiar with tool sets and how to create within and around. There are certain things like format forgiveness that must be understood, for you cannot simply snap your fingers for what you want to happen to happen the way you instruct it to happen, the way an actor in real life would simply comply.

There is a disconnect between the Hollywood creative mind-set and those who are used to being on a set and a machinimist who is sitting in an automated environment that is largely reliant on animation scripts for the execution of actions. Sometimes that can be incredibly challenging or frustrating. Hollywood is going to tap people who know how to do that, whose work they have experienced and appreciated, and who they believe will transcend that threshold from virtual to real audiences. Right now machinimists are making pictures for people who are machinimists from their content of origin, not necessarily for the mainstream.

We all have to think bigger, and that is really what I intend to do, encourage people to think bigger and don't think of yourself as a *Second Life* machinimist, *Sims* machinimatographer, or Moviestorm machinimatographer, rather think of yourself as a filmmaker and your platform is obviously your tool. Machinima is never going to encroach upon the real-world film industry; it may complement it in fantastic ways and has already started to do that. When I say I want people to cross that threshold into the real and not be limited or bound by their creation platform of choice, I want to encourage them to think what motivates them and consider what they want to achieve.

That is so non-specific in terms of tools because you have so many assets at your disposal. When people see *Second Life* they see the great colors, titles, details and that it is relatively easy to use; then they want to make a production. There has to be that desire to proceed forward beyond basics, some sort of antagonist challenge that makes them want to advance and progress and recognize the importance of improving standards in their work. For me, part of that is crossing that threshold and introducing my work to a larger audience. It's been largely strategic, starting with my experimentation in silent machinima, moving to talkies, and ultimately I decided when I learned a lot, to challenge myself further.

I dropped my *Second Life* character into the *World of Warcraft* platform which was never done before. I knew that the minute she didn't look like she belonged in *World of Warcraft* would be the moment I was going to lose both audiences, if I were not strategic. For me, it was largely about exposing a film to a new audience and not necessarily a *Second Life* audience, and that's what I think inhibits filmmakers today who largely create exclusively on platforms for their own respective communities, instead of extending toward a larger demographic.

Largely the machinima communities are supportive, and people would and should want to see other works from different platforms transcend boundaries and reach wider audiences. It is critical to introduce people to machinima generally, giving people examples of what can be achieved — of how you can take a story not exclusive to machinima that could also be viewed on a big screen in a huge theater playing around the world and produce it convincingly as machinima without losing any momentum or sense of the story. To prove this theory is why I produced the machinima *Harbinger*. As I have said, I am sort of like the accidental advocate for machinima, when I recognized that machinima was something that lends itself to my ideas in so many ways and nobody was telling me that I could not do it nor sending me a letter in the mail that said "thanks but no thanks." I became aware there were no walls being put up between me and what my end result could be. The art of machinima was something that was accessible to everybody and was a public medium.

There are so many artists, brilliant artists, with ideas, people who have been so needing an outlet, something transformative to them, in the way that machinima was transformative to me. It changed my opinion on everything about filmmaking and machinima's relationship to real-world cinema and with regard to its potential as cinema on a much wider scale. I believe machinima is going to be the next big type of media that will not require you to be a Pixar studio to make a wonderful movie where we laugh and cry, to create convincing characters that touch people.

The walls are down. People can create whatever they like, and the power of that is unstoppable. I think that we will see *Second Life*, Moviestorm, iClone, 3-D, and *Halo* (being obviously the first platform to become a cultural staple) take their place in history as formative of a brand new era of profound filmmaking, of filmmakers who struck a match to light a fire that will not be doused. It is not a replaceable or disposable format. I think the bigger we are as a community spanning platforms and the more people that lend their voices to machinima, creating machinima, putting machinima on YouTube, developing their own audiences and so forth, we will have a stronger voice as filmmakers.

We have put ourselves out there to create, and people have paid attention, applauded, and now enjoy machinima. You cannot put a cap on what is already out, and the larger world that cares about entertainment and media of any type is going to eventually, if not today or tomorrow, someday, accept machinima as a new genre to be widely accepted as an arts and interactive storytelling cinematic presentation. That to me is extremely exciting because we are on the cusp of greatness. When Hollywood became an industry and it was segmented into studios, it was taken out of the independent hands of Charlie Chaplin and all those who made films in that era. We look back today and say all that is archaic, black and white and grainy and you see props, but still no one knew at that time that these filmmakers, not even themselves, were starting the engine of a vehicle that would one day dominate the economy of nations. We don't realize or really regard how in society movies influence our lives, and this all began with an idea to capture and display action for all to enjoy.

We are in today's era of machinima, and still stumbling through, but we are entertaining people now as then. In 20 years or sooner, the machinimators of today will be as the Charlie Chaplins of yesterday. I definitely see machinima as having a strong place in recorded history, in terms of new media. Machinima is something that is incredibly powerful, and in the near future I can see it as a far more interactive, "choose your own adventure" type of series, where people are actively participating in the creation of moving stories by a collaborative means based on a real-time audience's votes or desires. We will go as far as our imaginations will take us because there is nobody telling us we cannot or should not proceed, or that we are doing it wrong, and that is the strength of the form — and it is liberating as hell because you have the world at your fingertips through the Internet.

The Machinima Interviews

This section provides in-depth examination of themes that emerged partly from the authors' roundtable discussions, as well as other conversations during the making of this book. Some of the issues explored through these interviews include cultural representation and perspectives through machinima (Al Peretz), the artistic evolution of and practice in machinima (Iono Allen), music videos made with machinima (Rysan Fall), and the challenges of machinima tools and techniques (Kate Fosk). The authors decided that *The Sims* (Decorgal [aka Judy Lee]) and *World of Warcraft* (Michael Gray), both with rich histories in machinima storytelling, should be examined at length. Other virtual platforms and environments are touched upon as well, but it is impossible to provide coverage to all. Restating from the introduction, this book deals with the second stage of machinima, the shift toward storytelling and crafting messages, and going beyond machinima as a mere means to capture and archive events and moments. Machinima is a powerful tool to create rich cinematic expression on both the small and large screen, with its makers striving to appeal to audiences beyond virtual realms.

The interview methods varied, mainly due to differences in time zones, work schedules, and life commitments. The purpose of these conversations was to enhance some of the machinima themes that surfaced during the process of researching trends and uncovering various perspectives on machinima. The interviews were conducted by the authors. Machinimatographers Al Peretz (USA/South America), Rysan Fall (USA) and Kate Fosk (UK) were interviewed at the offices and studios of Lowe Runo Productions, LLC, within *Second Life*. Both authors interviewed Peretz and Fosk. Johnson interviewed Fall, assisted by his long-time machinima friend Moo Money. Iono Allen (France) was interviewed by Johnson (with Money) at his *Second Life* art gallery. Treet TV Wiz Nordberg (Australia) and (USA) were interviewed by Pettit and Johnson through Skype, and Decorgal (USA) responded to the authors' questions via e-mail.

Al Peretz

Alfonso Kohn, known as Al Peretz in *Second Life*, had a career in media in Colombia for many years and was working as a channel director of a cultural and educational television station for several years as well there. He founded a media school in Colombia. His approach as a teacher was to provide tools to his student to facilitate their learning. He introduced them to some inexpensive tools, and in fact he was reading about machinima in *Second Life*. At the time, he was working with platforms like *The Sims*, The Movies, and iClone, but when he found out about *Second Life*, he knew he had discovered a fairly inexpensive way to tell his stories and to expand his potential at filmmaking. He began his journey in machinima about five years ago, and with that background we proceed with his interview. Kohn lives in the United States now, but his avatar filmmaker Al Peretz resides in *Second Life* making award-winning machinima. Phylis Johnson interviews Peretz with Donald Pettit.

Phylis Johnson: Well, tell me about your experiences with the different platforms from which you have created machinima. How do they compare? *Sims* is sort of like *Second Life*, in a sense, so what was your experience in *The Sims* for example?

Al Peretz: Every platform is really different. Some have things that you say, "Oh, this is cool," and the other one has another thing. All are different tools. In *The Sims*, you don't have the same power to work with others. That's the reason I really like *Second Life* because you have a lot of power, and you can work with other people. That is very important, because I think we need to produce machinima in the same way that you make any film. You have to make a team, and have people who can work on production, lights, dress, everything. Here you can work in that way. In *The Sims*, you can make a lot of things, and maybe you can work somewhat in the same way but you have to be with the team in your same space. In *Second Life* I can be here, and you can be anywhere. We can work together all the time. That's a very nice convenience in *Second Life*. I think *The Sims* was a good experience. I made one machinima, but I don't think I will go back there.

Phylis Johnson: What other platforms did you do besides *Sims*?

Al Peretz: The Movies. I did a music video there. It was nice, too. But you have to work with those tools, and you cannot be too creative. You have to work with their camera, and their avatars, and everything too. You cannot move too much. But it's good in its own way, too. Of course they have a lot of things that you can use, and it's nice.

Phylis Johnson: What is your favorite machinima that you've made so far?

Al Peretz: Any time you make a new machinima, you like what you have done now because the past always has to be better. I think in this moment *La Rumba Bacana* could be one of the best maybe because I did it in a different way — and I have a lot of different machinima. I don't have a preference. I learned when I make a new machinima, I put all my new knowledge into doing it better. It's hard to say which is better because they are all different in some ways.

Phylis Johnson: That's understandable. Obviously, you're from South America, and you take a cultural approach to your machinima. Do you think that sets you apart from others in *Second Life*?

Al Peretz: Well, the first thing is, in Spanish, it is difficult to work in machinima. Of course, I don't speak too much English. But I work with a lot of people who speak only English, for example. I learn other cultures through machinima. When I made a machinima in Spanish, I try to put all my culture in there, like that example of the music videos that I did.

Donald Pettit: *La Rumba Bacana*. It's very good.

Al Peretz: *(Laughs.)* Good.

Donald Pettit: So, si para que comos? *(Laughs.)*

Phylis Johnson: Your website has some examples of journalism. Have you contemplated doing any, or have you done any journalism as machinima? Any news pieces along that line?

Al Peretz: Yes. I like to make documentaries. It is a good genre, and it is like this interview. Maybe you are recording me. This is a kind of journalism, maybe a documentary about machinima. I like to find people here that are very interesting, that did or do something that all people want to know. I worked as a journalist for a lot of years. All the time, I say, "Oh, I can do this or that." But it's a hard genre here [in a virtual world]. In machinima, when you try to work on a documentary, it becomes a huge effort to explain to people what is going on, without making it boring. For example, when I made two documentaries about the Titanic, I tried to show different places and people there, and what they did. It's hard, yet, because you don't have too much movement. In the machinima, I need movement in the film for it to be good. If not, it's like a picture.

Phylis Johnson: What kind of documentaries do you think would be appropriate in *Second Life*, given that you've also worked in real life journalism in order to maintain some credibility?

Al Peretz: Well, I think this is a new culture — the future, the most important culture of the whole world. People are coming to learn about virtual worlds. Then, we have new associations and new relationships between people. I think it's important to show all the people in both *Second Life* and real life about business, love, communication, integration between cultures, and how we make a new culture here. I think there are a lot of things that we can make a documentary about, but it's hard because a lot of people don't want to give you their real names and that is hard for making documentaries. We need to show real people, and real names, so I would like to make some documentary in machinima, but mixing with real people. Then maybe I can go to your house, for example. I can show who are you in real life, and who are you in *Second Life*, and mix that to show the real people and the how of this world — work, culture, everything.

Phylis Johnson: Very good. We don't know if *Second Life* will be a platform in the future. What would be your next step if, for example, let's say that *Second Life* wasn't what it is today? What would you do? How would you continue to do your machinima? Where would you go?

Al Peretz: I would like to mix machinima with different platforms. I don't think the only one is *Second Life*, of course. I have seen different platforms similar, or different, but I think a good machinima could mix everything. The hard part is to, of course, exchange elements, like avatars, props, lights. I would like to mix it up.

Phylis Johnson: We really did want to know, is there a specific, unique market in the Latino culture, in terms of Spanish machinima? Is there a specific audience that would like to see more Spanish machinima? Is it growing?

Al Peretz: Well, I think in any language you talk, you will have a market, but it would have to be good. We have to make better and better machinima to open different markets. I think the Spanish machinima would be a very good idea to expand. For example, in my case, when I started making machinima, I had started reading about it because I had a school, as I told you. My students really didn't have many tools to make any kind of videos. It is a way to make non-expensive productions. Then, maybe if we do a good machinima — good quality, and express the culture, it would be good on any channel. I think in education and a lot of different kinds of programs that could be very good; then it becomes a market. I think it's ready to be opened.

Phylis Johnson: So, of all your work, what do you think was the best one that you've done so far? I know you say continually you like the latest one, but if you were to say, "This is probably my best" because not necessarily even the technical accomplishments but maybe the message that you wanted to communicate. Is there a specific title that you would want to share with us on that?

Al Peretz: (*Laughs.*) It's really hard. I told you. (*Laughs.*) Well, I think one of the nicest experiences was making *Be Love*. It's a nice film. I made it with a lot of French people. I think I spent a lot of time doing it. It was the first time I did a machinima with a lot of people. For me, that is important, because I think we need to make teams here. If we really want to make films — a real film — we need teams, including actors. We need actors. We really don't have, in *Second Life*, a lot of people who study to be actors. But we do have people who study to be models, for example. I know a lot of actors, but they want to be radio actors. They talk. They know how to express with their voice, but they don't know how to move their bodies. We need people who start learning about animation, how to move their bodies and everything. I think in *Be Love*, I have a lot of tools and people who know how to make animations, dress, lights, and different things. I think that was a very good video for me.

Phylis Johnson: Okay. Is there anything you'd like to add, if you feel there's something that I didn't ask you?

Al Peretz: I think a lot of people are making machinima, and I'm really happy about that. I think at the same time that people have to learn how to make machinima and what it is. I have seen a lot of people that think just filming here is producing machinima. I can't agree with that because I think then we will have a lot of machinima on YouTube and all becomes machinima without meaning. Just film, film, film, film. Other people may see that kind of machinima and say, "Oh, what is that? This is not a real art." People have to learn how to produce machinima as film, using the process like real-life film, and maybe we will make a better market for all the people who really like to make quality machinima. Now I am starting an online school for machinima in Spanish at www.machinimaespanol.com. I hope this will be a very important resource to all the people who want to learn.

Phylis Johnson: True. I would like to say that YouTube's filled with a lot of non-machinima that's trash too. *(Laughs.)* That's just the nature of people with cameras.

Al Peretz: Yes. A lot of people have cameras and film everything. They film everything, but they don't put it on YouTube, for example. I know some people that put out 500 movies. What is that? For what? It's not important to do that. I think the important thing is less film, more quality of course. Learn about how to do it better. Then you can put it out for everybody, and you can share with other people. I think it's important to educate people about this.

Phylis Johnson: I agree with you. But I'm culpable of that, too.

Al Peretz: I would like to share with you my first big machinima that was made in The Movies. It's with the same singer that was in *La Rumba Bacana*, the same because he's a friend of mine. I would like to share my link because that machinima was produced four years ago. That year was also the presidential election in Colombia. I was making a machinima to promote my candidate. *(Laughs.)* I make a lot of political commercials as machinima. I don't think too many people make political commercials in machinima.

Phylis Johnson: No. *(Laughs.)*

Al Peretz: But it was my opportunity to do this. The candidate's avatar was made in *Second Life*, and he talked about his politics. A lot of people saw my machinima commercials.

Phylis Johnson: Do you think they watched because it's just an interesting platform and people were curious? Or is it because it's an inexpensive platform and it gives different political groups access?

Al Peretz: The political machinima was produced for real-life people.

Phylis Johnson: Do you think this is a way for some politicians, some candidates, to be able to reach people inexpensively?

Al Peretz: They have a lot of money and they want to spend their money in the best way they think. I think this is a very good way to do that because you can show their politics in a different way and everything.

Phylis Johnson: Sure. That's an interesting idea.

Al Peretz: You can see how I try to make the avatar very similar to the candidate.

Phylis Johnson: Very good.

Al Peretz: I take all his voice-overs, and edit them into the commercials. It worked well. I have some videos with about 2,000 to 3,000 views in one month, and up to 4,000. All the viewers were real people [not necessarily affiliated with *Second Life*].

Phylis Johnson: Any other videos you would like to share?

(*Al Peretz drops in a few links in the public chat window.*)

Donald Pettit: (*Watching a video.*] Very entertaining. I like it. *(Laughs.)*

Al Peretz: La Abuela.

Donald Pettit: Si. *(Laughs.)* Mucho.

Al Peretz: I think I put some translation there.

Donald Pettit: Very good.

Al Peretz: It is difficult to learn English here in Miami. All the people speak Spanish. I really learn English in *Second Life*, and that was my second objective here. I came to see how to make machinima, but when I came here, I saw, "Oh, I can learn English here. Oh, it's perfect!" I have tried to learn in Miami, and I go to the gas station, or supermarket, everywhere, and people only speak Spanish — and bad Spanish. Then I lost my Spanish, and I didn't learn English. *(Laughs.)*

Phylis Johnson: *(Laughs.)*

Donald Pettit: See, I come in here a lot to meet Spanish people to practice my Spanish. *(Laughs.)*

Conclusion

Al Peretz is one of a growing number of Spanish-speaking machinima producers who bring a cultural perspective to its art and practice. His school targeted to helping the Latino community learn machinima is likely the first of its kind, particularly when looking for online instruction in this area. The machinima community in *Second Life* has encouraged such thinking, with the idea of acknowledging the accessibility and empowerment offered by this tool.

Recommended Machinima

Al Peretz Channel, YouTube, http://www.youtube.com/user/alorja1?feature=mhum
Al Peretz, Vimeo, http://www.vimeo.com/alkohn
Alfonso Kohn, company site, http://alfonsokohn.com/
Be Love by Al Peretz, http://www.youtube.com/watch?v=D_tCbIPUGo8
La Abuela by Al Peretz, http://www.youtube.com/watch?v=oReD2H5wjps

La Rumba Bacana II by Al Peretz, http://www.youtube.com/watch?v=K9UcCW2CZ0c
Por qué quiero ser Presidente by Al Peretz, http://www.youtube.com/watch?v=T-CFxJzQGb0
RMS Titanic in Second Life by Al Peretz, http://www.youtube.com/watch?v=Yo74qzjG2J8
Titanic in Second Life by Al Peretz, http://www.youtube.com/watch?v=JrBc4fhb6KM
The Sword by Al Peretz http://www.youtube.com/watch?v=Gz4Ri0IqoFA

Decorgal

We had the opportunity to present some questions to the talented *Sims* machinima producer Judy Lee, who simply goes by the name of Decorgal. She has a master of arts in sociology, specializing in race and class inequality and research methods, with advanced graduate work toward her Ph.D. Part of her recent experience included a position as senior research analyst in education for the University of California system, doing research and evaluation for K-12 outreach programs in mathematics and science. Her cultural and diversity studies, complemented with her personal experiences as a Korean-American, might be offered up as a unique lens to bring to machinima as a critic and producer. Certainly she brings a significant perspective as an extremely educated woman and machinimist. She is an innovator for what the authors see as the second phase of machinima since the early capture days of speed runs. She works independently, but spends most of her time with her recently adopted son from Korea. Her longtime interest in machinima has fallen to the wayside due to her parental commitments.

One of the first things that you learn about Decorgal is that she has been amazingly passionate about machinima, although she "never really had an interest in making movies or writing." She explains how all that changed several years ago:

> Prior to the release of *Sims 2* in 2004, I was a player of *Sims 1.* I had never even heard of it until my much younger brother (who is 13 years my junior) asked me to buy *Sims 1* for him. Once he showed me the game, he never again got a chance to play it I was so completely hooked. It didn't take long until I stumbled onto the storytelling feature of the game on *The Sims* website. I wanted to do the same so tried my hand at it but failed miserably because I wasn't a very good creative writer. When *Sims 2* was due out, I had heard about the in-game camera and decided I would try my hand at movies instead. When *Sims 2* was finally released, I saw some machinima, which was an unfamiliar term to all of us at the time, on *The Sims 2* website and began making my own movies. After my first machinima release in 2004, making movies quickly became a serious passion which I pursued with vigor, eventually neglecting all of my other hobbies.

After establishing some essential biographical background, our discussion proceeds to probe into the mind and creativity of one of the most prolific machinima makers of *The Sims*, created by Electronic Arts (EA). To date, she is best known for her *Adventures in Dating* series. Whether she remains on hiatus from machinima production or picks up her long-time passion again is left to the future course of interests and events in her life. She admits machinima is time consuming, and that is something she has little of these days.

Launching from that fairly terse introduction, what follows is Decorgal graciously responding in writing to a series of questions presented to her by the authors, and her answers subsequently help to provide some history on the development of *The Sims* machinima and some of its past and present challenges to machinimists.

Authors: Have you tried any other platforms, other than *Sims*— and what? Please compare them if so.

Decorgal: *Sims* is the only platform with which I have tried to make machinima. I did play *Second Life* for a period of time and did some filming in it but found the lack of control of the environment too difficult for making a movie. I do have a *Sims* friend, Trace Sanderson (Lainy Voom), who moved from *Sims* machinima to *Second Life*, who has successfully created some amazing and well-respected work with *Second Life* (see *The Dumb Man*). Her biggest argument for abandoning *Sims* machinima is the lack of ownership of the material — EA does not release rights with machinima created with *The Sims*.

I think I have enough knowledge through viewing machinima made with different platforms and discussing those platforms with machinima friends who have used them to make some comparisons. When I first started making *Sims* machinima, it seemed to me to be one of the most ideal programs for that purpose. I, like most others making *Sims* machinima at the time, mainly made music videos that focused on relationships and dramas. Because *The Sims* game is focused on living "life" and relationships, there are an extraordinary number of animations and Sims-to-Sims interactions that are detailed and, I would dare say, meaningful. There are, of course, those animations that the player can control, but there are also lots of autonomous animations that happen depending on the personality of your *Sims* and the circumstance in which you put them. Because of this, you really have to be a player and know the game intimately to effectively create machinima with it. The nature of the game lends itself to easy character and set design, giving the producer quick and great control over creating the environment in which to film. Another great thing about the game is *The Sims* community, which is strongly focused on custom content creation for the game. The game is designed so that custom content can be easily shared among players and installed. The techniques and programs developed for creating content are shared freely for the community to enjoy, and the vast majority offer their content for free. Although there was a dearth of content for the game when it was first released, just a few years later there were literally millions of items you could download for the game. Nearly anything you needed for whatever scene you had in mind was readily and easily available for download. In addition to custom content, there are game hackers out there, including myself, who give the player the ability to more easily control the game. Hacks range from eliminating annoyances from the game to lighting hacks to in-game camera control hacks.

I have gotten to the point where *Sims 2* has become much too limiting for me, particularly since almost everything I am interested in making now is talkies (dialogue-driven) movies rather than music videos. Filming dialogue is an incredibly laborious task since *The Sims* are much too animated when they talk, particularly for dramas. Lip-syncing is also nearly impossible since there is no in-game tool for doing so, and *The Sims* speak a fictitious language called "Simlish." There are tools and hacks I've developed to help deal with this, which I'll discuss later, but I find that I have to edit around my attempts at lip-syncing rather than editing the way I really want to. I find I have to cut much more than I'd like when filming conversations between two people, for example, just so the lips will match the dialogue better. It doesn't help that *The Sims* game is not designed for machinima but for game play, and that sometimes gets in the way. Again, hacks and tools help with this process, but depending on the movie I'm trying to make, *Sims* isn't always the ideal platform. I have been interested in using Moviestorm for my future projects, mainly because of the lip-syncing feature, and there is much more control in the program since it was designed specifically for creating machinima. I have to say though that I really despise the way the characters look and move in Moviestorm. There isn't the community of creators offering items for free in the game, and customizing content isn't as easy as it is in *Sims*. I do know there are some creators out there offering content for Moviestorm, but they are not free. For a one-person production such as myself and for creating machinima mainly for my enjoyment, paying for content is an unnecessary expense, as it could add up quickly.

Authors: What do you like about producing machinima in *Sims*? Some of your likes were touched upon in the previous questions. Could you expand?

Decorgal: When I first started making machinima, I made music videos. The thing that I love about *Sims* is the amazing amount of detail in the game, particularly in the characterization of *The Sims*. In addition to those that the player can control, *The Sims* have many hidden, autonomous actions and interactions of which only a true player of the game would be aware. For example, if you watch a pregnant Sim for a while, you'll notice that she will occasionally rub her belly affectionately. If one of your *Sims* is taking a shower and a family member comes in and flushes the toilet, the Sim taking the shower will get angry. It is in these details that one can discover the "humanity" of *Sims*, making them incredibly real. Discovering and using these moments, clever editing and the right music can create a deeply emotional piece with which viewers can really identify. Most of my music videos are just that for me — deeply emotional works. I consider it a compliment and honor when someone contacts me to let me know my machinima made them cry or touched them in some way. Lacking the experience from using other platforms, it's hard for me to judge, but I'm not sure I would have been able to accomplish this using anything else. I like making mostly talkies now, but even if I used something like Moviestorm for that, I would return to *Sims* for music videos.

Authors: What are some obstacles in production?

Decorgal: There are many obstacles in production depending on the type of machinima I create. For talkies, casting voice-over actors and lip-syncing with *The Sims* is definitely the biggest challenge. For all my movies, it's always a challenge to figure out ways to create a scene that doesn't exist in the game. A simple one, for example, would be a train scene I did in the *Adventures in Dating* series. Building a set and creative editing made it possible and relatively easy, but there are times when I have a scene in mind that I have to modify so that it's more doable with the game. Not being able to realize a specific vision I had and having to compromise is difficult for me to do as a director. Another problem I have is that I always seem to need a more powerful computer. I have had three different computers built for me specifically for making machinima over the years (although the first was just so I could play the game), but each quickly seemed to lack the power I needed. Filming is extremely resource intensive on a computer, so it usually takes me several minutes to film just a few seconds of footage. I also have an incredible amount of custom content in my game for moviemaking (I have three gigabytes of files), so the game is very slow to start up and to get in and out of sets. It will take me 10 minutes to start up the game with custom content, whereas it would just take a minute or so without. Editing is also sometimes difficult when making talkies because I'll sometimes be working with eight tracks, and it's hard to preview because it will be jerky. Some of these issues make creating machinima more laborious than it really is and can be discouraging when my free time and motivation are limited.

Authors: What tools do you use in producing your machinima?

Decorgal: The programs I've used for editing and writing have changed over the years as my skills have advanced. Currently, I use Sony Vegas Pro for the actual movie editing, Celtx for the script writing, and Sony Sound Forge for audio recording. To film in *The Sims*, I generally use the in-game camera but sometimes have to resort to using Fraps for slow-motion scenes or for extra high resolution. I also create many of my own *Sims* game hacks to make filming easier as well as to create new character poses or movements. For those I use SimPE (a *Sims* community-created program) and Milkshape.

Authors: What makes for a good story?

Decorgal: Even with "real" movies that I watch, I have always been interested in characters. I enjoy a good plot, but character-driven stories have always been my favorite. I love movies that make me think and those that stay with me and linger long past the credits. I love when movies make me reflect on myself or people in my life. I also appreciate movies that I may not love immediately after viewing but that stay with me and that I eventually learn to love as I think about and understand them better. I think one of the most important elements of a good story is that the writer and/or director has to have some real connection to the story and put a piece of him or herself into it. There has to be a link, whether that is through experience or a subject he or she is passionate about. I think that's what gives the viewer a connection to a character or story line that, to me, is essential to a good story.

Authors: What is your favorite machinima that you have produced?

Decorgal: The obvious answer to this question is my series *Adventures in Dating*. It was pretty much the only thing I worked on from 2006 to 2009 and pretty much consumed me, requiring more dedication and time than I had ever spent on anything else I had done as a hobby. The story was something I thought about and wrote months in advance, while gathering and building sets, characters, voice actors, and so on. It was my chance to really push myself creatively as well as technically since many of the scenes I had in mind were not preexisting features of the game. Also, Sims was and is not an ideal medium for a series focused almost exclusively on dialogue. In addition to lip-syncing being really difficult, the Sims' expressions, on the whole, tend to be comically exaggerated and are not very suitable for drama. My tendency is to underplay the drama and for the "actors" to under act. A subtle look or expression is more meaningful to me than something overt and obvious, and this was not something that *The Sims* characters did well. As I've touched on before, I felt I was forced to create hacks and tools to deal with these issues, and you can tell the series developed a much different "look" as it progressed. I am proud of being able to create such a large-scale production (probably one of the largest *Sims* productions) on my own and to stick to the series throughout the years and to actually complete it. My series is one of the few larger-scaled *Sims* series that was fully finished; most directors lose steam and leave their series unfinished.

One of my favorite music video pieces is *A Lack of Color* based on a song by Death Cab for Cutie by the same name. Although it was only the second video I'd ever made, the song has a deeply personal meaning to me and is one of my favorites. I find the lyrics beautifully simple yet incredibly meaningful. Despite its being one of my earlier movies and technically deficient compared to what I could create today, I love the emotion and mood of the piece and still find it moving to watch today. I would absolutely love to remake it using the skills and custom animations I can create today to truly execute my vision of the song.

Authors: What is your favorite machimima that someone else has produced?

Decorgal: That's a really hard question to answer since there is such a wide range of movies that I really love. If I was forced to choose my favorite, it would be the series *Metamorphosis* by Tamara Russell who is otherwise known as Artcgrrl in the machinima community. *Metamorphosis** is a *Sims 2* talkie series about an artist who has lost his muse and has a difficult time creating art. Consequently, he has reached a stalemate in life and has lost all passion for living. The series is really well written and has a very strong artistic and ethereal quality to it. The creator of the series is an actual artist and that's particularly evident in the beautiful cinematography. She really put herself into the series which is very character driven and rich in symbolism — all qualities I appreciate and enjoy. It's unfortunate but like many others who embark on a big-production series, Tamara left it unfinished so it was never fully realized and left me curious as to where she would've taken it.

Authors: Do you do anything media related in real life. What kind of media training did you have — or not? Explain as much as you want and can.

Decorgal: I have absolutely no media training. I don't think I've ever even taken a class or anything. I learned by pretty much throwing myself into the metaphorical water and managed to figure most things out on my own. The only informal "training" that I've had, if you could even call it that, was something that helped me with cinematography. My father was an artist during his free time and an avid photographer. He gave me a camera when I was in middle school and let me take as many pictures as I wanted, before digital photography existed and when film and photo processing were quite costly. Whenever I had a new package of pictures developed, my father would look at each one with me and point out the compositional problems and explain how to frame the picture properly. I think this helped me a great deal with filming machinima. Obviously, with more experience and a better handle on the game engine's camera, my cinematography also improved over time.

I've also had experience with some related media work throughout college and my career. I was co-editor of one of my college's newspapers, which I had no experience with prior to and learned while on the job. During my working years, I've recommended and created a newsletter, promotional brochures and materials and designed several websites. I've had no formal training in any of these areas but had an interest and wanted to learn, so I just pursued it without thinking twice about it or my abilities which were sorely lacking.

Authors: What does machinima mean for you?

Decorgal: Machinima to me was always and will always be a creative outlet and a hobby. Just because I call it a hobby doesn't mean that I don't take my work seriously or strive for excellence or perfection since I tend to be a perfectionist. I am the type of person who pursues my interests with incredible passion and dedication. But with something like that, it's hard to maintain that passion

---

Decorgal doesn't think this is available for viewing anywhere. Russell used to actually host her work on the now defunct SimsPremiere, which Decorgal talks about later in the interview. Russell no longer actively makes machinima but now creates custom content for sale in Second Life. Russell also starred as the voice of Ellen in Adventures in Dating.

over a long period of time. I find that my interests have waned a bit and I'm not interested in creating or even watching it as much as I used to be.

Authors: What are some machinima story lines or directions that you have been thinking about? How did you come up with your past machinima plots?

Decorgal: I have lots and lots of projects in the pipeline. I've been fortunate enough to always have ideas for projects. My problem lies in whether or not I have the energy or time to realize them. One of the projects I have in mind is a comedic instructional-video-style parody for women on the realities of relationships and marriage. The title, which is still a working one, is something like "The Single Woman's Guide to Marriage." It's meant to be completely silly and fun and an exaggerated spoof of the reality people encounter in relationships leading up to and in marriage.

Another project that I have in mind is a drama series, with each episode self-contained, called "Beyond Closed Doors." Each episode will feature a different couple, in various stages and types of relationships, and a conversation between the two. I actually have scripts written up for two of the episodes and have thought of several others. I got the idea for it from the notion that no one really knows what goes on in a relationship other than the two people involved. It's meant to be completely character focused as each episode takes place in one scene, over one conversation. This is a project I have in mind for the Moviestorm platform, not just because filming dialogue is easier with it but so that I can have full ownership over my work.

I get all of my ideas from my own life and the experiences of friends and family. Although all of my work is completely fictional, there are definitely grains of reality in them as characters and plotlines are loosely based on people I know or myself and our experiences. No matter what I create — music videos, comedy pieces, dramas — I always put some piece of myself in my work. Even when I'm not actively working on machinima, I'm always thinking of how this or that idea or experience would make a good movie.

Authors: Have you been involved in any type of machinima community, and can you specify and tell us how it has been supportive?

Decorgal: Being part of *The Sims* machinima community is why I became so intensely involved in creating machinima and the custom content and hacks that I use for my movies. My involvement began with the official *Sims 2* site's moviemakers forum. When *The Sims 2* first came out, this forum was mainly comprised of a small community of people who were very supportive and tended to be older (i.e., older teens and adults) compared to some of the other forums on *The Sims 2* site. There was a handful of more experienced movie creators on that forum who were really supportive of my work from the get-go and gave me lots of encouragement and pushed me to create more work. That forum eventually grew too large and too young for my liking, so I left that site, tried a couple of other forums but decided creating my own community was the best option. I had purchased a website pretty soon after I began making machinima because it was difficult to find places to host movies. *The Sims 2* site had a 10 MB and one-movie upload limit at the time. Places like YouTube and all the other hosting sites that are around today either did not exist or were not really well known at the time. Since I knew other machinima creators had the same issues as me and I had the means to purchase an additional website, I created *Sims*Premiere.com which was a place to showcase and host the work of talented, lesser-known *Sims 2* directors. It was through this site that I formed many close bonds with fellow machinima directors, and this was what spurred my own *Sims 2* machinima-focused forum. This drew lots of people more serious about their work and those interested in really nurturing talented people with lots of potential. It was an intimate forum and its members really went out of their way to offer advice, creative and technical feedback, support and assistance to each other. We also made a point to "spread the word" about machinima that we thought was good and should be seen. Although the majority of the creators worked with *Sims 2*, we did attract a few people who also used other platforms in addition to *Sims*. Many of us eventually became interested in using other platforms such as Moviestorm or *Second Life*, and some moved on from *Sims* to making other machinima, while many more just lost interest and stopped making machinima all together. This community tended to be older (i.e., adults) and really wanted to push machinima as an art form, appreciating works that stood out or pushed the creative "envelope." Many of the people whom I met through *Sims*Premiere are those with whom I became more intimate and continue to keep in contact with today despite my closing the site some years later.

Authors: Is there a unique role for women machinimists in *Sims*, or in machinima in general?

Decorgal: I think one has to be careful when making generalizations about the work of women versus men in machinima since it's so easy to stereotype, so my comments about the role of women should be qualified. Prior to the popularity of *Sims* machinima, which is dominated by women, it's pretty safe to say that machinima was male dominated and was based on games that were focused on violence. This doesn't mean that the machinima was necessarily violent but that the themes tended to focus less on relationships and more on plot or technical achievement. *Sims* machinima, due to the nature of the game, generally focused more on characters and relationships. Again, these are generalizations and there are definitely examples of women making plot/technically focused machinima or men making machinima about characters/relationships.

I think when *Sims* machinima first began to be recognized by sites like machinima.com, which was a non-profit venture at the time, there were some in that community that didn't take it seriously. I do think this may have been because most of the people creating machinima at the time were adult males who looked "down" upon *The Sims* because it wasn't a serious game and it attracted mostly teenagers and adult females. There was a lot of criticism of the game as a platform for machinima — that it was too cartoony, too limiting, the characters all looked similar, and so forth. I wonder too if some may have felt that the type of *Sims* machinima being produced, mostly by women, was just not to their liking — that is, the themes were just not interesting to them. I wasn't particularly involved in that community directly, choosing to stay within *The Sims* community, and have only heard things through people plugged into those circles. It's difficult to pinpoint specific negative comments or attitudes, if there were any, based on gender at the time. But then again, sentiments are sometimes just felt via instinct — like women or people of color have an instinct and can more readily recognize sexism or racism. I think sexism would be a much too powerful term to use in this case and would be inappropriate, but what I would say is that the general sentiment toward *Sims* machinima was negative at the time but it would be unfair to say that it was entirely a gender issue. Despite some anti–*Sims* sentiment, there were also those who supported *Sims* machinima. People like Ben Grussi who helped run the machinima.com website at the time was a big supporter of my work, and Phil Rice, who is a well-respected machinima director and musician, helped to promote my work and ended up dabbling in *Sims* machinima himself, getting some amazing recognition for his comedy piece *Male Restroom Etiquette*. Because of this, I didn't feel like I suffered any ill effects of any of the negative sentiments that may have existed at the time.

Several years ago, a fellow *Sims* machinima creator who happens to be an adult male, Todd Stallkamp, won best series at the Academy of Machinima Arts and Sciences organization's (machinima.org) annual film festival for his series *The Fixer*. Todd, who is a machinima friend (he was active at *The Sims*Premiere forum I ran), was absolutely shocked when he won, not just because he was humble about his work but because it was *Sims*. He was up against some pretty tough competition. I can't remember the specific series that he was up against, but some of them were created by more professional production teams rather than the one-person show, like me, that Todd was running (Phil Rice who saw the series when it was released got involved and agreed to score original music for it, which allowed Todd to enter the series since copyrighted material is not allowed in the competition). I was a fan of *The Fixer* when it was released and felt the win was well deserved. What I did think about though, being a woman, was that although it was *Sims* machinima, *The Fixer* "fit" into the category of the vast majority of machinima that was out there and in the competition. It was not at all character/relationship focused, even by Todd's own admission in my discussions with him, and it was violent and very technically (special effects) driven. It made me wonder if *The Sims* submission had instead been about something that women tended to make more of, a movie about relationships for example, could it have had a chance to win? There has been a dearth of *Sims* submissions to the academy for best picture/series awards. I think it's because most people making *Sims* machinima are like me — doing it for fun. It would be interesting to see how such a movie/series would do up against what you typically see in the competition. I have been out of the machinima loop for a couple of years now, though, so things could be much different today than they were years ago when I was more intensely involved.

With all that said, I guess I could say that women contribute to machinima by offering a different voice. Whether the type of machinima we make is technically focused, emotion focused, plot intensive, relationship focused, or whatever, we offer a woman's voice. I can't make a generalization about what that voice is since women as a group can't be lumped together and come from all different walks of life and experiences, but the perspective is indeed a different one from men.

Authors: As producer, how much do you work alone versus collaboratively? Do you cast for avatars? Or just create them? How do you cast for voices?

Decorgal: The beauty of machinima is that it really requires no prior experience or set skills. People like me, who have never filmed or edited before, can just do it without any real resources. Because of this, I think most people who make machinima are like me and work on projects as a solitary effort. That's what makes machinima so accessible and a great equalizer — you can compete as a one-person crew with professional production companies for an audience and recognition. Some fellow machinima director friends and I have attempted to collaborate on several projects, but with all of us creating as a hobby and in our spare time, it's been difficult to work together.

For most of my machinima projects, I have been the one to create the characters, sets, and so forth, but for the *Adventures in Dating* series, I had to use content created by others because the scope of the project was too big. The beauty of *The Sims* games is that content creation and sharing is an integral part of the game experience, and plenty of content, most of which is free, is easily accessible. Because of this, it wasn't too difficult to find lots/sets that I could retrofit for filming, objects to decorate, wardrobe, and the like. For the characters (avatars), I sent out a "casting" call and got submissions from which I cast. I did find that I had to create a lot of the characters myself though since I wanted to incorporate their personalities into their look. Voice-over casting is a difficult problem for me and for many fellow directors looking for volunteers. In *The Sims* machinima world, it is really difficult to cast for adult males since there are relatively few adult male directors/players, and in the non–*Sims* machinima world (the two don't often cross paths), it is difficult to cast adult females since there are few female directors/players. In addition to finding adult males, it's difficult to find people who are reliable and have decent-quality microphones and the ability to record clearly. Because of this, I'll try and cast machinima friends who I know will be reliable, have good microphones and have decent acting ability. I'll also cast myself and my husband, not because I want to but because I know I can rely on us. I personally hate casting myself since I don't like my voice and I can't really act, and my husband hates doing voice-over work. In an ideal world, a voice style to fit the character and acting ability would be foremost in casting someone, but it becomes less of a concern when you find yourself scrambling to cast people. Despite all this, I do find that I'm fortunate enough to have enough people willing to work in my movies, which they do willingly for nothing in exchange. I think building a solid reputation for creating good work and being active in/contributing to the community helps tremendously in finding volunteers.

Authors: Tell us about your content creation work. Do you make your own props for machinima? What type of content do you create, and how do you market them, for whom and where?

Decorgal: I do quite a bit of content creation for *Sims* which includes creating clothing, recoloring objects (i.e., applying different textures to new meshes created by others), and most importantly creating hacks. Although I had some interest in doing things like creating clothing and recoloring prior to creating machinima, most of the work was spurred on by my need for items that were hard to find or didn't exist. For example, when *Sims 2* was relatively new, there were few custom clothing items that weren't overly sexy (such as super low-cut shirts or skirts for women) because most of the people creating these items were either teenagers or young adults. I found these types of clothing to be inappropriate for my characters and had a need for more "normal" clothing so started creating them. I ended up sharing these items on my site and found that there were many others likes me, machinima directors and just players alike, who had the same need for their game.

I started creating hacks because it was incredibly time consuming and difficult to queue characters' actions and interactions. When I first starting making *Sims* movies, I would spend hours just playing the actual game in order to film *The Sims* doing something I needed, all just to capture a few seconds of footage. Years later, another machinima creator who goes by the name JayDee created a hack to queue some of the existing in-game actions so that directors could get *The Sims* to do what they wanted on demand. There are literally tens of thousands of animations in the game — the thought that went into making the game is incredible, and it's one of the reasons why I love using it for machinima but also what makes filming difficult. Another machinima friend of mine, André Lopion [author's note: see Totilo, 2005], who goes by the name Jixs, learned how to create the same sort of hack from JayDee, and then André taught it to me. That's when I really started dissecting the game and by adapting some techniques from André's hacks figured out a way to minimize the "cartooniness" and exaggerated animations of *The Sims*. I started making all sorts of animation hacks to make filming easier and more efficient for myself and shared them so that other moviemakers and storytellers could benefit and because sharing content is a *Sims* tradition. Eventually, I was able to piece together the knowledge provided by *Sims* hackers (there's a community of them) and figured out a way to create custom animations. All of this happened during the course of the three years it took me to film *Adventures in Dating*, and you'll notice the different ways *The Sims* move and talk as the series progresses. All of my custom content, except some of my hacks, is distributed for free and marketed on my website on the Designs page. I've got quite a few subscribers to the site so don't really feel a need to market them. There are also some *Sims* "finds" sites out there that report daily on new releases by certain designers, and I am lucky enough to be featured on several of these sites. My hacks I distribute mainly on a site called Modthesims2.com. Its origin was as a hacking site, and there were many hacking tools such as programs and knowledge shared on this site. Although they offer all types of custom content now, I distribute my hacks there because I appreciate all the help I've received from the site and because I'd like to contribute and "give back." Because I offer a large range of content from movies to clothing to hacks, my audience covers a range of users—from those who have never watched my machinima to fellow machinima creators.

Authors: Any other comments—something you would like to talk about?

Decorgal: I got the opportunity to go to the creator's camp EA offered just before the *Sims 3* was released. I had the chance to test-drive the game with some fellow players and try my hand at a machinima piece while I was there. It was an amazing experience. I really enjoyed the *Sims 3*, and there were many components of the game that were added to assist in the creation of machinima. The lighting design, for example, was really vamped up and it is much more nuanced and detailed in the game. The in-game camera was also improved significantly with finer controls on the camera and some new angles not offered in *Sims 2*. These improvements were due to Todd Stallkamp, who was a fellow *Sims 2* machinima friend with a television production background. When EA had an opening for a full-time *Sims* machinima creator, they hired him. As a machinima director, and with discussions with people like me, he knew what we wanted from the game and really pushed hard for these features in *Sims 3*. There were many other things we asked for, but since machinima creators are just a small part of the player base, additional features that we requested were not included. I have not purchased *The Sims 3* game and don't plan to. As much as I love the game simply as a player, I don't see using it as a machinima tool. While I was at EA, I made a movie and it was just like making movies with *Sims 2* in the beginning—incredibly time consuming and limiting because of the lack of hacks or custom items for it. I can't imagine starting all over again with such limits. There will come a time when there are lots of custom content and hacks for the game, but I don't want to start over and don't have the time to work on the type of hacks I've created for *The Sims 2* anymore.

As I mentioned throughout the interview, I do have an interest in using Moviestorm for some of my future machinima projects. But with a young child now, I find it nearly impossible to dedicate the amount of time it takes to create a machinima piece. I'm not sure if it's something I'll ever be as passionate about as I once was, but I'm still thinking of projects and still writing when I can and hope to make more machinima in the future. I do miss my hobby, though, so what I've been doing instead is making little movies of my son and am currently working on a short documentary chronicling our experience of going to Korea to pick up our son so that he'll know how he became a part of our family.

Conclusion

Decorgal was listed in Hancock and Ingram's (2007) *Machinima for Dummies* supplemental website as one of 16 women influential to machinima. Listed along with her were JayDee, Lainy Voom (Trace Sanderson), Kate Fosk, and Moo Money, all discussed in this book. Decorgal was described as a "prolific creator of *Sims* mods, models and recolors, including the ground-breaking lip-sync mods for *Sims 2*," and of course her *Adventure in Dating* series. Many talented women comprise the machinima field, and there is no way to discuss them all. Decorgal was instrumental to networking the machinima community, and her legacy to building that community and its resources—as well as the necessity to do so—will be remembered as a significant contribution in years to come, as we work together toward the next phase of machinima's evolution.

References

Hancock, Hugh, & Ingram, Jonnie. (2007). Women Who Have Changed Machinima. *Machinima for Dummies*. Hoboken, NJ: Wiley Publishing, Inc. See companion Web Site. Accessed January 7, 2011, from http://www.machinimafordummies.com/articles/2009/03/24/women-who-have-changed-machinima
Totilo, Stephen. (2005, August 23). Gamers Remodel R. Kelly's 'Closet,' Replace Sex with Cuddling. Video games provide tools for fans to (re)make music videos. *Simple Plan*. VH1.com. Accessed January 1, 2011, from http://www.vh1.com/artists/news/1508172/20050823/simple_plan.jhtml

Recommended Machinima

http://decorgal.com, *Adventures in Dating* by Decorgal
http://www.voom-machine.com, *The Dumb Man* by Trace Sanderson (Lainy Voom)
http://z-studios.com/collaborations/the-fixer, *The Fixer* by Phil Rice & Todd Stallkamp
http://www.jd-movies.com/movies.php, JayDee
http://www.koinup.com/Jixs/http://www.koinup.com/Jixs, by André Lopion (Jixs)
http://z-studios.com/films/mre, *Male Restroom Etiquette* by Phil Rice (Overman)

Iono Allen

Machinimist Iono Allen is an art collector, a machinima producer and even an artist, although regarding the latter he will not admit so. In his virtual gallery of *Second Life*, his art is exhibited as well as many other in-world pieces from a diverse selection of artists. One thing that really fascinated the authors is Allen's ability to capture the artistic sense of *Second Life* through machinima. He speaks little of his real life, but he has surrounded himself with art and cinema his whole life. *Second Life* has reawakened his love for film. Allen's work archives *SL* installations, builds, and virtual environment of other artists, and then he expands upon them, bringing in his own interpretation and vision. It is a mixed-up world for Allen, where one day he envisions bringing the real and virtual into one machinima to demonstrate the intersections between the worlds, giving us perhaps a glimpse of our future, where computers will continue to shape our understanding of humanity. Allen speaks to the art side of virtual worlds, and this becomes evident during our interview with him. Along with Phylis Johnson on this day was Moo Money, filming the interview, at Allen's art gallery.

Phylis Johnson: If you could tell me a little bit about your background, which led you to machinima, that would be great.

Iono Allen: The way that I have been educated by my parents, and everything else I've done in my life, has contributed to my work in *Second Life*. Actually, it's not about my work in real life, which has nothing to do with art, nor machinima, nor video, and so on. In real life, I regularly go to the museum, and I'm very, very interested in art. I guess that is one of the reasons why we are talking at my gallery. It's my place in *Second Life*. Even downstairs, there is some art in my garden. So I've always been interested in art, and when I came into *Second Life*, it was in 2007. It was a time when art was beginning to be really interesting with all the new capabilities from 3-D software — excellent software, like Blender, for example. Artists had begun to emphasize their ability to make art, and that was quite interesting. My real interest in *Second Life* is art, and that came about last year when I met White Leopard, who was the creator of Burning Life in 2009. Now we are very, very good friends. She showed me around Burning Life. I didn't know at all what it was. For me, it was a revelation. It was the way for me. I had already built this gallery. I had already chosen some artists to feature. It was the revelation that art was quite important in *Second Life*.

Phylis Johnson: It is obvious that your art has informed your machinima. Much of your machinima presents unique themes. What do you think has been your greatest work so far that you have been really proud of? I know you get better and better the more you produce machinima, but is there a piece of work that you feel that helps to define where you want to go, what you really like about machinima?

Iono Allen: That's difficult to say. One year ago, I hardly knew what machinima was, so for me I've been learning for the whole year. I've been exploring many ways. Yes. You're right. They are really different. And the artists I film are different. What I've said about Burning Life, there have been other artists that I have met like Rose Borchovski. For me, it was just an exercise for my eyes, how to catch the themes and an exercise to catch the ambience — especially with the Rose Borchovski's sim. It is not only the artwork which is important; it is how you capture the ambience that I'm quite interested in. I feel close to Rose's art. I'm a great fan of hers, actually. For me, it was important to catch the ambience, and maybe to add a bit of my personality. I don't know. That's difficult to say if I am transparent or if I put some of my personality in the machinima in doing that. I guess that where I want to go is to put, of course, more personality of mine into my work, but I also want to film stories like I did in *A Question of Honor*, which is not about art.

Phylis Johnson: Go ahead and tell me about *A Question of Honor*, as an illustration of how you like to craft stories. Tell me a little bit about that, and that direction.

Iono Allen: *A Question of Honor*. Well, I think that my best machinimas are those based on stories. The interesting thing, for instance, about *A Question of Honor* is that I made it very quickly on a kind of inspiration. One day, I said, "Okay. I think I have an idea. Let's do it." and I made it. At least the filming, the shooting was done quickly. The editing was its own project. When you have an idea, when you get inspired, you just go and film like you want to film. Especially in *A Question of Honor*, I had the idea of a sepulcher, and I found the light, as in what light setting I would use. Once this was established in my mind, I went there, and when you go there, you can't stop filming because the sim is really a fabulous work by itself. A very, very, very, very good build. Very good landscapes. But it's not too much. I like it very much, for it is a very good balance of landscaping and building, with even shopping. There are a lot of shops there.

Phylis Johnson: Typically do you do anything special to your filming environment? Like when you go into the environment and the environment is fairly much set for you, is it mainly a matter of how you work with lighting? Do you do anything special with lighting to create such beautiful images?

Iono Allen: Do you mean in Hosoi Ichiba?

Phylis Johnson: You can use that as an example. Yes, that was the virtual location for *A Question of Honor*. But I meant overall, what are some of your approaches to your lighting at a particular location?

Iono Allen: In general, I like to experiment with lighting, primarily relying on what is available in the environmental settings of *Second Life*. Even on my land here, if you use a setting, a night setting at midnight, you will see that I've worked a lot with the light. I really like that. In machinima, I don't add any light prim or such. I'm only working with the light settings internal to the virtual world. That is, however, in general. In machinima, I never used midday light and usually use the setting at nearly night when the sun is going down.

Phylis Johnson: Okay. That's interesting, even how you play with lighting on the grounds of your gallery and in your art, the use of color; you are very exacting in your work. So tell me a little bit about where you want to go from here. What do you envision for your goals?

Iono Allen: I have learned a lot in one year. I have learned many things to help me with making machinima. With virtual worlds, and especially *Second Life*, what I would like to make is a machinima which mixes reality into *Second Life*, meaning like we are here. We are human beings in *Second Life*. I look like a man; you look like a woman, Moo [Moo Money] the same, even if she wears a bunny outfit.

Phylis Johnson: *(Laughs.)*

Iono Allen: So what I would like to do is one day mix the real things that people have built in *Second Life* with completely imaginative things. In *Second Life*, a lot of people are building things as they were in real life. If you go to Paris 1920, it's very nice, but it's exactly Paris as it was. There is nothing new. There is no imagination, or it is just created as Paris at that time in history. I think it is interesting to mix both. I'm quite interested in mixing real images with virtual images. While some people do that already in machinima, I think that it needs to be more natural and not forced.

Phylis Johnson: That makes sense. You'd like to see more imagination with the recreations of even history, and plus see more of a mix between reality and *Second Life*. More fluid in the transitions between worlds.

Iono Allen: Yes because the virtual world is fluid. The virtual world allows you to emphasize your own reality. That's what I would like to do one day in a machinima. Kind of invent a story with this kind of approach.

Phylis Johnson: So besides *Second Life*, have you ventured into other virtual worlds?

Iono Allen: No. No. I know this one, and, well, I'm used to the build and can make small things here. So I manage things well here, I know this place. I won't go anywhere else for now.

Phylis Johnson: So you'll continue your gallery, as well as producing machinima. Are those your plans?

Iono Allen: My gallery. *Second Life* is a world of fantasy. It's my art collection. So my first fantasy was to build a gallery because in real life, if I were a wealthy man, it's what I would do.

Phylis Johnson: And your plans for machinima?

Iono Allen: Yes, yes, yes. Machinima is really an exciting thing, and actually, I think we are living in a very interesting moment. Very interesting period. It's a kind of, well, I guess we're attending to the birth of something which has no name for now, which is a mix between video, between cinema, between virtual worlds, where the images are built by computers. And I think that all this is going to be mixed, and there will be, in one or two years or maybe later, something with a name, which would be cinema, video, and machinima. There would be something; maybe it will be called machinima or not. And this period is very important. For me, it is like the period when cinema was born. For now, we just focus on some sharing platform, like YouTube, or Vimeo, and you are looking at some movie. Let's say a movie, which is built with images, which come from computers, cinema, movies, video, and all that, or even handmade animated drawings. I guess that all this is going to be mixed, and one day, you'll have a new medium, I think.

Phylis Johnson: Well, the angle that I thought was interesting was that you were capturing other artists' work. I think that's a really important and different aspect of machinima because you capture the beauty of others' creations in *Second Life*, an installation for example, and you document it. And then you recreate it, taking it to the next level. It's an interesting approach to viewing art through a machinima lens.

Iono Allen: I think that I have had some success like this because of my education. I told you about the art background, but what I didn't tell you is that when I was a teen, I knew everything about cinema. Classic cinema. I'm French so of course it was, at first, French cinema. French classic cinema. Then U.S. classic cinema. European classic cinema. I went to see other kinds of cinema too, but I knew everything at this time about cinema. I'm a bit older, about 50, and I never made any videos, never made anything with film until now. I had a camera to take photographs, but I didn't have any camera for filming. What I have learned recently is that I have all this knowledge which was buried for years about cinema, and about art. Well, art is always here, but now it seems in making machinima, I can create with my knowledge. My older knowledge, which was buried, buried, buried, wants to create machinima.

Recommended Machinima

A Question of Honor by Iono Allen, http://www.youtube.com/user/Ionoallen#p/u/5/YftouEm3CT4
Fears: The Story of Susa Bubble (An Installation by Rose Borchovski) by Iono Allen, http://www.you tube.com/user/Ionoallen#p/u/1/ByIIVpTvX38
Fusion by Iono Allen, http://www.youtube.com/watch?v=PaaQzut4Jio
Nine Steps to Heaven—An Installation by Betty Tureaud by Iono Allen, http://www.youtube.com/user/Ionoallen#p/u/0/HJB4OYb_p58
The Story of Susa Bubble by Iono Allen, http://www.youtube.com/watch?v=aJdVCqG3bZs

Kate Fosk

At the time of the interview, Kate Fosk was overwhelmed with preparations for the then upcoming Machinima Expo for November 20–21, 2010, in *Second Life*. She served on the executive committee, along with Phil Rice and Ricky Grove. She is an independent filmmaker from Northeast England, and is a business partner to Michael R. Joyce. Together, since 2007, they own Pineapple Pictures, a production company that produces machinima in a diversity of forms and genres. Fosk's machinima adventure began in *The Sims*, when she started building sets and creating her own content. Along the way, she met many interesting people when she started uploading some of her content to the Internet, and from there she would exchange it with others on *The Sims* Resource, which was the official way to share with other members. Fosk believes that a collaborative approach is at the core of what makes machinima unique, especially in platforms like *Second Life*. This is where we pick up on our interview with Fosk. The moderators are Phylis Johnson and Donald Pettit.

Kate Fosk: *The Sims* Resource was kind of like a slide show with subtitles at the bottom. So it was a really good introduction to storytelling. I used in-game engines. And then I found out that there was a community which made film and encouraged each other. I became involved in that. I got involved in *The Sims* machinima community — *Sims99* — and met Decorgal who was working on machinima. I quickly became friendly with lots of the particularly themer machinimators who I felt had a really unique perspective that I could identify with. Then from there, I was frustrated with the lack of lip sync in *The Sims* or overall the difficulty in creating the illusions which *Sims* had. When Moviestorm started it was in beta, but that was really the start of my moving out into the wider community. The rest of the machinima community went into *Second Life*. Lots and lots of machinimators that were not used to *Second Life* were invited in, and some of us really got hooked on it. After that, I really stopped exploring and seeing what other engines were out there. I got really interested in the community as well.

Phylis Johnson: Do you do anything else with *Sims* anymore? Have you gone back there in a while?

Kate Fosk: No. I think the frustrating thing with *The Sims* community was the issue on the licensing. I'm sure you must remember Phil Rice's film, *Male Restroom Etiquette*, that was really popular. It received millions of views, and he was invited onto prime-time TV shows to talk about his film, and he wasn't able to do it because of EA (Electronic Arts). I think there was some late-night chat show. There were a few offers to become much more mainstream, and Electronic Arts, who owned *The Sims*, just wouldn't allow it. So I think that was the ultimate wake-up call for me dealing with licensing. It's not really about money so much as having control over your films. And of course *Second Life* offers that as well. At the moment, I'm seeing that there's a divergence. There are people who are making films very much in game engines and enjoying doing it. And then there's another group of people who are really interested in the art of moviemaking and seeing machinima as a very accessible tool for doing that.

Phylis Johnson: And you see yourself as aligned to which community?

Kate Fosk: It's kind of hard to say, really. I think one of the characteristics that people would say about me is that I do tend to get about a bit. *(Laughs.)* I'm interested in the wider network of machinimators as a whole, but I think the communities that I don't take part in as much would be *World of Warcraft* because I don't have a license for that game, and I'm not that interested in the shoot-'em-up games either. I'm still interested in the films that come out of those engines. I think I've got a really hefty foot in *Second Life* even though I don't spend as much time here as I like. Probably the Moviestorm community is a bit where my heart is as well.

Phylis Johnson: How would you defend Moviestorm? There are some people that would say, "What is Moviestorm? Is it really machinima or not?" And so this kind of approaches the definition of what machinima is, so could you comment on that?

Kate Fosk: I have made quite a few blog posts. And I realize that machinima is a continuum, so you get people who are working in the office at Pixar who are making machinima. You wouldn't call it that because it's a professional organization. They're using very expensive machines. Any definition that would apply to machinima — there are people in professional organizations who make 3-D work and make machinima. I, in the end, decided that the thing that defines it for me is the community, that there is a definite approach to filmmaking within the machinima community, and that is the core for me.

Phylis Johnson: Just to clarify, what would that core be to the machinima community that would define it differently from falling into film or falling into animation?

Kate Fosk: It's a kind of a fuzzy description. It would be people who would turn live rendered footage into a film, but then there are all sorts of ways of helping you get your FPS (Frames Per Second) by using different tools. So that's not an exact definition. It's usually someone who's on a budget, who's at home, who's either making films for themselves or is interacting with us on the Internet. It does tend to be very Internet based. Of course, as you know, machinima has reached out more and more as we've gone on, and there have been numerous festivals which show films to people outside the community — art galleries and all sorts of places, which show and display machinima now, but it's still a fairly niche thing to be doing, I think.

Phylis Johnson: What type of work do you enjoy?

Kate Fosk: The things that I look forward to are the visuals and the sound design and the originality. So I'd really rather not mention anyone in particular because it feels a bit weird to do it when you're helping to run a film festival.

Phylis Johnson: No. I understand that. How about something personally that's close to you?

Kate Fosk: The film that we made. We finished last year. It was a film called *Park Tennis*. We made quite a lot of that in *Second Life*. It kind of looks like a bit of a trivial film, but there were a lot of things that run deep within it — the job market, people surviving in a world where there's a lot of economic uncertainty and people's survival strategies for that. It took a long time to do it. It was a two-year project. A whole year of that was spent investigating OpenSim. At the end of that year, I'd kind of had enough because it was too alpha for me.

It was not a spontaneous medium to work in or it isn't at the moment. My film partner is carrying on with that research while I deal with the projects, and we'll get back together and probably use it again once it's developed a little more.

Phylis Johnson: What genre do you like to work in yourself? Does it matter?

Kate Fosk: I always end up coming back to comedy because I love writing comedy and I love watching comedy.

Phylis Johnson: Is there a classic machinima example that you would like to pass on to people? I don't want to interfere with the expo, but we've been asking machinimists for examples to understand the essence of machinima's possibilities.

Kate Fosk: I think the film that I saw that really struck home and made me realize that there were possibilities beyond the comic and beyond the kind of trivial poppy films was one of the first made in *Grand Theft Auto*. It was sort of post-apocalyptic. There were two people on the roof talking. It was such a violent engine but they had made such a sophisticated story. It was the two extremes. It was showing that you can use machinima as a tool. You don't have to go with the feel of the original game, and as a director, you can go in and use that environment in any way that you like.

Phylis Johnson: I have another question along a different line. You have said machinima allows women to have a unique perspective. Let me pick your brain for what you think that unique perspective is or perspectives are that you've noticed. You have been doing this for quite a long time.

Kate Fosk: I've noticed there are some similarities between *Second Life* machinima and machinima made by good directors in *The Sims*. There's a real paying attention to the artistic cinematography of things—the color and the textures compared to maybe some of the rather movement-orientated films that could be made by beginning male filmmakers. There seems to be that kind of a gender difference. Of course, if there's an engine where there aren't that many female filmmakers, and one comes along, then you certainly see the engine in a different way. You have this female perspective on the color scheme and just the way of filming.

Phylis Johnson: Are there other examples—maybe with *World of Warcraft*? Phaylen Fairchild did some mixed machinima with *Second Life* and *WoW*.

Kate Fosk: If you're thinking of *World of Warcraft*, there's a machinimator called Legs Machinima. I don't know if you've ever seen anything by her.

Moo Money notes in chat that Legs was the one who produced the *Out in the Cold* video that she chose as an example in the author's call for best practice.

Kate Fosk: Yeah. You were talking about Phaylen's film, which I've seen. I love her writing and I think she's just got wonderful comic talent. I think Legs Machinima has the real visual quality. If you watch her work, she really makes the *WoW* engine look different.

Phylis Johnson: When you contribute to a piece, or you work with someone, as you do, do you feel like it's a female perspective, or is it Kate's perspective, or can you really separate that?

Kate Fosk: I think there's a bit of both. I know when I'm working with Mike and we're script writing, he will say that he thinks I have more talent for naturalistic dialogue. He will tend to think things through visually, story lines, whereas I can kind of hear characters talking in my head. I think that's a writing thing more than a female thing. I think I bring that kind of surreal going off-of-a-tangent creative process.

Phylis Johnson: What are some other issues you think that are really important? Any issues that are really close to your heart that you would want to discuss in terms of machinima.

Kate Fosk: I think machinima is such an enabling medium. You can make wonderful things at such a low cost. It means that people who would never ever have the chance to make a film are able to do it, and that is really important. Like a lot of other networks that are developed on the Internet, there's a meeting of minds which means that a whole greater sum of individuals participate; people are able to bounce ideas off each other. I live in a small village north of England. I would never meet anybody else who was making films, and I get to meet people every day who are making films from all around the world. There's the international community side of it. Obviously, as you said, there are the legal issues. I feel frustrated when people have spent what could be up to a year of their life making a film and they have not really understood that they didn't own their film at the end of it. Because they haven't known about the licensing issues in certain engines or they haven't realized that if they used certain music, they would be limited in what they could do with that film. I feel passionate about the education side of it — our rights. I think it's important that we have a clear understanding of what we own and what we don't own and take ourselves seriously enough.

Donald Pettit: I noticed that you and a lot of other high-end production companies started making your own sim on your own computer or your servers. I can see that as a natural reaction to these things where people lose — like you say — their ownership to their work only because of the legalities. I just want to say I see what you're doing and why that has been done. That would be very, very disheartening.

Kate Fosk: Personally, I've found it really difficult to get a sim working on my own PC, though my film partner, Mike, has managed it. You can make a film in *Second Life* and you can own the film. If you put a lot of work into something, you don't want to feel under risk.

Donald Pettit: That's correct.

Kate Fosk: I've been getting into a lot of open-source software recently. It's interesting how that is developing. You know, OpenSim and open-source software are in a very early stage. It feels like things are opening up for people.

There's a much wider group of people who have access to more complex tools. I think that's to the good.

Donald Pettit: I think so too. It gives you a safety factor. I was at some fair here in *Second Life* and they were giving away the code to set up your own little mini sim on your computer

Kate Fosk: Well, last year at the Expo, we had presentations for different engines. Not the whole lot, because there would be too many. It so happened that I was helping to present *Second Life*, and one of the things that really struck me about the benefits of *Second Life* is the possibilities of collaboration. In fact, it's difficult to make a film on your own without it being just a one-off film.

Phylis Johnson: Let me ask you about the educational side. Have you done things in terms of any collaboration with any educational facilities, or anything like that, or people along that line?

Kate Fosk: As part of the Expo, we're forging links with universities. One of the sites that we're using in *Second Life* is owned by a university in the south of England. The keynote speaker is a lecturer from a university in the north of England. We're just talking now. We have people in the background from the U.S. who are working in universities there, and hopefully they will be appearing as well. There seems to be a lot of research interest in machinima and new media. They see these types of gatherings as a good way to learn about these tools. So it's at that level. Maybe because I used to kind of work in teaching. I don't necessarily do a lot myself, but I very much support it when I do.

Donald Pettit: I think we covered a lot here. I am very curious, however, as I've looked at some of your stuff and I enjoy it. It's very, very interesting. With all the production you've done, do you have a favorite character you've produced?

Kate Fosk: I really like the pair from the last movie, *Park Tennis*.

Donald Pettit: What do you think makes a strong character?

Kate Fosk: It must be how much you can show emotion through animations, whether they're feeling anger or whatever. You feel like you're kind of going on this emotional journey with them, as the creator.

Donald Pettit: Sort of like an empathy thing. Have you had any issues like in costuming? Do you do your own, or do you contract people? Again, that's also part of your character and animations—those kinds of things.

Kate Fosk: The fantastic thing about *Second Life* is being inspired by other people's creations. You just find an outfit, or find an avatar that you like, and suddenly a story will appear out of it. I do make up my own clothes and skins and so on, but not to the quality of people who make them every day, and that's what they do. If I want something special, I'll make it, but in *Second Life* anyway, I would buy it because other people are just much more dedicated and able to spend a lot longer making these things. It's incredible what you buy for your money—how much time people have spent making skins and so on.

Donald Pettit: That's true. I find that myself. Sometimes it's easier to go out and talk with some makers and get some good stuff. I know that Beans/Kate has been on the MAG site for a long time. She's one of the old-timers on the site. She's been very supportive there. It is nice to get to meet you finally too.

Kate Fosk: It was lovely to meet you. I've been delighted to see how much work you've done with MAG, and I thought the site was a wonderful idea.

Donald Pettit: I really love to get people started and then just watch them grow. When they're new in *Second Life*, or in the virtual type part of it, I'll give them all kinds of advice and direction. I really enjoy the art form. I know it's going to be around longer than me and I hope that we turn out some really good machinimators. I think we are.

Kate Fosk: Part of my motivation for spending so much time on the Expo is that I feel strongly that there are people out there, outside the community of machinima, who would really love to see these movies. There's so much out there that they get lost. By grouping movies together and getting what a small group of people might think is excellent, you might spark some interest. There's a cumulative effect over time.

Donald Pettit: Well, I try to get people to move past the music video and into something more meaty, something that has a story involved. That always makes me happy.

Phylis Johnson: Kate, as we wind this interview down, let me ask, do you see other *Second Lifes* coming up? Or are there going to be other directions for which we should be on the lookout? Or woe to us, for we should be protecting ourselves because if something happens to *Second Life*, where will we be then? I know you're working on Moviestorm, but is Moviestorm really the same thing as your *Second Life* experience?

Kate Fosk: No, it isn't, and it's not meant to be. It's a filmmaking environment, whereas *Second Life* is a great deal more than that. My feeling is that I'm tending toward the 3-D web idea. As it becomes easier and easier for people to interact in 3-D environments, I think the possibilities will spread, and *Second Life* will be seen as one of the first. I think *Second Life* has shown a lot of people the possibilities of virtual life. There seems to be a definite pattern that people will not understand what you can get out of *Second Life* until they're here. The people that do, they couldn't have imagined. There's an experiential part of it that you just can't explain. You've just got to experience it.

Conclusion

Kate Fosk and her business partner, Michael R. Joyce, spend considerable time experimenting with machinima techniques and tools. They have helped to advance the field, while having fun creating machinima along the way. Fosk was instrumental in the planning and execution of 2010 Machinima Expo and continues to evangelize machinima as a unique way to entertain audiences. She

clearly understands the value of creating movies in and for interactive environments, and looks toward a host of virtual possibilities in the near future.

Recommended Machinima

Park Tennis by Pineapple Pictures, http://www.vimeo.com/10714505

Michael Gray

What interested the authors in contacting Michael Gray was his role as a
machinima reviewer for "*WoW* Moviewatch" for *WoW Insider*. Moo Money
had preceded him in that same position. Gray seems to have a very reflective
and objective viewpoint on what's out there in the way of machinima, what
kind of machinima is happening in *WoW* and why, and who the top people are.
He brings to his position an educational background in literature and English,
and his idea was to bring a comparative literature approach to his machinima
reviews rather discussing graphic quality and techniques. For Gray, it is more
about the producer's ability to communicate to an audience through well-
crafted storytelling than anything else.

Michael Gray: Actually, in a lot of ways, I lucked into being involved in
machinima at all. I did a certain amount of film studies in college, way back
in the day, of course. But that's not really exactly how I got into it. I started
working at *WoW Insider* coming up on three years ago as a general news writer,
because a lot of my background is in journalism and publishing. I started working with *WoW Insider* back then, and one of the things that we found ourselves
needing was somebody who could do a daily column regarding it. So I stepped
in very lightly. Even now, two years later, with this being something that I do
every day for a couple hours a day, I still don't have necessarily the technology
guns to always be able to review it on that level.

So when you look at machinima and the stuff that I see every day, for *WoW*
machinima, you have the machinima aspect of it — the machinima dynamic,
where you have people like Baron Soosdon and Gnomechewer who are doing
these absolutely glorious, incredible graphics and displays, and this very artistic
vision. Then, on the other side of the spectrum, we have someone like a gentleman named Crendor who speaks more to the satirical, tongue-in-cheek aspect
of *World of Warcraft*. There's kind of a sliding scale between the two in terms
of, "Are you doing something that's more about *WoW*, something that's more
about machinima?" and then you also have these folks out there who are doing
music videos, which is always very exciting for me, because my wife is a singer
and a performer, so I get very much into the musical aspect of it.

Cranius creates music, and work with, for example, Legs, a machinimator who just does an incredible synergy between the music he's doing and the graphics and the animations that she's doing. They really create something that's more than the sum of the parts. That's where I really get excited, where I see people blend together the different dynamics, something more than just a visual feast and something more than just a *WoW* story. I see so much different stuff, because I get some days 100 new videos sent to me, but all are not on the same level, and some of the material I just can't publish.

Phylis Johnson: Do you see a lot of blending between *WoW* with other games like *Halo* and those of a similar genre? Do you see more and more of that kind of blending going on right now?

Michael Gray: You know, with the technically and graphically advanced guys, definitely. Today's video actually was a rerun of something Baron Soosdon did, called *I'm So Sick*. Totally the work that he does is crazy, bringing together all these different games, and the models. He uses stuff like *Garry's Mod* (a sandbox physics engine).

Donald Pettit: Right.

Michael Gray: Soosdon and another called Myndflame are the two that are responsible for me getting into machinima in terms of why I took the gig when it came up, and why I got excited about it. I remember there's a story that I told a couple of times about my wife and I, back when we lived in a condo, and we were sitting and decided to go look through all of these movies. We started with Baron Soosdon, and I remember thinking, "Oh my god! If we could get this guy to use his powers for good!" Because *WoW*, the graphics and the stuff that he's doing, and one of his videos, I'm very sorry, I forget the exact name of it, but it's a riff on *Portal*. [Author's note: *The Device Has Been Modified*.]

Phylis Johnson: Yeah.

Michael Gray: And he did this *WoW* version of a video for *Portal*, where he's playing with a remixed version of *Still Alive*, and playing with *WoW* models, and playing with that whole concept — just really awesome stuff.

Phylis Johnson: I saw that.

Michael Gray: So he's definitely, more than anyone else I can think of off the top of my head, bringing in outside elements. But that's also why I talked about, you have the technical group like him, and then you have the folks who are very much focusing on *World of Warcraft*. They're not looking outside to the other camps at all yet.

Phylis Johnson: Okay. So you watch 100 videos a day. That's a pretty healthy machinima community. I have a series of related questions, and I will ask them all so you can see where I am going with this. How do people stay in touch with each other? Is it through machinima.com and things like that? Or is it through the *WoW Insider*? Or are there other communities? How does machinima play into the actual game players' routine as well? Is it something game players want to watch and find entertainment with? Or is it something more or less for the machinima community that is forming in *WoW*?

Michael Gray: Okay, so this is kind of the dangerous question — well, if you are familiar with the genre of *WoW* machinima called Belf Rap, you will know why. *WoW* announced that *World of Warcraft* has 12 million players. Concurrently. Right now. Twelve million people playing *World of Warcraft*, and that makes it one of, if not the, largest MMO (Massively Multiplayer Online) game. So when you're talking about a group of 12 million concurrent players, and then in addition everybody who has canceled their account, and then there's a lot of *WoW* machinimators who actually don't play *WoW*. Anyway, so you're talking about a huge community, and so there are a couple of genres, even inside *WoW* machinima. One of them is Belf Rap. *Belf* stands for Blood Elf. It's one of the races in *WoW*.

Phylis Johnson: Right. Right.

Michael Gray: This guy named Nyhm was actually, in a sense, the first Belf rapper, but that's not really what he was doing at the time. He just kind of spawned a generation. Belf Rap is kind of this genre where they take rap, or blues music, or hip-hop, and they do a parody based on *World of Warcraft*, and then they set it to machinima. Machinima.com has recently been reaching out to *WoW* machinimators in a way they never have before. I mean they're really out there, really bringing a lot of folks together. But before that, the Belf rappers communicated primarily on YouTube.

You would have somebody, Gigi she went by, who was huge in growing the Belf Rap community and a lot of *WoW* machinimators in the last year. There was a period where the art had really kind of slowed down. It lost a lot of steam for various reasons. So she went out to all the Belf rappers and really worked with them. In an interesting parallel to the real-world rap and hip-hop community, they all started doing collaborations with each other. That really kept them going at an insane pace that I've never heard of from anyone else in machinima. Because they really almost production-lined their work, where this person was doing the lyrics, and they were due by this Wednesday. Then by Saturday, somebody else would have a machinima up for it. By the middle of next week, they'd have the tracks all laid down.

Donald Pettit: *(Laughs.)*

Michael Gray: So, really, they were kicking out an immense amount of work. Then, also, one of the reasons we have these feasts and famines is because there's a lot of fan contests, where folks will get a hold of a beta key and say, "All right. Create a 90-second machinima." Or a 15-second machinima is the shortest one I've seen. Everyone and their sister will run out and try to create stuff to compete for that beta key.

Phylis Johnson: Right.

Michael Gray: And it's really where they are based. A lot of it is on machinima.com. A lot of it is actually YouTube, Facebook, and individual blogs.

Phylis Johnson: So what are some of the difficulties with — I know that

Blizzard is fairly friendly, in terms of machinima people — but what are some of the restrictions that confront machinima people in *World of Warcraft*? Are you familiar with some of those?

Michael Gray: Yeah. There are a couple of things that I hear about, and one of the first ones — a good friend of mine, a guy I have a lot of respect for, is Clint Hackleman, over at Myndflame.com. One of the challenges that he frequently encounters is that, while Blizzard is friendly to machinimators, they are very strict with controlling their brand and controlling their IP, understandably. So machinimators who want to do things like put ads up on their pages, or sell any kind of derivative work, are really kind of challenged. So that's one. [Author's note: see Myndflame's *Blizzard & Machinima Law*, 2009.]

The second thing that I hear is that some of the models have not been updated in many years. It's actually one of the reasons Belf Rap, for all that I talk about it, is a good example of this also. A lot of the viewing audience has gotten kind of burned out on blood elves, and they're tired of seeing them. The problem is that blood elves are one of the two most recent races with the most advanced models, the best resolution, the best emotes, the best innate animations to use for machinima. For some of the work that people do, there's the reality that if you put a blood elf and a human character next to each other in your animation, the human will look bad, because it's a four-year-older model and technology has come that far. So that's kind of an issue that they encounter. The third and last one is that there are trolls in any network. In a game with 12 million people, that's a lot of trolls out there to troll the world.

Phylis Johnson: *(Laughs.)*

Donald Pettit: So the characters, like I know in the platform that we're from primarily, they're getting ready to do a mesh improvement, which will improve everybody's avatar concurrently. I guess in *WoW* that doesn't happen. Your older avatars, or characters, stay as they were is what you're saying?

Michael Gray: That's correct.

Donald Pettit: Wow. *(Laughs.)* Okay. Wow!

Michael Gray: They'll change armor types and gear and such as they advance the character.

Donald Pettit: That's very interesting.

Michael Gray: One of the things Blizzard has talked about, about why that is, is that folks are very attached to their characters because it is an escapist game. And it's a character that you develop from level 1 to, coming up with the new expansion, 85. You get very attached, and they are apprehensive to start changing those character models because it may lead to a sense of disconnection from your character, and they don't want that.

Donald Pettit: So for a *WoW* player, your avatar's appearance isn't so much important as it's actually almost a badge of honor having an old character that has gained, like you say, levels, and obtained many things.

Michael Gray: Yep.

Donald Pettit: So, I understand. It's just a different philosophy. Gotcha.

Michael Gray: Correct.

Phylis Johnson: Well, the other thing I guess is the machinimist would have a different perspective on this, with them wanting a concurrent look and continuity in their machinima.

Michael Gray: Yep.

Donald Pettit: So you couldn't switch it on and off—the mesh and the resolution. It's too bad.

Phylis Johnson: That's an interesting point, which I didn't come across, on why there were so many of those elves in *WoW* machinima. Makes sense now.

Donald Pettit: *(Laughs.)*

Phylis Johnson: It kind of works. For me, it kind of works because it plays into the fantasy and everything, but obviously it lacks a lot of the other characters that maybe some of the older players can relate to. So who is the machinima audience? Who watches this, do you think?

Michael Gray: We actually have a lot of different demographics. We've seen a lot of different numbers about that. Sitting where I sit, I get to see who clicks on what. The machinima audience changes a lot according to the kind of machinima, which might be a no-brainer to say. But I'll say, for example, Belf Rap videos, which for all that it's worth are not appreciated as much among the more regular machinima crowd, have a very good showing with a money demographic being 18- to 25 year-old males. They get a lot of clicks from those genres.

By comparison, story-based machinimators, my favorite example of that is a woman named Selserene who does some absolutely gorgeous film noir work. She has a series called *In for a Penny*. She does very well with the slightly older female group. Who's the audience? *WoW* players, and occasionally one of the machinima kind of goes viral. For example, there's a *WoW* version of *Boom De Yada* that was done by Irdeen, and wow, everybody saw that. Everybody knew that. There's actually viewing demographics among our machinima. It makes a difference who's watching what. If I post something from Crendor, the game players love Crendor. The machinima watchers, not so much. Baron Soosdon—anyone who's ever liked machinima digs him. But then some of the game players do too. So there's a different audience per artist.

Donald Pettit: Okay. That's interesting.

Phylis Johnson: So how many female machinima makers are out there?

Michael Gray: Shooting from the hip, I'd say actually I deal with more female machinima folks than I do male.

Phylis Johnson: Impressive.

Michael Gray: The gentlemen tend to work a little bit more on the graphics. The women tend to work a little more on the story and music. But again, that's me shooting from the hip.

Phylis Johnson: Understood.

Michael Gray: I'm trying to think, and for every machinima gentleman,

I can think of a machinima lady, very easily. Personal opinions vary. "Do you think Crendor is as valuable, or as highly rated, as Cranius?" So that's a personal opinion, but they both certainly have a huge fan base.

Phylis Johnson: Interesting. So where do you think machinima is going to go? The *Cataclysm* game is about to come out in December [2010]. I mean, how is that going to change anything? I know there's probably going to be a rush of new machinima out there, but where do you think everything is going to go in terms of *World of Warcraft*? In the short run, probably a little bit more blending, maybe? What other things do you foresee for the future?

Michael Gray: You know, I would hope for more blending, but one of the things I expect to see happening is that there's a seasonal affect to *WoW* machinima so far, where somebody holds a contest. All of a sudden there's a lot more machinima out there. In the last six months, with the current expansion having become somewhat stale, there haven't been as many contests and attention. So what *Cataclysm* will really do for us is get sponsors again for contests, and get people moving again. So that's kind of exciting. For all that I see of a lot of machinima, how much do I see at the top tier? I haven't been seeing the top-tier stuff as much lately. I'm hoping with the BlizzCon machinima contest coming through, with the work of Machinima Realm and that of machinima.com, that we'll spark some more of these really refined artists.

Phylis Johnson: And who are these people that make *WoW* machinima? In the various platforms, we all come from different backgrounds and stuff, so I'm just curious. Who is this person? Is it somebody that has never picked up a camera before, and this just gives them an easy, accessible way to be creative? Or are they film majors? What was your take on the people's background that got them involved in machinima?

Michael Gray: A lot of the folks just seem to find themselves with a little bit of time on their hands, they're kind of curious, or they're inspired by someone. So they give it a whirl; they see what they get. Then someone like me comes along and will say, "Hey, everybody check this out!" and they get some encouragement. Then they go on and grow and they do a lot better. They just keep doing more and more. Those with a professional background, such as Crendor and I, and even I think Baron Soosdon, all decided they wanted to try it out, and they got into it; there's an IRC (Internet Relay Chat) channel where they hang out and talk and swap techniques, and they just keep doing more and more.

Phylis Johnson: What do you think the age range of machinima producers is?

Michael Gray: The youngest one I've encountered so far was seven, or was it eight? And that wasn't top-shelf stuff, but it was awesome for somebody at that age. And there's another young woman [Demachic], at 13, who did a series of Britney Spears videos, which got a huge following from a lot of ages. The eldest I know has a couple of children, is a very loving mother, and I believe she's in her mid–40s. So there's a fairly big range. *World of Warcraft* itself has a huge range of followers, and machinima kind of follows behind that.

Donald Pettit: Anything in particular that you think a newcomer to *WoW* should pay attention to, in terms of producing machinima?

Michael Gray: I would say the biggest thing is what I started off saying. *WoW* machinima, for all that it is, has so many different subgenres in and of itself that you kind of have to classify it a bit. I talk about the Belf Rap, talk about the Crendor-like satire, so if you have a successful machinimator, people are going to follow that style, and you see a lot of that. You can kind of trace the origins. To understand the music and the "filk" part that I was talking about, I would definitely check out Cranius, and one of our favorites by him is *The Ballad of Darrowshire*. Check out *Big Blue Dress* too, which is this incredible ballad he wrote inspired by a quest chain in *World of Warcraft*. Beautiful piece of music, beautiful machinima.

Phylis Johnson: But I think when you look at machinima, and storytelling, that there's a lot more in common with the people that like to do the storytelling in the films. A good story is a good story. It's all about characters.

Michael Gray: Absolutely. When you're spending that much work creating a video, how much time do you have to play the game? So maybe you're not as over-invested.

Conclusion

Gray is a respected machinima columnist who appreciates the accessibility and creativity of machinima, as a reflection of pop culture and the gaming world. He has been following machinima trends and reporting on how they relate to audience viewing beyond *World of Warcraft* to an increasingly mainstream audience. He has witnessed how women have brought their own unique perspectives to machinima as makers and viewers. Gray helps us to visualize *World of Warcraft* as a source of art and inspiration for virtual filmmakers.

References

Gray, Michael. (2011). *WoW* Moviewatch. *WoW Insider*. Accessed January 8, 2010, from http://wow.joystiq.com/category/wow-moviewatch/

Myndflame. (2009, May 4). Blizzard & Machinima Law — Part 1— Does Blizzard Hate you? What is Commercialization? *Myndflame Machinima Advanced*. Accessed January 8, 2011, from http://myndflame.gameriot.com/blogs/Guide-me-plz/Blizzard-Machinima-Law-Part-1-Does-Blizzard-Hate-you-What-is-Commercialization/

Recommended Machinima

Bear Cows by Myndflame, http://wow.joystiq.com/2010/10/22/wow-moviewatch-roflbear-the-bear-cows/

Big Blue Dress by Cranius, http://wow.joystiq.com/2008/04/14/wow-moviewatch-big-blue-dress/

Darrowshire by Cranius, http://wow.joystiq.com/2010/08/16/wow-moviewatch-darrowshire/

Boom De Yada by Irdeen, http://wow.joystiq.com/2010/10/12/wow-moviewatch-boom-de-yada/
I'm So Sick by Baron Soosdon, http://www.joystiq.com/2010/10/07/wow-moviewatch-im-so-sick/
In for Penny by Selserene, http://www.youtube.com/watch?v=VV_kw81CCUc
My Name is Nyhm by Nyhm, http://wow.joystiq.com/2008/06/30/wow-moviewatch-my-name-is-nyhm/
Out in the Cold by Legs, http://wow.joystiq.com/2010/12/24/wow-moviewatch-out-in-the-cold/
The Device Has Been Modified by Baron Soosdan, http://wow.joystiq.com/2010/09/07/wow-movie watch-the-device-has-been-modified/
The Guild Charter Guy by Crendor, http://wow.joystiq.com/2010/03/24/wow-moviewatch-the-guild-charter-guy/
The Interrogation by Gnomechewer, http://wow.joystiq.com/2010/12/30/wow-moviewatch-the-interrogation/

Rysan Fall

Rysan Fall has been involved in producing machinima for nearly three years and seems to be the perfect person to talk to when you want to know its potential. He has done about everything in machinima, from a forum for virtual newscasts complete with field reports, to short feature films, to filming weddings and events, to creating professional music videos for real-life musicians like Craig Lyons. His machinima production of *Across the Universe* for Lyons' team has received major accolades among not only his professional machinima peers, but from music video fans and producers. Fall fell into machinima, and it has taken him around the world, having presented his videos at various exhibitions. What started as a fluke has become a profession for him. In this interview, he shares his thoughts on what machinima is to him, defying any narrow conceptions or misconceptions of what is possible through its production process. Professional machinimist Moo Money assisted Phylis Johnson during the interview, filming it and injecting a few thoughts and questions off microphone, with one focusing on Fall's voice work in machinima and another about his views on pre-production. His primary software is Adobe Premiere, namely Adobe Photoshop and Adobe After Effects and Sound Booth for his audio. To Fall, machinima is the means, an artistic path, to capturing real life as it exists in virtual worlds and sometimes as it reflects reality; and it is also a way to reimagine media production.

Phylis Johnson: What I want to know, first of all, I've seen your work, and you've transitioned a lot. You've been continuously growing, so now, comparatively, how do you define what you did before in machinima, compared to what you do now?

Rysan Fall: Wow. That's a great question. I kind of got started in it as a way of practice for real-life film. I was editing a really short period of time before I found *Second Life*. I'd done only a couple of real-life things, and I had totally planned to go back to it, but the demand for machinima became so overwhelming that real-life video took a backseat to everything. At the same

·

time, each time I saw other people's work, pieces or certain elements that I admire of their work, I tried to incorporate them into my own, like clarity or the way they do transitions or whatever, and then put my spin on it. For the most part, I just keep practicing. If I'm logged on, I'm working on something. That's just some kind of indication of how it is. I've never expected that to happen. This was all a fluke on how I got into it, actually. I made the first machinima for a friend of mine just to try and practice some editing techniques and stuff. Then it just snapped from there. It was amazing. I really never expected to be in *Second Life* this long to tell you the truth. If it weren't for machinima, I really don't think I would have spent that much time with it.

Phylis Johnson: Right. Well, you've done a lot of different things. You've done machinima news, and all these other kinds of genres. What's your favorite?

Rysan Fall: Wow. What's my favorite? That's hard to say because they're all fun. You know what I mean, even a machinima of a lecture that I had to do for a law class one time, where they wanted me to film their machinima about criminal justice in virtual worlds, it was very interesting. They had a bunch of professors from real life that handled, dealt with this kind of thing — Internet crime and crime within virtual environments. I enjoyed that one. For the most part, the ones I like doing the most are the music videos. Anything creative, anything that I get to do for my own brain, or whatever, is the one I have the most fun with. Usually I'm making a video for somebody else. That's the cornerstone of my videos, actually. I'm out for hire. It has been that way since I started making it. So I very rarely get to do anything for myself. *Strange Fruit* was for me. A couple of other pieces were for me, but not a lot. Usually it's for somebody else, and I try to do the best I can.

Phylis Johnson: How do you take the criticism against music videos? I mean I enjoy music videos too, but there's sort of that debate between what is machinima. Are music videos "real" machinima, for example? A lot of people say machinima should be a story, or it should be this and that, but when people make music videos, they're not using the full potential of machinima.

Rysan Fall: Oh, no. Whoever is saying that is completely wrong. I think machinima is a reflection of real life. It's real-life video making. I think I mentioned that earlier. Anything that you could do with real-life video making, you could do with machinima, if not easier in some elements. You could recreate special effects at a fraction of the cost that it would take to do in real life. You know what I mean? To pigeonhole it into being for one type of video making, I think that would be wrong. I mean, there are all sorts of applications for machinima. Anything! Ever since I've done this, I've done so many different types of videos. I couldn't even see pigeonholing machinima into a certain genre or type. I think that would be absurd. Chantal Harvey did something amazing one time. She made a children's video using machinima, and machinima would be perfect for something like that — making children's stories, educational videos, tutorials or anything. Anything. There are so many applications to this.

Phylis Johnson: Okay. Well, I agree.

Rysan Fall: I think the only thing that's holding it back is the animation limitations. If it were not for that, you could do anything.

Phylis Johnson: What makes a good machinima? You watch a lot of machinima, so how do you recognize a good machinima? Usually it entails what?

Rysan Fall: A good machinima has to be kind of catchy, and it has to be really quick. It has to grab your attention quick, hold it, and then release it quickly. I've found that people's attention spans are really short with machinima. If you're going to make a long machinima, you'd better have a lot of content going on in that video. I think a lot of machinimators make the mistake of holding scenes too long on the same subject, and they're not cutting in between scenes fast enough, I think. They forget that. They forget what's going on in their background. You've got to make sure everything is clear, like no pose balls or voice dots, or anything like that. *(Laughs.)*

Phylis Johnson: *(Laughs.) Second Lifers* will know what we are talking about.

Rysan Fall: I can't believe how many machinimas where I see pose balls, or something in the background, which naturally wouldn't be there. It kind of takes away from the art of the whole thing. I think just paying attention to your environment, what you got going on around you, would help out greatly in a lot of people's machinima. What else? What makes a good machinima?

Phylis Johnson: Like what grabs you and attracts your attention?

Rysan Fall: I like artsier stuff. If you could have two people sitting in a room with nothing going on, but the conversation is great, I wouldn't even mind like that — something interacting between men and women, or two different types of people, or two different types of cultures, or something like that — something where somebody could learn from it, or whatever.

Phylis Johnson: You brought up the question of culture, and we talked about that previously outside of this interview. In terms of your views, in terms of the African-American perspective as well, I would like to ask you for your take on the cultural opportunities in *Second Life* to create art that reflects a diverse perspective and in your case, machinima would be the medium to do so. There isn't a lot of media representation, I think, personally, of race and ethnicity; especially I don't necessarily see a lot of black machinima, if you were to say there was such a thing as that. I don't really even hear that term. It would seem like that would be an empowering term.

Rysan Fall: Right.

Phylis Johnson: I wonder what your views are on that.

Rysan Fall: I don't see a lot of black machinima either, actually. Of the ones that I do see, it's more of that stereotypical stuff. You know, a lot of booty shakin', a lot of dance videos where it's projecting the stereotypes and stuff. As far as positive black machinima, there's not really.... There are a couple of machinima troupes out there that deal with basically just R & B videos. They're very good, but then again, it's nothing really progressive. You know what I mean?

Phylis Johnson: Right.

Rysan Fall: By way of any means of education. I'm all about teaching somebody something or learning something myself from somebody else's stuff.

Phylis Johnson: Well, your *Strange Fruit* was really good. And that was a service to Virtual Harlem.

Rysan Fall: Yes, there were things about the song and Billie Holiday that I didn't even know about before I made that video. It was really enlightening and I was surprised to see how well it was received, and I'm still getting compliments over it. I'm really glad that machinima is being recognized as a viable art form. I've seen it in so many places now. You see it all over the place.

Phylis Johnson: Right.

Rysan Fall: I actually had to talk about machinima for a presentation one time, and I had to look up some things about machinima. It had a really long history that goes really, really far back, to tell you the truth. It's just now cracking the surface, and mainstream film companies are using it, like I said, for special effects. They can get something done cheaper than they normally would be able to produce otherwise.

Phylis Johnson: So where would you like to go with all this? I remember the first time I met you was, I met you but you didn't meet me, at the second birthday celebration of the Machinima Artist Guild, and you had to do a presentation on the history of machinima.

Rysan Fall: Right. That's what it was. Yeah. That's it. *(Laughs.)*

Phylis Johnson: I'm just wondering, where do you see yourself going in the future, with all this?

Rysan Fall: In the future?

Phylis Johnson: Are you going to move machinima into real-life projects more, or you kind of did that with Craig Lyons' music video, *Across the Universe*. Where do you feel you're going with all this?

Rysan Fall: I have some opportunities already on the horizon that I am not at liberty to discuss at this point. Like I said, just everything that happened, from me making that first machinima, and me talking to you, being interviewed, being in magazines, and being flown out to California back and forth, just because of machinima. It's such a fluke. I never expected this. Really. This company flew me out to California, treated me like a king for a week, because of machinima.

Phylis Johnson: Who would you say is your inspiration for machinima? If you were to name maybe just three names and say, "Hey look at these people because I think they are it!"

Rysan Fall: I like SpyvsSpy. Lainy Voom, she made a machinima called *The Dumb Man*, and that's the one that I saw after I made my first machinima, and I kind of used that as a focus point, like I want to be that good. So Lainy Voom, definitely, you've got to mention her. I like SpyvsSpy because of his effects. He's really nuts with it. *(Laughs.)* I'm all about special effects and everything like that, but he's on another level with it, and I want to get to that level with him. Who else? I like Toxic's work. Toxic Menges and Chantal Harvey.

Phylis Johnson: You've told me in previous discussions that content is far more important than necessarily the effects.

Rysan Fall: Yes. I agree.

Phylis Johnson: So anything you'd like to pass on, in terms of advice, along that line?

Rysan Fall: Wow. There are so many things I could say. But I think that one of the great things about machinima is that it gives a schmuck, a nobody from Connecticut like me, a chance to do something great, like artistic, with very little money, and be able to express themselves artistically just out of the basement of his home. I think that's the beautiful thing about it. It affords the people the opportunity where they would never have had that before — to learn filmmaking and editing, and things like that. Stick with it. *(Laughs.)* Any new person is going to get discouraged with their work. I was too. I even thought of not doing it for a little while. If that's what you're into, keep learning as much as you can, from anyone who does it. That's the best advice I can give.

Phylis Johnson: So what about your voice work? Moo is asking that question in the background. You have a wonderful voice, and I have heard you on various projects before in *Second Life*.

Rysan Fall: *(Laughs.)* Awww. Shucks. I do voice-over work and for companies in-world also. Every once in a while if you're in a store, or something like that, and they have audio playing, like a commercial, and you hear somebody that sounds like me, it's probably me. *(Laughs.)* I've done machinima projects before that used my voice. I'm also playing Captain Stillson in Doc Groom's *Awakening*. That's another thing that'll kill a machinima too. If you have voice actors in a machinima and they're kind of like deadpan, really monotone which I hear all the time —"We're making a movie here. Find somebody that can talk well."

Phylis Johnson: Not only that, I think it's really important to be able to spend time on, just not the voice casting, but it's the whole sound bed that needs significant attention.

Rysan Fall: Sound is so important. It's the marriage between sight and sound that makes a good machinima. You must blend them well.

Phylis Johnson: Anyways. Another comment from Moo— she is saying a lot of machinimists do not try to set the scenes.

Rysan Fall: No, they don't. Storyboarding and everything like that is wickedly important. Can't tell you how much — yes, staging and all that.

Phylis Johnson: So basically you do a lot of planning then.

Rysan Fall: Oh, yeah. You must plan everything out. Honestly, I can't edit until I see it in my head first. I don't do a lot of storyboarding. I do a lot of it in my head, which I shouldn't do. But I have to put it in order of the sequence. You must know what you're going to film. You must know what you're going to do. If you're going to make a machinima, you should see it before you do it. Some people just film, just point the camera and just shoot — point and record. That's it. It's good. Post it. No, no. *(Laughs.)*

Phylis Johnson: And if you're doing this commercially, what happens is you're overwhelmed with hours of tape. It would not be effective for a client or anything along that line.

Rysan Fall: I agree.

Phylis Johnson: Okay, I am going to ask you about something you once mentioned to me, about what I will call borderline machinima, in terms of maybe unrated videos, with somewhat to extremely pornographic or violent content produced as machinima, in the genre of gothic or vampire, or other themes. Where do you see these themes fitting into the scope of machinima, because there is a growing online popularity for those types, as well as a niche audience? Do they detract from the machinima community overall?

Rysan Fall: Unfortunately, some of these things are negative. Yet, its mere existence gives legitimacy to the whole art of machinima. As a whole, you're not going to get away from it. Sex is saturated in *Second Life*. It's just ridiculous almost to think that machinima would be protected from that, or be exempt from that. *(Laughs.)* It would be kind of ludicrous. There could be a machinima about people having babies, or people getting married, or a lecture, a music video. There's sex. There's violence.

Phylis Johnson: Right. You do weddings.

Rysan Fall: Right. It just rounds out the circle, I think. *(Laughs.)* You have to take the good with the bad. If anybody has anything that's worthwhile doing, there's always going to be somebody that will focus on the negative.

Phylis Johnson: I've seen you grow professionally. It's been interesting and in a very short period of time, too.

Rysan Fall: Thank you. I'm learning and trying new stuff every day.

Conclusion

Fall is one example of how far one can go as a producer of machinima, with a dedication to learning his craft and a willingness to spend long hours building his portfolio and skills. He has excelled in showcasing music, history and social issues through machinima, and his gift has become recognized internationally on more than one instance. Fall has found his niche and continues to evolve, as does the field itself.

Recommended Machinima

Strange Fruit: Billie Holiday Tribute by Fall Films, http://www.youtube.com/watch?v=Q7Wo4RAmJcU
Across the Universe (Director's Version) by Fall Films, http://www.youtube.com/watch?v=MaRxjRlM
    TWg
Black Soul Rhythms Radio Commercial, Fall Films, http://www.youtube.com/watch?v=ZnY2hQsnAac

Wiz Nordberg

Wiz Nordberg is the chief executive officer of Treet TV, a virtual-world television station that creates broadcast content and streams it online across the world. The station began as *Second Life* Cable Network (*SLCN*) and evolved in the larger enterprise, Treet TV. Viewers inside *Second Life* have an opportunity to watch a variety of programming, from virtual sports and news to fashion on their *SL* television. They can also watch programming live and on demand on the Internet. The process for creating content is machinima. Programs are recorded live, often in front of a studio audience, and then made available for immediate or later viewing. The authors had an opportunity to interview Wiz Nordberg on how he became involved in machinima content creation and distribution.

Phylis Johnson: What was the process that launched Treet TV to the company it is today?

Wiz Nordberg: We were one of the, if not the leading, entertainment developers in Australian Internet for music companies. We had companies like Warner Music, for which we did strategic platforms for them. These were fairly big things. They were not like artists' sites. We worked with Sony BMG as well. We did the music sites for the largest telco here in Australia. We also happened to stream about 40 entertainment webcasts, three of which were the largest ever done in the Southern Hemisphere. That's loosely related because that is the way *Second Life* Cable Network got started — my partner Grace and I were in *Second Life* for about a year, purely because it was a diversion while we were involved in real-life things like running our company. Drawing from our entertainment background, Grace has established a relationship with the Australian Trade Commission, particularly because it was very interested in exporting Australian music to other countries. That was about April 2007, at the time of a South by Southwest Music Conference which became pivotal to our next move. The Australian government helps to fund several bands to attend the conference. At the same time, many were left out. We had the idea that — this was unrelated to doing video or anything — to actually get about seven or eight Australian bands who would have loved to have gone to South by Southwest to perform in *Second Life*. This was before we thought about television; the goal was to get people from South by Southwest involved.

In 24 hours, the Australian commission went from not being interested at all to consulting with public-relations people that said "you must do this." This was right at the height of people beginning to believe that *Second Life* was some sort of special phenomenon. So when we did that event because of our background in webcasting and Internet concerts and so forth, it seemed obvious to me, "Well, this should be a webcast." No different from when we would have the Red Hot Chili Peppers on stage or a similar event; to me this was the same thing. I realized the best approach was via webcast. We had the all equipment. I did some experiments and I suppose other people have done this but I set up a screen in-world. Basically, we had a "video" camera, a computer shooting *Second Life* video going through a streaming server that we owned, and it was being piped back into *Second Life.*

What was interesting is that it was similar to, let's say, an island in the South Pacific where people had never seen a transistor. People in *Second Life* would stand in front of the screen and watch themselves dancing! And the things that they would say were astounding to me. I realized especially at the time that there was no real technology or company or method that reflected the lives of people in *Second Life.* People were building things, having events, playing hockey and all kinds of sports—yet there was no artifact for many of those activities, no documentation, nothing of the sort. I think that accounted for the reaction.

Honestly I believe that was the day I registered *SLCN* on my computer. And I don't think I had any idea why this was so significant at the time for at least a year. *Second Life* seemed very much like another country to us. Governor Linden was a big deal to residents, and discussions on the need for governance in *Second Life* became prominent. *Second Life* felt like a country, and I thought, every country needs a TV station. There were metaphors for everything else in *Second Life,* but what seemed missing was television. This led us to create a prototype show called *That's Life,* which was produced solely to prove to ourselves how to get the techniques in place and to show how it was possible to integrate television into *Second Life.* A picture is worth a thousand words; a video must be worth a million. So that is how *SLCN,* now Treet TV, got started.

Phylis Johnson: Could you explain the workings of the television station?

Wiz Nordberg: We had a video studio in our actual Internet company with an editing suite. We had produced videos for music companies, so we had road cases filled with OB (out broadcast) equipment. This was our background, and sort of a life we knew well and understood. When we initially positioned ourselves in *Second Life,* we did exactly what an OB company did, but within a virtual environment. In fact, if you were to call a video production company today, many would say, you know, what Treet does is very difficult to accomplish.

Well, it is not very difficult. If you were to call a video production company, and say, "I would like a quote for a one-hour live Internet broadcast that will involve three different computers mixed together using video capture software," they would roll in with lots of rack-mount equipment to do this, and they would probably charge you about 20,000 to 30,000 dollars for that hour. It's an off-the-shelf service that companies in any city in the United States would do for that kind of price. We started out with the same type of equipment. We have Sony scan converters and vision mixing equipment. We do not capture the way machinimists use Fraps or similar programs. We have scan computers that are wired to assist in vision mixing. If you were to view the production of a three-camera sports broadcast from an OB van, you would see a setup almost exactly like the one we have today in our studio.

From a technical point of view, what we are doing is quite standard in the video industry. Yet there are many things that an OB company, if you called them, would not do compared to what we must to accomplish our goals. We have learned necessity is the mother of invention. We routinely mix Skype and *Second Life* voice together. We routinely mix audio from multiple cameras together with what's going on in *Second Life*. We record everything in broadcast format and mix it down from different sources. And we have developed these techniques tailored specifically to the broadcast problems inherent in *Second Life*. Some of those would be the same problems one would encounter with any sort of video in an animated "game" environment. We have gotten quite good at this to the point that our studio is ready 24–7, such as if you want to produce a one-hour show in 5 minutes from now; we could be "live to air" within 10 minutes, doing your show. There would be no problem. It is very predictable.

We have experience with real-life television workflow, so our background has been transferable to our *Second Life* operations. If you produce a live television show, you'll have a run sheet. You might have an asset manifest. We help our producers learn how to apply those types of concepts to *Second Life*. They send us run sheets with blocking and information about interstitials, so we can use that as a guide during production, especially because we mix it together live. We go through a workflow of encoding. We used to require three people in our studio all the time; now we can operate with two. So it's actually become quite inexpensive to produce our programs. For example, on our new schedule, we'll have eight shows being produced on Sunday. That will be eight hours of programming that will be completed by Monday. There are not many people who can produce eight hours of finished machinima in eight hours.

Phylis Johnson: Where are you going with all this—can you say?

Wiz Nordberg: I wonder myself. I don't know quite yet. That's the simple answer. One thing that is clear to me is that an insatiable desire exists among people to chronicle their online lives. Now this solely does not extend to video and machinima, and *Second Life*. This is all over the Web. But we are fairly much zeroing in on the kind of immersive recreations that people have with regard to these experiences. People have in-world meetings. They create sports. They have battles. Increasingly I hope people will begin to tell stories, which unfortunately does not happen as often. Our goal is to figure out how to empower more people to become involved. That is sort of our goal as a company. I think when you go through these start-up things, you learn a lot about what you are doing. One of the things we've learned that is critical to our success is the necessity of enabling tens of thousands, or hundreds of thousands, of people to do what right now only a dozen can do. That's very important to us. That's something we are investing in for the future.

Phylis Johnson: Any plans to expand your operations to other worlds?

Wiz Nordberg: We're interested in other virtual worlds. But I don't think the answer is quite that simple. With *Second Life*, we see something unique that, we believe, will become extremely popular and mainstream. That is not to say that I believe *Second Life* is going to be "it." But what we see in *Second Life* is the ability for people to fashion creations entirely of their own invention where there is no preconceived plot, story line or environment. It is to me a completely generic animated production studio. That is what *Second Life* is. When we look at other worlds, *World of Warcraft* being one of the more notable ones within the constraints of that world, people are doing some interesting machinima. But when we further study it, we see that is very limited compared to *Second Life*. The number of people who are interested in engaging in content creation in these other worlds is actually far less than *Second Life*. So one of the things that fuels creation of our type of machinima is empowering people to create what they want to create, not to create within a constrained framework. I believe those types of platforms that give people the power to create anything will become more and more dominant. That's the business gamble. Right now, *Second Life* is one of the few environments, almost the only, where a large percentage of people engage in unstructured creation. I suppose that is the criteria I see.

Phylis Johnson: What is the criteria for programming?

Wiz Nordberg: We get a lot of show pitches from producers, and our criteria always surprise them. We have two criteria in determining whether we support a show idea. Our first is actually a practical one. Is it producible? That is a much more difficult question than it seems. We are not really concerned whether people can do the first show, but more concerned with whether they can do the 50th. I think that doing a single creative half hour or hour is something that lots of people can do. They can amass a team; they can generate a lot of energy; they can do some remarkably creative things. That is almost a different type of process. What we want to be assured of is that all those elements will continue week to week. For that reason, "Is it producible?" means do the people that are pitching to us have a team, do they understand how to manage people, do they have the commitment, and do they really, really realize what they are getting into here? So that is one of the first criteria.

And the other criterion is what community the producers bring to Treet through that program, for which it becomes the magnifying glass for that audience. You see, I believe our role is not as creator; our role is almost to focus a lens on something and magnify it and chronicle it. It's very difficult to create something from scratch. We have many people pitch us programs like *I Want to Be a Lindenaire*, or lots and lots of other ideas. Everyone believes that the idea is what we are looking for — but that's not true because even if you have a really good idea, it takes a great deal of investment of time and energy to get people to watch those shows. It's sort of a risk mitigation thing I suppose. Is there any existing community around these people that are producing these things that will simply flock to what they are creating? It saves us wondering if there's going to be an audience. Then after that, we begin to ask a whole bunch of questions among ourselves. Does this seem like a good idea? But usually people who pitch us think that we are interested in the idea first, and that is usually the last thing we're interested in.

Phylis Johnson: What has been your best programming decision?

Wiz Nordberg: Our best decision in programming has been not to judge our programs ourselves but to try to let audiences assess them. That is probably the best decision we have made in programming overall. And we have had some programs that have been very successful — *Metanomics, Tonight Live with Paisely Beebe* and *Designing Worlds*. We have had other shows not as successful in terms of viewer numbers. We have learned something from all of them, and we work with all of them. I have to stress we have only had two shows that went out of production. A number of programs were series. We did one called *ISTE Eduverse Talks* [on behalf of the International Society for Technology in Education (ISTE)]. It actually went longer, but it was planned as an eight-week series. And we had a conference series based on *Virtual Worlds Best Practices in Education* (VWBPE). But only two shows — *Sail On* and *Music Academy onLive* — are no longer in production, both running two years. The rest of the shows that we started are still in production, with most of them having done well over 100 episodes. We have a total of over 3,000 episodes on our website. We have been fairly successful at making sure that we've gotten production teams that can really do the work. We don't pay them; it is a cooperative deal with all our producers. They work really, really hard. Each one of these teams has learned and developed their own valuable techniques for how to produce these types of shows.

Phylis Johnson: The best advice for machinimatographers?

Wiz Nordberg: The best advice is to make sure you understand why you are doing it. Really, I think that there are lots of different motivations. The thing I see most often is that people go into something believing that they are either going to make money or that they are going to be popular, or they have the illusion that if they create something people will automatically watch. And that's not true. "You build it and they will come" doesn't work. Often people who want many viewers believe that the idea will bring in the audience. But it's not really an idea that brings the viewers; it's promotion and other types of things. I am a very practical person, and I tend to think that if you are going to start something and you are really going to follow through on it, you don't want it to fail. And be sure you know why you are doing it. If you are not doing it for the money, make sure you don't mind if your bank account goes empty. If you are doing it for the money, make sure that you have a way to reach enough people to do that. I think that's a constant lesson that we're learning and relearning ourselves to make sure you have a very good understanding of what your goals are. The other thing, I suppose, is that the dream you have is always a lot harder than it ever seems, so make sure you want it so badly that you are willing to go through all the crap that you are going to end up having to go through to get there. Be ready. Be ready. That's advice from the trenches, I suppose.

We have a very different perspective on making these videos than a lot of people I talk to. We are very harsh on ourselves. We look at the things that we do. We listen very hard at what viewers say, and what viewers say is all that matters. I think you have to be harsh on yourself. You have to say, instead of saying "this is all wonderful," you have to say, who thinks it is wonderful and where are the people who think it is wonderful? You have to seek out those viewers, or if you want to call them customers, you have to be so focused on pleasing them that you are willing to put your own opinions second and put the opinions of others first. Now I do think what we are doing is a unique television thing. Machinima is very broad and it is a technique of producing something, so it can be done like television; it can be done like cinema. You can produce documentaries. I think there are different bits of advice that you can have for all of these forms. If someone is producing something very creative like a movie or a story, maybe the advice isn't "listen to your audience"; the advice is "listen to your heart." But I think for television, where our goal is to chronicle the lives and happenings of virtual people, what good is chronicling something if you have no audience? So for us, what the audience says is everything. I would think that many good television stations would echo that sentiment.

Phylis Johnson: How does your philosophy compare to out-world TV stations?

Wiz Nordberg: We monitor and collect an amazing amount of data, even do focus groups. We have viewing parties in-world where people watch our videos— anonymous people that don't know we're Treet watch our videos and we listen to what they say. And we have been doing that for a while off and on. So we're desperate to try to figure out exactly what people think. That drives everything we do.

Phylis Johnson: Could you expound on your company plans for the future?

Wiz Nordberg: "Do you want to be the next NBC of pixels?" some might ask. People in-world sometimes look at me like I'm *Second Life*'s Rupert Murdoch. It makes me laugh. In some ways, I suppose it makes sense. It's silly in some ways too. I've spoken at real-life film and television seminars and workshops in conferences. One of the big differences between the way that programmers at MSNBC or CBS would think and the way we think is that CBS, NBC, HBO, and others are interested in a small number of markets of millions. That's what drives those businesses, whereas we need to be interested in a million markets of small numbers of viewers. Not even a million markets, but we need to be interested in a large number of markets that have a modest number of viewers, because that's the way the Web works. In fact, that's the way this type of content will survive. So I think one of the dangers of anyone that is in video production online and trying to sort of compete and wedge themselves in using online as an opportunity, is that they often look at how traditional media reaches millions of people — like *Boardwalk Empire* was watched by 5 million people on its first night. That's what you want to do when you're HBO. Most empowering Internet companies do not work off of that type of model. So I think that reversal is probably the biggest thing I would add that can make what we do [online, virtually] successful.

Conclusion

Nordberg continues to push the boundaries of machinima content, seeking innovative means in creating original programming with unique ways to involve audiences within interactive environments. The consistency in quality programming developed for the Treet TV network, as well as the company's support of the crews behind the shows, is indicative of Nordberg's success at building an appropriate infrastructure that unites audiences to content creators. Machinima thrives under such conditions, and its definition continues to evolve within a television network model.

Roundtable One:
Terminology, Technology and Practice

A series of roundtable discussions on machinima themes were held in summer 2010 within *Second Life*. The first two sessions helped to define machinima — it strengths and weaknesses in storytelling and practice, technologies/techniques, and other related topics. All sessions were conducted on the Island of Fame at the offices of Lowe Runo Productions, LLC, within *Second Life*. The first session was held Friday, June 25, 2010. The second session, June 30, 2010, continues the dialogue among a different set of machinimists, as well as those involved in diverse aspects of the machinima community. Among the various attendees, there was a wealth of machinima experience with various software and game engines. The authors, Phylis Johnson and Donald Pettit, moderated the discussion.

Session 1

The authors, as moderators, introduced the series of roundtable sessions by examining different perspectives on machinima, examining its origins and present uses, as well as looking toward the future. As part of that defining process, the discussion touched upon the strengths and weaknesses of machinima. Attendees at the first roundtable included Alley McNally, Asil Ares, Evie Fairchild, Cisko Vandeverre, Pooky Amsterdam, and Tikaf Viper. As discussed in chapter 1, defining *machinima* can be contentious at times, and viewpoints differ greatly among producers and the various people involved in the creation process. The level of experience varied among the attendees, but all were familiar with the filming environment of *Second Life*, and many were familiar with competitive and complementary technologies, gaming platforms and virtual environments. With that in mind, the discussion begins...

Phylis Johnson: All your statements—spoken and written—are public record, and by being here today you provide your consent for your comments to be published in this book, and other related forums. Let's begin, with how you would define *machinima*. What is your definition?

Cisko Vandeverre: To me especially, it is to visualize ideas. I use these tools to make animation films; I use virtual worlds to capture films because I don't have to render. I can use this giant store for props, as I always say, props for peanuts. So if you want some special things which you are not able to build yourself, you can easily get it, in that it is Linden-dollar based, fairly fast; if you are going to pay, you are going to pay under 100 Lindens. Machinima is a professional combination of animation, cinema, and machines. But this is more or less recreational descriptions. To me it is the tools to make animation in real time.

Donald Pettit: So to me, you might be saying it is an economic way to get into animated 3-D filming.

Cisko Vandeverre: Yes, in comparison to classic animation and 3-D animation.

Pooky Amsterdam: I agree with Cisko that it is a way to make one's dreams and one's vision real, although I think that has been the province of the artist to interpret that in whatever medium they choose to use, whether that's stage, theater, painting, or writing. It is certainly a visual representation. It is again animated cinema done on machine, and it is through the use of graphical engines that already exist that we are able to use these platforms and create our characters, our sets, and scenarios with which we can then impose our will and film, as any film director does. I think it is an interesting distinction to make, though, and one I certainly think about a lot, between game engines like Moviestorm, iClone, and an engine of course like *Second Life*. If there is going to be a definition or distinguishing mark in machinima, I wonder if it will be there. Moviestorm of course is great. The director has complete control over so much, whereas in *Second Life*, because it is a virtual world, you don't have as much control, but you have so many more assets and so much more ability to create rich visualizations. And at some point, you endure trade-offs between engines, but that is a different kind of question. I would say that the core use of machinima use is the ability of the graphic platforms we have available through game engines to tell our stories. I think there was that demo function in Quake for a long time, [then] people recorded their kills or the level upgrades—but it really wasn't until *Diary of a Camper* that somebody used machinima to tell a story. That really paved the way for using a game engine to do this, and to create this, and we all are taking this, and using this, to push it as far as we can.

Donald Pettit: Pooky, since you have been involved in all this, how has it been enriching to you? How has it changed, how has it evolved? Basically in my life, I went and did little funny dance movies on my little bit of Linden property to making really big, really involved FX stuff which I didn't ever think

I would be into. So it has actually been a personal development for me. But are those things that you have seen evolved since you started, and especially with machinima since you have been working with it?

Pooky Amsterdam: I think you make an excellent point. And that is that the development and evolving of the medium happened through you. It's your evolution. That brought what you're doing with machinima to another level. And I think that might be how I have to look at it too. I mean the engine exists. Along the way, there are new technical things that have happened. Of course there is WindLight that has happened. And of course being able to use the Kirstens Viewer for shadows is a great thing. And with the new viewer, you have a lot of other tricks in that sense.

Donald Pettit: How about you personally — how have you evolved with your practice of it?

Pooky Amsterdam: It has enabled me to push my dreams even further. I also think machinima is a very intimate kind of experience. There is nothing I think that I can't do with machinima. I see this as a huge platform. As how it has pushed me, now I stay up at night and I watch old movies like total classic movies and I say, could I do that shot? How can I make that moment happen where he looks at her and where she's walking down the road? And how can I capture that feeling? because that is what we respond to as an audience and that's what we want to portray as filmmakers, or what I want to, because that is what I am involved into, sort of those intimate human moments, and that intimate human experience, that is unique and universal at the same time. I guess that using machinima has enabled me to say, "Yes I can do this. Yes this can happen." Machinima has freed me and has allowed me to have no limitations. I accept that I may meet them and find them, and I am willing to try every single time. It has given me a license to thrill; what can I say?

Donald Pettit: Cisko, in your personal life, how have you evolved with machinima, along with the same topics?

Cisko Vandeverre: It depends on what you want to see or cover as a story.

Donald Pettit: I would like to see your very first cinema.

Cisko Vandeverre: My personal style hasn't changed so much. With every production, the main thing, especially in *Second Life* or if you are using other commercial worlds, video games, platforms, or whatever to capture footage, the main thing especially on *Second Life* is how you handle the animations and all the alts.

Donald Pettit: A good point. Okay, I see another guest at the table. It's Ally McNally. Ally has done some features and she has a contest going on too now, I believe.

Ally McNally: Yes, I do. I am trying to encourage new machinima artists to give it a try.

Donald Pettit: We're talking about what machinima means to us, our definition of it, and we certainly would like to hear your opinion.

Ally McNally: For me, machinima allows me to experiment with projects that maybe I would not otherwise be able to do due to money and transportation issues that I have in real life. So I get to experiment with different things. The biggest thing for me is that I am still evolving with my art. I think we are all evolving. I have challenges like you, Cisko, with that the available animations are not what I would like them to be to really get the kind of story that I want so far. But I think it's definitely a great way for people to get a story told. I think I am a bit too wordy with myself, but it is probably coming from my theater background where words are so important. That's why I am having the contest right now that prohibits words.

Donald Pettit: Interesting. Very good. Very good.

Pooky Amsterdam: I have one quick comment, and that is, I think that it is very important in using machinima to play to the strengths of the platform and to mask the weaknesses. And that is something that I am also learning to do, and it's something I think is critical. Nobody sees because this is theater, right—*document réalité*. Nobody sees what goes on behind; the audience will only see the final product so you can mask and camouflage, and avoid the weaknesses, and I think that is important to do. I just wanted to make that comment.

Phylis Johnson: Could you expound on the weaknesses, Pooky, from your experience?

Pooky Amsterdam: When I talk about *Second Life* within that context, I can say facial expressions can be limiting. It is important to either catch them at the right point or match them at the right point or tweak the avatars. Inner structure. That is a weakness and has to be worked with. Lip sync is also sometimes a challenge as we know. And that is something that also has to be masked. Awkwardness in movement of the body — you know you cannot film somebody standing up in any kind of real meaningful way. I mean we understand it. But I do want to make machinima without apologies. I don't want someone to have to be a *Second Life* resident in order to appreciate the film that I am doing. We make a lot of excuses for machinima, and I want it to stand on its own. Movement, facial expressions, and lip sync — I think those are the great challenges. Also the prim, the way the physics is, it is very hard; I will stop there because I am mainly talking about [machinima] film. I am not talking about the shows or the interactive television or the social TV, which I certainly see myself on the forefront of. But in terms of film, this is an amazing engine for prototyping. Also think about it for prototyping expensive commercials or television films. And I see us where Francis Ford Coppola was years ago when he started using video for editing, when he'd shoot it in video and started video storyboarding to save himself time and make his presentation richer. Just imagine — we could do explosion after explosion here and it's extremely cost effective, beautiful and possible.

Donald Pettit: Thank you very much, Pooky. That is a very good observation.

Ally McNally: It is interesting what Pooky said about lip sync. I personally despise it. Generally what I do with my films is get rid of it altogether because a lot of times I am dealing with Furries, so it doesn't look right. I think the biggest thing for me is that I get to have big expensive sets for fairly no money because I can build it myself. I used to be a builder myself. Also almost anything I can find somewhere in *Second Life* or I can build it myself and roll with it. There's also the transportation issue. I just stay in my room instead of trying to go half across town.

Phylis Johnson: Ally, where would you like to see machinima advance?

Ally McNally: Where would I like to see it go? It would be interesting to see a way for us to go more organically to record machinima. Now, for me, it is a very laborious process to get the film to feel very organic. The animations I have to use have to be sliced together to make it feel organic. We have a character standing, let's say, and I want her to laugh or to cry; I have to use a HUD. It is easier to just go through a list of the animations if she is going to stay in the same spot and click those animations and in post select the one that I want — the section of it that I want. It would be great for me to be able to have a show that would be live to tape, where I wouldn't have to do that. Because right now if I do a show (I have done this too in *Second Life* where I have performed), I am either sitting the whole time or I am standing and you get to see my radio (voice) waves, and as far as I am concerned that is not a very interesting machinima show. Generally what I do in SL, I don't keep the audio. I record all the audio later and put it on the piece.

Cisko Vandeverre: When you record lip sync, you should record the sound.

Phylis Johnson: At what point is the concept of machinima lost, if it is, when the producer incorporates post-production elements not internal to a game engine? Or, how about those that might argue that storytelling is central to the definition of machinima, or it cannot be validated as machinima?

Pooky Amsterdam: I think if you do a film and you film with a film camera, a commercial or a movie or an industrial, it is still considered film. You are making film. I think that is the same thing with machinima. You use the game engine, the graphic game engine, to create a product whether or not it's a real-time broadcast, or a training film, or we just completed something for Moog Market which is absolutely stunning. That is, as far as I am concerned, a machinima, where you are using the graphical platform. We're using elements of *Second Life* to create this. So I think it will be helpful for us as we all move forward to say that animated cinema done on machine is machinima. How different artists and different people and different filmmakers use it is a testimony to its adaptability and value as an engine for use. It cannot be boxed into a category. "It has to tell a story or it is not a machinima" — I don't think that is valid any more than you can say that somebody doing a film or putting out a video is an actor in a video. If they are doing an interview, for example, that is a video; what else would you call it? To legitimize the term of *machinima* to make it more broadly used and adapted, I think it is helpful to include it as a genre and medium itself.

Ally McNally: I agree with what you are saying, Pooky. It is kind of like saying that a person who modifies a computer per se is not a hacker. That was the original term, and that meant you hacked away something to make something new. I think the only main variation, like gray area, is when you are combining machinima and film. Otherwise if it is recorded using a video camera of any kind, it's film. If it's recorded using some sort of game engine, it's machinima. It really is that simple. It can be anything within that spectrum.

Donald Pettit: Very good observation, Ally.

Phylis Johnson: So that takes us back full circle to the definition of *machinima*.

Cisko Vandeverre: I think the meaning of *machinima* is actually, you can make animation frames—you can use these—there are so many sorts of ways of doing animation films. And if it is called video, film or machinima, I do not think it is important for a filmmaker. He has to choose his platform or his tools. And if the tool is called *Second Life* or it is called Virtual World or a video engine game or whatever, then it's a tool to produce his story if it has a story. So I don't want to be too strict on the meaning of *machinima*: we have the machine, we have the animation, and we have the cinema. These three combined represent the meaning of *machinima* for the main public. It starts to get recognized as such. In the past, we had cartoons, and what were the first cartoons? It started with Mickey Mouse, Superman, and all this stuff, so we have this genre emerging and maybe machinima is truly a comic from the future, the 21st century, the digital society. Maybe machinima will become the books of the digital society, which I strongly believe in because nobody is reading in the future. And so this is my thesis that machinima and its future adaption is a tool to produce stories; and I don't want to go against writers and authors, but for generations that are coming up, the ability to read will go down definitely. They will read maximum the headline, and the rest will be shown through picture or told.

Donald Pettit: This is something that has always been a curiosity to me. I have iClone on my computer now. I have Moviestorm. I have been playing. I play with it once in a while. And then you have something like 3ds Max, which I also have. Let's say I produce a feature on each one of those platforms. Are those all machinima?

Cisko Vandeverre: No. When you do it in the classic computer animation, then it is computer animation. I think the rubric between machinima and computer-generated images, well, they are still or moving; but these are two different technologies.

Donald Pettit: So iClone would not be considered machinima?

Pooky Amsterdam: How can you not consider iClone or Moviestorm machinima?

Donald Pettit: This is why I am asking?

Pooky Amsterdam: I can understand 3ds Max as being computer effects, but how can you say that people who do work in Moviestorm and iClone are not doing machinima?

Cisko Vandeverre: No, they are doing computer-animated films. I mean I don't know where that discussion will go.

Pooky Amsterdam: So let me ask you this, so are we not also doing computer-animated film? We're animated through the computer.

Donald Pettit: (*Laughs.*) Again this is why I asked. The concept of machinima is becoming harder to pin down in some respects.

Cisko Vandeverre: To me machinima is not the real-time aspect that makes a computer-animated film into machinima.

Donald Pettit: I will interject one little thing. Some of my newer features—and I will say this, it incorporates *Second Life* mixed with 3ds Max, mixed with other programs—and to produce my final thing to *WoW* people, without the tool of all those tools, I would not be able to make a very interesting feature. So I am going to say I use all of those, and I don't think that disqualifies my machinima, but again I think Cisko has a valid point. When you use just one of those, and I would call them your PC-based software, you do take away some of the spontaneity of machinima capture. Say, without that spontaneity, you could never do a live show like *Dating Casino* on 3-ds Max. You just couldn't do it; well you would be doing it, but you would already know the results. I would interject the same goes with Moviestorm or similar platforms.

Pooky Amsterdam: I would also like to ask, a movie that uses green screen technology, does that mean it is not a film anymore because they are not using actors in a room of a set and filming them? They're putting on an overlay of something that might be in fact computer generated. And how could one say a film that uses a green screen is not really a movie, not really a film in the classic sense of, let's say, Brunelle. It's a film, it's a film. It is legitimate as that.

Phylis Johnson: So might we say that when a machinima becomes a tool rather than a technology, it is no longer about creating a story or archive of virtual life, but it is employed as a tool to cross over for real-world applications? (Thanks, Moo Money, for the question and possible delineation.)

Cisko Vandeverre: As I said, for me, the main difference to call a piece a machinima or a computer-generated mixed reality or whatever is when you capture something in real time that the engine you are using and the platform you are using gives you the footage in real time. Then you can say it is machinima.

Donald Pettit: So real time for you is the kicker, the main point?

Cisko Vandeverre: Of course.

Pooky Amsterdam: I just don't know what isn't real time. You film even on Moviestorm in real time. The difference is that it is not coming out of a multi-user virtual environment. That is something I brought up in the beginning. It is a very legitimate distinction and a very interesting one.

Cisko Vandeverre: When you see *Avatar*, a top-notch computer-generated movie, would you call that machinima?

Donald Pettit: No, I wouldn't. If you created a machinima version of it, I would; but you would have to do it like that. You would have to come in-world, go to one of those role-play *Sims* (inspired by the movie) in *Second Life*, and deal with the owner, and film it.

Phylis Johnson: Could you do it on Moviestorm?

Donald Pettit: Sure you could.

Cisko Vandeverre: Moviestorm is a tool which was developed by filmmakers to do pre-production.

Pooky Amsterdam: You don't have any pre-or post-production in your films.

Donald Pettit: My early ones did and they were awful. One case in point, a girl dancing on a platform; that was my early one.

Cisko Vandeverre: I would like to clarify, a technical problem. Computer-generated images need a lot more machine power. Twenty years ago, we were far, far away from real time and the more complex scenery. The more time you need to render such images and the game engine's simulation platforms like *Second Life*, your computer needs to be able to render that.

Donald Pettit: And consequently it is a big plus. The spontaneity is.

Cisko Vandeverre: As we see especially in *Second Life*, we are real-time and 3-D puppets; we want to see the same thing at the same time. We have the graphics—at the moment we see other platforms that are stand-alone which are becoming photo realistic.

Pooky Amsterdam: Have you never inhabited another avatar, Cisko, for film? Then that's not you in real time. You have created a puppet to act how you want.

Cisko Vandeverre: Right.

Pooky Amsterdam: ...on *Second Life* which is a graphical computer platform. That is also a definition of what you would do if you wanted to use Moviestorm, and let me say I am sitting here—actually standing here now because I am all excited. I have never used Moviestorm although I am going to be investigating that—I have never used Moviestorm and am not a fan of it because every woman looks the same. In fact, I have written a script for a film that is a cross-over between Moviestorm and *Second Life* that I would very much like to do over the summer. You know I am a huge advocate of *Second Life*, and this platform as well, and I will say you create the character in a graphical engine—you make that character speak and move how you want. To me, if you are in *Second Life* or if you are in Moviestorm, that's a big similarity.

Cisko Vandeverre: As for the outcome, I agree; but the technical behind it, it's completely different, and that makes it necessary to distinguish between what is machinima and computer animated.

Donald Pettit: I think there is a bit of rivalry between people who do machinima among various platforms.

Pooky Amsterdam: They don't understand it, and that's why I think Cisko taking his extreme position is very valid and very important in this discussion. While I may sit here and give another opinion, it's very important for Cisko to be there saying it has to be on an engine like this in order to bring *Second Life* forward into the machinima platform. Look at machinima.com. They have such few *Second Life* videos there.

Cisko Vandeverre: Right, right. There you see the main content is from *Halo* and all these war games.

Donald Pettit: Cisko, we have heard you and Pooky. Tikaf Viper and Asil Ares have joined us in text chat.

Tikaf Viper: Machinima is a visual story created through whatever computer science technologies or virtual platforms are available.

Asil Ares: The technical definition of *machinima* is filmmaking within a real-time, 3-D virtual environment, often using 3-D video game technologies. As for story or story making, I would say that it's just another way for people who make movies to tell their stories. It's the medium that makes it unique — unique in much the same way that video technology was unique when it was first introduced. For makers, video was a revolution because of its cost-effective nature. Now, without going into the politics of which media are "better" (35 mm, 70 mm, analog video, digital video, high definition, etc.), what makes machinima unique is how it frees the maker from the real-world constraints of the "camera" as a physical object in the world around which you construct a shot. In the game engine, the camera can go anywhere, have any POV. Now, there are certain camera conventions (like depth of field) that you can't recreate in real time. But we have post-production tools that can assist with this.

Tikaf Viper: But then, Asil, no difference with Japanese animation movies, right?

Asil Ares: Tikaf, I would say that it is a way to make movies. How folks use it is affected by culture.

Pooky Amsterdam: That's fairly much the history of machinima and how it has evolved over time.

Asil Ares: The most important issue for me is how will people using this technology make money with it?

Pooky Amsterdam: Wonderful.

Asil Ares: If a media is to thrive, it has to have a viable commercial aspect. Look at this thread: http://promag.ning.com/forum/topics/red-dead-redemption?xg_source=activity. Most of the game engines will *only* allow the maker to use it for noncommercial purposes or their own promotional requirements.

Tikaf Viper: The difference is between having a job and doing machinima for fun.

Donald Pettit: Asil and Tikaf have given very good discussion points.

Asil Ares: Here is the thing with being able to make money. There are many ways this can be used. Not only in the direct aspect of making a machinima for paid consumption, but as a tool for pre-production of a different kind of film. And I think it is important to recognize how the online distribution works within these environments. I would also recommend looking at this online book, http://neovictoria.ning.com/group/admin/forum/topics/the-psychology-of-cyberspace. Dr. John Suler's hypertext book explores the psychological aspects of environments created by computers and online networks. The other person I'd recommend following is Mike Jones, http://blogs.digital-mediaonlineinc.com/digitalbasin/entry/20070410. He's an educator and highly technical, but it's his thoughtful analysis of the virtual camera that is definitive for me.

Pooky Amsterdam: I think that the original definition of *machinima*, as I said coming out of something like *Diary of a Camper*, was a revelation — the revelation that this could be used to tell a story. And because of that, filmmakers began to see machinima as a storytelling device. With what I am doing with the *1st Question*, and the other game and media shows I am developing, is using this for more than a beginning, middle or end story — although indeed the show has a beginning, middle and end just like a television game show. Now, would you say that *The Twilight Zone* wasn't television but *The Price Is Right* was? You can't say that. Or *Kraft Mystery Theater* wasn't television. It's television — it's on the TV. You see it there, and for me, because I use *Second Life* as a media platform and I have taken it a step further, I do indeed know that what I present each week is a real-time live interactive media show which is filmed and broadcast as machinima. I think in order to make machinima more legitimate and broader in the coming years we should extend our definition of it. That of course is my personal feeling. I don't mind if people call *The 1st Question* machinima or not; I just want them to watch it. That's my media product, and it's different.

Cisko Vandeverre: It's actually moving pictures. Whether you want to call it video or film, or machinima or YouTube or whatever, it depends on what platform or what system your creation would be displayed on. When you are in an IMAX theater, it's called film. To take SL machinima and blow it up as an IMAX presentation, that is ridiculous and no one would appreciate that. You really have to keep in mind what kind of media you want to serve with your creations. I think with the so-called digital society which is still arriving as yet, things will change. This will also revolutionize the viewing of media. I think the system you are using for your creation becomes secondary when it is digitized in areas of various displays in various modes. The fantastic thing is that the looks of all these different media are becoming more and more equal.

Pooky Amsterdam: I think that our evolution of technology has created the confusion; for example I was watching Maurice Chevalier sing "I'm Glad

I'm Not Young Anymore" from the Vincente Minelli film *Gigi* on YouTube. As technology has evolved, our definitions have been forced to broaden, and it is within that context that we have the free flow of video to animated movies— and I just want to make that point. It is also because of where we are today with the availabilities of technology that we also have a confusion and confluence coming together of terms that we might not have had before.

Cisko Vandeverre: Yes, that's the meaning of evolution.

Pooky Amsterdam: I have to say because I have a lot of respect for Cisko and he for me that we can debate and learn as we do.

Cisko Vandeverre: As I said we are all learning. It is also important to realize that machinima makers are dealing with at least 10 jobs at the same time.

Pooky Amsterdam: Absolutely.

Cisko Vandeverre: If you are a director, you have to be a set designer. You have to be a clothing designer. There are so many issues that you have to handle. Often the question is, how good are you in all of them? Are you a pro in all these jobs that you have to cover?

Pooky Amsterdam: I think that is very tough. My goal, to be quite frank, is to be the Sherry Lansing of machinima. In no film, Hollywood film, does the director be also producer, also clothing designer, also scriptwriter, so what I envision is a studio where people who are remarkably adept in each of those categories come together to participate in the filmmaking machinima process to create better and better and more beautiful and great film because we get to each play to our strengths in our field.

Session 2

Session Two of Roundtable One asks the same questions as in Session One, but to a different group of people involved in machinima production. Attendees included Baird Barnard, Chantal Harvey, CodeWarrior Carling, Kit Guardian, Larkworthy Antfarm, Gene Williams, Penumbra Carter, and Suzy Yue. Again, all participants were familiar with the *Second Life* platform to varying degrees, and many others had professional experiences with other gaming platforms, including other virtual worlds, environments, and technologies.

Donald Pettit: Welcome to our second session of the Machinima Roundtables.

Phylis Johnson: We start out by defining machinima, and then we tackle its strengths and weaknesses. All your statements— spoken and written — are public record, and by being here today you provide your consent for your comments to be published in this book, and other related forums.

Suzy Yue: I'm going to be in a minority on this, but I'm kind of a novice though I discovered machinima about two and a half years ago. I'm kind of old fashioned in the idea that it's live, basically. It's recording someone driving an avatar's actions and a story, and so, in particular, I have a problem with using/defining *machinima* to include things like Moviestorm, mainly because that's just animation. It's not any different than any other animation tool. The thing that makes machinima different is that it's a marriage of live action and animation in a very unique way. So if you're programming in movements and repeating them over and over and over again and recording that, you're not doing anything different than Pixar, so it's animation. But machinima is in fact something quite unique in that you're recording the actions someone else or even yourself is doing at that moment it's happening. I know the definition of *machinima* is changing to include other elements. But if you're going to say that using Moviestorm to create a movie is *machinima,* then so is what Pixar is doing or any other 3-D animation production company. So that's just me, but I'm way in the minority, I know.

Donald Pettit: Very good. Very interesting!

Chantal Harvey: I have a different opinion, of course.

Donald Pettit: Well, then come on Chantal, what is machinima to you?

Chantal Harvey: Machinima, in my opinion, as a definition, is computer-generated filming in a virtual world or a game. That's it. I'm including all.

Kit Guardian: Machinima is probably newest to me than everyone else in this room because I actually do live theater in SL, and so machinima to me is a tool that I'd like to learn to use so that I can film my theater productions and be able to put them on the Web. So yes it is both of what has been said here. I've got friends that have been doing machinima for a long time, and I have looked at their films and am quite fascinated at what's capable. And I'm also going to use it as I prepare to create my real-life feature film. So for me, it's an educational tool to see if certain shots might work in real life using avatars and might be a lot less expensive in that fashion.

Suzy Yue: That's absolutely the best way you can use it.

Penumbra Carter: I guess what machinima has meant to me since I've been in *Second Life* is basically I have mostly recorded experiences that I've had here, exploring places and making somewhat stream-of-consciousness types of film. That's what it's been for me. At least right now, I love to capture not only places that I explore, but look at *Second Life* installations

Donald Pettit: Okay. Anyone else?

Larkworthy Antfarm: When I first encountered machinima, it reminded me of the Japanese art form Bunraku (boon-RAH-coo)— puppetry in which you have people who are behind the scenes moving the puppets to tell a story. In that way, they are alike. We're the live actors, and we run these avatars. It's kind of fascinating to be involved in that. And for me it's been about the art form. I've been interested in the arts and poetry and music. Telling stories. I really love the fact that we can collaborate with each other and that I can find musicians in SL who help me to tell my stories, that I can find people for my videos, and I've been in lots of other people's videos. It's really fun. I don't want us to forget that it's fun. It's not just like a professional thing for me. It's just I enjoy what I'm doing.

Donald Pettit: Excellent. Excellent.

Suzy Yue: I don't see how you could forget that — it's art. It's unique in what it is. It is puppetry. It's like kind of almost the ultimate puppetry, which is why I think of it as being different than, again, using any kind of animation tool that takes the person out of the loop. Because when you watch a puppet performance, you know some of the really amazing ones, the actor — the person moving the puppet, manipulating the puppet — embodies that. And so I think that's what makes machinima kind of unique among animation forms is that it is moving. I can have an actor do a scene two or three times and yes, they're using animations, maybe they're scripted, of course, but I still get a different performance every time. And *that's* one of the things that makes it incredible. Very much like film. Very much like stage — live stage performances. You don't get the same performance twice. It's the live performance that makes it really interesting and unique. That's just me.

Donald Pettit: Okay.

CodeWarrior Carling: The answer on that one is ... no comment. I think going around the table, you've covered a lot of different viewpoints and you're not going to get everyone to agree. I think you prefaced your question with that. So you know there's nothing to really add to anything anyone said.

Donald Pettit: Cool.

CodeWarrior Carling: Other than that, maybe just *machinima* is a label that gets applied differently by different groups of people. Laypeople don't necessarily agree with people who make machinima; even people who make machinima don't necessarily agree with each other, so....

Donald Pettit: Yeah, we're finding that out at these roundtables.

Gene Williams: I've had a background for several years in animation and I think a few people on the panel have as well. And you know a lot of people are making that comparison to those in the animation field and machinima. And I think for those of us who have actually done animation, we know that it takes a *really* long time to do animation. I went to art school, you know, back in the day, and, you know, for me to do a 30-second animation clip, it took *months*. I don't know if anyone has spent as long doing a machinima as those (doing a similar production) in the animation field, and I don't know if professional animators might look on machinima as the same type of thing or if they'd even respect it, but I think it is its *own thing*, and the fact that I was able to create machinima in a matter of days, the same type of thing that it would have taken me months to do if I were to animate it, that helps me out a lot. It makes it really accessible to other people too. So now anybody can create, as long as they have a good computer.

Kit Guardian: I have to agree with you there only because I just got my Fraps last week and I by accident turned it on when I was shopping and I had all these stills from shopping. I thought, "Oh Wow! That's kinda cool!" so I can cut and paste that like into something very quickly if I wanted to. And I work in the film industry but I've never worked in animation, but one of my friends just did *Mary and Max* last year and it took them, you know, a very long time to construct that, and *Harvie Krumpet* and stuff. So, yeah, we know we have to thank the Linden Lab for all of its animations because they've really done the groundwork, haven't they?—along with all the people that create animations that you can buy and gestures available. I learned all that with the theater. I only just figured out in the last six months how to use a HUD and an AO (animation overdrive), but it's all here in *Second Life*. All the tools are here. It's fabulous.

Suzy Yue: Well, they're being created too, and that's the thing. I mean, Linden basically did the groundwork, but the creators, the content creators, the animators, the scripters, the builders, they're the ones who were really doing the job for us. Many of the things that you don't have you can actually find somebody that can do it for you. That's the difference between *Second Life* and somewhere else.

Phylis Johnson: Any final thoughts on this discussion thread?

Suzy Yue: Can I just say something? I have a lot of friends in the industry also, and animators I have absolute respect for. I don't want to try to say that machinima is better or worse than traditional animation. That is to me comparing apples and oranges. They're both good. If you do it well, they both take a lot of talent and a lot of time. And I know basically you can draw stick figures on sheets of paper and lay them out and film each one and come up with an extremely moving story. Or you can have something that is just, I don't know, like *Avatar* or something, where it takes animation to the extreme. But I think that the thing is that, yeah, *Second Life* is a different environment, and it seems to marry the best things of both worlds, both animation and live action and you could conceivably create something in a few days or a few hours. But also there are those things that take months really to get it right. I know that in the pieces that I've done that involve *lots* of people coordinating, you can take months to get everything exactly the way you need to. On the other hand, working on the 48 Hour Filming Project last year, I did a bunch in 48 hours! *(Laughs.)* More than I ever thought!

Donald Pettit: Very good. And that was very good work!

Suzy Yue: Thank you.

Baird Barnard: Machinima to me? That's a question I'm constantly asking myself. Sitting around here listening to everybody talking about all the different points of view, I guess it's the opportunity to take what I love doing in the real world and applying it to a virtual world and having more opportunity to have creative control. You can create or collaborate with more people on projects that you wouldn't normally be able to budget for in real life. And it's a lot of fun. I'm having so much fun doing it. And I get to wear different hats. When you're working in the industry, you're only allowed to wear maybe one or two hats. And in-world here, I can be set director, or if it's a small group of people I can be an actor. I can bring out an alt and be two actors. I used to make the joke when I worked in theater before as a technician, so when I made the transition into film, I used to go Wow! Like film production is like theater production on crack because you're just running around and dealing with multiple departments, all working on your crunch time. Elements are changing constantly and you're going with the flow. It's not sort of linear, like theater is. And machinima is another level on top of that where you're taking elements of filmmaking in the real world, but it's enhanced by camera techniques that you can use. You can add animations. If you're really lucky, you can get some motion capture and then you can sort of cross into that uncanny valley, depending on how you cut it. You sort of have to work around the hurdles that you have to deal with in SL. Every few months, somebody comes up with a new solution or technique or gadget that sort of fixes that, or makes it more interesting, or makes it easier to work with. I find machinima, specifically in SL, constantly an amazing evolution of people, coming up with new ways to create a genre that nobody seems to have a definite definition on yet.

Donald Pettit: I'd like to point out that for me jumping/finding ways to jump over the hurdles—creative ways—is half the fun. Like using part of a dance to do an action animation to get that punch no one knows, unless you really watch and do that dance all the time.

Baird Barnard: Exactly.

Phylis Johnson: Did anyone learn about *Second Life* by watching machinima online?

Kit Guardian: I just want to say that, for me, my first experience with machinima was [from] friends that actually do television [work] and have very large audiences. For me, watching other people use machinima to create something where thousands of people can watch it again later or watch it online instead of being in-world, that is what Baird and everyone else is saying. It really bridges the two worlds together in a really great way because it gives people that don't even do SL an opportunity to see what we're doing in here and become a part of it and hopefully make people take it more seriously. That's all.

Donald Pettit: Very good. Next question.

Phylis Johnson: There is a lot of discussion around the virtual water cooler about machinima's role—is it a tool or mainly a genre in and of itself to tell stories? Some insist that machinima, purely defined, is a storytelling medium.

CodeWarrior Carling: I think that's sort of looking at machinima as an object or a product as opposed to a tool. And I see machinima as a tool that can be used to produce videos or film or whatever you want to call that, and not as a *thing*.

Donald Pettit: Code has these direct—(*Laughs*)—really direct answers.

CodeWarrior Carling: Well you wouldn't ask this question of a type of camera, like what genre are you going to use this camera in. It just doesn't make sense to ask that question of machinima.

Phylis Johnson: Sure. Doesn't anyone else want to respond?

Suzy Yue: I think I understand Code's comment, and I understand yours as well. But I think, yeah, for me, personally, if I'm going to say what I think — I think of machinima as just another form of expression, for whatever it is you're trying to express. If you want to create art using machinima, it's the same as creating art using film, or paint, or something like that. So, same thing, if you're creating a commercial. You might do it for radio, television, film, a billboard, or machinima. I tend to actually steer away from, frankly, the term *machinima* because I tend to think of it as film. Period. It's just a different kind of film. It's like animation.

CodeWarrior Carling: Yeah, that's what I meant. Totally agree with Suzy there.

Suzy Yue: Right.

CodeWarrior Carling: My comment earlier was sort of using her definition of *machinima* as something that you do live and you capture game footage. But the end of that, it's just a section of video tape or a piece of film, and then all of the normal editing processes take over, and before you capture that bit of Fraps footage, all of the pre-planning and all of the other things that apply to either television or film or commercials or any method of production of video media applied before you actually capture the Fraps footage and then after all of those things apply as well. So the machinima part of it is just a little small narrow tiny piece in a very big tree that already exists.

Suzy Yue: Exactly.

Kit Guardian: To follow up on what was asked, something like "does machinima have to have a story line?" I think if someone wants to just film something because it's organic and they're just walking through a sim or something, that doesn't necessarily have a story line. That's more of an improvised meeting with other people or an event, but definitely like everyone is saying, it's another format of filming, and the story line is important if you want to get something across, like a message of some sort. But you can still just film if you want and just make nothing, but *(Laughs.)* generally you do have to tie all your shots together to make some kind of sense out of it for your audience in the end.

Gene Williams: Yeah, I agree. That's like with an artist like Rysan Fall. He has a great video of a concert of U2 performing in *Second Life*. It's just a concert performance. There's no story involved in it. But it's still a machinima.

Larkworthy Antfarm: If I could build on what all of you have been saying, I also think sometimes we are filming stuff that cannot be reproduced in real life, as with the artists that create stuff in SL that can only be viewed in SL. Those are valuable things to get on film. I think we're documentarians sometimes. I've noticed how many things I've filmed in SL; *The Sims* (the original) no longer exist; the things are gone. We're the only record of them being here.

Phylis Johnson: Exactly, well that broadens the definition of machinima immensely outside of storytelling — live captures of music events, art installations, special occasions, etcetera.

Larkworthy Antfarm: And that is really an amazing thing. I also think it's interesting that we control the content of what we do. We are not being told what to do by other people. And we're an amazingly creative group, and that creativity spreads across *every* genre, *every* form of art. It is really something that we should all be proud of. And I think we're pioneers in what we're doing here.

Suzy Yue: Larkworthy, I totally agree with you — it doesn't to me differ from any other new form of expression. Every new form of expression that there's been since cave drawings has either documented what was happening at the time or told stories of things that were in people's imaginations. I think machinima is certainly that also. You're absolutely right. We are documenting, in a lot of ways, the things that exist in *Second Life*, or in any other environment like *Second Life*. I think *Second Life* is unique *among* those environments, but we certainly *are* capturing that, but I think that in much the same way as writers, painters, filmmakers, and photographers. I don't know if it's that much different than cavemen actually at all. I think it, in fact, they were, the people who made cave drawings, the filmmakers of their time. They told stories of what was around them, and they're the *only* record — those drawings are the only record of that time. So, I mean, we are in fact that. Yeah, that's what I'm saying. They were storytellers, but they were also historians.

Donald Pettit: So Suzy, you're saying we're the Neanderthals of the media world? (*Everyone laughs.*)

Chantal Harvey: I would like to tweet that. Cave drawings are machinimas. That's a good definition.

Suzy Yue: Don't you dare send that! (*Laughs.*) But I was saying that those drawings were in fact their art expression.

Chantal Harvey: I would like to address the question about storytelling and machinima. I think I've tried it all. I have tried the recording when you run into an event or something happening in *Second Life* to extreme manipulating of situations or doing films or machinimas from a storyboard with a script that worked out every shot exactly with point of view. I've done fantasy ones. I've done documentaries. I think I've tried it all. And for me, it all boils down to, yes, you need a story, unless you want to put unedited material online because editing on its own is telling a story. Machinima is about storytelling, even if you do an art event or music clip. Yes. Public events. Anything.

CodeWarrior Carling: There's also from the viewpoint of the laypeople or just the general populace that doesn't necessarily come into virtual worlds, but there's sort of an iconography of virtual worlds that they recognize when they see it on television in shows like *South Park* and *Robot Chicken* that are made from avatars. People sort of recognize that, and it's part of popular culture, but they don't really care about *how* it's made. I mean it could be full CGI animation, like the movie *Avatar*. People don't ... the general public doesn't care that that avatar wasn't rendered in real time. To me, the whole term *machinima*—when we look back in a hundred years—is going to have a period where it really had some meaning and then it will become meaningless.

Suzy Yue: Like "talkies."

CodeWarrior Carling: Yeah.

Suzy Yue: Like the term "talkies."

CodeWarrior Carling: Like you were saying earlier, it's really difficult to get any credibility. As we all up our game and learn things, we start mixing it with other things. Real filmmakers aren't going to be limited in what techniques they can use, so machinimatographers are going to say, "Why can't I use real footage or full CGI or whatever tool I have available?" When we get the stuff in Premiere, we put effects on top of it and do stuff with it, so it's already impure there.

Suzy Yue: Yes. Uh huh.

CodeWarrior Carling: It's just a very fuzzy argument.

Suzy Yue: I always thought that at some point the lines were going to be blurred between live action and animation anyway once the computing power came—and it's still increasing, the ability to be able to meld those two. The lines are getting blurred every day *much* faster than I thought. I remember thinking five or six years ago that at some point the Academy of Motion Picture Arts and Sciences was going to say, okay, we're going to have to define how much animation makes an animation film versus a live action, and they haven't done it yet. The minute you start putting a completely animated character's performance up against a live performance for best actor, then you're going to see those arguments come about. *(Laughs.)* But, yeah, I think machinima is a term that's eventually going to just go by the wayside because everything is being blended now. Every form of expression that we call film is being ... it's all being judged together, like with the 48 Hour Film Project the idea that they accepted machinima.

CodeWarrior Carling: Well, even the Pixar stuff you were talking about. I've seen the direction they were going is to ... like with *Beowulf*. They all want to sort of digitize the actor and then hook up sensors and have the actor really driving the thing. If their render farm could produce in real time, well they'd be like, "What's it called? Machinima? We love it!"

Suzy Yue: Oh, exactly. Well, I always wondered whether or not at some point they were just going to do away with actors, which is a point I want to talk about. *(Laughs.)* Do away with actors completely, because directors and everybody else hates actors.

Gene Williams: I would like to address what Code was saying about the name, or the term, *machinima*, because I do agree, and it's difficult, because the films that I make, I make for outside of *Second Life*. And normally, when I show it to people, I have to go through the whole thing of explaining the word *machinima*. And as far as they're concerned, it's a video. So sometimes it saves time just to say, "All right, it's a video. I used game graphics for it." Without going through the whole terminology or explaining the meaning of the word *machinima* or where it came from. But I was thinking about what Code was saying and knowing my history of animation, like when we look at something like Gumby, or Davy and Goliath, for those of you old enough to remember those [offscreen someone laughs and says "I do."], we still call it claymation! They never really called it animation. They called it claymation. And the Ray Harryhausen films, they're always stop-motion. So I don't know. Now I'm thinking about it, the word *machinima* might have legs. It might still stick around for a while, longer than we expect it to.

Phylis Johnson: Good point.

CodeWarrior Carling: I mean, the meaning has actually changed quite a bit from what the very, very first machinima were. And in fact, Suzy, they were recorded game sessions in Quake that weren't videos. They were like demo-mode recordings.

Suzy Yue: Uh huh.

CodeWarrior Carling: So they had to run the same version of Quake and then load in your demo recording. In a sense, you were saying that a human has to sort of drive. In a sense, they were driving, but their joystick movements were recorded. The term has already come a really long way from its original meaning, and there are some large market forces and some of the original people expounding the change in the definition to include things that Suzy was saying were more animation programs.

Suzy Yue: I think I'm watching a whole other conversation going on in chat, and whoever said that anybody could do it, yeah, absolutely, is wrong. It's like anybody can also point a camera and turn it on and call themselves a filmmaker. But that's not what you're doing. I mean, you can call it a film, but that's where it begins and ends. So anybody can do machinima, sure, if they have a computer with the power and software to capture it, but as far as creating something worthwhile, no, of course not. Not anybody can do it. You have to have somebody who wants to put some time in and wants to create something, someone that not only has the drive, but the energy and the talent, and everything else.

Penumbra Carter: Right, I said that anyone can do it, meaning that you don't have to have a background to start doing it. I'm not asking for an opinion on my work. But I'm just saying that you can come in here and start experimenting around.

Larkworthy Antfarm: Well, yeah. I absolutely agree. I mean you don't have to; it's like [how] Robert Rodriguez basically started. I mean a lot of filmmakers started just filming things with their cameras, and they didn't necessarily go to school for it. They didn't necessarily have expensive equipment or anything like that. They didn't even have the terminology, but they created something with what they had. That's what a lot of filmmakers are doing in-world, Penumbra. I think that that's how this whole thing came up. That's how most art forms happen. People start expressing themselves with the media.

CodeWarrior Carling: A better term for the thing that would clear up, sort of unify a lot of the different viewpoints, would be *virtual film*.

Phylis Johnson: True.

CodeWarrior Carling: Because that encompasses some of these other things that are trying to squeeze their way in. You can synthesize everything in here and that removes all the barriers that normally would exist for individuals or small groups to create works of cinema.

Kit Guardian: I think it's really good to have a vision and a lot of people have vision qualities, but they don't have machinima qualities or the ability to make machinima and vice versa. And I think the most important thing that we're talking about here and in this industry is that we team together like we do in real life because there are some technicians and there are some that are just visionaries.

Suzy Yue: Exactly.

Kit Guardian: I mean I love to visualize what I think I can do in SL with film, but oh my gosh! *(Laughs.)* I buy the programs and I go, mmm, maybe not. It's a little daunting because my head's already full of all the visuals and buying costumes and props and furniture and animations and getting the actors. So like what Baird was saying, here you can wear a lot of different hats, and that's true, but I think a true machinima director really has to spend a lot of time learning the craft and editing and all that.

Suzy Yue: I didn't know what machinima was when I started. Somebody said that they were making a film and they needed actors, and I just said, sure, I can get actors together and everything. I ended up directing that series, and that's what I do. I felt, actually, kind of outside the machinima community for a long time, because I worked with a team. And I wasn't capturing and performing and doing the voices and finding the music and everything. I was directing and coordinating production, so I *had* actors and a machini-matographer to do filming and the editing, and I had input in that editing process as a director would. And we had costumers and designers and builders. So for *me*, that process was natural. That's what I brought in from the outside. That's the only way I knew how to work. Then I found out that most people were doing everything themselves and they would ask me, "Are you a machin-imatographer?" and I'd say no, I was a director and that would be the end of the discussion. A lot of people are starting to not necessarily dismiss the idea of having a director on set and a single artistic vision working with the machinimatographer or actually having actors and actual voice talent. I think more people coming into this field or using this media, this art form, are going to start understanding that, like any other form of storytelling. A lot of this is a collaborative process, and even though one of my machinima friends says it's more like being a painter, and it *can* be, but I think we need to expand that.

CodeWarrior Carling: Well, it's probably not as well suited for drama because the facial expressions aren't that mature, and it's difficult to do that in really good post. It can be done, but it's just very difficult to do it. So if you really wanted to do that, there are easier things than using *Second Life*.

Chantal Harvey: Yes, but it's very hard to do a good emotion. Emotion is so hard in avatars. And I'm not saying *Second Life*. I tried *Twinity* and some of the other games, but emotion, body language, and facial expressions, you can manipulate them. I did that with all these HUDs you can wear and mix, but you don't really get real emotion. It's a suggestion of it. And also filming in virtual worlds, well, any genre will work or not, depending on how good you do it and how good you use it, and avoid limitations. If you know a world really well, then you can avoid those things you run into during filming.

Suzy Yue: I don't think there's any limitation here in terms of doing dramatic works. I think that, yes, there are certain subtle facial expressions that aren't going to be available and maybe even certain body movements that aren't going to be available, but you edit, or you work around, you shoot it differently, or you have, what we *really* should have, more *really* good voice actors being utilized in-world. Because a lot of emotion, as you can shoot from the back, can be easily expressed in voice. So I honestly believe that, no, I don't think it's a limitation — it's hard, but what isn't, really? — if you really want to do it. There have been plenty of great performances done by Muppets, and you got a lot of really good expression out of it without much movement in the face.

CodeWarrior Carling: Yeah. I mean that's very much the case with nothing is impossible, but some things are easier and some things are harder. And I think it was Baird who said earlier that "you can do the impossible in here," but on the other hand, you can't open a frickin' doorknob.

(*Everyone chimes in and laughs.*)

Donald Pettit: Yes, hands are difficult.

CodeWarrior Carling: So you just have to deal with the limitations and do what you can. It's the same with any other medium.

Baird Barnard: You gotta fake it 'til you make it. You have to say "Okay that's not working. Let's take this weird thing and shoot it at this angle and add some music to it."

Suzy Yue: Yeah. It's just like you cut away or something. Yeah. The challenge is shooting in the environment with its limitations and pulling the most that you can out of it. And I've seen some amazing things as far as machinima is concerned that's coming out of *Second Life* that will make you laugh and cry.

Gene Williams: See, but once again, you're talking about what's already available to you in *Second Life*. Now if you're using an outside program like Poser 4, you can create those animations that you're looking for. You can create the facial expressions. It's just going to take more time. You can create those gestures to stand up from a chair, or even, well I don't know about the doorknob thing. That's going to be hard. *(Laughs.)* You're right about that. The hand thing is really tricky. It's just going to take more time for you to do those things. You have to actually create those animations and those gestures.

Suzy Yue: You know what? I'm sorry, but Marlon Brando didn't have many expressions *(Laughs)*, but he's considered a pretty good actor. So I think that you work with what you have.

Chantal Harvey: Has anybody seen the film that Liz Solo made? *Machine I Am.* That really moved me. That was in the MMIF [MaMachinima International Festival]. That's part of herself in real life. At one stage in the film, I had to look back because I couldn't remember if it was her real life or her avatar. You know, the story got me, and for me, it mixed totally. It was really amazing.

Donald Pettit: Thank you all for coming. When I started the MAG (Machinima Artist Guild), I began to get to know you. And now it's like every time I see one of your movies, I just feel so happy. Each one of you. Chantal, Code, Suzy, and Larky. I just feel like it's a great family to be in — and Gene, Baird, and Kit, all of you here and others. I just want to make sure everybody knows I do enjoy watching your stuff and I learn from you every day.

LINKS RECOMMENDED BY ATTENDEES

http://ideajuice.blip.tv [CodeWarrior Carling]
http://machinima.eu [Chantal Harvey]
http://www.lizsolo.com/machineiam.html [*Machine I Am*, by Liz Solo]
http://www.youtube.com/watch?v=uSGZOuD3kCU [*Diary of a Camper*]
http://www.pookymedia.com [*The Dating Casino, The 1st Question*, Pooky Amsterdam]
http://vimeo.com/27852715 [*Wizard of the North*, Kit Guardian/Al Peretz]

Roundtable Two: Collaboration, Commercialization and Content

This chapter focuses on the second roundtable series of discussions, broadly themed collaboration, commercialization, and content, Specifically, professional machinima producers, talent and creative support, responded to six themed questions: Are machinimists pioneers propelling advances in virtual filmmaking? What is machinima's role in advancing art and technology through and for commercialization? Is machinima at its best created through collaboration? What are some thoughts on collaborating as a team versus working solo? How has machinima inspired partnerships with community groups or businesses? What are some overall strengths and weaknesses of machinima? Can machinima be an intimate experience for the producer and viewer, and how so? And other themes that emerged along the way.

All sessions were conducted on the Island of Fame at the offices of Lowe Runo Productions, LLC, within *Second Life*. The third session was held Thursday, July 15, 2010. The fourth session, Friday, July 16, 2010, continues the dialogue among a different set of machinimists, as well as those involved in diverse aspects of the machinima community. Among the various attendees, there was an abundance of machinima experience with various software and game engines. Attendees at the third roundtable included langelcares Writer, Code-Warrior Carling, Evie Fairchild, Clover Fenwitch, Gwenette Writer, Joel Savard, LaPiscean Liberty, Kara Trapdoor, Gene Williams, Pamala Clift, and Suzy Yue.

Session 3

The authors, Phylis Johnson and Donald Pettit, moderate the discussion.

Phylis Johnson: All your statements—spoken and written—are public record, and by being here today you provide your consent for your comments to be published in this book, and other related forums. Let's begin with our first question, are we pioneers of a new form of virtual filmmaking? And if yes, how so? You can speak from your experience with *Second Life*, or any other machinima platform.

Donald Pettit: Okay. Anyone like to answer that question?

Evie Fairchild: Well, I was just going to say that I'm probably prejudiced being this is the only place that I have made machinima, but it seems to me that we have some unique tools here that you don't find others places. So the ways that we do this are pioneering in our own methods and the things that we have to create to make a machinima.

Donald Pettit: That's very good. Excellent observation. Anyone else like to chime in?

Gwenette Writer: I have a question. Isn't most of the machinima made in [virtual] worlds that are already pre-made? Isn't it kind of unique to be able to make the world? I mean with OpenSim, yeah.

Evie Fairchild: Yes, that's kind of my point.

Gwenette Writer: Yeah.

Evie Fairchild: That we have a different set of rules to make machinima in *Second Life*, and, if for no other reason than [that], this is pioneering.

Suzy Yue: I mean, well, when you think about it, when you talk about the pioneers of the Old West, or anybody going toward something, it's like, yeah, maybe it's uncharted, unmapped, undiscovered country. I think what we do with it is very individual. I think we talked about this before. You have an art form, so you take film then as an art form; people have different ideas about what they want to do with that. Some want to make art. Some want to make money. Some want to make a combination of art and money. Some want to just reach people and teach lessons. So I think that even though it's not that new, it is new in terms of being part of an art form or a new way of making films— it is still, I think, an individual choice as to where we want to go with it and what we want to do with it like any other filmmaker.

Suzy Yue: I invited 1angelcares Writer. She's an actress, so I thought her perspective would be welcomed.

1angelcares Writer: And that is like what the pioneers did when they all had different reasons for why they wanted to come west.

Suzy Yue: Right. Exactly. Some wanted gold. Some wanted land.

Pamala Clift: That's the idea. I would say, collaboration is so much better.

1angelcares Writer: I think once machinima — I'm only half joking here — using the same analogy — once machinima reaches that moment where we're almost there, wherever there is, I think we all need to kind of remember this. Just sitting around with each other and talking and where we came from and where we started. I think eventually, it's going to become — you know, it could become cutthroat. It could become very competitive, and I would hate to see that happen. I like for us all to be comrades in this.

Donald Pettit: I don't see a point to being competitive personally because, number one, we all have different styles and different things we like to produce.

I like to jump around and do different things, but I see as the machinima, or movies in virtual worlds, a very open thing. I don't think there's a niche thing yet. At least I don't think so. I think there's room to grow and live together.

1angelcares Writer: To me there's room for all of us with our various goals.

Pamala Clift: Creativity is different for everyone as well as styles. *(Chat text.)*

Suzy Yue: Well, I think there's room, definitely room, and I think anytime you have a group of people, a group of creatives, especially people with ideas, you're going to have competition. There's no getting around that. It's in our nature to want to say — it's the old joke, "How many actors does it take to screw in a lightbulb?" One hundred. One to screw it in and 99 to say, "I can do that better."

Donald Pettit: Right. Exactly.

Suzy Yue: Healthy competition encourages growth in an area. Sharing knowledge is a part of that. You can say, "Oh I found a better tool. Let me share that with everyone. Let me share what I found."

Donald Pettit: Well I, for one, am pretty generous because of the way I'm structured, and I don't want to talk about what I do, because that's not what we're here for, but I do structure my website and everything else to invite new people in. And they always do music videos. That's how everybody starts or something similar. And then they look at something that we're doing that's much more complex and they want to do it too. And so, you can't stimulate the newcomers to get better without having a little bit of copying. And that I don't mind as long as they don't take one of my scenes and copy it verbatim. *(Laughs.)* Then I probably would be kind of upset. But me, I'm very, very, very open to new people. I don't mind them. I don't mind sharing techniques and what I do. If someone has a project and they want me to help them with something that I have an ability to do, I would help them. If they asked, I would help them. So I believe — I know for my company, what I do — Lowe Runo Productions, I feel that I personally have a decent concept of collaboration.... I'm a very private person sometimes, but that doesn't mean I'm here building something and not letting anyone else in. That never would be the case.

Gwenette Writer: I have one observation about the pioneering aspect of it. Because I'm a person who talks to machinimists and needs machinima and wants to grow up and be a machinimist kind of thing, but I've not done it yet. I have noticed two interesting things that have happened in the last couple weeks. Someone came to me that's never been a machinimist and has decided to do it — not because they love it but because they see there's money in it — and I think that's a new kind of perspective I'm seeing more often and it's somebody who I think might be thought of as a long term futurist and very much involved in the business section of SL.... But the other thing that I saw is that I've spoken with somebody who is developing some tools about how to shoot — camera tools, basically. This is stuff that's going to be kept proprietary.

I mean most everything I've seen has been kind of open source or available for sale.... So I think that's a sign that you are pioneers because the other folks are clamoring in on top of your pioneering work.

Evie Fairchild: You know, I was thinking about when SL was brand new. The people that were here all went out of their way to help each other to learn the tools and were incredibly generous. Everybody would help *everybody*. You need a texture. Here's a texture. You need to know how to do that? Let me show you. And then the people who thought they could make money somehow here came in and all the sharing stopped, and that's what I'm a little bit worried about with machinima. We're still in the learning stages and we'll develop the content and the tools and the thoughts about it, and then other people will come in and try to make the money off of it, and in a way ruin it for all of us. Or make it different. Maybe I should say it that way. Make it a different atmosphere.

Donald Pettit: This is cool. I love this! I love the participation! It's very good.

Suzy Yue: I did just have a quick comment and then we can move on. I hope that there is room for people who are currently here to make a living doing machinima in-world. I'm an artist. I was born and raised in all that theater stuff and all of that related, but I think what I would like to see is room for discussion among people who are in fact trying to make a living at this. I'm one of those. I do always seem to come in on the minority side of that discussion. I think there's room for people who want to do this as a business, as well as an art. I understand that there are people coming in from the outside who, yeah, will probably be capitalizing on technology and practices that people who have been doing this for awhile have developed, but I think that's just the nature of any developing art craft/business. It was the same thing for filmmaking, television, whatever, radio even.

COLLABORATION

Phylis Johnson: Let's try this next question: is machinima at its best created through collaboration, and what are some of the advantages and disadvantages of working solo versus as a team?

Pamala Clift: I just listened to a TED [TED.com] talk that was discussing very distinctly about why we didn't fall apart in the 60s and 70s when everything sounded like the whole world was going apart. And that's because we were sharing.... And what happens is that you actually — even though I might make, for example, a spear and an axe, in two hours each, and Adam can make a spear and an axe in one hour. Well, to specialize and just say, "Okay. Well, you make the axe and I'll make this." When they trade the axe and the spear, it actually cuts down the hour for both parties, so collaboration — those who do bind together and share their techniques and make a bond, are going to move faster, better, and more completely...

Suzy Yue: Okay. My first group in here, Suzy's Super Cast & Crew, came out of that idea. It's the only way I've ever worked in the arts. A director, producer, a designer, a costumer — all of that — even on a one-woman show you have a crew. You may have only a cast of one, but you have everything else, and I get no fulfillment out of — I mean that's me personally, obviously — working on something myself because even when I direct, when I was directing the theater, there were those moments when I'm like, "I have no idea what this is looking like. Let me bring in somebody else" and call another director and sit down with me and say, "What are you seeing? What's wrong?" I think it's so much more fulfilling. It makes for a great cast party too. So I just think that, yeah, there are some things that are solitary. I think there are certain — even within the team — solitary ideas, moments. A costumer has her own ideas or his own ideas. A lighting designer has his or her own ideas. But it all comes together. It all comes together as a team effort, and a collaborative piece is such a beautiful thing to see.

Donald Pettit: I'll interject a little thing here. When I'm working with, and I find people that collaborate with me on a project, if I'm doing a special effect, like say we're doing something futuristic and all, and I have to shoot things over and over, and there may be a big green room, or something strange — I find it drives everyone nuts because I'm a perfectionist; I'll do it over and over and over. So either they'll give me their avatars, or tell me how to make their avatars, and I'll end up doing their voices; but I'll make a copy of their avatars and actually use them for the scene because I just can't inflict that kind of pain on them to make them hang around that long while I'm producing a particular effect. So there are times that it's not practical — for me anyways — to have a crew there only because the nature of the project I'm working on at that instant in the feature would not lend itself to sanity for some people to just do those things over and over. Okay. That's just me. Anyone else?

Clover Fenwitch: Well I think that I'm a writer first, but I do well producing. And I'm kind of the hub as far as the thing that we're working on right now. So from like a producer standpoint, I like my job because it's organizational and I can get everybody kind of together. People that sometimes create aren't the best at finishing the project, or really knowing what to do with the creations and sometimes it's like a thought funnel. One of my builders, he just doesn't build really. But give him a project, give him a timeline, and it's a whole different situation, and he produces some really great stuff. But I think you have to have all of that — and there's ONE single thought — which is my thought: how it's going to work, how it's going to look, and the end result. But I'm always up for everybody else's ideas and thoughts and stuff. For me, personally, it has to be everybody, because I'm not good at a lot of the different things. I can build sort of, I can do a little bit of animation, I can do some basic machinimatography, but I would rather produce it and get the people that are better at it. And write and just produce, instead of putting it all in myself because I don't know how anybody else gets it done that way.

Phylis Johnson: Others?

Gwenette Writer: I think that collaboration in general allows you to see possibilities and potentials in a project that you didn't foresee at all until someone else's energy came into it. That's true in anything that I've done in SL, whether it's building, or an event, or publications. So I'm certain that it would be true in machinima. And I know that sometimes artists are driven by their visions and it has to be just this way and they want everybody to fall in line and do it that way, but I don't actually consider a team like that to be collaborating. They're just like working on a project.

Pamala Clift: Is there a way that we can truncate and do assignments? And say okay, well, I'm a technician, I'm a filmer, I'm an editor, I'm a producer. Can we cut them into small enough pieces that we have specializations? And we acknowledge the specializations, and we collaborate, [and design] the team in that manner.

Donald Pettit: I know in my projects that's kind of what I do. Again, because of the nature of certain effects and things, I have to work differently.

Pamala Clift: I think only if we're stepping outside of our boxes. You know, we have writers and everything, so if we step outside of our boxes, we're going to have conflict. "I should do it this way. You should do it that way." But if we all contribute, then it goes in our little specialty field, then the, "Oh, My feelings are hurt. You're in my space" is going to be minimized.

Donald Pettit: Right. And some projects, certain teams won't even see the other people that I have involved in it sometimes.

Suzy Yue: Keeping that in mind, though, I think it's really important to have a unified vision. So the director, creator, however you want to put it, people who are used to working like this aren't going to have an issue with someone who is the director of the piece saying, "That works, but that doesn't." They'll probably have a problem, but they will get over it, because they understand that it's all going toward a particular vision. Otherwise it's a big mishmash. "I think it should look like this." "Well, I think the costumes should look like this." You know, "I think we should have space costumes even though it's set in the Old West because I like them." You need a unified vision that says, "Okay. This is what it's supposed to look like," and has the power to say, "That doesn't work," or "That does." *(Laughs.)* It's not a new method at all, but it does take people understanding that the goal of the piece is the piece itself, not the ego of the person making it, which is why I think a team works really well. Because it does—you know, you get a group of people, and it takes a while to get them working together. Just falling into a team is really not that easy, but once everybody's on board, and you get some time in together, it's a lot easier. And it becomes extremely fulfilling, I think. Learning to manage that process is a skill in and of itself. I had to learn that the hard way. I almost lost a really good costumer on a show once because she came in with something that I thought, "Well, ehhh..." and I went out and found some things myself and brought them in, and she said, "Well, you can do it then," and left. And I got in my car and chased her down and said, "*Please* come back! I brought you in on this project because I trusted you." So I shut up and let her do her job, and we got wonderful reviews as a result. She was brilliant at it, so I mean it's one of those things you have to learn, but I think it really is something that should be encouraged — and especially in machinima. And I say especially because there is the ability to do so much on your own. You know, I can build a little bit, I can go out and buy some costumes, and I can even sculpt an avatar, or whatever. I film it, and then I can edit it. But I think that, again, then you're getting one person's little thing, and how much more wonderful would it be to have someone else involved in that process and actually see something you may not see?

1angelcares Writer: As a machinima actress, I think I get the best of both worlds because when I'm on a set, or I'm working on a team like the 48 Hour Film Project [for machinima] or something like that, the energy is so wonderful. You get to really bounce that energy off of your fellow actors, and the time flies by — for me at least. I can't speak for all actors, but I really enjoy that creative process. I see it sort of as I give the director that, I guess that respect, and just knowing that he or she knows where this is going. And I see my role as an actor to help the director achieve that goal. I tend to keep my mouth shut until I'm asked to say my lines. I don't want to become the director. I want to be the actor and do the job that I was hired for. On the other side, I do a lot of voice work by myself in front of my computer, saying my lines with absolutely no direction whatsoever. And a lot of times, I literally have to guess, just basically from the script what the director would probably want. In fact, a lot of times, I end up doing two or three different takes of a line reading, because no one is there telling me how to say it. And that's kind of good and bad too, so I enjoy both aspects of working with a team, or with a group, on a set. And also just kind of being trusted and being left to my own devices. And knowing that if the director doesn't like how I did a line, then when they get the voice files, [he or she] can just send me an e-mail and say, "Hey, could you redo this line or say it this way?"

Evie Fairchild: Having worked with angel a few times, it always seems to me that when I have any question about, "Hrmm, maybe we should do this another way?" and ask an actor, I always learn something. I learn something every time I collaborate and trust other people's vision too. And obviously somebody has to have the final say, but everybody brings something wonderful to a project.

CodeWarrior Carling: What I'm trying to do right now is connect with *local* artists. I have a lot of friends in *Second Life*. They're all great people to collaborate with, but I'm not connected to my local arts community. So I joined

Twitter a while ago and I've been sort of cultivating contacts in town here, which has actually led me to join a video organization where I can now rent things like dolly equipment, cameras. They have editing suites. They have people who can advise me on getting grants, and all that sort of stuff. And so what I've done is I've made a machinima with characters that I'm soliciting local people to write the story behind them, and to volunteer to do the voice-overs for them as a way of connecting with the local community and collaborating in that way.

COMMUNITY SUPPORT AND GIVING BACK

Phylis Johnson: On that note, let's move on to the idea of giving back to the community of people who support the machinima, and help in its production, including establishing business partnerships, and also the idea of producing for non-profit groups as a sort of give back.

Donald Pettit: Hmm, the business and PR side.

CodeWarrior Carling: Well, there's always the traditional giveback in that normal film and video will put a plug for you — product placement. When we did our 48 Hour Film Project machinima a couple of years back, just the fact that we were going to display the signboard above the theater, it would promote that sim. And that's how we got permission to use the sim, and it's a fair quid pro quo. I don't think we need to give more than that. Same thing with the avatars. We've often approached avatar makers to use their avatars and got them free, you know, because when you're doing it for machinima, you often need the same avatars — three or four copies — so different actors can use it, or we've had to ask avatar makers to give us a modifiable version of an avatar, or that sort of thing. So we get a lot of help from the community, and you sort of give it back by promoting them in the credits at the end.

Donald Pettit: That's correct. And it is good advertising. It is for them. And it helps us get our things done economically because otherwise we'd be having several-thousand-dollar budgets ourselves that we can't scrape together.

CodeWarrior Carling: Yeah, we sort of all know how the fashion people in *Second Life* prey on the newbie machinimists for their first year or so and get us to all do fashion shows for them. *(Laughs.)*

Donald Pettit: Yes, they do.

Suzy Yue: Yeah. I tend to give as much credit as I can and then I always pay, even if it's a token fee to a sim owner or something like that. A lot of people are just like, "It's great for you to film here!" But I want to give something, and they pay a tier. I want to make sure people know, "Hey, this is a great place to go." So I'm going to try to give credit, if I get a chance to do it — if a client allows it.

CodeWarrior Carling: The other thing that you do, Suzy, in particular, that I'd like to be able to do too, you try to pay the actors. If you want to sort of talk about moving dollars around, it should probably go toward some of the people who volunteer and spend so much time doing the stuff.

Suzy Yue: Yep. That's my big bugaboo. I've had some arguments about it. But I do try to make it happen.*(Laughs.)*

CodeWarrior Carling: One of the problems with machinima versus, for example, live performance in *Second Life*—live performers in *Second Life* can put out a tip jar. So on the one hand, machinima is great because it lets us record what goes on in virtual reality and expose the wider world to it, but on the other hand, it's not so easy for us to put up a tip jar on the video and funnel that money back down to the people who made the stuff.

Suzy Yue: True. Yeah. Absolutely.

Donald Pettit: Very good observation.

CodeWarrior Carling: I don't want to dominate, but my favorite answer to non-profit groups has been for a while to introduce them to Livestream and to encourage them to have some of their members learn how to use Livestream, so that anytime they want ... because the way Livestream works is you create a channel. And for a non-profit group or anything like that, it makes a lot of sense for them to create a Livestream channel and then anytime they have an event, that event's video is added to their library on their channel. So I like to encourage them to own their channel and have some of the members learn how to use that—their capture tools—and they can brand it themselves and own all that kind of thing.

Donald Pettit: That's a very wise idea.

CodeWarrior Carling: Well, there's already people making money. Some people make money fairly consistently. I would guess that most of us have made a little money in the form of Lindens at least to help pay our tier. Not necessarily a real check in the mail in real dollars, but personally I turn down a lot of opportunities so that I can focus more on what I enjoy making.

Suzy Yue: Pass them my way. *(Laughs.)*

Evie Fairchild: Yeah. I was going to say.

Donald Pettit: Well, it depends on the nature of your project. I'm finding like if I have a great idea for a machinima or a movie, it might be a great one to watch, but there's not going to be a lot of sponsorship. Well, actually, if you do one good successful one, probably your second one or third one down the pike, there probably is some good opportunities for sponsorship and maybe some advertising. I know the last one I did, the bigger one I did, had some sponsorship, and it was nice. I hope to do it again. But again, I have to agree with Code that you don't make a lot of money at it. Let's face it. At best, you cover your costs usually.

CodeWarrior Carling: There's a hope in the sense that when you buy a lottery ticket, there's a hope that you might win.

Donald Pettit: This is correct.

Suzy Yue: I hope I can make a living at it.

Evie Fairchild: Actually, I'm thinking of using it to complement screenplays that I am trying to sell. Instead of just sending out a screenplay to an agent, I send out a machinima of the first chapter.

Clover Fenwitch: Me too.

Evie Fairchild: I don't have any idea if it's going to work yet, but it's a lot of fun to do.

Clover Fenwitch: That's my goal with what I'm doing right now. It is the same thing, sort of like a virtual tour of the script.

Evie Fairchild: Exactly!

Suzy Yue: A proof of concept, or...

Evie Fairchild: That's a good way of putting it.

Suzy Yue: Yeah.

Evie Fairchild: Well, it's like a fancy trailer, you know?

Code Warrior Carling: I think it would take some work, but if you're able to consistently produce every week — or even daily — but at least every week, say a 10-minute webisode that's funny or whatever that appeals to the general public, and not just VR [virtual reality] people. Although there's some — the name of it escapes me — but there's a web series about the gamers. Felicia Day is in it. It's actually won awards. It's competed with web...

Pamala Clift: It's called *The Guild*.

Code Warrior Carling: *The Guild*! That's right! Now, that's not machinima, but that sort of shows you that the audience — there's enough people that understand the gaming concepts.

Donald Pettit: Yeah. I watch that one.

Code Warrior Carling: There's actually a TV show [Internet distributed] called *Pure Pwnage*, so the demographic is starting to be there of an audience that understands gaming. But I think that's the key, and it's possible that you could produce machinima — I mean *Robot Chicken* is kind of — it's not machinima, but it's *South Park*. Animation is possible to become a mainstream hit sort of thing, but it needs to be consistent, regular, and appeal to an audience, and not sort of stray. It's got to be the same thing every week. And you've got to be committed to doing it for six months before anyone even notices you.

Suzy Yue: The story...

Evie Fairchild: Well, there though. There is where we need our tools to evolve because we can't compete with Pixar with the crap that we have in *Second Life*. *(Laughs.)* But it's entirely possible that our tools will evolve to the place that we can produce a really fine product here.

Suzy Yue: But if we concentrate on the tools...

Code Warrior Carling: But I mentioned *South Park*, because the tools they use have gotten better over the years, but in the beginning, it's like they were using cutout 2-D things with Photoshop. They could almost have done it with paper and scissors. It just goes to show, you need writing, and...

Suzy Yue: You need writing.

LaPiscean Liberty: So then it's the attraction to the artist and not the art at that point. *(Chat text.)*

Code Warrior Carling: You need to, yes, be consistent, and they're out there for a year and the people who like *South Park* got to know about it. They spread by word of mouth. If *South Park* had started out with that style of humor and then changed writers after the first year and gone in a totally different direction, they would have lost it. It's just you have to *be there* for long enough, consistent stuff, to build your audience.

Suzy Yue: You have to have a story, you have to have ... the story, the story, the story. It is the story and how you tell it. It doesn't matter how good the animation is here. We can't compete. We're *never* going to compete with Pixar. By the time this gets to Pixar, they'll be someplace else. It's not about the technology. It's about the story. This is just another way to tell the story.

CodeWarrior Carling: Yeah — and the delivery by the voices. I mean, it's the voices of the people in *South Park* that are doing most of the emotion. Just the little, well, if I make the eyebrows like this, that means this. But it's the voice that sells it. So we *have* that. We need the writing, and the story, and we need to get it out there, just sort of have the faith that it'll attract an audience. It doesn't always happen. Go look at Broadway, or movies, or whatever, there's a lot of failures of good things. Even if it's good, and it's consistent, you put it out there for a long time, it's still a roll of the dice. It's changing the odds. Instead of buying a lottery ticket, now you're playing blackjack or poker. It's a 50/50 chance instead of a one in a million.

Suzy Yue: It's showbiz. Exactly.

Evie Fairchild: Well, I entirely agree that the only thing that's, well, obviously the most important thing is the story. I think my point is just that as our tools get better, we're going to be taken more seriously. And it might be a little easier to get that audience. I don't know. But obviously the story is so much bigger than all the other issues.

LaPiscean Liberty: I also think that we need to add real-life acting in the machinima, say like *Roger Rabbit*. I think Phaylen had the right idea in a short machinima, using expressionism. Think about this— podcasts sell, and no animation. What you guys are doing right now is good content. How many movies do you watch that are 10 minutes or less? If you are going for that 30-second capture, then you are making commercials, or longer, music videos, etcetera. *(Chat text.)*

Evie Fairchild: Well, obviously we don't wait for the right animation. The thing that my partner and I say to each other all the time is, "Just tell me a story." The story is everything. In *Second Life*, you have to make do without the animation, or doing it with a different kind of camera shot, or whatever it is. But it really is the story, and the idea, that makes everything else work. And I have to say, has everyone seen Chad Vader? Darth Vader's little brother who works in a grocery store? *(Laughs.)*

Suzy Yue: Oh my god! That is so funny. *(Laughs.)* That's one of the funniest things...

Evie Fairchild: *(Laughs.)* Talk about a ridiculous idea that some college students got and are making some serious money. So obviously the idea is the thing.

Donald Pettit: Very interesting. Yes, I have seen Chad. It is funny.

Suzy Yue: I think, yeah. I think the thing is we just have to get it out. I mean, that's the thing that, if nothing [else]...

Evie Fairchild: Well, yeah. We have to moan about what we don't have and then go ahead and get it out anyway.

Suzy Yue: Yeah exactly. That's the thing that I've found. SL has been my joy in being able to make things happen — kind of more easily, more quickly, meet people, collaborate, all of that. It's not about what it hasn't turned into yet, what car you're driving or what restaurant you go to in Hollywood to meet the right person. *(Laughs.)* It's easier now here to make a connection, to put together a team, to put something out there. We just have to get it out there. Because, I can tell you one thing, they are watching. They are watching. People are watching for the next thing all the time. The fact that there are websites devoted to web-created content, that more people are starting to watch than network TV tells you — that they're watching to see what's coming out of who knows where. Chad Vader. *(Laughs.)* A lot of people credit the *Star Trek* tribute television series that was on the Internet for about three or four years before they even thought about the new *Star Trek* movie as getting enough interest, getting enough viewers, then they thought, "You know, we could probably make another movie and sell it." So, it's out there. People are watching. All we have to do is get our stuff out there, be good at it, and who knows? Who knows who's going to see it?

LaPiscean Liberty: Content is free; access is what you pay for. *(Chat text.)*

Evie Fairchild: And like what Code says, "and be consistent." Because if you put out one really good thing and then can't follow up, it dies on the vine.

STRENGTHS AND WEAKNESSES

Phylis Johnson: What are the limitations of machinima? What are some work-arounds?

Clover Fenwitch: You know, my biggest thing so far has been getting everything ready, and then realizing that the machinimatographer wanted 60 animations and I'm thinking just shut me mentally down on that. And you guys are saying stuff like, "Just get it done." It makes me want to pick it right back up and start it again like tomorrow. *(Laughs.)*

Evie Fairchild: Well, you should.

Clover Fenwitch: It's one of those things where you're like, "How am I going to make this possible?" As long as the writing is there and as long as the people are there...

CodeWarrior Carling: Okay. I have a cure for that. What you do, type in claymation and go watch a few of those, and then you realize that you've got it easy.

Clover Fenwitch: Right.

CodeWarrior Carling: *(Laughs.)* Yeah. I think that's a big key for writing *Second Life*.

Suzy Yue: Absolutely.

Evie Fairchild: And they're not being very creative about the way to use SL.

CodeWarrior Carling: You really have to, even if you've got a screenplay, or a play, or whatever you've got to do. I've worked a lot with theater groups that do live theater, and they really have to look at all the plays they do and adapt them so they can be done in *Second Life*. You can't just take anything and directly go, "Okay, we're gonna do this, we're gonna do this, we're gonna do that." You have to understand the limitations. There's odd things like, for example, as a director...

Clover Fenwitch: Right...

CodeWarrior Carling: ...you tell an actor to go and stand somewhere and face a certain direction. They will go and stand there and face *exactly* the way you told them, but you won't see that. No two people will see the same person in the same spot. So there's a lot of pitfalls that you need to be aware of and you need to adapt or rewrite a script to be shot in *Second Life*, before you even have a chance of doing it.

Suzy Yue: And get creative.

Evie Fairchild: Well, but by the same token, *Second Life* affords you things that would be much more difficult. When we did our 48 Hour Film thing, we had a spaceship already up in the clouds, and weird looking animations. And we could be aliens in five seconds flat. That's not so easy in real life, so there are a lot of drawbacks, but there are a lot of things you can do here that would be wildly difficult in other places.

Suzy Yue: Oh. My husband got his degree in scenic design for theater, and one of the things he realized after a while in SL is like, "I can build those sets" that he proposed in some of his design classes. They said, "Oh, yeah, you can't do that." You know, on a real stage. So that ability opens up a whole world of possibilities for him. By the same token, there are things that you can't do in SL exactly. Maybe you *can*. Maybe it's just not been tried yet. Maybe there are things that people will say, "Well, we can't do that." And I think, "well, you know, how do we get around it?" My husband was told once he needed to fly something in a black box that had no fly gallery. And they said, "Well, you can't do that." And he said, "Watch me." And he figured out a way to do it. So it takes imagination. We all have that or else we would not be in this room right now if we didn't have the ability to disregard the fact that we are all meeting in a space that basically exists on a computer someplace — it's just a bunch of pixels — and interact the way we do. If we didn't have imaginations that wouldn't happen. So you work with what you have, but within maybe some limitations; you just find a way around it which is really beautiful — SL's like the ultimate theater for me.

INTIMACY AND EMOTIONS

Phylis Johnson: Can machinima be an intimate experience for the producer and viewer, and how so, especially compared to other media forms?

Evie Fairchild: Oh, yes. I remember one that touched me deeply. It was just a very simple story of a girl falling in love. There were no words, but it was just so beautifully told that I think what we were feeling and what she filmed got directly to me. So I do think it's entirely possible.

Donald Pettit: I've had machinima make me cry. Oops. Don't want anybody to know that. No, but really, though.

Evie Fairchild: *(Laughs.)*

Donald Pettit: It can touch you. It can.

Evie Fairchild: Well, I think that's the whole point of any art. It's to move you to a different place. And I don't think machinima's any different.

Suzy Yue: It's like any other film.

Donald Pettit: I forget who the director is. It's on our site, but we had one where it shows a couple meeting each other, and then growing old together, and then one passes on. And that whole thing made me cry. I remember that. *Love* that thing.

Suzy Yue: I actually posted to somebody recently who put up a link to their machinima in our group that it was the only thing that I'd seen ever that made me think about the possibility of getting a prim baby. It was the funniest, cutest machinima in the world that was an ad for prim baby companies. *(Laughs.)*

Donald Pettit: I've seen it. I've seen it.

Suzy Yue: You saw it? Wasn't that hilarious — the imagination that went into that. I mean just coming up with that story line was brilliant. You have to see it because it was *so* funny. It was just funny. I'm going to find the link and I'll send it out again because it was — it starts out...

Donald Pettit: It was cute. I remember that.

Suzy Yue: It started out as being, "Oh, god. It's another one of those." And it turned into something beautiful. Yeah. I think that like any other film, the story, if it reaches you, it does. It certainly can be a very intimate experience.

Evie Fairchild: When you were talking about intimacy, were you thinking of machinima as different from some other kind of art?

Phylis Johnson: Yes, does machinima have the ability to connect to audiences in an intimate way — more so, or the same as other media?

CodeWarrior Carling: Have you seen the Old Spice guy on YouTube lately? Like in the last couple of weeks. It's very interesting what they've done. The Old Spice people — you know the commercial I'm talking about. There's a guy with a towel and he's on a horse at the end.

1angelcares Writer: Oh, yes. I've seen that.

CodeWarrior Carling: That guy now is on Facebook and on Twitter, so you ask him a question or something like that. Within a day, he will actually make a video, and it will be on YouTube. And it will be *that guy* with *that voice* answering a Facebook person by name. "So and so, you asked about this. Well let me tell you...." And it's all got to be sponsored by Old Spice. It's selling the brand.

Suzy Yue: Hysterical.

LaPiscean Liberty: Humor is as viral as intimacy. *(Chat text.)*

CodeWarrior Carling: It's a really unique branding thing that they're doing. Go to YouTube and look up Old Spice guy. There's got to be hundreds of posts there now. And the reason I bring that up is machinima has the capacity to do that kind of thing. Like with *Second Life*, a person has to drive an avatar. But to use the example of iClone, you just kind of feed in the audio, and it does the lip sync. Or CrazyTalk is the same sort of thing. So I can conceive of a little bit more technology behind that website, or something that's hooked up to Twitter where an automated response could be turned into a video—a machinima-style video—as a response to somebody's question on Twitter or whatever.

Evie Fairchild: You know, I went to journalism school before I changed majors twice, and one of the things they teach you about writing a story is that it needs proximity and intimacy. And what Code was just describing is the new world's version of exactly that. If you can put something on YouTube that responds to somebody within a day, that is proximity and intimacy virtually. I think that that is something that you can do in *Second Life*, or on YouTube, or whatever. Respond more quickly, and stay more current, because we don't have to take a year in development, and a year to film it, and six months to edit it, and blah blah blah. We can be more intimate because we can be more immediate.

Kara Trapdoor: That's what a lot of the teens are doing on YouTube right now, too. They're asking a question at the end of whatever their segment was—asking a question of their audience.

LINKS RECOMMENDED BY ATTENDEES

http://nwn.blogs.com/nwn/2010/07/machinima-tips.html
http://nwn.blogs.com/nwn/2010/04/shanghai-machinima.html
http://www.blamesociety.net [Chad Vader]

Session 4

Roundtable Two, Session Four, had fewer participants than Session Three, and all of them were experienced with machinima in virtual worlds to varying degrees. *Second Life*, *World of Warcraft* and *The Sims* series were the leading platforms, among those experiences. Some had substantial experience with strategic multi-player role-playing games, as well as Moviestorm and iClone.

The primary discussion points again centered on collaboration, commercialization, and content, with the latter category, content, examining the importance of storytelling in achieving a sense of intimacy with the audience. Embedded within those topics were perspectives on what tools and skills are needed to advance the craft and profession. Attendees included Alley McNally, Moo Money, Laurina Hawks, Thinkerer Melville, and xox Voyager. The authors, Phylis Johnson and Donald Pettit, moderate the discussion.

Donald Pettit: Welcome to our Second Session of the Machinima Roundtables.

Phylis Johnson: All your statements—spoken and written—are public record, and by being here today you provide your consent for your comments to be published in this book, and other related forums. Backtracking to the reason that we wanted to conduct these roundtables derives from the perspective that those here today are pioneers. I know some people say we are in the second phase of machinima, for there has been quite a lot of evolution since the early days.

Laurina Hawks: Well, so the question was whether we are pioneers? *(Chat text.)*

Phylis Johnson: Yes, in a sense you just being here indicates that beautifully. You all are pioneers to some extent. Our participants established in yesterday's roundtable that we are pioneers, and that was fairly much the opinion in the prior sessions as well. So let's move on, for time is limited, and let me ask, is machinima best created through collaboration? That's really the first question today that will begin to reveal our pioneering nature in producing machinima. Our discussion begins with the theme of collaboration in machinima production. There are two general camps of machinimatographers, those that prefer to work alone and the others who build machinima teams, from actors to directors to others fulfilling different roles.

Thinkerer Melville: Well, I'm open to starting.

Donald Pettit: Excellent.

Thinkerer Melville: I will respond to what was one aspect of your larger question: are people working together or as individuals? Basically, I've been working in related fields, as well as making videos for several years, actually, probably since 2006 or something like that. In the first place, if you're going to make a video, you probably need some other people working with you. You need several, you often will need actors, you need set builders, and people to write scripts. I couldn't imagine working without lots of people. I think one of the nice things about *Second Life* is we have lots and lots of people who are interested in doing things like that, or related things. I've had large numbers of people working with me. So basically my concept is if I'm going to make videos I need somebody to write scripts. I have two writing groups on the Cookie sim in *Second Life*. They write scripts. They write other things too, of course. You need somebody to perform. I have a major acting group, the Avatar

Repertory Theater, on Cookie. Incidentally, most of the people that I'm working with in that theater have union cards. So they're not totally amateurs. In some cases, they have physical limitations or illnesses that would prevent them from being on stage.

Donald Pettit: Very good. Anyone else have anything to contribute?

Moo Money: Oh, I don't really make art. I'm a corporate machinimator. I'm kind of the flip side. I was shopping a lot, and the former Ben Linden hired me to promote and educate machinima. I started making it on my own in May of 2006. Shortly after, I started getting asked to make it for other people. While I've freely given information on how to make machinima and everything, I'm kind of a recluse when it comes to sharing machinima and doing it and everything like that. I prefer to work by myself because my clients approach me. They want a video fast. Sometimes their budget is limited, and really I call myself a corporate machinimator because I work with a lot of real companies that come into *Second Life*. What I face is, I'll TP [teleport] people in and they'll have problems with other people there and they'll argue. Or they'll just kind of goof off. Or they'll take an hour to change because they literally have nothing in their inventory that's modest. What I've learned is that I like to chroma key myself in a lot of places. I have avatars of all different kinds — skins, clothing. I can be hundreds of people, or species. The other thing I do is I mask myself in scenes. I would say most of my stuff, because it's corporate, is not on the art side of it, so they come to me and they've already paid someone to build their island. They have a general idea on a script, or sometimes they just hand me a script and they say, "Film this. Help us with the audio." Sometimes they have the audio. I've done work for Cisco, Linden Lab, machinima.com, etcetera, and they usually provide everything for me. So the flip side would be I'm a loner.

Alley McNally: Well, I don't get paid, but what I've found — like you Moo — is that a lot of times, actors can be a royal pain. Sometimes, due to computers, or the lag in the place, a shot can take a while to get done right. If you have a human there, they'll go away, get cranky, complaining. What I've found is, generally, what I want from the actors, I can get from a bot because I replace the audio from *Second Life*. I generally do the dialogue myself. Or I have real actors from my local area provide the dialogue. So it ends up coming down to an issue of how quickly can I do this.

Donald Pettit: Very good. Anyone else?

xox Voyager: I want to say that I am a mix of the two. I'm an artist.

Phylis Johnson: So when would collaboration work well?

Alley McNally: Most of the productions I do are less than five minutes in length. It's fairly minor. But if I wanted to do a full feature-length film, which I've never even attempted, I'd definitely *have* to go to actors. And I mean *real* actors. Probably have to go local. There is collaboration there, particularly if it is a long feature film. I can't really edit it myself because I despise editing. I could do it for short stuff, but for anything that's probably over 10 minutes long, I think collaboration would come into play there, over what I typically do.

Phylis Johnson: How might collaboration assist you, Alley, in other ways, technically, let's say?

Alley McNally: I've had issues, too, as far as quality where I've had to go at low quality, or medium quality, just to get the shot done. So I have a hard time with high quality. So definitely collaboration, the technical stuff, where you would have to—if you had more than your computer could handle for, like, alts. Mine, I think, this computer can handle up to three or four alts at low. Then, the other one I can't have alts on there so much. If you need more than *that*, you *have* to go to other people. Otherwise it's impossible.

Moo Money: I work faster alone. *(Chat text.)*

Laurina Hawks: More interesting would be to ask *how* collaborating could be done at all. *(Chat text.)*

Thinkerer Melville: Depends on objective. *(Chat text.)*

Laurina Hawks: Depends also on technical possibilities; for example, I cannot use a second camera operator since I need all the footage on my computer. *(Chat text.)*

Thinkerer Melville: I have had second cameras. *(Chat text.)*

Moo Money: I've sent DVDs, external hard drives, etcetera. *(Chat text.)*

Thinkerer Melville: I have sent files compressed. *(Chat text.)*

Moo Money: There are certain ways that you can compress footage that's pretty lossless, but still allows you to edit it. I did some footage for Linden Lab where they wanted it in MPEG2—I believe it was? So they could put it on a website for news sites to download and then edit for television production or web production. It can be done. It's not *optimal*. I would prefer not to do that, but it can be done. I prefer to send hard drives or DVDs or something like that. Sometimes it's just prohibitive if it's a ton of stuff.

Donald Pettit: I use ZumoDrive and I put stuff on there, and people can pluck it off if they see fit. It's an Internet-based hard drive.

Thinkerer Melville: I have shared file sites. *(Chat text.)*

Laurina Hawks: Yes, but I don't trust any other camera. I have very precise pictures in mind. *(Chat text.)*

Thinkerer Melville: The only way I think collaboration will work is if the people who are collaborating are seeing that as a value to them. That is partly a matter of shared goals, shared objectives. If two of us working together believe that working together will get us better results than working separately, we will collaborate. I think it's mainly a matter of, for example, finding the particular elements that we need. If you need writers—you need somebody else to do the writing—then that's important to have that person. Cookie was set up as a place for video making and a place for writers and actors. Sure enough, after we got them there, they began to work together. That was one of the objectives that I had for it.

Laurina Hawks: Of course, I use actors, prop designers and stuff, but the major part in filming, writing and post-production is done by myself alone, and I see no way to collaborate in these parts. *(Chat text.)*

Alley McNally: I was thinking about one way that people also collaborate. What you said, Thinkerer, about the actual locations and that way you're collaborating — one way that could be strengthened if we wanted to use that term is in the tools or machinima. What I mean is not necessarily the recording tools, but in the tools to help you get more realistic animation — more fluid movement, more ease to quickly and easily get the shot. If we got more of *that*, it would make machinima easier, faster, *more* possible to make a full feature-length film relatively easily within a relative short period of time and for probably a fraction of the cost of a normal film.

Thinkerer Melville: Yeah, I think that's a good point, and actually that's one of the things, for example, about having an acting and movie production group. In our groups, we have, of course, people who make avatars and provide animations and have to have various kinds of animations. One of the *advantages* we have is that we have a lot of experience. Our people have a lot of experience in making animations. Of course they have probably a lot of animations just in their inventories. All of those things can be available, probably are available if anybody asks, for collaborative work on other shows. I hope — I look forward in the future — to be able to have our people provide assistance to other video makers or other theatrical performers. For not just animations, avatars, costumes, whatever is necessary, but all of those things we've been through. We don't have the solutions for everything, but we do have some substantial solutions for numerous problems, like using two sims.

COMMERCIALIZATION

Phylis Johnson: Some of you have conflicted thoughts about making money with machinima. Think about this question: what is machinima's role in advancing art and technology through and for commercialization?

Thinkerer Melville: I am all in favor of people making money. *(Chat text.)*

Moo Money: I have no artistic goal, but I did just produce a video for some artsy kids last night. They appealed to the fact that I had a goal of doing *one* artsy video in my life. It was still limited to their vision, but artsy. *(Chat text.)*

Alley McNally: I think the ultimate path that machinima is going right now is slowly toward a commercial, viable path, well for the vast majority who are doing machinima. It is something that's in the back of my mind, as I'm building my skill. I think, too, having the money backing, being able to make money off of your film, will encourage you to pay people for useful tools. You'll be more willing to spend the time to do this if there's a monetary goal behind it. I don't think artistic goals will ever go away. Even for me, I enjoy making stuff for no monetary benefit at all. A lot of the stuff that I make, there is absolutely no monetary possibility at all out of it. It costs time, it costs money to pay for the tools, it costs time if you're using actors, to pay for the actors. Sometimes you have to go and communicate with sim owners and other stuff. It costs money, so why shouldn't you be paid for good work?

Moo Money: Well, because a lot of artists are starving artists. They have a vision that no one else sees. I'm not putting it down, but I'm saying you basically have to be someone else's play toy — someone else's minion — to make money. I make boring, lifeless machinima because that's what corporate clients want. I am entirely capable of being creative — not in an artsy "What on earth is going on? I have no idea" way. But I am capable of being creative with my work, and they don't want that. They want point A to point B, point B to point C outlined, put on the script, don't deviate from the script, and that's what they want. However, when you're talking about commercialization, commercialization is what's putting it into the mainstream right now. Machinima.com was nothing in 2000. It was a small, niche group. Hugh Hancock was struggling with the server fees, sold it to Philip DeBevoise, and the DeBevoise family — Aaron, Allen, Philip — worked and got funding, 4 million dollars of funding. I was part of their funding hires for a while. They strike deals with popular video games, first-person shooters. *Hot Tub Time Machine* has machinima. *Lie to Me* had an interesting segment where this guy had PTSD (post-traumatic stress disorder) and they used a "simulation" — and I say that in quotes — and it was just like a war game, and they probably used some open-play mode for it and specified how they needed it (like for filmmaking in games like *Unreal Tournament*). I'd say that's the kind of machinima. So you see this stuff on TV and you know it comes from a video game or an animation, or something like that, and you might be curious. You see the *Dragon Age* machinima. You see all sorts of machinima and that intrigues people. And then Hollywood learns that it takes a fraction of the cost to make the setup. When you look at the *CSI* build in *Second Life* — 7 million dollars in funding from whatever Big Three network that was. I don't watch *CSI*. But I'll bet that machinima was a very small part of the cost compared to hiring the greeters, hiring the builders, the sim costs, the development costs. I'll bet machinima was just a tiny chunk of that. So I think commercialization is key for growth. You have sell out before you can make the art mainstream in and of itself. So that's my thoughts on it. [Authors' note: article link, *Business Communicators in Virtuality*, http://freshtakes.typepad.com/sl_communicators/2007/10/csi-new-york-in.html.]

Phylis Johnson: Any other comments on the commercialization versus art-/not-for-profit theme?

Alley McNally: I think just because not everyone has monetized it, or will monetize it, doesn't mean that it's a bad idea to do that. I think at the end of the day, like you said, you have to feed yourself. You have to live. And frankly, if I could make a living out of doing machinima, I'd so do it. It's fun! Even if it is "soulless work," it's still on the line of what I've trained to do.

Moo Money: I do enjoy it. It's just that; it can be soulless, but it can also be fun. I should specify that since we're recording. I just wish that someone creative would hire me to do a video. *(Laughs.)* Like I said, it's like hanging out after work. You can only do it so much. For making the hobby machinima after you spend all that time making the machinima you were paid to do, it can be tough, because you just want to relax and get away. In *Second Life*, I'm always *on*, always machinima.

Donald Pettit: I'd like to interject something, if I could. What I find good is to maybe do a few paying jobs, and then just do one of your own, something that you like. Just go out there and have fun with something. Try to mix it. I think that's what I do when I get to where, yes, when like you say you're not allowed sometimes to stretch your creativity or change outside of the script, so this is a way to vent your frustration, get a little bit more creative, enjoy it, have fun. So I would recommend like maybe for every three paid jobs you get, just do a small featurette, like three or four minutes. Something you like to do, whatever it is, and just do it. That's just me. It's for mental health.

Thinkerer Melville: I might add one other comment. There's a different issue. My theatrical group has already set itself up — or at least part of the members have — as a non-profit corporation. They are — once they get final approval, I guess in California, and then they will be getting approval I guess nationally in the United States. I don't know quite their status, but anyway, they intend to raise funds specifically for theatrical activities in virtual worlds — not specifically *Second Life*, but in virtual worlds. This will be fairly much the same thing as community theater. Community theater has always existed at least partly on contributions. I don't know what the outcome will be, but they seem to be pretty optimistic — and they're fairly experienced people — that they will be able to get enough funding to run some theatrical events which would be both video/machinima and live events — and of course probably live events with something like Procaster so a large population of people could watch it from the Web.

INTIMACY IN MACHINIMA

Phylis Johnson: Thanks for those comments. Okay, we touched upon collaboration, commercialization versus creativity as well as some limitations. The next discussion theme pushes the art and aesthetics concept further; here we consider the role of storytelling in machinima. We ask you to consider the role of machinima in creating intimacy.

Laurina Hawks: Intimate? *(Chat text.)*

Phylis Johnson: Can it trigger an emotional connection with the viewer to the characters and subsequently tap into the producer's point of view or goals?

Laurina Hawks: Hmm. I don't understand the question — do you mean, is it possible to have any emotions like in Hollywood movies? *(Chat text.)*

Donald Pettit: Can I interject something? This is an example. For instance, in our website, we have a little bit of a library, a collection, and I do peruse them. There's one — I can't even tell you the maker — it has an original artist that plays piano throughout, and shows this couple meeting, and then they meet in a bar, and then they show them falling in love, then they get married, then they get old. The person did a really great job with the avatars. She aged them together. Then the very end, one of them passes on. It was just a very, very touching machinima. And I actually cried — I hate to tell this to people — but I actually shed a tear. I cried. It moved me. So machinima in that instance, I consider that intimacy because it had an effect on my emotions. So what I would say, it could be comedy, where you just have a big old belly laugh, or it could be any major emotion that touches your heart. You see what I'm saying. So I think that's what we're talking about. Does machinima have a place there? And in my case, it did on that particular instance. It doesn't happen very often, but on that particular instance, it did.

Alley McNally: As far as emotions, I'm not sure if this is any more special or different than I would say a piece that's done live. But one piece that I did just recently that I called *The White Room* — I really liked it. I felt it kind of had the emotion that I was looking for. It was a woman who was quite literally going crazy. The cool thing that I did — I did this show first originally live in an actual stage production, and I have it recorded onto the Internet — and then I did it through machinima. And I like that I could get the camera really, really close to her face. You could see her suffering. You could see the world that she saw through her perspective, and you could actually see her delusions. You could see when she thought of herself as a monster. You could literally see the monster in the water. I'm not 100 percent sure I — at least me personally — could do that other than with machinima. Maybe someone else could. The monster in the water, I don't know if I could. It was something that even though I did it, I know I still felt at least somewhat moved by a machinima piece. I don't know how many times that something amazing like that happens.

Alley McNally: http://www.youtube.com/watch?v=P-FDxCscS4c *(Chat text.)*

Moo Money: So you're looking for the emotions that machinima can create? Is that what the question was? I actually have an example that's human and I can't talk about much of it because it didn't go well based on being tied up in corporate issues and everything like that. I was hired by a non-profit in *Second Life* — a fairly large one — to do a 17-minute documentary interviewing four people, maybe five, where they discussed their experiences volunteering with the group as it related to their medical issues or someone they know that had medical issues. It would make you cry. They were purely motivated by love and concern, and everything like that. I'll admit I cried when I couldn't release the video because of a logo issue. Anyway, that's probably my greatest regret, is this video that I made — and I made it for like dirt cheap for them — and it was a huge hassle, but it was a labor of love. I'm still devastated two years later that it can't be shown at their events.

Phylis Johnson: What about other types of movies that trigger emotions—like action movies?

Laurina Hawks: Sure! I watch my movies or those of Lowe Runo! *(Laughs.) (Chat text.)*

Donald Pettit: Oh, man. Don't stereotype my movies, please. *(Laughs.)* I want to do some other stuff. I do other things besides action. Just good at action.

Moo Money: Who made *Tales from Midnight City*? *(Chat text.)*

Phylis Johnson: Lainy Voom.

Moo Money: That was fairly action oriented. *(Chat text.)*

Laurina Hawks: Our action movie was incredible. *(Chat text.)*

Donald Pettit: And the lady [referring to Laurina] comes to my meeting with a gun. *(Laughs.)* And I'm behaving, too!

Phylis Johnson: Any other examples of machinima that moves you in some way?

Alley McNally: One of my favorite films that I've watched that I love to go back to over and over again is *Man vs. Second Life*. He literally just shot in Linden areas for the most part and one or two other places. That thing makes me laugh every single time I watch it.

Donald Pettit: See there? There's an emotional response. So machinima—we're all kind of in consensus that machinima, if it's well done, can evoke emotions.

Laurina Hawks: We still have big problems with facial expressions in *Second Life*. *(Chat text.)*

Moo Money: My definition is probably controversial, just because I've been around. *(Laughs.)* Machinima, to me, is still the movies made in 3-D gaming platforms, but I have something against PVP (player vs. player) and game play videos. I've done a lot of *WoW* (*World of Warcraft*) and other machinima reviews for different MMOs (Massive Multi-player Online) on *Massively*, *WoW Insider*, and whatnot. You might have a music video if it has a script and dialogue, or something that has some kind of coherent editing. If it's just a bunch of people playing animations and filming it straight and then cutting it to like Jay-Z or something, that's not machinima. That's game play footage. And I've gotten into debates over whether this counts, whether music videos count as machinima. *(Laughs.)* I think that there's a genre for them, but I really don't think that counts. You basically have to edit and cut it into a story. Tell me a story with this machinima you're making. That to me is machinima. It doesn't matter whether it's a commercial, or an action film, or a documentary. It still applies to the real-life categorizations, but it has to come from somewhere, not just a straight video dump of footage.

Alley McNally: So like say you decided to make a music video about Michael Jackson using one of his songs; if you just took a bunch of different scenes from *Second Life* that you got and mashed them together, you would consider that just game play footage?

Moo Money: Well, yeah. It really depends. It has to be cut into a story. You had to have seen those horrible, horrible, horrible music videos where they get some new dance from Vista Animations—I'm not knocking Vista Animations; their stuff's really good. But when they're just playing it on the screen and filming straight and they don't cut away or anything to get different angles of "booty shakin'" or whatever is an example of what I mean. Actually, I recently met the guy who does Vista Animations. I walked up to him and I said, "I have to say, I don't hate your machinima!" *(Laughs.)* Because he makes these product videos where it shows the person dancing. The cuts are interesting. But then he also takes time to put alongside the dancer the person doing the mocap (motion capture/tracking) live. So you get to see a side-by-side comparison of what you're seeing in *Second Life* and what happened in real life to get to that point. I think that's awesome versus something straight. He could just show his dances and be like, "Here they are." It really depends on the content of the video, the way it is cut, the story it tells, and all those factors.

Alley McNally: I totally agree with the idea of, say, you go into *Half-Life 2* and you record your most awesome frag with your friends having a great time. That's not machinima. That's weird game footage. But if you have something like *Red vs. Blue*, where there's a little bit more story to it, then that becomes machinima. I think that the music videos can be a real gray area whether or not they are machinima. I think if there's a little bit of a plan, a little bit of an intention to it, then it's probably machinima. If it's just your great time at the dance club mixed to music, no, not really at all.

Moo Money: Depends. Are you cutting a straight angle of him and lining up the audio later with his lip-syncing? Or are you just filming a straight-on angle? So I can answer this in a way. In 2004, Paul Marino wrote a book called *The Art of Machinima*. He talks about the early days of machinima and how it came to be. In '97, I think it was, someone made a video called *Diary of a Camper*. That was when it didn't have a name yet, but that was what was considered machinima. It's fairly telling that they didn't choose to call the game play footage that was floating around machinima. They chose to call *Diary of a Camper* machinima because it was edited into a cohesive story line, as limited as it may be in Quake.

Alley McNally: I think that we should—at least for a long time—not answer this question, just because it's so new or still working on its boundaries, what it is and what it isn't. It's not really in an early phase like *Diary of a Camper* anymore, but we still are trying to feel out what it is and how to do this and how we turn this into something so awesome that everyone wants to be with it. So I think we're a bit on a pioneer edge here. Maybe we're the second phase of machinima and it's too early to answer this question.

Laurina Hawks: We must honestly ask one question to us all: are we doing machinima because we are not capable of making RL films, or are we doing machinima because we love this genre and see it as something new and special? I am honest; I would make real-life movies if I had millions of dollars. But I love the genre too. *(Chat text.)*

Moo Money: It would take forever to establish yourself in the RL film market. *(Chat text.)*

Laurina Hawks: That's the point, Moo. It takes ages. I can answer this question very simply: I am a book author in Germany. I published seven books, and I found a way to bring my last book to the public with machinima. During this process, I learned about the possibilities, and now I make different machinima which are projects not solely based on my books. *(Chat text.)*

Moo Money: Time has evolved my feeling about machinima. My definition of it — I don't know if it's good or bad. I look forward to seeing it grow.

LINKS SUGGESTED BY ATTENDEES

http://avatarrepertorytheater.blogspot.com [The Avatar Repertory Theater]
http://ideajuice.blip.tv [CodeWarrior Carling]
http://sasharudie.com [Moo Money]
http://www.timetravellertm.com [xox Voyager]
http://avatarrepertorytheater.blogspot.com [The Avatar Repertory Theater]
http://www.youtube.com/watch?v=P-FDxCscS4c [*The White Room*, Ally McNally]
http://www.youtube.com/user/tracechops#p/u/5/PCSknY0Sa6I [*Tales from Midnight City*, Lainy Voom]
http://www.youtube.com/watch?v=pFS4l5B547s [*Man vs. Second Life*]
http://vimeo.com/8476413 [*Action Flick*, Lowe Runo Productions, LLC]
http://www.youtube.com/user/PhoenixEmbers#p/u/0/aM1UTigbj04 [*The Simulacron: Prologue*, Laurina Hawks]

About the Contributors

Iono **Allen** is an award-winning machinimatographer and was the official University of Western Australia machinimatographer.

Pooky **Amsterdam** is the CEO of PookyMedia, an award-winning machinima company.

Larkworthy **Antfarm** is an award-winning machinimatographer, artist and writer.

Asil **Ares**, machinimatographer, is owner of the NeoVictoria Estate in *Second Life*, including the NeoVictoria and Machinima sims, part of which includes a free-form role-play environment set in a virtual version of Victorian London.

Baird **Barnard**, machinimatographer, is a producer for Metaverse Television based out of *Second Life*.

Russell **Boyd** (Rosco Teardrop, SL) is the award-winning resident director for PookyMedia Films. He began producing films in 2005, drawing from his background as a flight-sim enthusiast and leader.

CodeWarrior **Carling**, CEO of IdeaJuice Studios, is a leading machinimatographer with cutting-edge knowledge of virtual reality, game engines, and other 3-D-related technologies.

Bryan **Carter** is an associate professor at the University of Central Missouri (USA) and the founder of Virtual Harlem in *Second Life*, a place where art, history and technology converge with immersive education experiences.

Penumbra **Carter** is a *Second Life* filmmaker, content creator and more recently involved in radio.

Pamala **Clift** is a professor at Rockcliffe University, and is the founder of The Roadside Philosopher discussion group in *Second Life*.

Decorgal (also known as Judy Lee) is well known as a leading machinimatographer and machinima expert on *The Sims* platform. She has a graduate degree in sociology. To date, she is best known for her *Adventures in Dating* series.

Draxtor **Despres** is a renowned machinima journalist/producer in *Second Life*. His professional experience has included producing news for a Los Angeles station and a National Public Radio affiliate.

Evie **Fairchild** is involved in many aspects of machinima, from directing to Foley to acting, and has worked with many leading machinima producers.

Phaylen **Fairchild** is a leading machinima producer with a strong background in writing, well known for her comedic series *DiVAS*, among other features.

Rysan **Fall** is CEO of Fall Films and a professional machinimatographer who is best known for his music video *Across the Universe*. He has presented his work internationally.

Clover **Fenwitch**, of Emerald House Productions, is a script writer and artist in Second Life, presently working on commercial and entertainment projects.

Kate **Fosk** is an independent filmmaker who co-owns the machinima company Pineapple Pictures with Michael R. Joyce. She served on the executive committee for the 2010 Machinima Expo.

Michael **Gray** is a *World of Warcraft* reviewer for "*WoW* Moviewatch" in *WoW Insider*.

Kit **Guardian**, CEO of KG Shine Productions and Shine TV, creates productions for theater, film, and television. She is a board member of Women in Film and Television (WIFT) in Australia.

Chantal **Harvey** is an international presenter and leading machinima advocate. She is founder of MaMachinima International Festival and an award-winning machinima producer.

Laurina **Hawks** is a novelist and award-winning machinima producer.

Todd **Herreman** is a copyright expert, music producer, songwriter, composer, engineer and session musician, with a client list that has included Prince and Michael Jackson. He teaches at Southern Illinois University, Carbondale, Illinois.

Jay Jay **Jegathesan** (also known as Jayjay Zifanwe) is the manager of the School of Physics at that University of Western Australia. Jegathesan manages the UWA presence in *Second Life*.

Phylis **Johnson** is a professor and former chairperson of the Radio-Television Department at Southern Illinois University, Carbondale.

Yani **Jowisz** is a machinimatographer, political machinimist blogger, and has been actively engaged in the machinima community as an actor and producer within *Second Life*.

LaPiscean **Liberty** is the founder and CEO of Aview TV network, and technical director of Cutting Edge Concerts.

Alley **McNally** is a performer and comedian and a machinimist of virtual worlds.

Thinkerer **Melville** is the founder of Thinkerer Studios, a support network for those interested in video storytelling in virtual worlds.

Toxic **Menges** is an award-winning machinimatographer, corporate machinima producer, and filmmaking artist, and has been heavily involved in virtual community development.

Moo **Money** is a professional machinimatographer specializing in corporate projects. She is a former reviewer for "*WoW* Moviewatch" for *WoW Insider*. Her past clients include Cisco, Linden Lab, Manpower, and the American Cancer Society.

Wiz **Nordberg** is the founder of Treet TV, a virtual content provider.

Al **Peretz** has experience as a channel director for a cultural and educational television station and founded a media school in Colombia, South America. He lives in the United States but his avatar filmmaker resides in *Second Life* making award-winning machinima.

Donald **Pettit** is a free-lance photographer and videographer, and the CEO of Lowe Runo Productions, a media company that features machinima and video production.

Jonathan **Pluskota**, sound engineer/scholar, is an assistant professor in the mass communication department at Northwest Missouri State University, Maryville (USA). He was a director at the Art Institute of Austin, where he developed audio and video curriculum.

Kara **Trapdoor** is an event correspondent and reporter for *Best of Second Life* magazine, as well as a machinimist and blogger.

xox **Voyager** is an artist, writer and curator of virtual spaces.

Gene **Williams** is a machinimist, educator and musician, with a strong professional background in animation.

Gwenette **Writer** is a *Second Life* campus developer, educator, technical writer, artist and poet, and is involved in the machinima community.

Iangelcares **Writer** is a voice-over actress of virtual worlds with many machinima productions to her credit.

Index

DATE DUE

GAYLORD   PRINTED IN U.S.A.